Alexander the Great Avenger

Dedicated to my teachers:

Adriani Varnava, for being the paradigm in teaching a class.

Yannis Danos and Dionyssis Fragatos, for tutoring me in Sciences.

Thanasis Roustas, for teaching me to properly write and develop an argument.

Aristea Velegraki, who taught me the intricacies of publishing and *Eu Zein*.

Giannis Kantartzoglou, for tutoring me in martial arts.

Manos Heliades, for tutoring me in Operations and Intelligence.

Spyrarchos Al Huzur, for mentoring me in technology and tactics.

Aggeliki Mastoraki, for teaching me English.

Pipitsa Lagogianni, for teaching me Ancient Greek.

Aggeliki Athanasiadou, for the course in social manners, especially tactfulness.

Nicolas Manaios, my best man, who inaugurated me in the world of the CQB.

The shadow of Stavroula Korompoki, for showcasing the balance between propriety and warmth.

The shadow of my grandmother Pitsa, for introducing me to geography.

And, above all else, the shadow of my grandfather, Manousos E. Kambouris, First of His Name in the family, for exposing me to the miracles of The Lore and the bliss of storytelling.

In gratitude,

                                        Manousos E. Kambouris, PhD

Alexander the Great Avenger

The Campaign that Felled Achaemenid Persia

Manousos E. Kambouris

Pen & Sword
MILITARY

First published in Great Britain in 2023 by
Pen & Sword Military
An imprint of
Pen & Sword Books Ltd
Yorkshire – Philadelphia

Copyright © Manousos E. Kambouris 2023

ISBN 978 1 39907 392 9

The right of Manousos E. Kambouris to be identified as Author of this work has been asserted by him in accordance with the Copyright, Designs and Patents Act 1988.

A CIP catalogue record for this book is
available from the British Library.

All rights reserved. No part of this book may be reproduced or transmitted in any form or by any means, electronic or mechanical including photocopying, recording or by any information storage and retrieval system, without permission from the Publisher in writing.

Typeset by Mac Style
Printed in the UK by CPI Group (UK) Ltd, Croydon, CR0 4YY.

Pen & Sword Books Limited incorporates the imprints of Atlas, Archaeology, Aviation, Discovery, Family History, Fiction, History, Maritime, Military, Military Classics, Politics, Select, Transport, True Crime, Air World, Frontline Publishing, Leo Cooper, Remember When, Seaforth Publishing, The Praetorian Press, Wharncliffe Local History, Wharncliffe Transport, Wharncliffe True Crime, White Owl and After the Battle.

For a complete list of Pen & Sword titles please contact

PEN & SWORD BOOKS LIMITED
47 Church Street, Barnsley, South Yorkshire, S70 2AS, England
E-mail: enquiries@pen-and-sword.co.uk
Website: www.pen-and-sword.co.uk

Or

PEN AND SWORD BOOKS
1950 Lawrence Rd, Havertown, PA 19083, USA
E-mail: Uspen-and-sword@casematepublishers.com
Website: www.penandswordbooks.com

Contents

Plates vi
Illustrations x
Maps xi
Acknowledgements xii
Introduction: The Men and Their Times xiii

Part I: The Troops 1

Chapter 1 The Knights 3
Chapter 2 The Line Infantry 18
Chapter 3 Archery in the Army of Alexander the Great 47
Chapter 4 The Elites 49
Chapter 5 Innovating and Conserving 58
Chapter 6 Phalanx Warfare 69

Part II: The Campaign 95

Chapter 7 Before Alexander: 200 Years of Greek Efforts to Neutralize the Asian threat(s) 97
Chapter 8 The Invasion of Alexander 106
Chapter 9 Granicus: The Battle for Asia Minor 115
Chapter 10 Asia Minor: A Year-long Campaign 137
Chapter 11 The Battle of Issus 165
Chapter 12 The Battle of Gaugamela 202
Chapter 13 After Gaugamela 250
Chapter 14 In the Heart of Persia 258
Chapter 15 Game Over 271

Bibliography 274
Index 281

Plates

1. The mosaic from Pompeii shows a confrontation between Alexander and Darius and is supposedly a snapshot of the Battle of Issus, or of Gaugamela. The former is more probable as Alexander wears long sleeves, something incompatible with the heat of the date of the Battle of Gaugamela (Arr Anab III.7,3). Also, the slaying of the Persian cavalryman in front of the chariot and the presence of another nearby sword at hand probably refer to the intervention of Oxathres, brother to the King of Kings, who possibly saved the life of the sovereign (Diod XVII.34,2-4; Curt III.11.8). There are many important details, here indicated with arrows: Alexander has a composite cuirass with flaps at waist and arms, and a straight sword as evident from the symmetric hilt. He uses a long spear, probably a *xyston*, with the underhand grip, although a Companion behind him (the Boeotian helmet can be seen) evidently uses his weapon from the overhead position. Alexander's mount wears partial barding (horse armour) including criniere (neck armour) and chanfron (facial armor), although a peytral (chest piece) cannot be seen. The Imperials use both straight and curved swords. The trooper killed by Alexander has the latter half-drawn, as identified by the asymmetry of the handle, whereas the trooper behind him has his straight, rhomboid-bladed weapon drawn – the new model of Greek swords of the late fourth century, to replace the leaf-like blades of the original hoplite sword of the sixth and early fifth centuries. An Imperial falls under the chariot (notice the immense wheels and the boxlike vehicle) and has an Argive shield, meaning he is a *kardaka* hoplite. Spent or lost weapons lay on the ground: a *palton* double-role javelin, of knotted wood (Sekunda 2001) and with its launching loop attached at the centre, and a straight sword, the hilt of which is similar to the one of Alexander, and its holster, more to the right. At the left lower corner, a bow and arrow lay on the ground as well. The Achaemenids wear flexible corselets while Darius, with his headgear upright (the King's prerogative) holds his bow and reaches for the horse offered to him to mount, leaving the chariot, once more the episode reminding of the Battle of Issus (Arr Anab II.11,5). (*Courtesy of Brigadier General B. Papathanasiou, Hellenic Army-Ret*)

2. Greek shields of line infantry at the age of Alexander III. Compared to the Argive *hoplon* shield (C–D) the Macedonian (front (A) and back (B) views) buckler has a baldric for hanging from the shoulder; it is shallower and rimless (thus occasionally called *pelte*, and in this case the armband or *porpax* is off from the centre. Front (C) and back (D) views of the Argive *hoplon* shield of the southern Greek allies and mercenaries outfitted as hoplites. The armband or *porpax* is a bit off, as it should be placed squarely on the diameter, to allow optimal coverage. The handle *antilabe* is also seen, along with the inner aspect of the rim and the internal suspension cord for carrying the shield hanging at the back and packing stores in it. (*Courtesy of Brigadier General B. Papathanasiou, Hellenic Army-Ret*)
3. (A) The underhand use of the *xyston*. The prominent butt point, of a shape intended as a warhead before anything else, plus the moderate length identify the weapon (Sekunda 2001). The helmet rather than the Phrygian model that would imply a lancer mounted scout (Sekunda 1984) is a crested version of the standard-issue *konos* (Juhel 2009). (B) A very popular interpretation of the Macedonian Phalanx shows the bucklers (Plate 2 C–D) simply hanging like talismans, from the neck and the arms extending, uncovered, around the bucklers' rims to brandish the *sarissa* pike to waist or chest level. (C) The fresco of the very renowned Macedonian tomb of Lyson and Callicles shows different painted items of weaponry. The flexible body armour with two flights of flaps or *pteryges*, the standardized *konos* helmet (Juhel 2009) with cheek-pieces and horsetail, the greaves are all easily discernible and imply an officer. The shield resembles the highly concave later model rather than the usual phalanx buckler and there is one sword and one sabre in their sheaths with baldric. One can tell the weapons apart due to the asymmetry at the edge (pommel) of the handle of the sabre. (D) The Mycenaean line infantry use body shields hanging from shoulder straps and handle their *egxeia* pikes with both hands to shoulder level. (*Courtesy of Brigadier General B. Papathanasiou, Hellenic Army-Ret*)
4. The varying details of the Alexander Sarcophagus show Hypaspists, identified by the combination of Argive shields (Plate 2 A-B) plus Phrygian helmets (Sekunda 1984). They are presented both in nudity, for mobile missions, and with body armor with flaps and obviously flexible materials, with or without metal inserts between the layers of the leather or the fabric (Sekunda 2000). The difference in armor may reflect different chiliarchies, or missions. The Macedonian cavalry are Companions with Boeotian helmets (Sekunda 1984), while Alexander has the signature one recreating the lion's head insinuating Hercules' lion skin. Oriental

infantry can be seen using Argive shields, implying *kardaka* hoplites, and scalloped shields, definitely *takabara* (Sekunda 1992) plus the Persian headgear. Greek cavalry brandish, according to the position of the arm, shafted weapons or sidearms, the latter possibly including *kopis* sabres (Plate 5). The fallen hoplite under an Achaemenid cavalryman may be a Hypaspist operating as *hamippos*, trying to disembowel the enemy mount (Sekunda 1986). (*Courtesy of Brigadier General B. Papathanasiou, Hellenic Army-Ret*)

5. Greek *kopis* sabre reconstructed to the right along with *pelte* crescent moon shield, typical for Thracian troops of the fourth century and signature of *peltasts*. The spear is most probably the Persian infantry model, with spherical butt, while there are two axes, a Scythian-type straight one (*sagaris*) and a conventional *pelekys* possibly used by Persian infantry, especially veterans, as a CQB item. (*Courtesy of Brigadier General B. Papathanasiou, Hellenic Army-Ret*)

6. The reconstruction (A) refers to the linothorax of Alexander, enhanced with metal foils, interpreting the famous mosaic (**Plate 1**). The cuirass of Callicles (B) interprets the fresco from the Tomb of Lyson and Callicles (**Plate 2C**), in here made by leather and reinforced in select areas. The cuirass of Vergina (C) is represented as a composite design, formed to the lines of usual linothorax but containing metal plates sandwiched between the layers of fabric. (*The recreated cuirasses, displayed at the Museum of Ancient Greek Technology in Athens, were created by the professional armourer D. Katsikis (www.hellenicarmors.gr) and photographed by D. Karvountzis*)

7. Native infantry of the larger Macedonian Kingdom. The Peltast-javelineer may be similar to early Macedonian infantry and definitely to the Thracian confederates/ vassals/allies of the throne of Pella, and to the Agrianian troops who became elite. The suspension system comes from vase paintings and suggests a double-handle, conceptually similar style to the hoplite shield, but with a different makeup. Its use to wear the shield on the back looks obvious. The shorter javelins have short, penetrating points. The Pikemen, both in attention and in assault positions, wear body armour fabricated from perishable materials augmented with incorporatted *pterygai* flaps, as suggested in the fresco (Plate 3C). They sport different types of helmet, the one on the left being a later, more exquisite model of the Phrygian lineage. The small buckler has no rim and is tidy to allow the left hand to support the pike at the assault position (right), the length of which and its small penetrating warhead are well-attested at the standing position (middle). (*Re-enactment photographs courtesy of Koryvantes Association of Historical Studies*)

8. The plain attire of this hoplite, limited to basic and ubiquitous items (conical Laconian *pilos* helmet, argive *hoplon* shield, spear and sidearm as indicated by the baldric, probably *kopis*-type sabre) would be the standard for mercenary hoplites fighting both for and against Alexander. The basic and thus affordable kit allows for high numbers and also extreme operational flexibility, from pitched battle to territorial, mountain and urban warfare. (*Re-enactment photographs courtesy of Koryvantes Association of Historical Studies*)

Illustrations

1.1	Philip's initial cavalry force	7
1.2	Macedonian cavalry *embolon* of forty-nine cavalrymen in seven rows	8
1.3	Possible formations of tertiary *ila*, with three fifty-man wedges	11
1.4	The three formations of the cavalry binary system	16
1.5	A Thessalian rhomboid of fifty horses	17
2.1	Possible formations of the three *lochoi* of a tertiary *taxis*	23
2.2	The fourth-century ideal Greek force structure	24
5.1	The Macedonian conscription system by Sarantis, 1977	62
5.2	The Macedonian conscription system by Hammond, 1988	63
5.3	The Macedonian conscription system by Rzepka, 2008	66
6.1	The basic layout of the phalanx unit	74
6.2	Changing the depth and front by file	75
6.3	Changing the depth and density by file	77
6.4	Unit deployment	78
6.5	Army in marching order	80
6.6	Army deployment	81
9.1	The campaign of Granicus	123
9.2	The battle of the Granicus	126
11.1	Riverine deployments	168
11.2	The battle of Issus – the deployment of Alexander	170
11.3	The battle of Issus Phase 1	173
11.4	The battle of Issus Phase 2	176
11.5	The battle of Issus – The Thessalian use of rhomboids	177
12.1	The battle of Gaugamela – The sequence of events	225
12.2	The battle of Gaugamela – Alexander's deployment	229
12.3	Oblique order	235
12.4	Organization of the Macedonian phalanx at Gaugamela	245
12.5	The tertiary basis of the phalanx	245

Maps

1. Greek World-Persian Empire — xv
2. Asia Minor Invasion Vectors — 104
3. Recruitment Areas — 116
4. Campaign in Asia Minor — 117
5. The road system (two axes) in Asia Minor – Armenia Asia Minor options from the Hellespont — 137
6. South-East Asia Minor – Cilicia – Mesopotamia – Issus Campaign — 138
7. Phoenicia-Egypt — 183
8. The naval theatre — 195
9. Gaugamela, Chorasan and the three Mesopotamian roads/ Persian gates – Ecbatana — 202

Acknowledgements

The recreated cuirasses are displayed at the Museum of Ancient Greek Technology in Athens, manufactured by the professional armourer D. Katsikis, (www.hellenicarmors.gr) and photographed by D. Karvountzis.

The paintings in the colour plates, the shields and the offensive weapons are exhibits in physical form or as imagery at The War Museum of Athens, photographed by Brigadier General Basileios Papathanasiou, Hellenic Army (Retired) and collated or further processed by the author.

Introduction: The Men and Their Times

The campaign of Alexander changed the path of history, but it is seldom seen in context. It was an event of conquest, grander than anything previous but not that much: Cyrus the Great and conquerors from Egypt and Mesopotamia had astonishing careers, such as Sargon. The campaign of Alexander, though, was a turning point. Before Alexander, Ahura-Mazda from his abode in Bactria (the Greeks mistakenly thought it was in Persia) overlooked the mountains from the Himalayas to Tmolus and Ida in western Asia Minor. With Alexander the believers of Zeus would travel, trade, bicker and wander from Spain to the river Indus. It was vindication for the outrage committed against the Greek holy mountain of Olympus by Xerxes 150 years previously.

Before Alexander, the hoplite, evolving and wandering, was the paramount military figure around the Mediterranean. With Alexander the pikeman was supreme. His death showed the frailty of things: his imperial Successors lost battles to rebellious hoplite armies, occasionally decided without the heavy infantry ever clashing. Things were settled amongst cavalry forces, something unheard of in Greece.

Before Alexander, the Achaemenids ruled supreme and were recuperating after some decades of decline, to the horror of Greece. After Alexander, Greece had nothing to fear. Greece was feared and respected everywhere and the Achaemenids were history.

Before Alexander the mercenaries were the ultimate tool of war. Sparta not only embraced them; in her home territory, Cape Taenarum, there was the biggest, official mercenary market. This would have been unbelievable to the generation of Leonidas. When Alexander died, mercenaries were for garrison duty mostly; nations-in-arms and citizen-recruits were back in the vogue.

Some mediocre, though capable, chieftains and nobles, marginally adequate for minor theatre-wide campaigns, under Alexander became world-conquering marshals, roving over vast expanses and commanding great multitudes. Once Alexander died they were at each other's neck with lightning speed and hardly ever added an inch to the empire.

Alexander demonstrated the effect of synergy. What happens when all the pillars of military power, such as technology, tactical and strategic brilliance, training, motivation, courage, leadership, organization, integration and morale co-exist in a single military establishment? Not prioritization of 'this rather than that'; total supremacy, total superiority. And this, in an army not conceptually different from its opposite number and *definitely* smaller.

It is regularly overlooked that the two clashing armies of the imperial Achaemenids and royal Macedonians were very similar in nature. They were both imperial armies, with a hard nucleus of the Master Race, the core ethnicity or nationality, augmented by mercenaries, allies and subjects. The army of the Athenian Empire was such, especially in Sicily in 415 BC; the army of Agesilaus, invading Persia, even more so (Xen Hell III.4,11). The army of Alexander had the Macedonian national army as a nucleus (Burn 1965), the contributions of the League or Alliance of Corinth (actually the *second* Alliance of Corinth, the first being the one established against Xerxes in 481 BC) were the allied elements, and there was also a contribution from the Macedonian European empire, namely Thracians and possibly Illyrians, although the latter may have been allies as well, as were the Agrianians. And there was always a mercenary element (Cretan archers being paradigmatic), as Philip and generally the Throne of Macedon used to employ mercenary troops, similarly to every self-respecting state in Greece. Since the days of Agesilaus, Sparta started using such services, a thought intolerable in the past, and the king died of old age as one such *condottiere*, fighting for pay – always against Persia.

Similarly, the Persian army had its vast number of subject nations under arms, a significant number of Greek mercenaries, other mercenaries as well (such as Carians and Arabs), crack Persian troops and also some allies. Such were the Scythians from the lands beyond the realm, although they were not fielded on all occasions; needed not to, anyway. So, there was no national army against imperial host, no inclusive, multinational army against a cohesive, homogeneous force, although in cultural terms Alexander's army, at least initially, was more cohesive than the Persian multinational and multicultural host. True, Illyrians, Thracians and Greco-Macedonians had differences in religion and customs but they were able to interact and communicate more readily than the Persians with the hundreds of nations of their realm.

A repercussion of this fact is that most probably the accounts of both Achaemenid and Greco-Macedonian forces do not regard combatants, but the sum of the flock. Even if not all of them had to be fed from the sovereign's treasury, the local resources, from space in camp to drinking water had to be taken into consideration. The numbers of the Persian invasion in

Introduction: The Men and Their Times   xv

Greece imply exactly this fact. The Greeks at the time were counting only combatants, to establish strength; the Achaemenids total count, to arrange logistics. When the Greeks started with expeditionary or imperial warfare, as in Sicily, they also started counting total numbers and not 'shields'. Simply the Macedonian national army, with one retainer per 10 phalangites and one per cavalryman, was leaner – and meaner – than Persian armies, or Greek hoplite armies with one retainer per hoplite.

And the spectacular success of Alexander came in the face of a formidable enemy. A look at the map (**Map 1**) says a lot for the imbalance of power, and it is common sport to degrade the performance of Darius III so as to belittle Alexander, or at least to rationalize the staggering magnitude of his achievement even if without malice (Hammond 1989). That is the outcome of the campaign, and, most importantly, its rapidity; just 5 years to topple the Achaemenid dynasty. Darius III was no fool, and no weakling. He was both cruel and efficient; perhaps more of the first than of the second, but actually both. Being able to make the murderous Chief Eunuch Bagoas, who made him king, drink the poison intended for Darius III himself, as he had done with the previous 2 sovereigns, does not qualify for cruelty. Executing his most devoted chief of mercenaries because he was – truthfully – offensive regarding the courage but most importantly the efficiency of the Persian warfighting abilities was cruel and unjust: the champion of the God of Truth and Light should not have executed someone for speaking his true mind, especially since it was, if a bit exaggerated, accurate and correct. But massacring the sick bay of the army of Alexander at Issus, just before

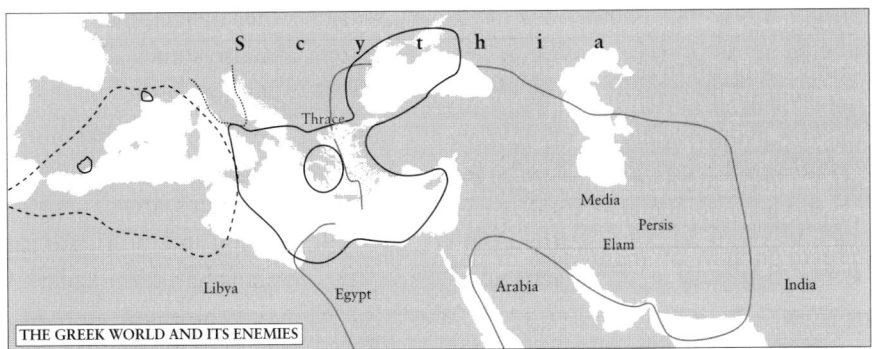

Map 1: Greek World-Persian Empire.

Key: Dotted line: The Etruscan Confederacy/Italics.
Continuous grey line: The Achaemenid Empire.
Continuous black lines: The Greek World from its core (small circle) to the full extent (closed lines).
Dashed line: The Carthaginian Empire.

the battle, and with tortures, is nothing short of a crime, similar to the executions of loyalist troops in hospitals by the Communist insurgents in the Greek Civil War, and the burning of Greek ambulance coaches full of incapacitated troops by the Turkish guerrillas and regulars in 1921 in Asia Minor.

Still, Darius was capable and efficient. He was able to recruit – or to retain – former imperial insurgents and other fugitives of high standing that had found safe havens in the court of Philip, and also senior members of the Macedonian opposition. This was a feat and a staggering success, to reacquire services of valuable associates who had previously fled in terror, and with their good services the Throne had also acquired an intimate knowledge of characters, thoughts, conditions and persons of the Macedonian court, an invaluable bonanza of intelligence.

It is not clear when exactly Darius was enthroned, but his and Alexander's ascendencies were in the same year. The assassination of Philip might also be credited to Darius and should have much to do with said intimate knowledge and contacts, if not network, established by the double-deserters as the brothers Memnon, Mendor and, most prominent of all, their former employer and in-law, Artabazus.

A very tell-tale proof of Darius' personal radiance is the devotion he commanded amongst his Greek mercenaries; a feature similar to the magnetism and leadership of Alexander – but of a lesser calibre. Yes, he was toppled and assassinated by his court and commanders; but Alexander had escaped repeatedly by a thread or less. This is no indicator of the respect they commanded. It is true that the Greek mercenaries – throughout the ages one may add – showed exceptional loyalty. Their attitude to the US Marines in the Tripoli campaign is revealing. But in the case of Darius it was not loyalty, it was devotion. They followed him till his last breath, committed to safeguard his person amongst a sea of conspirators and such attitude was quintessential to their ultimate acquittal by Alexander from the crime of sacrilege and high treason. Alexander could not execute someone who became traitor by honouring his previously held commission in the spirit of Loyalty.

The respect paid by Alexander to the murdered Emperor was political, but also of his own chivalrous disposition. But it was, to some extent, earned by Darius' merits as a character and not merely as a sovereign and commander. Darius has been belittled by many historians as below-average commander and sovereign (Hammond 1989), with the double intent either to belittle Alexander's achievements ('not too difficult to beat a lesser opponent') or, quite the opposite, by his eulogizers: he was so much better than his opponent, a light and darkness case, the utmost antithesis.

Darius was able to enact changes in the military, despite the backward and reactionary nobles; he delegated command, conducted different kinds of war, was extremely fast to adapt from one battle to the next and heard any advice that could solve a problem without prejudice. Technical, tactical, operational advice he noted and quickly implemented in a decrepit and declining, occasionally rotten mechanism. He was perhaps the most capable soldier and commander ancient Persia had to show. The verdict of the war was against him only because he faced a far better man. He was top of his class. Alexander was another class and history owes the cruel but mainly unlucky sovereign a favourable note.

The last issue is exactly the conduct of war. There are many doubts there: how can a competent commander lose his whole empire in 4 years and be crushed in battles where he chose the terrain and had numerical superiority? The answer is simple: if his enemy is much better – and perhaps with some luck. Luck is the subordinates being of vastly different calibres. Indeed, the rednecks of Alexander were not corrupted by gold and purple; this would come in time, but at the time the corruption championship was going to the Persians, hands-down.

The evidence though is clear: Darius was ready to hear sound advice and to delegate power and command. He did so correctly: the campaign of Memnon, with a small elite force of 4 or 5,000 crack Greek mercenaries made the bridgehead of Philip's troops under Parmenio and Attalus, established to the whole northwest corner of Asia Minor, from the Hellespont all the way to Ephesus and to Erythrea, opposite to the island of Chios where it was possible for Alexander to make a crossing. This foothold was enough to cause the fall of the empire, but this cannot nullify the success of the campaign of Memnon, compared to the impotence of satrapal levies. Darius further supported his choice without prejudice and after the Battle of the Granicus delegated full authority in the theatre to Memnon, perhaps making him *Karana*, something really rare if not unprecedented for a Greek or any nationality outside the core of the Empire (Persians, Medes, Elamites/Susians and Bactrians).

He did let the local forces, headed by local aristocrats, take care of the initial invasion, as they were familiar with the terrain and the resources, whereas mobilizing a host would have taken much valuable time; even if he was to command local forces in person (a case of micromanagement) to save time, travel for the King was a major and time-consuming enterprise. And time was of essence. He did provide units, especially cavalry, from the royal host, but left the locals to manage their operation. He must have also provided treasure, otherwise the swelling of the number of Greek mercenaries from the 5,000 under Memnon to the 20,000 at the Granicus, plus the garrisons of Ephesus, Miletus and Halicarnassus, cannot be explained. The locals' failure was not of his making, as they most vehemently opposed the naming of Memnon, a foreigner, as *Karana*.

Then, judging correctly that his intervention was needed, he mobilized. The lightning campaigns of Alexander, especially during the winter of 334–333 BC and his use of siege engineering, toppled his plans and Darius found himself to have lost the whole Asia Minor, in mere months, Cilicia included – the veritable gate to the Asian mainland. He judged correctly that his defeated aristocrats were fools, thickheads and incompetent to the point of criminal negligence – his Commander-in-Chief (*Spadapatish*) committed suicide. But no cowards; they paid the ultimate price at the Granicus without fear. This fact, if we have the story correctly, is as good cause as any to have Charidemus executed, if he indeed belittled the Persian valour. In his grand army Darius incorporated the mercenary forces of his navy, which was proven incapable of producing any decisive results to the rear of the invaders. He used this mercenary branch at the decisive battle, concentrating his assets where they mattered; and he used this particular asset as instructed by the experts, his mercenary generals, and attempted to re-equip accordingly his own home army (*Kardaka*). His abject failure bears evidence of his good judgment over a lost battle for an ongoing cause; a valid eye for fixing deficiencies and for hybrid warfare: instead of regrouping everything in the interior, survivors of the battle were vectored to the rear of the invaders, trying to destabilize if not reconquer – the Macedonian – Asia Minor.

Darius identified the defeat at Issus as due to tactics (he used Greek ones, in deep deployment of hoplites and in battlefield fortification by trenches) and to the tactical surprise of the Macedonian weaponry: especially the lances. He was more adaptable than many great marshals and at Gaugamela he had devised answers: linear deployment for flanking, mainly cavalry for mobile action, scythed chariots to break the enemy formations (a very keen observation on the nature of the superiority of his foe) and long lances to tackle the premium tactical advantage of his opponent. Alexander adapted his tactics again and conquered. This was not due to the inefficiency of Darius, who took every precaution: he kept his army in battle order to avoid any nocturnal surprises, he cleared and levelled the terrain to allow his wonder weapons (introduced some 70 years before at the latest, but perhaps even earlier) and formed combined forces of cavalry and infantry, something unprecedented for Persian armies, where even the combined *use* was something of a prodigy: the only such case reported has a Greek mercenary tactician in a key position.

Thus Darius III Codomanus was the best the Achaemenids – or the Achaemenid Empire, as he himself was of dubious lineage (Badian 2000) – had to show to intercept Alexander and go in a blaze of glory. Anything short of this dictum is unfair for the last Achaemenid. He valued his troops and did anything he could. He went on resisting even when deprived of country, family and treasure, as a guerrilla in the mountains. His slayers were lesser men, statesmen and warriors, than himself. The superiority of the invaders was not his fault, nor the decline of his realm. He saved the decency of his state, something Bessus, his murderer and usurper, never did, plunging his faith and religion into ignobility.

Macedonian institutions

The administrative mechanism of Alexander was fully fledged and developed when he assumed the throne; optimizations were carried out but nothing major. The institutions of Macedon were a combination of different influences. First, it was the local peculiarities plus the heritage of the previous Greek eras, especially the Bronze Age/Homeric societies. Second, the institutions many ancient monarchies shared as a parallel evolution or due to a deterministic factor. Then, the third factor, was the southern Greek influence, from democracies to tyrannies (as in Sicily) and oligarchies. Influences from the central Balkans, Thrace and Illyria was another constituent and the last, and much more important than assumed, is the Persian empire.

The last one is downplayed because modern scholars have biases: when they admire the Achaemenids, it is degrading to admit that their arch-enemies used some of their own assets against their inventors. Then, there are many scholars hostile to the Achaemenids, some from powers outright hostile to contemporary Iran, and some others from the contemporary Iran itself, whence the social and especially religious standing of the Achaemenids.

For example, the pike phalanx was a recast of the Mycenaean one, while the funeral games and athletic contests were a direct survival of the Mycenaean practices, the latter throughout classical Greece, the former discontinued in the urbanized south. The *sarissa* pike as a weapon might have been adopted from Thracians, although adapted and modified for the infantry Philip envisaged, itself a spinoff of the Iphicratean peltast. And then, there is the expeditionary quota. Alexander left behind roughly half his Macedonian force, the difference from the perfect half possibly (but not necessarily) explained by the personal guard of the King. This is the Persian standard as mentioned by Xenophon in Cyropaedia. The Spartans and the whole Peloponnesian alliance had a 2/3 expeditionary quota as mentioned by Thucydides, the Athenians none known. The only evidence is the decree of Troezen, ordaining 50 per cent but this was a naval campaign and eventually it was not implemented. Our understanding is that the Athenians mobilized judging by the conditions and the objective, not by some standard; still, the rationale and algorithms for such determinations of mobilization scales escape us.

The select bodies of troops being the King's bodyguard is a common element of monarchies throughout the Globe and many cultures; still, the Companions of the Macedonian Kings might have been a transplantation of the King's Relatives of the Achaemenids. Similar is the issue of the Royal Pages, while the Macedonian line infantry was deployed with the southern standard eight-strong file, while the nomenclature (*dekas* – ten) implied a ten-based file, the *Achaemenid* standard. It *could* be a slip of the tongue (or pen) due to the *Roman* standard, familiar to historians (i.e. Arrian) but the Achaemenid standard is a better bet for an organizational fossil. Given that Macedon came into the Persian orbit when Darius I, a great administrative mind, was on the throne, modelling of the Macedonian court and administration is a given. It must have been encouraged, if not imposed, as the administrative standardization across the multicultural and multinational empire would simplify command and control. Thus, Alexander was able to absorb the conquered territories immediately by simply delegating his own choices as Satraps. This means his staff knew well how to run a satrapy and what resources assets, and obligations such a position entailed.

Part I

The Troops

Chapter 1

The Knights

The *asabara*

Our reconstitution of the Persian military establishment of the early fifth century provides for cavalry or *asabara* (Fields 2007; Sekunda 1989 & 1992), organized in units used for independent action, flanking attacks and assault with missile weapons. These latter were mainly javelins (Her IX.18 & IX.49), which reminds one of the *palta* of the time of Xenophon (Xen Hell III.4,14; Xen Anab I.8,2) but bows were used as well (Her IX.49); still, at this time – and possibly earlier – it may perhaps be presumed that horse archers were a different arm than the *asabara* knights (Humble 1980). Peculiar metal helmets (Her VII.84) and perhaps panoply under the clothes were used, as insinuated by the scale armour of one of the high commanders, Masistius (Her IX.22). Thus, either the full cavalry force or a part of it (Delbruck 1920; Nefedkin 2006) may have been already armoured, as might be deduced from the obscure reference of cuirassiers (Her VIII.113), regardless of conventional scholarship, which considers the fourth-century armoured Persian horse a development due to the unpleasant contact with the mainland Greek *hoplite* heavy infantryman (Sekunda 1989 & 1992; Nefedkin 2006).

Still, their armour in the fourth century is more prominent (Xen Anab I.8,6), and during the fifth century, the Persian cavalry supposedly charged only broken, frontally engaged, numerically insignificant, out of formation or fleeing enemy infantry units and implemented raiding warfare and hot pursuit autonomously (Hammond 1968). It is more than possible that the Persian *asabara* was, at the day, armed with *both* javelins and bow, plus sidearms (Charles 2015). After all, this was the Scythian standard and, actually, the Byzantine and Sassanid standard of a later day. Similarly to *sparabara* infantry, this approach effectively doubled, in functional terms, the available manpower and was far from marring the focus of the knightly warriors, who had time and means aplenty for this dual training. This format was very important given that cavalry was supposed to fight isolated and with a numerical disadvantage. It is supported by Herodotus' statement that 'The Persian cavalry were armed like their infantry' (Her VII.61,1), implying directly both spear, or perhaps shafted weapons in general, and bow (Her VII.84). This is corroborated by the royal self-introduction of Darius I (DNb 2), repeated verbatim by Xerxes (Xnb): 'I am a good archer on horseback and on foot, I am a good spearman on horseback and on foot' (Llewellyn-Jones 2012) and also by a list of the armament of the Persian cavalryman during the last quarter of the fifth century, where javelins, shield and quiver were included in the kit of the mounted warrior along with sidearms (Fields 2007).

The lore that limits the education of the Persian scions to riding, archery and candour (Strabo XV.3,18; Her I.136) refers obviously to *azata* nobility and directly implies the ability of *all* cavalry, not of a portion, to shoot the bow. The insightful analysis of Matthew (2013) which concludes that the Persian shafted weapon was not only shorter but also thinner and flimsier than the Greek *dory*, with a very limited reach as it was balanced at the middle so as to be suitable for casting, too, most probably refers to the cavalry weapon (*palton* or javelin) and explains a certain reluctance of the Persian nobles to come to grips with hoplites, in stark contrast to knightly forces of Medieval Europe armed with the long, stout lance, held underarm. But by the time of Xenophon and then of Alexander the Great, the *asabara* had evolved: his armour had been enriched (Xen On Hors 12,1–7) and his main weapon was the pair of *palta* (Xen On Hors 12,12; Arr Anab I.15,5); no spear and no bow (Nefedkin 2006).

The Persian cavalry did not shirk from close engagement: adequately protected and suitably armed, with the advantage of the mass of their mounts, the Imperial *asabara* cavalrymen would close in with enemy infantry, even unbroken, to trample and slaughter (Sears & Willekes 2016). The first is attested for Artybius' horse, which reared and kicked enemy troops (Her V.111,1); the latter by Xenophon, when a Greek trooper is mentioned as holding his entrails with his hands (Xen Anab II.5,33); a secure indication of a slashing blow by sabre, not piercing thrust by shafted weapon or arrow. But smashing onto a phalanx front where *dory* spears were inclined densely and in successive lines, wielded by armoured infantrymen, partly impervious to initial missile barrage during the charge, that was another thing altogether.

The decimal organization of the cavalry and its assignment by units to infantry armies indicates a highly organized and disciplined force, standardized and thus organized centrally and consequently not suffering from a number of limitations and drawbacks inherent in knightly armies. As the governance of Darius I was highly centralized, the carefree European knight might be an unsuitable paradigm for his and Xerxes' cavalry. But there were no combined arms. In many descriptions of battles, even before the invasion of Xerxes, the cavalry is missing from the accounts, and it is *never* reported as taking position on the flanks of the infantry line. It is always in one body, not divided between wings or any other tactical entities; this is implied at the battle of Malene (Her VI.29,1) and explicitly stated at Plataea, (Her IX.32,2). The Achaemenid cavalry operated independently at Plataea in 479 BC (Her IX.14; 17,3; 20,1;40; 49,1) and before, at Eretria in 490 BC (Her VI.101,1) and when pursuing the Paeonian fugitives in 499 BC (Her V.98,4).

The size of the Persian mounts, coming from the Nyssean Fields in Media, was astonishing (Her IX.20; VII.196) and a factor contributing to the success of such cavalry. Additional momentum when charging or casting javelins, higher seat for downward crushing and cutting blows, higher speed and the endurance to carry weaponry and additional armour; all contributed to the legend and mystique of a force actually much smaller than indicated by its lore. The usual proportion was supposedly less than 1:10 cavalry to infantry (Sarantis 1975; Ray 2009), the latter being the *Greek* optimum (Plut Aris 21,1). At Marathon, a force of at least 18,000 and probably 24,000 infantry was probably supported by *one* single *hazarabam* (meaning 1,000 troops) of cavalry (Lazenby 1993). The rate is similar in the host of Xerxes (100,000 cavalry, 1.8 million infantry, 1:18) and at Issus (30,000 cavalry, 600,000 infantry, 1:20)

One thing rarely explored is the supposed cooperation of the Imperial cavalry with their infantry. It has been argued that there was no such cooperation as we understand it in Combined Arms terms (Kambouris 2022a/b/c). The *protaxis* arrangement, combined with the reports of the Scythian campaign by Herodotus, show that there was one form of co-operation: if defeated, the Persian cavalry sought refuge behind their infantry (Her IV.128,3), which had adequate anti-cavalry drill, something quite natural for massive archery protected by field fortifications, as were the *spara*-walls (Her IX.99,3). This explains the *protaxis*: the cavalry had the infantry watching their back. There must have been some drill for the infantry to open corridors for the cavalry to pass behind, and, most naturally, to pass in front for the pursuit or, if things went south, to cover the infantry flight (Her IX.68).

The Companions

When exactly the feudal cavalry of Macedon became the Companions is a valid query, but the Achaemenid influence and example of the late sixth century sounds a fitting start, under Alexander I. They were the aristocrats of the realm; filthy rich and the cadre of the higher social status from where higher officials and administrators were coming. There is no distinction between Companion cavalrymen and Companion courtiers as suggested (Rzepka 2012). They were the close associates of the King, they could be found either in the court or at their estates at different times and upon the whim of the king as standard in courts throughout the ages, and they were fighting as cavalry, obviously mustering at their home units. The staff of Alexander (Hammond 1998) was made of his most trusted men of the Companions social stratum called from their estates to his court.

Said cavalry, a knightly force of the landlords of the realm and thus feudal to its core (Fuller 1958; Rzepka 2012), was of superior quality during the Peloponnesian War, and it was the only arm that could be called upon by King Perdikkas against the invasion of King Sitalces of Thrace, with the human flood of the Balkans following him (Thuc II.100) – masses of cavalry included (Webber 2003). Competent such forces characterized the kingdom and the next iteration is after the disastrous Macedonian defeat by the Illyrians in 359 BC, which brought Philip II to the throne (Diod XVI.2,4). Philip reorganized the army of the realm and his cavalry, 600-strong in the beginning, was instrumental in defeating the Illyrians for good in 358 BC at Erigon River and reversing the results of the previous defeat of 359 BC (Hammond 1966, 1998). This is the very latest possible date for the emergence of the name Companions (*Hetairoi*). The number 600 should imply a 100-horse *Ila* or squadron (**Figure 1.1**) from each of the six territories of the Kingdom (Hammond 1992), at least initially; the conscription of these troops under Philip and Alexander is discussed in detail separately.

This organization is similar to that of the southern Greeks, or is copied from there. There were many insertions of military know-how, from doctrine and organization to weaponry from the times of Alexander I at the wake of the Persian invasion. Most importantly from Athens in 480s when the export of timber for the fleet of Themistocles brought the two states together, or later, at the times of the Athenian empire – still importing Macedonian timber – and from the Spartans under Brasidas in mid-420s (Thuc IV.124,1). The list is long, but two events are important: Iphicrates, the renowned Athenian general serving as a mercenary in Macedon and being adopted by the King (Matthew 2015; Nepos Iph 3.2), and Philip's sojourn as a hostage in Thebes during the heyday of Epaminondas (Diod XVI.2,2–3). This means his cavalry, possibly an institution in name and social function copied from the Achaemenids since the days of Xerxes and Alexander I, was of the most modern southern example, and was meant as a

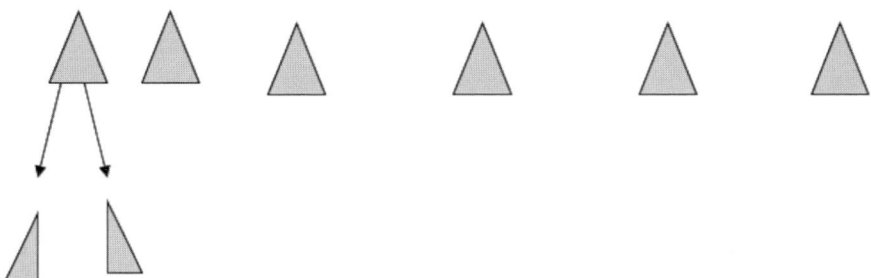

Figure 1.1: The initial cavalry force of Philip was 600 strong, evidently six hundred-man squadrons or *ilae* each raised in one of the six lowland districts of Lower Macedon. Each squadron was divided to two subunits of fifty, in accordance with the organization systems of both Greek and Achaemenid pedigree.

shock arm (Sidnell 2007). This again means *ilai* of binary type, 100-strong, divided to two fifty-strong troops (**Figure 1.1**). The name of these troops in Macedonian service escapes us but it *could* have been *Tetrarchia* (Arr Anab III.17,5), although perhaps at a later date. It should be noted that the name of the fifty-strong cavalry subunits is not well-attested for southern Greek cavalry, neither. Their presence is well-attested, but only the Spartan *Oulamos* (Esposito 2020) is known by a name.

The name *Tetrarchia* may be an anachronism on two grounds: either from the time when the *ila* had expanded to two cavalry *lochoi* (Arr Anab III.16,11) and thus reached four such subunits (see below). Or it could have been used by Arrian given that later tacticians referred in such terms to the 64-strong infantry unit (Arr Tact X.1), and at some point the said cavalry unit must have expanded to 64 as well (Arr Anab IV.3,7). The standard southern deployment of the equivalent unit would be oblong, five deep and ten wide most probably (Arr Tact XVI.11) but this may vary by the actual strength, as four-deep seems perfectly acceptable (Xen Hell III.4,13).

The outfit would be similar to the advice of Xenophon, the Greek sage on equestrian military issues in fourth-century Greece. It consisted of a heavy cavalry cuirass with flaps for the waist, Boeotian helmet, sabre, pair of *palta* double-purpose javelins, horse armour (**Plate 1**). Additional armour pieces such as neckguard, simple or the elaborate type that covers up to the chin, thighguards, tubular Persian armour for the left arm and armour patch for the right armpit (Xen On Hors 12,1–10) may have been included; the first was attested for Alexander (Plut Alex 32,5). The Companions had infantry shields, most probably Argive *hopla* (**Plate 2**) which they used for infantry assignments (Arr Anab I.6,5), but could not use in mounted operations, as the weight, volume and handling peculiarities of the *hoplon* were not compatible with riding a horse and holding the reins.

At the very least since the Second Battle of Mantinea in 362 BC, southern cavalry formations were charging against intact hoplite phalanxes hoping to cut through them. For such tasks, a wedge formation had been developed (Xen Hell VII.5,24), a better and much more elaborate arrangement than the deep column of the Achaemenid *asabara* reported since the early fourth century (Xen Hell III.4,13). The Thessalians had developed rhomboid formations (Arr Tact XVI.3; Strootman 2012) but the Macedonians were using wedges (Hanson 1999), probably copied by Philip from Thebes, despite views that the original may have been developed by the Scythians, based uniformly on a questionable interpretation of sources (Arr Tact XVI.6); there is no way that either the Thebans or the Macedonians under Philip had come into contact with Scythian battle prowess and the Thracian Connection is a rather shaky proposition.

There are two different possible conformations of the wedge (Petitjean 2017): the most likely is the 1–3–5 etc., with each rank being two troopers wider than the previous and keeping the rest of the rank directly behind

Macedonian cavalry *embolon* of 49 cavalrymen in seven rows. Each row covers the rear flanks of the previous, thus explaining the famous incident at Granicus (Arr Anab I.15,7-8); Cleitus must have been positioned left, second row, to have a shot at the armed hand of the flanking Spithridates. Aretes right, second row, so as to be fighting and easiest to reach out for Alexander, when requesting a fresh spear. Demaratus, having a spear intact, must have been middle, second row, yet unengaged and near so as to hand the fresh weapon to the king

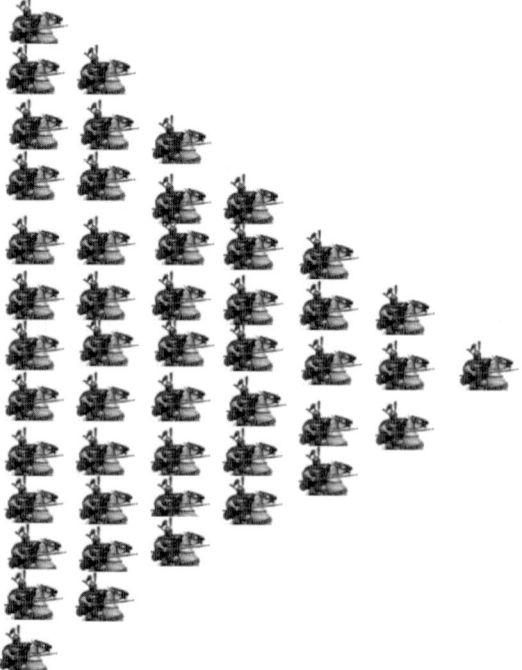

Figure 1.2: A Macedonian wedge of fifty horse (two wedges per squadron). Successive ranks differ by two troopers (1-13).

the troopers of the rank in front. With seven ranks, the sum would be 1+3+5+7+9+11+13 amounting to 49 cavalry (**Figure 1.2**), very close to the magic number 50. The 15 of an additional rank would bring the total to 64, corroborating the sixty-strong unit (Arr Anab IV.3,7), obviously a round number, if not trimmed by casualties. Additionally, this model lends itself well to a valid theory of the 'casualty logistics', regarding the ability of a cavalry squadron in a seven-rank wedge to cut clean through a standard, eight-deep phalanx (Markle 1977). Alternatively, if the troopers of each rank are positioned behind the spaces between the troopers of the previous rank the progression goes 1+2+3+4+5+6+7+8+9(+10) to a total of either 45 or 55. The addition of one more rank would result in 66 troopers, somewhat greater a diversion from the sixty mentioned (Arr Anab IV.3,7) and totally incompatible with the infantry numbers.

Despite the – hazy – proceedings in Chaeronea (Sears & Willekes 2016; Markle 1977; Rahe 1981), at the crossing of the Hellespont the Companion cavalry under Alexander was as above, lethally efficient but unremarkable. They were using javelins (Arr Anab I.2,6) and the basis was the 100-strong *ila*, compatible with the 200 horse brigaded on each wing in the campaign at Pelion (Arr Anab I.6,1) and the 200-strong detachment of Companions in Ionia, after the Granicus (Arr Anab I.18,1). They did use the mass of the horse to shove in contact (Arr Anab I.2,6) but this was still standard practice for cavalry through the centuries (Sears & Willekes 2016.).

But then, in the Battle of the Granicus, where the first massive engagement of Companions versus *asabara* happens, they did not use javelins. They used spears or, rather, lances (Arr Anab I.15,5), probably tipped at both ends (Sekunda 2001), as were the hoplite spears, and thrust at the enemy's face (Arr Anab I.15,7), while they most probably used both underhand and overhand thrusts (**Plates 3 & 4**), as this explains better than any other interpretation the sequence of the duel of Alexander and Spithridates (Diod XVII.20,3–6). Moreover, the wedge formation explains the geometry of the engagement that culminated in the famous event of Cleitus the Black saving Alexander's life (Arr Anab I.15,8).

Arrian explicitly states that the Persians themselves were using wedges, although the Greek term *Embolon*, literary 'ram', applies to column formations as well. Still, the proceedings of the personal engagement of Alexander and his entourage with the Persian leadership insinuates two wedges meeting head-on, with the lancers (Macedonians) beating the quasi-spearmen. The latter must have expended their spare *palta* while at the riverside, shooting against the Macedonian assault.

At the Granicus the Companions definitely used lances as mentioned above; whether at Chaeronea they had done the same (Markle 1978) is debatable. Thus, this weapon may have been a surprise for the Achaemenids; perhaps partial, a first use of the Macedonian cavalry lance in cavalry against cavalry format. It may have been a *total* surprise, the first time the Persians were facing, literally, the dreaded *xyston* (the term actually means 'shaft' in Greek). The weapon was made of cornel wood and was long, but not awkwardly so; shorter than the cavalry *sarissa*, somewhere near the length of the hoplite spear and thus allowing its comfortable use by one hand in both overhead and underarm modes (Gaebel 2002), which is the correct interpretation of Diodorus' version of the engagement of Alexander at the Granicus with the Persian aristocrats (Diod XVII.20,3–6).

The *xyston* brandished a spearpoint following the lines and specifications of *spears*, with a wide slashing warhead for maximum flesh damage and easy extraction, due to the inherently limited penetration into soft tissue (Howard 2011; Sekunda 2001). The wide warhead, intended to bleed unprotected body parts of mount and rider or of fleeing infantry, when thrust onto an enemy's cuirass, would present an increased chance for shattering and thus the butt point would be used immediately – this time for a face thrust. The butt point of the *xyston*, contrary to other spears and pikes, was identical in shape to the spearpoint (Sekunda 2001), a precaution against the bearer being disarmed when breaking and also to allow quick succession of thrusting fore and aft in melees and the use of techniques such as the Syrian Parry.

The weapon was a true technological miracle, and it was invented before Philip's time as it features in southern Greek pottery (Sekunda 2001). It was sturdier than the flimsy cavalry *kamax* spears of the classical age southern Greek cavalry (Sekunda 1984, 1986), which were meant to skewer infantry downwards but shattered when used against charging cavalry with frustrating frequency (Xen Hell III.4,14), thus prompting the Greek equestrian connoisseur Xenophon to demand their replacement by pairs of the Persian two-role *palton* (Xen On Hors 12,12).

The squadrons (*ilai*) of the corps were obviously of standard strength, a most prudent policy in raising, training and using an army. A year before the invasion, at Pelion, they are evidently 100-strong, as the two cavalry wings of 200 horse each (Arr Anab I.6,1) cannot imply any other arrangement than 100-strong *ilai*. And this must have been their strength at the Granicus, as no restructure of the cavalry has been reported. It still was so in Ionia, after the Granicus (Arr Anab I.18,1). But suddenly, one year later, in the opening moves of the Battle of Issus, it is explicitly mentioned that Alexander left two *ilai* of Companions to ward off any diversionary enemy action, and that

The Knights

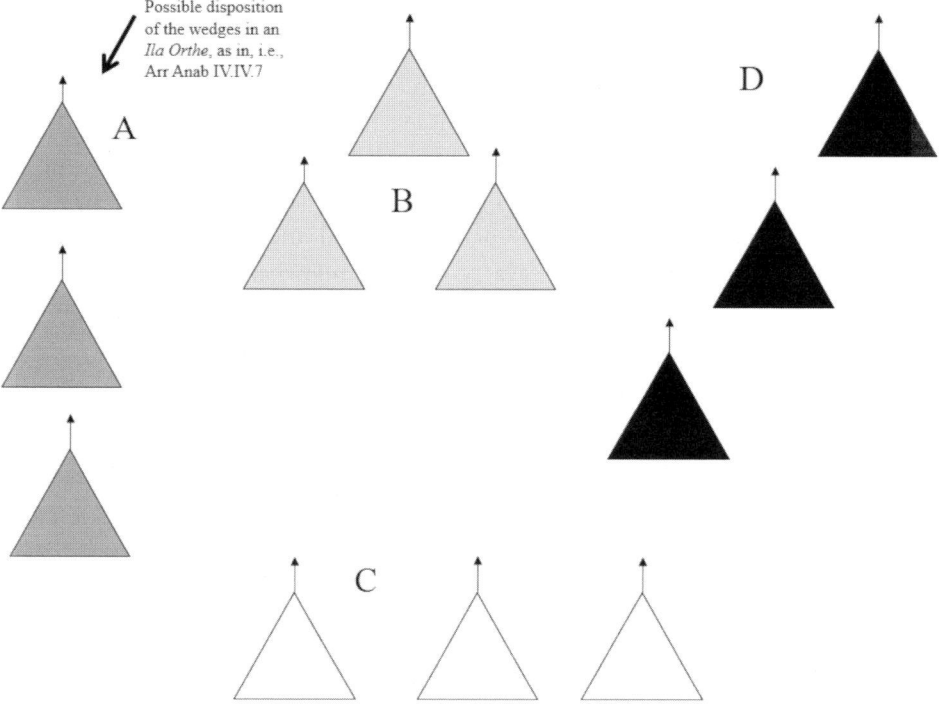

Possible formations of tertiary Ila, with three 50-man wedges

Figure 1.3: The tertiary system allowed a cavalry *ila* to deploy in depth/line ahead (A), in V-shape or hollow wedge (B), in line-abreast (C) and oblique (D), with one side projected and the other denied.

this amounted to 300 cavalrymen (Arr Anab II.9.3–4); a rare detail even for Arrian, who also mentions the names of the two units. Since this point, the Corps must be understood to comprise 'triangular', or rather tertiary, *ilai* of three squads of fifty each. This has tremendous tactical impact: the unit may take a number of formations to suit terrain and mission (**Figure 1.3**).

It is not certain that the increase of the strength of the *ila* and, more importantly, its novel structure, happened at some time between the battles of the Granicus and Issus; it could have happened any time after the campaign at Pelion, especially just before the launching of the invasion, although this might be contested (see Chapter 5). But the arrival in early 333 BC of reinforcements from Macedon, the new recruits of the year (Arr Anab I.29.4) would have enabled Alexander to raise the strength of the *ilai*. It is in vain to try to compare the number of the cavalry of the invading army, or any group, as is the 1,800 Macedonian cavalry supposedly taken by Alexander to Asia (Diod XVII.17,4), to deduce units and unit strengths.

There is no solid indications for the number of the *ilai* of the Companion cavalry; Arrian takes good care *not* to present a figure (Arr Anab I.14,1) while in other respects he gives a detailed account.

The next evolutionary step is after Gaugamela. New arrivals at Susa allow once more the swelling of the numbers; a fourth subunit is added, bringing the *ila* to 200, double its original strength, and an intermediate echelon is established, the cavalry *lochos* (Arr Anab III.16,11), two per *ile*, each with two subunits. The next step was the addition of men into the subunit; one more rank to the wedge would account for 15 more men and bringing the strength of it to 64, which corroborates well with 60 (Arr Anab IV.3,7) as already mentioned. The *ila* would sum up to 256, the same strength as the basic infantry unit, the renowned 16X16 building block of the Macedonian pike phalanx (Nefedkin 2011) which amounted to half a *lochos* (Company). This suits perfectly the 500-men cavalry detachment reported at the Persian Gates; two new *ilai* or squadrons (Arr Anab III.18,4–5), actually a *hipparchy*.

The other direction of the evolution was the grouping of *ilai* into *hipparchies* or regiments. One would expect once more a binary structure with the standard *ilai* grouped by two. In here there would be an exception, the cavalry guard, the Royal Squadron (Arr Anab III.1,4), possibly renamed at some point to Cavalry Agema (Arr Anab V.12,2) to match that of the infantry (Bosworth 1988). Its special status would suggest double-strength (Rzepka 2008), meaning 300 cavalry; whether it followed the rest of the Companion Cavalry and increased to 400 is uncertain, but probably not. It must have remained 300-strong (Bosworth 1988), as was the case with the Hypaspist Corps which never exceeded 3,000. Thus, the two elite units must have kept the standard cavalry-to-infantry 1:10 ratio in Greek armies (Plut Aris 21,1). But one could propose that before the regular *ilae* went to 150 troopers, the Royal Squadron would have been 200-strong, to be double the standard, 100-strong squadrons. This would suggest a Hypaspist Corps initially of 2,000, two chiliarchies, very similar to the two Achaemenid infantry guards (Spearbearers and Applebearers), each 1,000-strong (Her VII.40,2–41,3).

The hipparchies were four in number, as a fifth is explicitly mentioned to have been recruited from Orientals (Arr Anab VII.6,3), although there is some inconsistency over their number. Contrary to taking the terms at face value after half a millennium, it is possible to assign the discrepancies *not* to events and tacit reorganizations, for which one should guess or make up content, context and timeframe (Brunt 1963; Bosworth 1988), but to the difference in terminology in sources spanning over five centuries, when the *Find* function or the index, for that matter, had not been invented.

What is important is that once organized into Hipparchies, the Companion Cavalry absorbed the Macedonian light cavalry. The Scouts might have been elevated, at royal expense, to true Companion status, or they may have had their *ilae* (squadrons) incorporated into the Hipparchies as a light element (Griffith 1963; Bosworth 1988), which would make the Hipparchies brigades rather than regiments. In the Persian Gates a detachment of 500 cavalrymen is reported (Arr Anab III.18,4–5) as mentioned above. Rather than one *hipparchy* of two squadrons of 250, it might have been a hipparchy of two 200-strong Companion squadrons plus one 100-strong squadron of Scouts.

There is an unresolved issue on the subject of the Companion Cavalry. It is unknown how many squadrons there were. Arrian enumerates six phalanx *taxeis* all the way to Gaugamela (Arr Anab III.11,9–10) and then a seventh (Arr Anab V.11,3 & 12,1–2) in the Battle of the Hydaspes, but not the number of the Companion *ilae*, possibly because he was at a loss, too; numbers generally given are speculative. Only at Gaugamela there is a detailed account of seven Companion squadrons and on top of them the Royal Squadron (Arr Anab III.11,8). This anomaly is convincingly dealt with (Rzepka 2008) by reckoning that the Royal Squadron had been divided in two commands for this battle, thus increasing the total of the Companion Corps to eight units of rather than the usual seven (six territorial and the double-strength Royal Squadron).

But, most importantly, given that Alexander took half his army to Asia, there is a valid question on the nature of the draft. It could be that some parts of Macedon furnished cavalry and others infantry. In this case, half of the draft of an area was left behind and the other half followed the campaign, as obviously happened with the Persians (Xen Cyr I.2,9, 12). This would suit perfectly with the notion that Alexander by choice took with him the veterans of the Macedonian war machine, not the troops in the prime of life (Just XI.6,4–6). The other possibility is that each recruiting area would furnish both cavalry and infantry to satisfy some quota; this is how things were in Athens, Sparta, Boeotia etc. (Xen Const Lac XI.4; Xen Hipp II.2). In this case, Alexander had taken infantry from some areas and cavalry from others, leaving the opposites back home with Antipater (Burn 1965).

The Hippeis

The Scouts

The *Prodromoi* or Scouts are not mentioned before the reign of Philip II and this might imply they were one of his innovations (Hammond 1998) or just reflect the inadequacy of the sources. They had to be lighter and were not aristocrats; their recruitment is not convincingly determined, but their equipment definitely lacked in armour, especially the metal cuirass and the other parts as detailed above, but for exceptions (the helmet must have been standard, and fabric (linen most probably included) or leather jerkins cannot be ruled out).

To increase their survivability, a longer weapon was issued, possibly as an innovation of Alexander (Snodgrass 1967); whether only for field engagements in set-piece battles or in the scouting missions as well is not clear, as such weapons provided a very real range advantage. The weapon was called *sarissa*, and it was a version of the infantry pike but evidently shorter (Noguera-Borel 1999; Sekunda 2001; Markle 1977, 1978), as it should be wielded with one hand. It may have been couched underarm, as the medieval knights did with their lance, or it may have been used mainly for underhand thrusts and perhaps in ways similar to the moves of the lancers of late eighteenth and early nineteenth centuries. Still, in a cavalry era without stirrups and proper saddle, the long weapon had to be brandished mainly with one hand (Hammond 1998), as couching it underarm would pose severe issues of balance upon impact (Samuels 1997). Moreover, the left arm was engaged with the bridles – although this does not exclude its auxiliary use to aim the weapon; contrarily, the infantry *sarissa* was wielded exclusively with both hands (Polyb XVIII.29,3). Last, but not least, concerning the form of the cavalry *sarissa*, one would expect it to follow the typology of the *xyston* (Sekunda 2001) in order to incapacitate cavalry mounts and thus be large-bladed, something possibly accounting for such findings (Andronicos 1970), which do not warrant the ritualistic explanation (Sekunda 2001) of whatever does not fit a predetermined '3F' (form, fit and function) blueprint.

There is no reason to doubt that they could fight in wedges; their weapons would fit nicely into this context and the training syllabus would be common with the Companions. Which implies that they would be proficient with the javelin as well, irrespective their SOP (Standard Operating Procedures) regarding weaponeering (Hammond 1998). Their squadrons must have remained 100-strong; they assumed no missions requiring tertiary organization and thus being 150-strong as occasionally suggested (ibid). The number of said squadrons is usually understood to have been from four to six. If the former figure is correct, it suits nicely the number of the hipparchies, and one scout *ila* must have been incorporated in each hipparchy bringing the total strength to 500 or 600 cavalrymen (depending on whether the Companion squadrons were made of subunits of fifty or of sixty-four troops) and providing organic scouting capabilities. This version of events suggests that the *Scouts* (lancers) remained as such, but not in a separate corps. Their *ilai*, of 100 each, were absorbed as true separate *ilai* into the hipparchies. If the latter figure is correct, it suits well with the elaborate recruitment scheme assigning them to the same conscription areas as the infantry and the Companions (Rzepka 2008). Their social identity is elusive; there is no reason to consider them of Upper Macedonian stock, as the area provided excellent heavy cavalry; nor of any area out of the realm (Hammond 1998). Being subjects of the King but not Macedonians (perhaps southern settlers) is a possibility (ibid.), but it needs not be a common background for all of them; there were southern settlers serving as Companions, after all (Arr I.15,6). Non-aristocratic lineage from affluent, horse-owning and breeding social strata, including farmers, is not implausible.

The Thessalian
The Thessalians were the ultimate cavalrymen in Greece, due to socioeconomic reasons. They were the only opportunity of the Greek Alliance to secure some cavalry against the Persian invasion in 480 BC – a hope dashed as the Thessalians turned pro-Persian readily. They were raising their *ilai* in their districts, in feudal fashion and at the time of Alexander they must have numbered ten such territorially raised *ilae*, with one being of increased strength as the guard of the *Tagos*, the appointed federal Supreme Commander of Thessaly in times of duress (Strootman 2012). The fact that this was the squadron of Pharsalus (Arr Anab III.11,10) implies that somehow, the two Argeads, Philip II and Alexander III, were recognized as their *Tagoi* (Diod XVII.4,1; Just XI.3,1–2; Hammond 1994, 1989; EB 1911) and must have been affiliated or adopted by this specific city, Pharsalus, previously a hotspot of anti-Persian resistance back in the 480s (Westlake 1936; Green 1998).

In terms of equipment they were up to date, with heavy armament. They were excellent riders (after the death of Alexander they repeatedly beat Macedonian cavalry) and at some unknown time but perhaps around 371–70 BC, under their military reformer Jason of Pherae, they invented the rhomboid formation for their *ilai* (Strootman 2012). No invention of weapon or doctrinal and organizational advances are recorded thus they must have deployed standard binary *ilai* (**Figure 1.4**), being armed with the javelin, their national weapon. The loop attached to the classical Greek javelin in service since archaic times (sixth century BC at the latest), to provide better accuracy and higher velocity and thus penetrative power (Xen Anab IV.2,28), was called the 'Thessalian Thong'. Thus they must have stuck to the javelins once these came into fashion due to the somewhat painful oriental experience

16 Alexander the Great Avenger

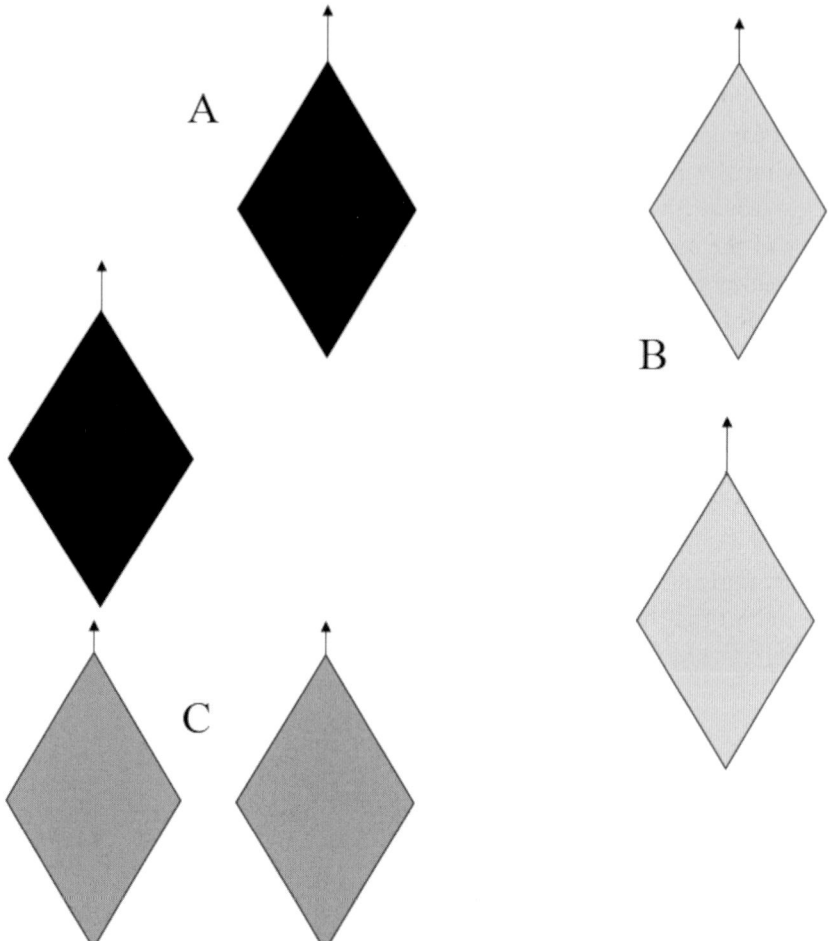

Figure 1.4: The binary system in cavalry allows only three formations: The side-by-side (C) is the most usual to cover space and increase the use of troops. Tandem (B) and slanted (A) arrangements (for penetrating deep and flank covering respectively) were also possible.

of Greek cavalry forces in the early fourth century (Xen Hell III.4,14); after all, the Companions also occasionally were using javelins (Arr Anab I.2,6). But given that the *xyston* was *not* a Macedonian invention (Sekunda 2001) it could have been adopted by other cavalry units of the time, either within the context of the army of Alexander, or, more probably, within the framework of their state of origin equipment standard.

The rhomboid was a tactical masterpiece. Made to penetrate and cut through any oblong, phalanx-like formation of infantry and cavalry, it was immensely responsive; with each trooper turning by 90 degrees, the whole formation was facing sideways; or backwards in the same manner. All other formations had to change direction by performing open, concerted turns, which produced windows of vulnerability (Xen Ages II.3). The rhomboid changed promptly; this would be vital to move instantly out of the way of the Persian cavalry columns charging with great momentum, but generally following the leader, by some tenths of metres sideways and the Persian charge would hit empty space and their vulnerable flank would be exposed to one of the corners of the rhomboid as the latter would wheel back by the troops simply about-facing.

True, for a given number of men, say fifty, the standard subunit (a 100-man rhomboid would have been very awkward) their breadth would be only seven men, compared to the thirteen of the wedge (**Figure 1.2**). The sequence for the rhomboid would be 1+2+3+4+5+6+7+6+5+4+3+2+1, contrary to the kind of sequence used for the wedge (**Figure 1.5**). A waste of manpower for frontal, set action, where a front should be covered with a given number of men and extend as wide as possible to allow flanking. The charge would develop fairly straightforwardly in most cases, thus why spend men in the back half of the rhomboid?

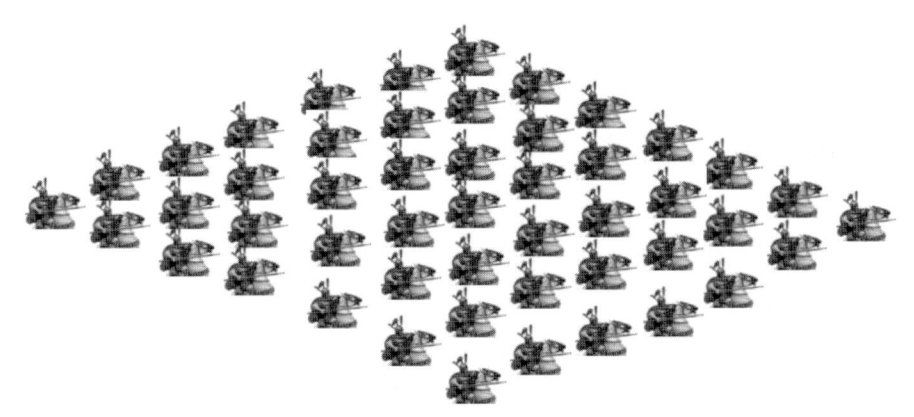

Figure 1.5: A Thessalian rhomboid of fifty horse (two rhomboids per squadron). Successive ranks differ by one trooper (1-7-1).

Chapter 2

The Line Infantry

The Foot Companions or Phalangites

It is well-established that the traditional Macedonian military branch was the cavalry (Thuc II.100), definitely feudal in nature (Rzepka 2012). This may have been due to social structure, Achaemenid influence or the suitability of the ground to both raise horses and use them in combat. But with Philip this changed: the infantry became prominent. It was massive, cheap, disciplined, useful in defence and offence, in combat engineering tasks and siege warfare. Thus the commanding officers (CO) of the infantry instalments, the *taxeis*, were Generals; the commanding officers of the equivalent cavalry formations, the *ilae*, were not of equal footing, nor were the commanders of the *chiliarchies* of the Hypaspists. Equal standing to these generals had only the Commander of the whole Companion Cavalry and of the Hypaspist Corps (Bosworth 1988) – and higher seniority, at that – and perhaps the COs of allied and mercenary divisions and contributions, brigaded together into homogenous groups. This sits well with the view that the two forces, the Companions and the Hypaspists, were the royal part of the Army, along with specialists and mercenaries, while the Foot Companions were the territorial part (Burn 1965; Fuller 1958).

The line infantry of Alexander III, and Philip II before him, was the Foot Companions who formed the Macedonian pike phalanx. The name 'Foot Companions' was a surrogate for the noblemen who were named the Companions, as a way to allow a measure of prestige to the rank and file infantry, raised by the commoners (English 2002). This implies that Philip II christened them, as it was during the early months of his reign that such measures were desperately needed, to reman and reform the crashed and depleted national Macedonian Army (Matthew 2015). Or Philip, by conscripting the sum of the Macedonian human resources into his new-model Phalanx, rather than a meagre proportion (as was the southern hoplite raising system) expanded the status of Foot Companion to all enfranchised Macedonian males drafted into the infantry under the colours of the King. The Hypaspists, who would also take the field as pikemen, must have been his own invention as well, in mimicking the elite standing armies of the southern Greek military establishments, but at a massive scale, rather reminiscent of the Persian Standing Army, the Immortals. Of course there are different opinions on the matter, founded to different ancient sources, but unfortunately such sources do not coincide and the interpretation becomes a bit subjective and precarious; not erroneous by definition, but less convincing.

The Foot Companions were line infantry. Like the *sparabara* and the *hoplites* (the latter after the Persian Wars) when they were sent on expeditions they would have been employed not only in set-piece battle but in other types of warfare, over broken ground and in loose (if any) order. At least since 400 BC the hoplites were habitually performing assaults over rough terrain in no linear order, but in column formations, similar to the 'Towers' of the Mycenaeans (Hom Il IV-334) and the similar arrangements of the Napoleonic Wars. The exemplary use of this mode by the 10,000 of Xenophon (Xen Anab IV.8,14) implies it was not something new; it was standard drill and the troops and officers knew how to execute and to adapt it to the specific tactical context. This understanding suggests conclusions regarding equipment and organization of the Macedonian infantry, especially given their distinct origin from the destroyed army of Perdikkas III and the new army of Philip.

Development and evolution
The evolution of the Macedonian phalanx stems directly from the hoplite ancestry, but with some more ingredients added. The expedition of Brasidas in the last quarter of the fifth century BC (Thuc IV. 126) perhaps led to the development of a Macedonian hoplite arm, but the results must have been ambiguous at best: a mix of tradition and socioeconomic factors made the transplantation of the hoplite system a rather risky attempt. Despite considerable successes, with the model being exported to Carthage, Etruria, Phoenicia, early Rome and most probably Illyria (Salimbeti & D'Amato 2014; D'Amato & Salimbeti 2018; Sekunda 1995) there were some mixed feelings on the subject: some Greek areas never really adopted it, although situated in the midst of the Hellenic peninsula, and some other neighbours such as the Thracians clearly desisted (Webber 2001).

Moreover, a truly effective hoplite arm demanded high costs and efficient training and this had a socioeconomic impact (Taylor 2021). It was perhaps cheaper to hire mercenaries for the campaigning season but the solution was untrustworthy; mercenaries could always cause more trouble than they solved, and the expense was counterproductive. The user or employer was left with no residual increase of his deterrence when the mercenaries were decommissioned (Randall 2012). When Iphicrates, the famous Athenian general and *condottiere* found shelter and employment in the court of Aegae, he introduced his military innovations to the Macedonians (Burn 1965) and was acknowledged or adopted as (step)son of the ruling monarch Amyntas, father of Philip II (Matthew 2015). An ardent disciplinarian and a professional soldier, Iphicrates had been working with the problem of introducing considerable hoplite-quality infantry to counter dense infantry formations in short time for a wealthy master with ample human resources, without the extensive training period and the liabilities as the intimacy with the immediate comrades in battle needed for achieving unit cohesion. During his service with the Persians in one of their invasions of Egypt in early fourth century, he based his new troop type, the *Iphicratean*, on the peltast (Diod XV.44,2–3), a model in abundance and of which he had exceptional experience. Operating under the auspices of Athens against Sparta in the Corinthian War as a Commander of Peltasts, he had become a hero (Xen Hell IV.5,13–17).

Although in Greek service peltasts were used for skirmishing and ambushing only, given that hoplites performed most of the other functions (and at no special cost, for they were draftees or fixed-contract mercenaries), Iphicrates was acquainted with the original Thracian example. In Thrace peltasts were the main troop type; they featured differentiated armament and fulfilled any number or roles, including that of infantry of the line ('line' being inaccurate a term for the peltasts; 'close contact' or 'mass' may be more accurate). Their kit included hand weapon, javelins *or* spear and any defensive item (helmet, corselet, greaves) one could get his hands on (Webber 2001, Best 1969) plus the *pelte* shield. Thus, Iphicrates improved and standardized the – extremely basic – kit of mercenary peltasts. He issued circular or slightly oval bucklers instead of the crescent pelte (but of similar construction), standard boots, light body protection from perishable materials (Garlan 1994), helmet and armed the new model with longer offensive weapons; both a longer sword and a longer spear (Matthew 2015). These longer-standard weapons may well have been typical in Thrace in some form or other. This way the new troops, being much easier and cheaper to equip, would retain mobility and would have been simpler to train as very close contact and cohesion/ coordination were not needed.

Still, they would be able to face hoplites, trying to secure victory at the first contact, during spear-thrust exchange (*doratismos*) and before coming to grips. Once successful in the spearfight, thanks to the reach of their longer spear, their inferiority in pushing or shoving, the factor behind the high demands in training and the high cost of shield/hoplite kit (Kambouris et al 2019) would not matter. A great many hoplite battles had been decided before pushing, much less shoving, were ever needed (Matthew 2012).

This troop type would had been the best solution for Macedon. Coupled to rigorous training and ample manpower, it could have been all that the kingdom needed. But it was not. Most probably this troop type also required a tactical flair in its use, which was not available after Iphicrates was gone; and also a social revolution.

The crushing defeat by the Illyrians in 359 BC provided the social revolution Philip needed to pass his innovations. To them, another ingredient was added later, the tactical brilliance combined with iron discipline, both lessons learned from Philip II as he was a young hostage in the environ of Epaminondas in Thebes. A philosophical, dialectic approach to command and tactics instead of the civic decadence to professionalism and tradition in Athens and Sparta, resulted in high troop morale and loyalty among the Macedonian peasantry that had been mobilized massively to deliver the country from the Illyrian menace. The loyalty and the desperation allowed rigorous training and drilling; the latter offered extreme confidence, improved the morale and increased the troop effectiveness. Philip used all these ingredients on the basis of the Iphicratean trooper (Burn 1965); after all, both Iphicrates and Epaminondas were firm disciplinarians. And he added the extra-long *sarissa*, held with two hands; the longer Iphicratean spear was probably still wielded with one hand.

The length of the *sarissa* of the days of Alexander is handed over to us by Theophrastus, a student of Aristotle and direct contemporary of the campaign. The size demands wielding by both hands, which poses specific requirements to the shape, size and outfit of the shield, the training syllabus and the posture of the body when engaging. This two-hand pike idea was nothing new as it was current in the past and current in the East (Howard 2011; Heckel & Jones 2006). It reflected older Mycenaean lance practices as depicted in the Dagger of the Hunt (**Plate 3**), and was perhaps enacted at the time by the Thracians (Anson 2010) and the Chalybes in Asia Minor (Xen Anab IV.7,16). The former used it in disciplined and drilled formations, the latter ad hoc and over favourable terrain (Andronicos 1970; Best 1969; Webber 2001), possibly – but not probably – (also) in cavalry applications (Markle 1978) but definitely as a weapon for peltast-type infantry (Best 1969). Philip had fell victim to one such weapon brandished by a Triballi tribesman, whether on foot or mounted on horseback, in 339 BC, which lamed him and killed his horse under him (Anson 2010). As a result he was personal witness to its lethality and efficiency. Whether he had appreciated the weapon long ago or just then (Markle 1978) is open to discussion; one does not need to feel it to appreciate it, especially its obvious range advantage over the hoplite spear (Heckel & Jones 2006).

Still, such a concept allowed a far sturdier weapon with the prospect to pierce shields *and* armour and not just to snipe over them, as with the hoplite spear. Its sturdiness allowed even better repulsive effect against cavalry, which was evolving to more and more heavily armoured types, especially in the Persian Empire, conceivably to some extent due to the traumatic results of the contact with hoplites. The new Persian cavalry was much better protected against hoplite weaponry (Sekunda 1992), a fact that amplified the effectiveness of the adoption of the Greek kopis and of the traditional javelin armament. But with the Macedonian infantry adopting the *sarissa*, these factors changed again, in favour of the infantry.

Organization and deployment
The recruitment was most probably on a provincial basis (discussed later in detail) and perhaps followed Achaemenid practice, at least in expeditionary quota, meaning the dispatch of 50 per cent of available forces (Xen Cyr I.2,9). The organization of the force followed southern examples, Theban or Athenian (Rzepka 2008). The *taxeis* were territorial divisions (Diod XVII.57,2). They were usually named by their commander and not by the recruitment area, but the commander is always a local, corroborating a territorial army structure (Bosworth 1988; Heckel & Jones 2006). The southern *taxeis* were 1,000-strong, and in the Athenian army they are made of two 500-strong *lochoi*, under *lochagoi*. These officers are mentioned to attend a war council under Alexander (Arr Anab III.9,6) and thus were more important and less in number (Bosworth 1988) than the file leaders under the same title of later days, as described in post-fourth century tactical manuals (Arr Tact V.4–6). As the Greeks favoured width in their deployment, both to outflank the enemy and to avoid it themselves, the two *lochoi* were usually deployed side-by-side (**Figure 2.1B**). In some cases tandem deployment could be used **Figure 2.1A**), and 'en echelon' (**Figure 2.1C**) was an option if a number of units – an army – was involved, although there are no records of such an arrangement, with the possible exception of Leuctra, 371 BC by the Thebans under Epaminondas.

This means that the Macedonian *taxis* was 1,000-strong, and the figure 1,500 which is usually associated with the unit refers to its tertiary transformation (**Figure 2.1**). This fits the 150-strong *ilae*, corroborating the 10:1 ratio of infantry to cavalry (**Figure 2.2**). Furthermore, 1,500 is the result produced by the division of the number of the Macedonian infantry reported for the initiation of the invasion, i.e. 12,000 (Diod XVII.17,3–5),

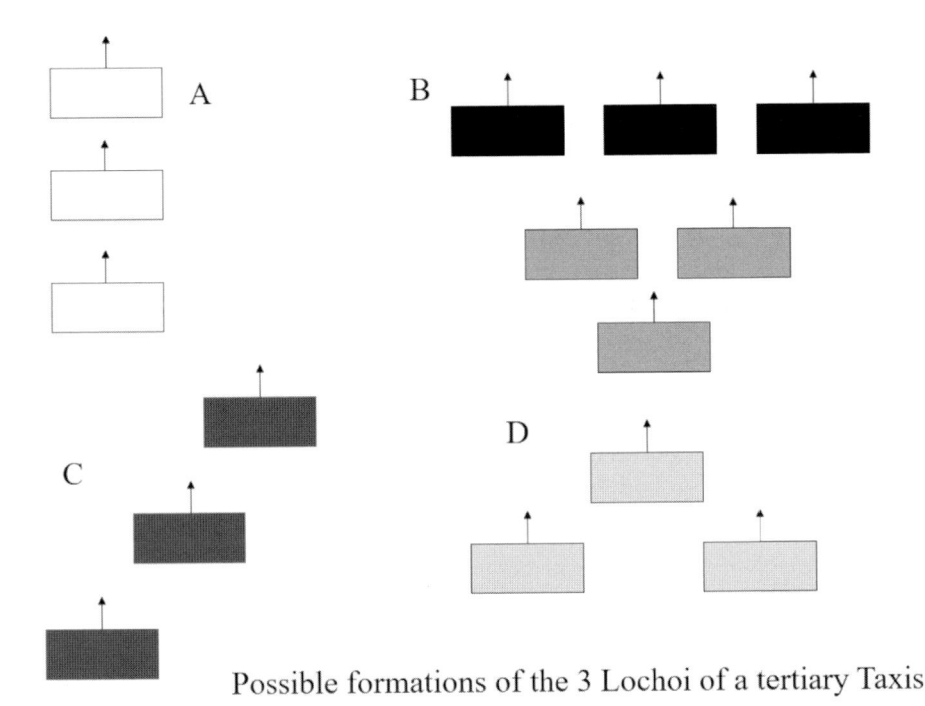

Possible formations of the 3 Lochoi of a tertiary Taxis

Figure 2.1: The tertiary system allowed an infantry *taxis* to deploy its three *lochoi* in depth or line ahead (A), in line-abreast (B), obliquely (C) with one side projected and the other denied or in V shape or hollow wedge, both standard and inverted (D).

minus the Hypaspists (3,000) by 6, the number of *taxeis* mentioned at the Granicus (Arr Anab I.14,2–3) by the simplest interpretation of said text, as there are some complications. But the latter is misleading: the number of the Hypaspists in the beginning might have been lower, say 2,000. Additionally, there is no specific mention that there were *only* six *taxeis*: other Macedonian units or subunits of considerable strength had been dispatched to strategic points (Arr Anab I.28,3). And finally the number of the Macedonian infantry is a bit vague: whether the number of Diodorus includes any Macedonian light infantry, including but not limited to Macedonian archers and/or Macedonian troops of the advance guard that were stationed in the bridgehead in Asia (Pol Strat V.44,4–5; Diod XVII.7,10) is not clear. The reason for the difference in the strengths of the invading force recorded in the sources (Brunt 1963): 35,000 (Arr Anab I.11,3) vs. 36,500 (Diod XVII.17,4–5) vs. 45,300 (Plut Alex 15,1) may well be the men already in Asia, but also the unaccounted-for auxiliaries, especially the members of the medical, the geographical and the engineer or siege corps.

Figure 2.2: The fourth-century Greek ideal in force structure is one cavalryman and one light infantryman for ten heavy infantry, of which one tenth is elite, in permanent high-readiness. The 1:1 ratio of elites, light infantry (which should have been in abundance for social reasons) and the cavalry could imply that the light infantry had the function of *hamippoi* in combination with cavalry and/or the *parentaxis* combination of hoplites and missile troops.

Arms and armour

Most of the information on the phalangite gear comes from later periods; in fact there is no record of the campaign of Alexander by any contemporary source. It is usually conjectured that a state that created the pikeman for lack of funds to make hoplites was not able to outfit such troops with panoplies, neither as standard issues nor in the form of subsidies (Anson 2010; Heckel & Jones 2006); and they were not able to afford purchasing them in a purely individual basis (Anson 2010). This sounds logical, but Philip may have created pikemen by choice. The type is suitable and compatible with impoverished populations, as were the medieval Swiss, the archetypal pikemen in Europe (Anson 2010). But there are other significant advantages, tactical and logistical. The range advantage and the asymmetric nature can be listed among the former. The latter is not limited to acquisition, but includes direct and indirect costs (including time, a most unyielding necessity) regarding training and organization; the pike, when limited to basic skill, requires less training than the basic hoplite gear (Anson 2010). *All* these were essential factors.

Philip's finances were in bad shape; his army was in worse, and the army was the priority. With an effective army the finances would come around by not paying national treasure as compensation, tax, fee, bribe or losing it as loot; thus *any* currency available, in cash or credit, would have gone to the army anyhow. After all, poverty was not incompatible with hoplite warfare. Not all the hoplite mercenaries of Cyrus the Younger were gentlemen-adventurers. Very poor candidates from Arcadia and Achaea made up quite a proportion (Fuller 1958).

In any case, in 334 BC Macedon was in a much better shape than when Philip created the phalanx and the expenditure for issuing defensive items could be undertaken by the state, at least partly, by subsidizing individual investment, as implied by the actual existence of panoplies in the line infantry (Matthew 2015), even if of perishable material (Garlan 1994). The

Romans did that for armour, the Athenians for cavalry mounts and fodder – and this without taking into account the standard issue of spear and shield to create sizeable hoplite armies. If Athens could issue shield and spear, Macedon could as well – and did. This means that the pikeman was a matter of deliberate evolution, not a forced move due to lack of funds.

Arrian directly states that in an engagement in Pisidia, after winning the battle, the Macedonian infantry of Alexander were not able to pursue effectively the enemy because the latter were lights and the former *hoplites* (the term used in the text) and thus heavier (Arr Anab I.28,6–7). The helmet and the Macedonian shield, if at the time it was the buckler of the second century BC, do not account for such description; body armour is implied, but this might well have been greaves and cuirass in a provisional basis: they may have been issued to part of the phalanx, front ranks, obviously, the ones most exposed, but also the first to give chase and thus encumbered by said items (Matthew 2015; Heckel & Jones 2006).

Changes in the kit are expected and have happened, as when *hemithorakia* (half-cuirasses, covering only chest and belly but not the back, where the straps met and crossed) were issued as a disciplinary measure for the massive flight in some battle (Pol Strat IV.3,13). In such a case, when refitting the army after the wear and tear became insurmountable, a massive re-issue of equipment took place, to raise the spirits and strike awe to the natives. It was a massive investment with 25,000 new panoplies issued and the old suits burned (Curt IX.3,21). The process shows an honoured retirement of the old, worn-out equipment, reminiscent of many troops throughout the ages who name their weapons (especially swords and bows and, in Ancient Greece, shields), honour and cherish them and consider them comrades. The event directly implies non-metallic equipment, similar to *linothorax* (**Plates 3, 4**).

Furthermore, the distribution of armour was not uniform. The code of Amphipolis makes clear that the file leaders had armour (and were fined for losing it) whereas the rest of the file did not. But this code refers to a steeply declining Macedon in the third and second century.

On the other hand, it is regularly stated that the best armed *and* lightest of the phalanx (Arr Anab IV.28,8) were used for some missions requiring mobility. This does not refer to whole *taxeis*. When one or more *taxeis* were selected for a task, this is directly stated (Arr Anab III.24,1) and it is not mutually exclusive with the selection by the suitability of the kit (Arr Anab IV.28,8). So when the *lightest* are mentioned (Arr Anab III.23,3), this refers to some division *within* the *taxeis* and most probably uniform to all of them. One would suggest an age differentiation, as in the Republican Roman legion, where the younger ages, the *Velites*, had lighter gear (Polyb VI.21,7 & 22,1–3) and amounted to a quarter of a legion's strength (Polyb VI.21,9–10). Closer to Macedon, the southerners had developed the *ekdromoi* extra light hoplites, darting out of the phalanx to pursue enemy skirmishers and missile troops such as peltasts. These are directly mentioned for the first decade of the fourth century (Xen Hell IV.5,14), but probably were operating since much earlier, if not during the Persian Wars as well (as at Marathon), trained in the sports event of *hoplitodromos* (Kambouris 2022a,b). The equivalent of the *ekdromoi* in the Macedonian phalanx must have been the 'most suitably armed and lightest' as mentioned – and referenced – above.

The helmet was an indispensable item, as head wounds are always incapacitating and usually fatal and both Greeks and barbarians used cutting (chopping or slicing) sidearms, anything from cleavers and sabres to axes and clubs (**Plate 5**), studded or not. Initially the draftees may have had a choice, any helmet they could find as a family relic, a gift, a fine purchase or a prize. The whole range of southern types must have been used. Once finances allowed, uniforms were introduced, a step to produce a larger, more prestigious and more cohesive military. Regarding such standard issue practices, the *konos* helmet appeared (**Plate 3**), a vastly improved version of the Laconian *Pilos* helmet. Like its progenitor it was mass-produced (Juhel 2009) while the Hypaspists were probably issued with elaborate Phrygian helmets (**Plate 4**) and better, possibly metallic, or metal-reinforced armour (Sekunda 1984; Markle 1977). The Companion cavalry under Alexander must have standardized to the Boeotian type (English 2002; Sekunda 1984; **Plate 4**) as suggested by Xenophon (Xen On Hors 12,3).

The signature pike of the phalanx infantry was the *sarissa*. Its length was at the time, by the authority of Theophrastus (Hist Plant III.12,1–2), a contemporary of Alexander and a Master in Botany, something like 4.5m (Sekunda 2001) although the measurement of Theophrastus allows alternative interpretations to 5.8m (Connolly 2000). The explicit remark of Theophrastus to the 'longest *sarissa*' means there was at least one shorter example already in his days (Markle 1977), and this must have been the cavalry model.

The weapon had, per standard Greek practice, a butt spike used as a counterweight, but mainly to plant the weapon upright for some time, as when at camp or in waiting for the enemy. It could be used, most probably, to fix it at a slant so as to make it steady for impaling charging cavalry – or infantry – and thus repulsing assaults, especially of armoured cavalry and troops riding large animals, such as elephants and camels. And finally, if the warhead was chopped off or broken off, a secondary warhead was available (Andronicos 1970; Markle 1977; Connolly 2000; Sekunda 2001); not a very effective one, but much better than reverting to the sword in a line engagement.

The archaeological findings do not unanimously reveal the nature of the *sarissa*. It is a matter of some debate whether it had a rather small, penetrating primary warhead to defeat shields and armour (Connolly 2000; Sekunda 2001) or a large one (Andronicos 1970; Hanson 1999, Sears & Willekes 2016), to intensify bleeding and bone and muscle damage, especially against large targets such as horses (Sekunda 2001) and restrict penetration to facilitate extraction of the weapon. Though, there is no reason for taking one exclusive position: even at the very same military context, there could have been two cases of points, the penetrative for infantry pikes and the large, intended for major soft tissue damage in cavalry examples, following the similar configuration of the cavalry *xyston* (Sekunda 2001). It is not very probable, but should remain an object in discussing the weapon.

Large, wide warheads, even when not achieving penetration, could prove detrimental for the enemy personnel, tactics or materiel. They could damage and degrade the integrity of some defensive weapons, the example being light shields. This is especially so in the case of layered or composite construction, as were the Roman *scuta*, the Persian *spara* and *taka* and the Thracian and Greek *peltai* (**Plate 5**). Furthermore, especially when used in a combined, synchronized manner, they delivered considerable stopping power against well-protected enemies (Matthew 2015), pushing them back, stopping their forward momentum and knocking them out of balance, to impede an onslaught and slow down or stop cold their advance. Given that oriental long shafted weapons such as the *naginata* had massive warheads and that the European armies, using pikes with small, penetrating points, also used long halberds, the comparative argument against massive warheads for the *sarissa* (Sekunda 2001) is not entirely convincing; especially as the Mycenaean pike, the *egxeia*, had a massive thrust and slash warhead, although narrow in width (Kambouris 2014; Howard 2011).

One may ponder whether different parts of the phalanx, meaning different ranks, were armed differently not only in terms of armour, and thus likely to be divided to lighter and heavier (Arr Anab IV.28,8) but also in terms of the tip of the *sarissai*, which would explain the division between 'better armed' (for a specific occasion) and the rest (Arr Anab IV.28,8). It is an interesting thought, though a long shot, to suppose some kind of association between the type of *sarissa* point and the extent of the kit; whether lighter-armed troops had been issued preferentially one type of *sarissa* while the others used the other type.

And this may be followed further, to age and pedigree: younger or older Foot Companions were preferred for a type of weaponry, as with the Roman Triarii, and this might have something to do with previous experience in hoplite warfare: the survivors of the army of Perdikkas of 359 BC, when trained as pikemen, had already some knowledge and skill in hoplite warfare, which the new recruits, especially the ones from Upper Macedon, had not. It stands to reason that the former hoplites were issued heavier gear and may have progressively passed from the phalanx, by merit, to the Hypaspists or Argyraspids.

Another issue of debate is whether the *sarissa* was unitary, in terms of shaft, or composite, of two parts held together by a metal sheath as found in Vergina (Andronicos 1970; Markle 1977). The sheath could be very practical even for a unitary weapon as a handle, but for a composite one it was indispensable, as the two parts were brought together in it. This implies that the warhead was fixed onto a shorter shaft, perhaps as short as half that of the full *sarissa* (Andronicos 1970; Matthew 2015) which could be used as a hoplite spear whenever the Phalanx, any part of the phalanx, Foot Companions (Hammond 1994; Markle 1978; Heckel & Jones 2006) or Hypaspists (Montagu 2000; Anson 2010; Markle 1977) were to engage as hoplites, or, at the very least, with a hoplite spear instead of the full-length but more cumbersome *sarissa*. This arrangement also facilitated transportation, maintenance/replacement and safekeeping of the weapons.

This theory is attractive in the implication that one part of the weapon, the front, could be used as a hoplite spear for any kind of engagement, especially close ones, as in storming operations, naval battles, mobile or counterinsurgency operations and so on (Markle 1978; Hammond 1994), as was the case with the rather short spear of the Persian *sparabara* (Kambouris 2022a), though this kind of modularity is not attested as a standard practice for the era nor is it recorded as a priority of the commanders and warriors. Most importantly, it is somewhat difficult to prove how such a weapon would be durable on impact in any degree, or even rigid enough to aim properly and steadily. The manufacture of European pikes from the trunk of suitable trees (Sekunda 2001; Connolly 2000) allows for one-piece shafts and there is no example of the rigid weapons of this kind coming from Europe to be of such modular construction, possibly for very good reasons...

In many cases, art shows infantry of the army of Alexander using hoplite shields, as in the Alexander Sarcophagus (**Plate 4**). At one incident, in Thrace, the phalanx troops laid down and covered themselves with their shields to avoid hand-wagons loaded with stones wheeling down an inclination against them (Arr Anab I.1,9). This incident implies unequivocally large, robust hoplite shields. This may refer to a unit of the Hypaspists, as such shields seem to go part-and-parcel with Phrygian helmets (**Plate 4**) and they are known to have used Argive shields, at least occasionally (Sekunda 1984; Kambouris et al 2019).

Still, although there is consensus that the phalanx used bucklers, this is a bit retro-projecting. Bucklers are securely attested for later phalanx (Plut Aem 19,1); they were less concave and smaller than the Argive shield but still circular in shape, although rimless, to allow use while the left hand, passing through both the central grip, *porpax*, and the secondary, *antilabe*, protruded to the right to support the *sarissa*. Their carriage, strapped diagonally over the neck and shoulder and the double hoplite grip comprising the porpax in the middle and the antilabe near the edge (**Plate 2**), the latter possibly an extension of the neck strap (Matthew 2015) is nothing more than an evolution of the internal carriage of the hoplite shields as depicted in art.

And then there is the very concave Macedonian buckler, still rimless and of smaller size than the Argive shield, shown in representations. The use of this item remains elusive; using it with the *sarissa* is impossible, but the prominent concavity allows excellent deflection of missiles and blows. Still, it is a late arrival, from the time of Antigonus Gonatas (in the third century BC). It is larger than the buckler, which is less concave than the *hoplon*, while the late Macedonian item is *more* concave (**Plate 3**) than the *hoplon* (**Plate 2**), and it is not a part of the era of Alexander (Markle 1977).

The greaves were the signature item of the panoply for the Greeks. In the Iliad, the Greek troops are many a time called 'the Greeks bearing nice greaves' (Hom Il I-17). Possibly suspended during the expeditionary phase of hoplite warfare, in the mid- to late-fourth century, it is just as possible that the scarcity in late classical representations refers to the subsidized hoplites rather than the true hoplite class and/or purely economic realities. In any case, panoplies returned to favour in the mid-fourth century (Sekunda 1986). An excessive item for surrogate hoplites as the first phalangites might have been, under royal subsidy (Diod XVI.1,3) it is highly likely that in the days of Alexander at the very latest they were back in vogue (Hammond 1994), and Arrian names the greaves in the kit of heavy infantry (Arr Tact III.5) and not the cuirass (Pol Strat IV.2,10). It is expected that the Hypaspists and the file leaders of the *Pezetairoi* would have adopted the greaves, but the rank and file would also, if they had the means. It is not only the expected rough terrain in Asia. It is the limited protection afforded by the buckler and the incapacitating blows one would expect to get from missile troops firing massively and low, in order to disrupt a phalanx advance. The *sarissai* do not protect from direct, low shots as they do from ballistic ones (Polyb

XVIII.30,3) as detailed later. They are presented shortly before impact, in order to allow the troops to manoeuvre unmolested, and also to spare the following ranks from the buttspikes of the *sarissai* of the preceding ranks, especially in certain, more care-free conditions, as during an approach, or under duress (Heckel & Jones 2006).

The sidearm is the last issue in the outfit of the phalangite. At this time sidearms were made of iron, perhaps totally replacing the bronze that had survived – though minimally – as the material for the blades. In terms of shape and type, the original hoplite straight broadsword, an excellent cut-and-thrust weapon originating from the bronze-age Naue II and evolving to a leaf-shaped, medium-size two-edged blade with ridge, was superseded. The *Kopis* cleaver or sabre (**Plate 4**) was popular, as it was easier in using and handling (Snodgrass 1967). Such weapons must have been immensely popular in the army of Alexander, amongst both cavalry and infantry; Cleitus the Black must have used it to chop off the arm of a Persian noble at the Granicus, at the nick of time to save Alexander (Arr Anab I.15,8).

But when Iphicrates developed his medium infantry troops (Konijnendijk 2014), who might have been the inspiration of Philip for his phalanx, he armed them with a longer sword (Diod XV.44,2–3). To discuss the issue of length, true swords, not sabres, are compared and stabbing action is considered the primary assault mode. This weapon of the literary sources may just account for a rhomboid-bladed, straight broadsword present in contemporary art (**Plate 1**). Given that Iphicrates spent some time in Macedon and his innovations were followed, if not implemented as they were, this item may have been in vogue, especially within the infantry. The longer Iphicratean sword was technically an innovation, antagonizing the established cleaver, and allowed more elaborate use to well-trained bearers. It was available to the troops probably on the basis of personal preference rather than standard issue. This suggests it was for the armies of Amyntas and Perdikkas, which preceded that of Philip and which were smaller and most probably hoplite-orientated.

The Hoplite

When the Persian Wars (*sensu lato*) erupted in the late sixth century, the hoplite, as a warrior and a socioeconomic entity, had undergone profound evolution since the original concept of the seventh century and operated mostly within the phalanx. In conceptual and technological terms he had evolved even more. And from the Persian wars to the campaign of Alexander, the evolution was still more noticeable.

The panoply had evolved in all three main parts (helmet, cuirass, greaves) and most of the secondary parts, such as thigh and arm guards and lower-belly guard had been discarded long ago to reduce weight and cost. From this stage, the standard during the Persian Wars, more armour items were discarded partly to allow lighter formats for the expeditionary warfare of the Athenian Empire and its antagonists, and partly so as to field more hoplites with state subsidies. Once spear and shield were issued, and training was under state sustenance and oversight, the acquisition of the rest of the kit, meaning sidearm and helmet (both considered non-essentials but rather nice to have) meant affordability to an unprecedented number of citizens and resident aliens.

The *dory* spear, after some evolution (as in the pair of single-pointed, cast-and-thrust weapons of the sixth century), had been standardized to a single, thrust-only weapon, hurled as a missile only in extreme conditions (Xen Hell IV.6,11) but perfectly weighted, so as to *be* a missile should the need be, despite its length. It was powerful enough to penetrate armour and long enough to counter cavalry and protrude beyond the front of the hoplite phalanx in order to intercept the foe before a physical impact on the shields of the first rank (Anderson 1991; Snodgrass 1967; Matthew 2013). It was outfitted with a leather strap or rope thong (visible in art and misidentified regularly for the launch thong of javelins) attached to a similar handle to secure the grip even when sweat, blood and fatigue made the shaft slippery. And there was a butt-spike (*sauroter*) to allow solid fixing in the ground, without corroding the warhead. The *sauroter* could be used in an emergency as a warhead, i.e. in cases of shaft breakage due to hacking or shattering, and offered a counterweight that made a hind grip possible, to capitalize on the length of the shaft in terms of reach (Matthew 2012). The hoplite spear was used in low, underarm or overhead grips, with the scholarly debate on the subject still raging. There was also the reverse overhead (Matthew 2012), with the spear positioned as in overhead but the arm and hand orientated as in low.

The low and underarm grips, preferably with the shaft at a high angle, so as not to cause injuries to the troops that followed, could be used at a run, as they permitted free movement of the torso and lower body, accurate aiming and transfer of the kinetic energy of the body to the spear-point for a lethal penetrating effect through armour. Both low and underarm grips were adequate to spar with an enemy and repel cavalry; the latter suggested a semi-kneeling position. But with a closely packed phalanx, in *synaspismos* mode with interlocked shields, the overhead grip was the best choice, similarly to the practice among *sparabara*. The interlocked shields could not open for a thrust: re-enactment has shown that the right part of an Argive shield must be placed *behind* the left part of the shield of the trooper to the *right* to produce a line withstanding the shock delivered by enemy troops crashing on the shield wall.

In such cases, low or overhead grips are possible, but not underarm. Contrary to some views (Matthew 2013; Matthew 2012) the overhead grip was immensely practical and is well attested in art, although *some* confusion with javelin casting did occur (Matthew 2012). The overhead grip gave a shorter reach indeed, but when used from a standstill, as in a phalanx confrontation, it was putting a much higher proportion of the body weight onto the thrust, thus achieving better penetration. Additionally, the downward thrust was delivering the blow *behind* the shield of the enemy and between the latter's shield and helmet, to either unarmoured or less armoured areas. Such were the vicinity of the lower part of the face and the lower neck, at the upper side of the ribcage, especially when linothorax jerkins were used instead of the full metal cuirass of old. The spear-head of the *dory* at the time of the Persian Wars must have been narrower than it had originally been during the sixth century, in order to achieve better penetration, whereas the very wide base of earlier models was intended to maximize wound width and bleeding and restrict the depth of the penetration so as to facilitate extraction of the weapon without losing the spearpoint.

The *hoplon* shield – another term for the Argive shield and the origin of the name of the hoplites – had been improved in terms of ergonomics and manufacture; its bowl was deeper and bronze-faced and so more resistant to tear from slashing weapons (**Plate 2C,D**). Additionally, it was handier against contacting enemies, allowing the wielder actually to wear it and put his weight *in* it, to shove off opponents and also support friendlies within the phalanx when shoving. Its carriage, especially the peculiar central arm-band, the *porpax*, improved it in terms of technology and handiness as well, as did the complete suspension subsystem, with the long-haul cords and bands which made the shield an expeditionary sack for utensils and supplies when on campaign, wearable as a backpack.

A rather long, straight, rhomboid, ridged cut-and-thrust sword had been available (and perhaps standard-issued by some states) by the late fourth century at the latest (**Plate 1**), the evolution of the sixth and fifth century leaf-bladed example, which had replaced the longer, straight or triangular one of the geometric era as slash-and-thrust sidearm. The extremely short Laconian dirk, a shrunken version of the standard fifth-century blade, intended for stabbing in congested conditions in absence of metal body armour required utmost dexterity – and courage – in its use (Plut Moral 6, 69) and must have fallen out of favour since the Spartan decline of the mid-fourth century. The field belonged to long, sturdy weapons.

A concave curved sabre, the *Kopis* ('cleaver') had come into fashion at roughly the time of the Persian Wars, give or take, (Snodgrass 1967; Anderson 1991) and became immensely popular by the early fourth century and continuing in use during the reign of Alexander. The *kopis* could be mass-produced and was intended for slashing blows with less dexterity and skill, especially in a vertical or diagonal direction against enemies bereft of heavy headgear. In its most advanced, forward-curved version (**Plate 5**) it allowed a thrusting blow by skirting the upper face and rim of the hoplite shield, thus targeting the face of the enemy with minimal warning. It could be driven behind the shield by a diagonal thrust up and forward, piercing either the neck or the upper torso (Kambouris 2000).

Collectivity and coordination are quintessential for a phalanx, outputting much more than the sum of the parts – a real synergy. Such collective action demanded a very high degree of familiarization among troops, as seen in contemporary re-enactment experiments, drills and exercises. Thus, the phalanx was not a well-dressed assembly of troops, but a precisely (*sensu lato*) positioned entity, the precision particularly important in case of shoving or manoeuvring. The hoplite had to know, feel and create empathy with the troops surrounding him, and thus the positions were set within a phalanx and altered only during drill and transformations. A century later Xenophon declared that Spartan Peers were the only hoplites trained to fight in phalanx next to any of their Peers (Xen Const Lac XII.7) and that they could manoeuvre in combat, changing front, depth and density in a way simply impossible for other hoplite forces.

The abovementioned drill changes the relative positions of individual hoplites within a phalanx and is practical only with warriors able to fight effectively in the vicinity of any of their peers, or at the very least of a rather large selection of said peers. It follows that a phalanx of a certain city or community may become, with training and drill, a rock-solid formation, or even a nimble and somewhat flexible, still solid, formation. But a phalanx of *different* states fighting next to each other is another thing altogether. This might have been a valid reason for numerous hoplite defeats: especially in the years of the Ionic Revolt, posting hoplites of different contingents, which had never trained together and perhaps each group were using different tactics (depth and density, mode of advance) might have invited defeat.

Mobility supreme
The new, better, closely fitting and more protective greaves increased the mobility in rough terrain and the protection from missiles when the formation advanced, compared to the shorter previous models. Still, the

radical expansion of the recruitment meant that fewer troops could or would afford them, especially expeditionary-minded mercenaries or (semi) professional troops, although the elite corps would have included them in their arsenal for set-piece battles, but not for mobile operations.

The semi-open helmets like the Chalcidian model that increased awareness, which seems unnecessary in the confines of a phalanx, but becomes a must whenever concerted, coordinated action is at a premium, were partially discarded for fully open models of cheaper design and mass production. Such was the Illyrian model, leaving the face open but affording cheek protection (thus it was rather semi-open), the exemplary Laconian *pilos* helmet and the vastly superior Boeotian model, affording cover to the back of the neck and some shade too. Combined with the linothorax, which was occasionally stiffened with metal additions such as scales (**Plate 6**), the sum allowed more flexibility, manoeuvreability, awareness and mobility in general, which translate into capability for mobile tactics.

Thus, the standardization actually recedes. Young troops were trained for extreme mobility, to rush to the charge so as to avoid aimed volleys of arrows by alternating the distances in both direct and indirect shooting and to deny the enemy time for more volleys. They were the *ekdromoi*, renowned by the early fourth century thanks to Xenophon; the respective drill though must have started as early as the late sixth century. The *ekdromoi* were the younger hoplites, usually 20–30 years of age, (Xen Hell V.4,40 & IV.5,15; Sekunda 1986), able to charge at a run, as the one attested at Marathon and practised in the guise of *hoplitodromos* since 520 BC at the Olympic Games and other Panhellenic festivities and sports events (Sekunda 2000). The *ekdromoi* may have initially adopted lighter body armour, such as linothorax, leather jerkins (**Plate 6**) or used no body armour at all to gain additional mobility.

The Specialists return
The phalanx was an offensive and a defensive formation, the competent use of which required excellent commanders and decently trained men. Still, a conquering phalanx does little more than disrupting the enemy formation. To increase the loss exchange, the winner would ultimately engage in close-quarters combat with the vanquished (Plato Laches 5), but from an advantageous position. This close-quarters battle, reminiscent of the highly dexterous heroes of the past, was a personal matter – at least in Athens. The *Hoplomachoi* (literally 'Weapons-fighter') were the Close-Quarter-Battle instructors (Sekunda 2000 & 1998; Anderson 1991) who taught, for a handsome fee, the proper use of shield, sword and spear, their combinations, proper moves with and without them, evasions, parries and so many more

intricacies. In these conditions the Greek hoplites had better weapons, training and skills than the barbarians, Persians included, and engaged with an advantage. The Athenians introduced the skill into the syllabus of the reshuffled Ephebeia in 337 BC (Recaldin 2011) as state-sponsored skill learning.

The catch is that men trained adequately in such combat may prove unwilling to remain within the phalanx where success and failure – which means death – are outside their control, as they depend on sheer luck and on concerted action. It is a return of the Hero and thus Plato vehemently opposed and discouraged such practices with the doubtful argument that the Spartans did not allow such ilk to teach to Lacedaemon; not even to enter the borders (Plato Laches 6). This is a rather misguided conclusion: the Spartans were already masters of such skills themselves; they drove CQB gurus away because they did not *need* them and because they were fearful of their expert prying eyes (Krentz 1985).

Professional, mercenary hoplites were the last phase of the hoplite Epos, closing full circle. Starting with the voluntary military service of the fourth century for imperial campaigns by both Athens and Sparta, the expertise in the new set of skills became once more the property of few; civic bodies of full-time soldiers, the Elites or Picked ones (*Epilektoi*) appear once more since 418 BC at the very latest (Thuc V.72,3). Professionals are not by definition mercenaries; still, by the time of Alexander the Great, true mercenaries were most common. They were the norm in every state army, to augment local elites and draftees, especially for extended, year-round expeditionary or guard service – a trait transferred to the Macedonian phalanx conscripts (Hanson 1999). Sparta had admitted them into service, something Leonidas and his contemporaries would have rather died than accept, and the last great Spartan King, Agesilaus, who introduced them *en masse*, died fighting as a mercenary to raise some treasure for his declining state in the mid-fourth century (Plut Ages 40,1–2). During the campaign of Alexander, in the beginning far more *Greek* mercenaries were fighting for the Achaemenids: the battles of the Granicus (Arr Anab I.4,14) and Issus (Arr Anab II.8,6), taken together, meant a staggering 50,000 such troops in Persian pay.

The Persian infantry

The Sparabara
The Persians had recast the already ancient fighting *duo* of shield-bearer and archer, seen in Mesopotamian illustrations and occasionally mentioned in the Iliad (VIII.266–72), so as to maximize the firepower. The Persian

version included one shield-bearer (similar to the *pavisarii* of the Middle Ages) followed by nine archers, in a single file, which provided a deep landing zone of the arrows (Sekunda 1989). This depth accommodated for errors in aiming and was also excellent for assaulting in depth an enemy deployment, destroying its cohesion. It also insinuates that the archery duels were fought with arrows flying at relatively low angles, in direct shooting; else the *spara* shield would offer but little protection to the rear ranks. The high angle used by the English archers during the Hundred Years' War may not be an accurate paradigm. Xenophon, having fought both against and alongside Persians, mentions high-angle shooting by Cretan archers as an oddity due to the lack of proper ammunition (Xen Anab III.4,17) and, while corroborating Herodotus on the large size of the Persian bows (Xen Anab III.4,17 and Her VII.61,1) he makes clear that their range was less than the range of the Rhodian slingers (Xen Anab III.4,16), implying direct shooting.

Moreover, all archers were armed with spear and sidearm: sabre, dirk, such as the '*akinaka*', or axe, such as the Scythian '*sagaris*' (**Plate 5**). The same was true for the shield-bearer. As a result, they could all engage in hand-to-hand combat (Raaflaub 2013); again the reader of the Iliad feels at home (Il XV.466–75). Once the arrows caused casualties and disruption, a violent charge was disintegrating the enemy, and this onslaught was performed by all the fielded troops, increasing both impact power and killing efficiency.

This was the Persian line infantry, called *sparabara* due to the *spara*, the long, rectangular leather-and-wicker shield of the file leaders (Sekunda 1989 & 1992; Dahm 2019); very different and lighter than the (mainly) plank-constructed pavises of the Middle Ages. Other nations of the area, like the Medes, used it or a version of it and, in any case, adopted it under the Persian sovereigns. It is possible that their use of such kit predated that of the Persians, but this cannot be proven. Herodotus describes at least three more national contingents outfitted similarly to the Persians (Her VII.62).

The *spara* was rectangular and flat, thus providing standard coverage without any seams and openings, especially when in contact with the other *spara* of the rank. It was easy to set on the ground, so as to create a seamless barrier or rather field fortification from where to shoot in relative safety, without burdening the wielder's hands and interrupting his firing sequence. It was very light, which allowed the wielder high mobility, such as forced marches, violent charges, manoeuvring at a jog and pursuing fast and hot. Its beauty was, though, that it was not issued to all troops, but only to file leaders.

It is unclear whether *all* troops of such a combined formation were called *sparabara*; this issue relates, most probably, to the existence or not of shields for the nine archers-spearmen. Greek pottery shows Persian archers with sabres,

The Line Infantry 37

with or without a cuirass. The reliefs of Persepolis show Persian archers in ceremonial dress, with conventional quivers or combined *gorytos* quivers and bow-cases, carrying spears and occasionally straight dirks (*akinaka*). What is a bit confusing is that Greek pottery shows sabres or rather cleavers, but the Persian reliefs and Herodotus refer to *akinaka* dirks (Her VII.61,1). The cuirass might have been issued selectively (Charles 2012). The obvious choice is to the *dathapatish* file leaders of the *sparabara* who would bear the brunt of close-quarter combat and perhaps missile barrages; such armour must be identified with the Egyptian-style mentioned in Herodotus (Her I.135) and seen in Greek art. Additionally, the other type of cuirass, the iron-scale type (Her VII.61,1) was issued to or otherwise used by cavalry, at the very least by noble cavalrymen (Her IX.22,2) if not by the entire mounted host of Persian stock, and/or by the elusive cuirassiers (Her VIII.113,2), should they have been an infantry unit (Charles 2012) as suggested here.

It is also unclear whether the *spara*-bearing file leader, portrayed with cuirass or jerkin (obviously the Egyptian-style mentioned in Her I.135 made by stuffed linen) in Greek pottery, had been an archer as well. The *spara* could be solidly planted on the ground, as seen in said pottery, so both hands were free, but only a portion of the abovementioned representations show bow (but not quiver), for *spara*-carrying troopers (Miller 2006/7). Herodotus (VII.61,1) confusingly endows all Persian national infantry with a full kit of wicker shield of unstated shape and size, short spear, long bow hanging from the shoulder (from where it could be brought to notch position with just one move within the left palm), with one quiver at the back (for fast drawing of the reed arrows), with iron scale-armour and with a dirk hanging from the belt to their right side. And here lies a problem: there is not one image of a Persian with so full a kit, making the description of Herodotus reading like the inventory of the infantry, not the standard-issue kit of the infantryman.

The *spara* was quite a feat of manufacturing, despite the mundane materials; and of sizeable footprint. The size and form of the *spara* allowed the formation of a veritable shield wall, as mentioned above, with the file leaders planting their *spara* one next to the other to create a portable and movable linear field fortification, from which they were entrusted to repulse by spear-thrusts any enemy resilient enough to cross the hail of arrows and assault their shield wall. It should be noted, though, that there can be little possibility for more than one *spara*-bearer per *dathabam* (ten-man file). Even less so for an adjustable number of spear-bearers according to the tactical situation (Ray 2009). The idea that an array of weapons was available to all soldiers and the selection was done before deployment is impractical in anything but pitched battle, as it denies the ability to deploy promptly after a forced march or in battles by encounter. It may be suggested that all *sparabara*, all ten warriors of the file, had a *spara*. This would corroborate the abovementioned text of Herodotus (Her VII.61,1) as well as texts from Xenophon (Cyr I.2,9) and Strabo (XV.3,19) although this would change the whole concept of *sparabara* as we understand it.

Thus the Persian armies had multiplied their firepower, as almost all of the (first) line infantry shot bows and then doubled as shock troops (Raaflaub 2013). The Persians had practically doubled the effective size of their armies, and by fielding quite large ones they were truly able to cloud the sky with their arrows (Her VII.226). An ethnic Persian boy was taught from the age of 5 till 24 to ride, shoot the bow and speak the truth (Her I.136; Strabo XV.3,18), and then he was to follow either a military career or be released to the civilian life as a reservist, always subject to mobilization (Xen Cyr I.2,13). There is a slight problem, though: the infantry was by far the Persian decisive arm; Xenophon (Cyr I.2,15) estimates the Persians, obviously the conscription-liable, fully enfranchised ones, to be 120,000 in number. The bondsmen or *bandaka* were the intermediate social stratum, between the slaves or *mariaka* and the aristocrats or *azata* (Sekunda 1992) and accounted for the equivalent of the free citizenry, who obviously were the bulk of the manpower. These could not own a horse and had no war use for it. So how, and, most importantly, why should they have to 'learn to ride since childhood'? Most probably, the renowned motto referred to the scions of the Persian nobility, similarly to the slightly more expansive and diversified syllabus of Homeric heroes and medieval knights. Alternatively, this kind of training was provided to all enfranchised Persian youths who could afford the public training (i.e. *azata* and *bandaka*), possibly under the collective term *Kardaka* (see below), since the acquisition of a horse could happen during manhood due to gains or promotion and respective training in their early years should have made such provision a possibility.

The long Persian bow, firing a long, hollow arrow shaft (Her VII.61,1) had quite a range (Xen Anab III.3,15). The massive firepower practically reduced any need for defensive weaponry, which brought down the cost and increased the flexibility, speed and endurance of the troops. Although Persian troops are regularly mentioned as unarmoured (Her IX.62,3), Herodotus mentions iron-scale cuirasses for the Persian national infantry, possibly implying the first-rank *sparabara* (Her VII.61,1) but this may be a mistaken supposition.

In any case, such armour was a quantum leap compared to the bronze-scale panoplies of centuries past. Moreover, quilted jerkins and equivalents to Greek *linothorax* models are shown in pottery for Imperial troops –

basically archers and/or *sparabara*. By any account, the protection afforded by the Persian shield and armour was optimized against arrows, as they were the only actual threat to the Persian war machine, and secondarily against the chance slashing blow in the melee. Still, this picture of both literary and representational evidence is very far from the picture of 'naked', fully unarmoured troops explicitly referring to the Persian line infantry and considered a focal reason for their defeat in Plataea in 479 BC (Her IX.62,3).

The short spear with the apple-like (or spherical, *sensu lato*) counterweight (Her VII.41) was more important than usually acknowledged. Short in length, it was handy in congested conditions, such as the melee after a storm of arrows. Its spherical counterweight and short length (**Plate 5**) made its use safer for the rest of the ranks, contrary to the constant danger for the following ranks represented by the butt-spike of the Greek spear. This, usually disregarded, spherical counterweight allowed holding the shaft far towards the back end, which allowed maximization of the *useful* length and reach within a handy total length with minimal projection backwards – a feature further enhancing the collective safety and reducing the cumbersomeness of such a weapon. It must be noted that the Greeks had difficulty in spearing in congested conditions and preferred spear-fights at a distance in set-piece battles and/or on open ground. The Persian spearman, due to his more nimble Achaemenid spear, could be more mobile in the open and more dexterous in congested conditions, although at the cost of a somewhat reduced reach. Some projections assign central grip at an overhead position as the sole technique of using the Persian infantry spear, resulting in limited reach, 1.4m. Both this conclusion and the notion of fragility due to smaller diameter (Matthew 2013) might be due to a misunderstanding that confuses the dual-use *palton* of the cavalry with the counterweighted infantry spear attested by Herodotus (VII.41,3) and shown in various reliefs. The counterweight allowed, as mentioned before, a very asymmetrical hold, near the rear tip, and also both high and low positions, with the latter offering longer reach and being reminiscent of the *Iklwe* of the Zulus under Shaka; the former was the only suitable grasp for use from behind a fully deployed and dense *spara* wall, where spearing over the upper edge of the *spara* was mandatory.

Moreover, the counterweight allowed a police function, as a less-than-lethal club for riot control, and an alternative military function: as a lethal club to strike at heads and to break inflexible shields and armour, thus giving the user a dual-use weapon: a battle club with quite a reach paired to the conventional spear. This is by itself a noteworthy innovation compared to the armament of the Assyrians in the Army of Xerxes, which included lance, club and dagger (Her VII.63).

Furthermore, it is as yet unresolved what the Persian spearman-archer was doing with his spear when shooting arrows: leaving it lying on the ground would make picking it up rather difficult; the possibility that the sphere allowed it to balance upright should be taken into consideration and tested, at different types of ground. Without the butt-spike of the Greek weapons it might have been planted on the ground head-on (Ray 2009), which would expose its point to damage and rust; but also infest it with soil microbes, adding a septic dimension to any wound.

After all, the *sparabara* may have not been intended for the defensive pinning and bleeding of the enemy, as is commonly projected (Ray 2009). Their purpose must have been the decimation and stunning of the enemy. This would allow to tilt sideways or retract by any other means the few and light *spara*, thus enabling massive egress of the spearmen-archers. The latter would deliver a violent charge with CQB weapons to disintegrate the enemy by eroding his unity and dissolving his line, very much like the practice of the Roman legionaries some centuries later. Without this in mind, one cannot explain the use of spears hardly reaching a target positioned two ranks ahead by all the 10 ranks. Practically the fighting style of the Persian infantry was very Roman-like, perhaps lacking the body armour in kind or, at the very least, in type and using the bow instead of the javelin as a missile and the short spear instead of the *gladius*-type sword for close-quarter melee. Still, everybody had a close combat weapon (Xen Cyr I.2,9 & 13; Her VII.61,1; Strabo XV.3,19).

The file of ten men was both operational and administrative. It was the administrative unit, but also the standard file of one shield-bearer who led and commanded the file (*Dathapatis*) and nine – most probably, but not definitely, unshielded – archers. All ten men were armed with spear and sidearm. Thus, the standard file depth of a Persian unit was ten, and to increase depth for better defensive function or adaptation to confined space, the successive deployment of units in consecutive lines was most probably the standard procedure. If a higher echelon was depleted or undermanned, the personnel was reassigned and restructured to create full units. For example, a Persian century (*Satabam*) may be understrength, chiefly because some *dathaba* are taken for other – guard or outpost – duties; thus less than ten *dathaba* were present. In mobilization, such detachments would return to bring it up to strength for expeditionary duty. Still, low manning and casualties are also reasons for understrength *dathaba*. Consequently, a *satabam*, if left with seventy men, would cut three *dathaba* and use the manpower to fill seven *dathaba* to full strength (Ray 2009; Sekunda 1992). The net result was that understrength units may cover smaller fronts but always had a steady, ten-man deep landing zone for their arrows, assaulting the enemy at depth. The decimal organization, explicitly reported (Xen Cyr VIII.1,14), does not exclude the possibility of a binary tactical division, where in each echelon one half would be under the vice-commander (Xen Cyr II.1,22–6). The fifty-strong companies of *Kardaka* trainees (Strabo XV.3,18) suggest such a scheme, perhaps from the *dathabam* (two half-files of five) to the *baivarabam* (two commands of 5,000).

With Herodotus there is a tacit question. After the engagement at Plataea, the Imperial Army finds refuge in their fortified camp, and they repel Spartan assaults. How exactly do they do that? The ready answer is 'with their bows and javelins'. But they do not carry many javelins; the cavalry, if they follow later practice with *palton*, have a pair, one for hurling one for thrusting (see above), and in that day they just have shot all the available ones – and perhaps then some. The infantry had their bows. They were shooting relentlessly and in some cases throwing their bows to revert to sidearms during the battle. Thus, many had no arrows, others no bows. And if the case made below for the CQB-orientated cuirassiers holds water, some had no such weapons altogether. What were they using?

The Kardaka
The answer may be 'their slings'. Roman legionaries are supposed to have training with this weapon as standard, and use it to repel attacks at their fortified camps. Perhaps due to this knowledge Strabo says that all *Kardaka* (meaning fully enfranchised draftees) have slings (Strabo XV.3,19). And the sling takes no volume and has no weight, thus the veterans may carry it even when they deploy for CQB, with sidearm and shield. And use it when and if needed, as in hunting. This suggestion does not abide by Xenophon, who does provide some useful details for the tactical use of the sling by the Persians (Xen Anab III.3,17 & 15 & 7) but explicitly mentions the slingers as a specialized branch of the Persian army, not the everyday rank and file (Xen Anab III.3,6 & 4,2). This, of course, may be due to the Greek practice, where nobody knew how to use a sling but for some Rhodians, serving as Hoplites but having training, skill and knowledge in slinging as a national habit, sport or customary weapon (Xen Anab III.3,16). Although Xenophon is highly unlikely to be anything but perfectly informed on things Persian (he campaigned with Persians, side-by-side, for a year or so) it is the only plausible explanation.

And not unprecedented. It is still a mystery how the Greek hoplites were fighting off their enemies in broken terrain; when in the defensive, how were they able to repel the attackers. They were not trained slingers, and by casting stones and rocks they could not expect to stop hoplites, although it certainly did help. But a most successful use of stones cast by hand is described (Thuc I.106,1–2) as a peculiarity, a prodigy due to the very peculiar conditions of the terrain. What were they using in regular conditions, for example the hoplites defending the Long Walls? The spear was useful at the last two or three metres. Not taking advantage of the exposed enemy for some tens if not hundred metres was a waste, regarding the investment in fortifications. Perhaps all these should imply a tacit case for the javelin. All the manpower was trained to use it; it was the weapon of the hunter as the Greeks had no love for the bow. The insistence of Xenophon for the usefulness of the hunt as training for war (Xen Cyr I.2,10) cannot be explained if the hurling of javelins is not considered a skill needed by everybody, hoplites included. The peltasts and other lights (and the cavalry since the early fourth century) *kept* using it even in field action and set-piece battles, where the hoplites would trust their spear. Whether the Persians would make a similar case (Xen Cyr I.2,8), instead of the abovementioned for the sling, remains plausible.

Xenophon mentions that the Persian infantry was divided by age criteria into a standing and a reserve component (Xen Cyr I.2,13–14). Both components could be used for expeditionary service abroad, and they differed in both tactical employment and equipment; this differed from fifth century Greek practice but is similar to Roman (Connolly 1981). In terms of tactics Greeks in the fourth century did differentiate their infantry by age, but the basic gear was that of the hoplite. The mobile *ekdromoi*, the younger hoplites that assumed mobile tactics (Xen Hell IV.5,14–6) were deployed minus the body armour, but in essence they were able to fight as the veterans did, in phalanx. Non-phalanx infantry was not selected due to age, but to social status (Hanson 1983 & 1999).

Thus Xenophon directly states that the Persian national infantry had differentiated armament according to its active or reserve status: the former were archers, the latter assault troops armed with hand-to-hand weaponry (**Plate 5**) and issued with cuirasses (Xen Cyr I.2,13). By this piece of knowledge, two major issues in Herodotus' account are resolved immediately: the first is the identity of the Persian cuirassiers that Mardonius selected to remain with his host for the 479 BC campaign. They are the veteran Persians of the infantry, and not some cavalry regiment, as supposed based on the explicit mention of the cuirass of the cavalry commander Masistius (Her IX,22.2), on the context of a 422 BC catalogue of cavalry equipment (Charles 2015) and on the explicit mention by Herodotus that the Persian infantry engaging the Spartans had by armour (Her IX.63,2). This common interpretation implies that there was Persian cavalry *without* body armour, something unsupported by evidence (including but not restricted to the abovementioned catalogue) and very unlikely due to their feudal status.

The second is the battle order of the Persians in successive lines, as effected by Mardonius (Her IX.31,2). It was simply two different lines of two different troop types. The younger troops, making the standing army, were bow-armed *sparabara*. Behind them were the veterans, in cuirass and CQB weapons; they may well have been the *takabara* (Sekunda 1992), but this will be discussed later.

There is an issue with the secondary equipment. The interpretation followed here accounts for the *spara* shields, carried by the commanders of the ten-man file, the *dathabam*. But leaves open the issue of individual shields for the rank and file for use in more contested conditions, as in the assault after the barrage. Herodotus implies that the Persian archers were equipped with some short of close-rank weapons (Her IX.62,1) as secondary armament, but this is all. Shields are not mentioned explicitly. By the same token, the veterans are explicitly mentioned by Xenophon to bear armour and contact weapons (Xen Cyr I.2,13), but the examples he provides are limited to axes and sabres, plus a very clear but unhelpful mention attesting that their shields were accurately depicted in contemporary art. Whether spears were issued remains controversial. It is confusing that Xenophon insists, as does Strabo, too (Strabo XV.3,18–19), on the issue of a pair of dual-use spears (*palta*) while ceremonial and artistic depictions from Persia and Greece show counterweighted thrusting spears, corroborating Herodotus (Her VII.41,3).

The Greek art represents Achaemenid troops with cuirasses, axes, sabres, small scalloped shields or bodyshields. Initially the Greek artists would have had witnessed live Persians themselves, or at least the gear taken as booty, but eventually pottery copies might have become a product of higher volume and lower fidelity. Patterns may have been created by different workshops and applied en masse; thus some types of cuirass could be used whenever an armoured figure was needed, Greek, Persian, Amazon or whatever. This would explain the use of Greek-type linen corselets (*linothorax*), complete with Greek symbols, by Achaemenid troops, instead of the iron-scale type mentioned by Herodotus (Her VII.61,1) and Strabo (Strabo XV.3,19), although in later years acquisition of weaponry, especially some items, did find their way across the borders, as in the case of the army of Cyrus the Younger (Xen Anab I.8,7).

Whether Persian infantry with scalloped shields and spears may be identified with Xenophon's Persian veterans is a valid question, whenever cuirass and sidearms are not shown; when they *are* shown, the identification may be considered secure. Archers with small, scalloped shields may refer to Scythians/Saka or to the rank and file of the Persian line infantry (Head 1992).

Herodotus mentions javelins only as a weapon of Persian cavalry only, and as a main weapon at that (Her VII.61,1 & IX.17,3). Both Imperial and Greek representations support this view, showing clearly spears, not javelins, for the Imperial infantry. The spherical, apple-like counterweights in Imperial representations indeed imply spears, not javelins, for two reasons: the obvious one is that they would weight down a missile, reducing its range and spoiling its balance. The less obvious is that they are immensely useful for spears: they allow a longer reach and perhaps a secondary use as mentioned above.

Greek art shows Achaemenid troops with spear or sidearm and small shield. These are usually identified as *takabara*, and it has been suggested that they were garrison troops rather than expeditionary troops (Sekunda 1992). This might be the case, but it is just as possible that these were the veterans mentioned by Xenophon and were encountered more often when the Greeks took the offensive, possibly deprived of the support of expeditionary elements if the aggressors were achieving surprise. The cuirass may have been worn over or under the garment (Her IX.22,2). It is an issue whether double-scalloped shields in Achaemenid representations of spearmen suggests *takabara* and/or veterans (if the two are not the same).

The difference in equipment between the expeditionary and the reserve parts of the Persian national levy (Xen Cyr I.2,13–14) might be evident more than anywhere else during the reign of Darius III. In the Battle of Gaugamela there are no masses of *sparabara*, nor storms of arrows. *Sparabara* units are not reported for Issus either, despite modern projections on the issue (Dahm 2019). A backward, pastoralist tribal unit from Persis, the Mardians (Her I.125,4), are explicitly stated to be archers in the Achaemenid deployment at Gaugamela (Arr Anab III.11,5), as if to underline that the other Persian infantry were not. Actually, Arrian mentions two wings of 30,000 *Kardaka* each at Issus and thus totalling 60,000, describing them as hoplites (Arr Anab II.8,6). The number reminds one of the extrapolated strength of an Achaemenid Army Corps (Her IX.96,2 &VIII.126,1) and could well imply a common drafting area; Persis should be understood, due to their elite status, to flank the invaluable Greek mercenaries (Arr Anab II.8,6). The number also suits perfectly the Achaemenid practice of sending half the available manpower on campaign (Xen Cyr I.2,9) applied on the estimated pool of Persian conscripts of the time of Xenophon, i.e. 120,000 (Xen Cyr I.2,15).

Thus, Arrian should be understood as mentioning Kardaka *outfitted* as hoplites, not Kardaka *being* (by definition) barbarian hoplites. What the

Herodotean term was for such troops is elusive and would have shed light to their identity; the suffix *–ka* means 'man', generally a human subject (see *amrtaka, bandaka, mariaka*) but *not* trooper, which is *–bara* (*arshtibara, sparabara, takabara*). Per Strabo (XV.3,18) indeed this is the case and the meaning is *looter, robber* or *manly one*, possibly a wrong interpretation. As is, Arrian might refer to some effort of the known military innovator and exceptionally brave Darius III (Badian 2000), who issued enhanced offensive arms (Diod XVII.53,1) and fielded scythed chariots massively (Arr Anab III.11,6–7; Diod XVII.53,1–2), plus elephants (Arr Anab III.11,6), to recast the Persian national infantry to hoplite form (Charles 2012; Bosworth 1980a), so as to follow the most successful paradigm of the day, that of his Greek mercenaries and *frenemies*.

Whether the mercenary commander Charidemus of Athens was behind this rebooting is anyone's guess. His insistence on leading a campaign against Alexander with a specially raised army (Diod XVII.30,3), not a regularly drafted one, shows some anxiety over the selection, training and abilities of troops and perhaps a concern to test his creation, which would have been heavily criticized, at the very least, by Persian aristocracy. His anxiety was so acute that it cost him his life and the Persians their empire (Diod XVII.30,4–5). But the Achaemenid deployment at Issus, with a first line of 90,000 heavy infantry, a third of which were Greek mercenaries (Arr Anab II.8,6) sounds suspiciously close to the proposal of Charidemus (Diod XVII.30,3), the 10,000 balance conceivably being cavalry, as per Greek standard.

If indeed the *Kardaka* were the expedition-liable fraction of the Persian host (Xen Cyr I.2,9 & 13), the over-age militia (Xen Cyr I.2,14) must have been left with the standard kit (Xen Cyr I.2,13). These were the 40,000 infantry troops mobilized by Ariobarzanes to defend the Persian Gates (Arr Anab III.18,2). The division of a levy in two parts, with the younger, active-army being reorganized while the rest was left in the traditional outfit, may be detected in the purported Seleucid creation of Romanized infantry out of their active army phalanx units (Sekunda 1994; Meiklejohn 1938; Polyb XXX.25,3).

If Xenophon's testimony and that of Strabo are combined, they produce a coherent picture: the Persian males are divided by age to children, from five or seven to sixteen, youth to twenty-five, grown men to fifty and elders over fifty (Xen Cyr I.2,4 & 8 & 13). When the Persian youths are mentioned they are only the enfranchised part of the male society, which graduated the public education system (Xen Cyr I.2,15). They qualify for leadership positions (Xen Cyr I.2,13). They serve from seventeen to twenty-five as the standing part of the Persian army (Xen Cyr I.2,12) – the Spartan counterparts served from twenty to thirty. If the *Kardaka* were the expeditionary-grade part of the Persian nation, meaning from sixteen to fifty years of age, they were originally outfitted with two different suits of weapons (Charles 2012), as described for youths and men (Xen Cyr I.2,9 & 13 respectively).

Given that *Kardaka* refers to both cavalry and infantry draft (Strabo XV.3,19), it is not a troop type. It is a term for sociomilitary classification, before and beyond any assignment to particular arms. What is very obvious, though, is that although Xenophon's account refers to the proceedings of some royal city (Xen Cyr I.2,9), this is not so; it applies in other parts of the realm, where the highest authority is not the King; at least not for the running of routine functions (Xen Cyr I.2,5). The same social mechanics apply in different cities both in Persia and in the Persian colonies planted in different satrapies, where the highest authority is the satrap (Strabo XV.3,18).

Last, but not least, Xenophon (Cyr I.2,8–9) and Strabo (XV.3,18) do not agree with Herodotus in one most important issue: the javelin. In Herodotus javelins are the main (perhaps not the only) weapon of the *asabara* cavalrymen. The infantry has short spears, and there are no mentions of casting them. Xenophon and Strabo both agree that the kit of the *Kardaka* includes the javelin. There is no mention of just one spear as is implied in Herodotus and seen in the representations. Either the infantry gear had been recast, with the *palton* replacing the short spear, or the use of *palta* is applicable to cavalry service (Strabo XV.3,18) but part of the common training syllabus, as is the bow. It must be noted that in Arrian and Xenophon the Persian cavalry does not use bows, they fight with palta and sidearms, contrary to Herodotus, where the bow is also used.

Chapter 3

Archery in the Army of Alexander the Great

We have no record of arms, or armour of the archers of the army of Alexander, but an indication that some are lighter than others (Arr Anab III.18,5). His main archer force were native Macedonians and mercenary and allied Cretans. The army of Alexander is not different from other Greek armies of the era in any revolutionary way. But it incorporated so many evolutionary changes, both of his own and of other quasi-contemporary generals that the whole was revolutionary. We know a lot about archers' organization and operations. The tactical units are the 500-men *lochoi*, and this was the probable strength of the archer arm when the expedition began (Diod XVII.17,4), to climb to perhaps 2,000, half Cretan and half Macedonian 3 years later (Arr Anab III.12) – before large numbers of Asian natives are incorporated in the army. Their use was according to the late fifth century Greek doctrine: not massive fire but mobile fire available in 3-D context and over broken ground. They were supporting flying columns and special operations, as in storming a mountain pass (Arr Anab I.27,8). They were being incorporated in every fast detachment/task force led by Alexander to lightning action. They were used in support of shock troops in urban warfare and in siege warfare but also in the open, providing suppressive fire (Arr Anab I.1,11–12). They took casualties, especially if trapped by heavy opponents in limiting ground, as in Thebes, where they suffered a terrible blow when cornered by hoplites (Arr Anab I.8,4), as the shock action they supported did not break through, to allow them to burst into more open terrain and deliver volume fire. Most incredible is the casualty rate of the Master of Archers (*Toxarchos*), with three fatalities in less than two years (Arr Anab I.8,4 & I.22,7 & I.28,8), two being in siege action (Arr Anab I.8,4 & I.22,7), as they always supported the storming parties. In set battle they were mingled with shock troops – especially heavy cavalry (Arr Anab I.14,1) – to offer fire support in a fluid and concentrated manner in time and space; or they were assigned to certain parts of the line to provide massive concentrated fire (Arr Anab II.9,3).

The distinction of their service and the way they were used shows a culmination of all previously spotted features and assets: mobility in terms of speed and dealing with difficult terrain, stamina, initiative, adaptability, ability to shoot fast and accurately and deliver a considerable volume of arrows in time- and space-sensitive conditions and resilience. These imply lack or lightness of armour, an array of arms (perhaps javelins and surely side arms such as swords or sabres), small shield and possibly helmet, and the ability to shoot fast and accurately while standing and on the run; perhaps not while running, but stopping for a shot and then running again to a new position, like modern infantry in assault.

Chapter 4

The Elites

The Immortals/Kinsmen

Herodotus explains that the name *Immortals* for the Persian elite 10,000-strong division (*baivarabam*) was due to the immediate, possibly overnight making up of any casualties (Her VII.83). This indicated a standard *baivarabam*, but of special status and privileges (Her VII.83,3); usually Imperial units were expected to operate understrength and had procedures to redistribute the available manpower for more efficiently doing so (Sekunda 1992). The name 'Immortals' was known to the Greeks far before Herodotus; at the very latest by their spies dispatched to Sardis in 481 BC. The probability that all of their sources, spies, prisoners of war, deserters, ex-Medizers etc. had mistaken the Persian term *Anusiya*, meaning *Kinsman* (or other similar Greek translation, including Attendant, or Companion) for *Anausa*, meaning *Immortal*, is possible and even plausible (Waterfield 2006), but somehow unconvincing (Ray 2009); instead, the term *Amrtaka* has been proposed (Sekunda 1989 & 1992). Although it has never been found or read in ancient sources, it may be a correct approach.

Still, the usual explaining away of the unit missing from the explicit narratives of the era of Alexander III the Great (Arr Anab III.11,5) is that the Corps might have been disbanded after being implicated in the coup against Xerxes and the power struggle(s) since. This is even less convincing: in the Battle of Issus in 333 BC Arrian directly points to Xenophon's description for the deployment around the King (Xen Anab I.8,21), a moderately informative text. But in the Battle of Gaugamela (331 BC), whence the deployment plans of the Achaemenid staff fell to the hands of the Macedonians after the battle (Arr Anab III.11,3) – not to mention the archives of the Persian state some weeks or months later – Darius III had arrayed around him his Apple-bearers explicitly mentioned by Herodotus and the 'Kinsmen' (Arr Alex III.11,5). The latter term is the most proper for translating *Anusiya*, recommends the highest honour and was eventually adopted by Alexander III (Arr Anab VII.11,1 & 6) and his Successors. Actually, it may have been the model for the inception of the Companion Cavalry (Arr Anab III.14,2) by the early Macedonian kings Alexander I and his father Amyntas who were vassals to the Persians (Her V.17,1 and VIII.136,1 respectively).

There are some more details to contemplate upon. The Immortals were a field unit of *sparabara*, perhaps an elite standing army within the national Persian army, the *kara*. The notion of *kara* is a term, possibly equivalent to the Homeric Greek term *laos* which in Modern Greek means 'the people'. From its full levy emerged each time, upon mobilization, the *spada*, which was the actual, drafted plus standing, army (Fields 2007), possibly enhanced by vassal units and allies. The Guards of the King, on the other hand, were the Spearbearers; the actual term is *Doryphoroi*, the direct Greek translation of the Persian word *Arshtibara* (Sekunda 1989 & 1992), a unit in which Darius I had partaken (Her III.139,2) and most probably Xerxes too (Holland 2005). Thus, the *Arshtibara* mentioned as Spearbearers in Greek amount to two *hazaraba*, both identified by Herodotus in the Persian Parade Order (Her VII.40,2 & 41,2–3). It is possible that the *hazarabam* closest to the King, with apple-like counterweights, and of aristocratic lineage are understood to be the Applebearers, while the other *hazarabam*, with pomegranate-like counterweights, were drafted from the Immortals and made up by Persian commoners promoted on merit and valour (Charles 2011). One cannot fail to notice the symmetry with the Hypaspist units of Alexander III (Kambouris et al 2019), which included one battalion recruited from the entire nation (Hypaspists) and another from the aristocracy (Royal Hypaspists); still, the analogy is perhaps misleading, as the Hypaspists were a field unit and thus counterpart to the Immortals. The Immortals also had pomegranate-like counterweights (Her VII.41,3) and were an elite field, not guard, unit (Charles 2011). They must have been the same as the Kinsmen, as the two units are never mentioned together and their names are related; but the latter are usually understood as cavalry!

The Immortals actually might have included troops from the other core ethnicities, the Medes and the Elamites, too (Charles 2011; Miller 2004). Still, this is based on the representations of the official uniforms of the corps. Herodotus insists that the Immortals were Persians only (Her VII.41) and it is possible that the court attire included the national costumes of the three core ethnicities without drafting being proportional or representative of all of them; it could be a symbolism, not a factuality. Such practices can be identified even today in many guard units, which include costumes from different localities and/or from different times; the really minuscule Presidential Guard of the Hellenic Republic has currently no less than eight (8) official, ceremonial costumes.

The Hypaspist Corps

The elite Hypaspist Corps was a special unit, inherited by Alexander along with the other components of the Macedonian army. The paramount importance of these troops not only during the great battles of Philip and Alexander, but in almost every clash during the campaign of the latter, ignited the interest and curiosity of many scholars. Though the absence of contemporary literature, the huge time gap between the events and our most reliable source, Arrian's *Anabasis* (approx. 500 years), the shady descriptions of Arrian and the frequent reorganizations and restructures of the Macedonian army under Alexander have caused extremely diverse opinions. The unit was renamed Silver Shields – *Argyraspids* (Arr Anab VII.11,3; Justin XII.7,4–5) – and there is consensus on the issue in modern scholarship (Anson 1981) although some solitary voices support a *de novo* establishment of the latter (Lock 1977). In any case the Silver Shields were orientated towards strictly line infantry operations, retaining their enhanced elite status, but not their former special-warfare status, a development most understandable due to their advanced age. The special force, mobile elite infantry function should have been assigned to some other unit of younger troops (obviously retaining the unit name Hypaspists).

Regarding the Hypaspist Corps as such the functions and internal organization are rather straightforward before it became the Argyraspids. Parallels with Napoleonic 'Guard' Units (Hammond 1991 & 1997; Bosworth 1997), are irrelevant *before* the advent of Argyraspids. There are some basic things to remember when dealing with the Hypaspists. First, when Philip ascended to the throne, the unit – or its precursor, the *original* Foot-Companions, if Theopompus, F348 is to be trusted – might have been at first some 500 or 600-strong. The first figure refers to the standard strength of a Greek *lochos*-unit as mentioned elsewhere, but also to the strength of standard units of the Corps later (Arr Anab III.29,7). The second figure is a bit more complicated: it would match perfectly the original number of the Companion Cavalry, as per the ideal Greek army (**Figure 2.2**). It would also suggest a double-strength elite warrior unit similar to those of Southern Greeks that were usually 300-strong, as were the Theban Sacred Band and the Spartan Knights (Kambouris et al 2019). The Syracusans had such a double-strength unit in 414 BC (Thuc VI.96,3). But then it may also have been modelled on the Achaemenid connection: the Satraps and Regents or viceroys had a personal bodyguard of 1,000 *arshtibara* and/or cavalry, although the latter could be as few as 600 for any reason, as was the bodyguard of Cyrus the Younger (Xen Anab I.8,21).

Whatever its original strength, the Corps expanded, possibly in multiple iterations, to its ultimate 3,000-strong status during the campaign of Alexander: 'three chiliarchies' (Arr Anab V.23,7). This reference also resolves any issue on the possible organization of the Corps. Its manpower of 3,000 is divided to three 1,000 strong units-*Chiliarchies* (Arr Anab III.29,7), each commanded by a *Chiliarches* (Arr Anab I. 22,7) and this remains unchanged throughout the campaign.

The name of the unit means 'shield-bearers' and in such capacity and strength they may be associated (loosely?) with the Companion Cavalry, at the beginning of Philip's reign just 600 strong (Diod XVI.4,3). Before being detached from the Companions and reformed as a Corps *per se*, the Hypaspists might well have been embedded to the cavalry, as the squires of the Companions, following their masters in battle, perhaps in the like of the southern *hamippoi* (Heckel 2012) and/or carrying the heavy hoplite shield (*aspis*) of the Companions. Not only has this been a practice well-followed by southern Greek hoplite and cavalry troops, who had squires called Hypaspists (Xen Anab IV.2,20), but a task force composed of Companions and Bodyguards (most probably Royal Bodyguards) were specifically ordered by Alexander in one instance to 'take along their shields, half of them dismount and charge on foot mixed with the other, mounted half' (Arr Anab I.6, 5). This means that they *did* have shields, for cases where they had to fight on foot, i.e. sieges. These were not carried when fighting mounted. One cannot refrain from an association with the hoplite-type shield found by Prof. Andronicos in Vergina, which would serve its owner well in such a task. Southern Greek cavalrymen also had shields, as the elite and usually wealthy cavalrymen, including Cimon and Alcibiades the Younger, might be called to serve as hoplites, either ad hoc (Plut Cim 5,3) or by the decree of the muster.

From carrying the shields to using them in battle themselves, when their masters had no need (i.e. when fighting mounted) the distance is rather short, especially if they were fighting near and to support said masters. To further enhance this view, Arrian himself specifically talks about the 'Companions' Hypaspists' under Nicanor (Arr Anab I. 14,2) at the Granicus. This corps might well have been a standing army, at least since Philip reorganized it to a special, independent unit (Anson 1985) very much like the southern *Epilektoi* including the Arcadian *Eparitoi* (Xen Hell VII.4,22–25 & 33–34) units, which first appeared in Argos in 418 BC being 1,000-strong (Thuc V.67) and then spread out to many states and confederacies. The term *epilektoi* is used by Diodorus for describing Macedonian Army units understood to be the Hypaspists – or their predecessors (Diod XVI.4,3 & XVI.86,1). Such a relationship could also make their training to hoplite tactics (phalanx and the new, skirmishing and mobile kind of hoplite warfare of the fourth century BC) much more probable and explicable. Hoplite-style warfare ability of the Hypaspists is demonstrated in the Alexander Sarcophagus (**Plate 4**),

The Elites 53

with infantry troops with hoplite shield and Phrygian helmet presented to engage both nude (when fighting as light infantry) and in panoply. This fact, along with the multidimensional training inherent for standing *Epilektoi* units of southern Greece as repeatedly mentioned by Xenophon in *Hellenica* contradicts opinions that the only difference of the Hypaspists to the Foot Companion phalanx rank and file was the *esprit de corps*, training and discipline (Milns 1971). Thus, being a standing professional army, they would have been trained to hoplite warfare (phalanx, mobile and combined operations with cavalry) and then also to their state-standard *sarissa*-armed phalanx, fighting as such at least at the Hydaspes (Arr Anab V.12,2). There is absolutely no ground for supposing that their *sarissai* were anything but the standard of the pike phalanx (Ellis 1975); this would have destroyed the idea of the phalanx. The thing is that they were deployed occasionally with different gear and were a much more flexible force, intended for different missions with different gear.

During Alexander's campaign we hear of missions assigned to detachments of 500 and 1,000 Hypaspists (Arr Anab III.29,7), which are rather logically whole units of the corps. This binary organization differs from the eventual Foot Companion *taxeis*, 1,500 strong each and consisting of three 512-troop units or six 256-troop *Syntagmata* (the latter term refers to later establishments, of the Successors, and is rather anachronistically used here). But under the tactical level (*taxis* and chiliarchy) the scheme may well have been common. The organization would well be binary to both line infantry corps (Foot-Companions and Hypaspists) up to 500 men, and from then on the Hypaspists retained the binary organization to the tactical level (1,000-strong *Chiliarchies*) whereas the Foot Companions changed to tertiary: 1,500-strong *taxis*, which allows for more arrangements (**Figure 2.1**). In linear line-up (**Figure 2.1B**) an independent infantry line with two wings or *kerata* ('horns') and one centre could be produced, compared to the ancient binary division in left and right, traditionally invented by the God Pan (Pol Strat I.2,1).

On the other hand, the binary division is much more suitable for the kind of mobile medium infantry missions the Hypaspists had been usually undertaking. Three subunits offer more tactical combinations and flexibility (which is the reason to adopt it in line units) but 2 subunits are easier to command in mobile operations than three; this posed no problem for the Foot Companions, for, despite being regularly used for operations in uneven ground, they were primarily infantry of the line and not elite or special infantry.

This binary structure in three chiliarchies is also compatible with the theory that the elite unit was by definition twice as large as a standard infantry unit. But the chiliarchies may be reminiscent also of the Achaemenid practice, as already noted: the King-of Kings (Shah-an-Shah) had *two* guard units, one of commoners and one of the aristocracy (Her VII.40–41). Thus the Macedonian king did the same; the Hypaspists being from the commoners, who were raised from the retinue of the Aristocrats, and the Royal Hypaspists being from the Aristocracy or other elite strata of the population, as the citizens of the new cities build by the state, the enfranchised immigrants in the eastern, new territories etc.

One should also pay special attention to the fact that actually the abovementioned passage of Herodotus reports *three* Persian 1,000 strong elite units. The Spearbearers, the Applebearers and the thousand-strong part of the 10,000-strong Corps of the Immortals with golden pomegranate-like butt-ends, 'arranged as to surround the other 9,000' (Her VII.41,3). The function of the latter suits perfectly the Macedonian title *Agema,* which was the third unit of the Hypaspist Corps.

The seniority of the three chiliarchies might not be associated directly to their year of establishment; perhaps troopers that excelled in the two first chiliarchies were honourably promoted to joining the *Agema*. Contrarily, since the word *'Epilektoi'* for the elite Macedonian infantry positioned at the rightmost of the phalanx in the Battle of the Erigon Valley, 358 BC (Diod XVI.4,4), is a synonym for the *Agema,* precedence of the *Agema* might be considered seriously (Milns 1967) which could have been integrated into the Hypaspist Corps, once the latter was established, somewhat later, since Demosthenes knows nothing of the Corps while mentioning the Foot Companions and the mercenaries (Dem Or 2.17).

The corps being recruited geographically from the whole of Macedon, as Theopompus (F348) mentions and as the standard practice of *Epilektoi* units prescribed, contrary to the territory-based recruitment of the Foot-Companion *taxeis* (and the Companion Cavalry *ilae*) explains the sporadic use of the term *'Macedonon Agema',* which liberally translates to 'the foremost among the Macedonians': they were selected by virtue and enrolled from the whole of Macedon.

The other important aspect on the subject is the use of the corps in battle. Arrian may refer in different words to the *Agema,* sometimes just *'Agema',* other times as 'Royal *Agema'* and even *'Macedonon Agema'.* But he is rather cautious – let's not forget that he writes half a millennium later – to the use of 'the rest of *Hypaspists*' and the '*Royal Hypaspists*'. He confuses these two terms only twice, in Thebes (Arr Anab I.8,3–4) and in a far later incident (Arr Anab IV.24,10). This really points to three, distinctively named *Chiliarchies* forming the corps. Alternatively, one might think that one *'pentacosiarchia'* is the *Agema*, another is the Royal Hypaspists and the remaining four are 'the rest of Hypaspists'. The latter view is neither proven nor disproven in the text of Arrian; still it is indirectly contradicted by the description of the battle outside Thebes and also in Arr Anab V.13,4, as will be discussed shortly.

The command held by Nicanor, son of Parmenio, who usually commands the Hypaspists (his brother Philotas commands the Companions) is given by Arrian to comprise only two units in some cases, Gaugamela being one of them (Bosworth 1997). Another might be at Issus (Arr Anab II.8,3), but this is controversial, as the wording might imply all three units after all. At Gaugamela, only the Companions' Hypaspists and the *Agema* are mentioned as part of the battle line. The Royal Hypaspists are mentioned, along with the grooms, halting the scythed chariots that had passed harmlessly *through* the phalanx (Arr Anab III.13,6). This implies that Nicanor's immediate command comprised all three Hypaspists' Chiliarchies, in a very modern two-in-front, one-in-the-rear arrangement. The inconsistency in numbers (two units in front, one in the back) could well have been remedied by the rear unit being deployed in half the front ones' depth, thus equalizing the front of both echelons. This concept, if followed for all the heavy infantry deployment, meant a 2:1 distribution of manpower in favour of the first line, and is explored further in the chapter on the Battle of Gaugamela.

In the battle outside Thebes, the first line of Macedonian infantry is made up of two *taxeis* (Arr Anab I.8,1–2) due to terrain. The two *taxeis* probably numbered at most 3,000 men, more possibly 2,000, if the tertiary structure was not yet adopted. The Hypaspists were posted next to the *Agema* (Arr Anab I.8,3) forming the second line; but just some lines later the fleeing Foot Companions where received by the *Agema* and the *Royal Hypaspists* (Arr Anab I.8,4). The interpretation may be that in this case all *three* Chiliarchies were lined up, *Agema* in the middle. Due to ground factors, the retreating Foot Companions might have well retired through the two of the three side-by-side Hypaspist chiliarchies. Retirement *through* the second line, *a la Romana* (Kambouris & Bakas 2015) could explain how the Thebans received and repulsed two Macedonian attack lines before breaking at the attack of the third (Diod XVII. 11,1–12,4). Which units comprised the third line of the army – or rather the third assault line – (Diod XVII.11,1) is difficult to suggest.

The third of the Royal Hypaspists was dispatched to a certain task (Arr Anab IV.24,10). It is widely thought to mean the third of the Hypaspist corps, i.e. 1,000 Hypaspists. But in such a case Arrian would have clearly stated that a chiliarchy of the Hypaspists was assigned a task, as he does elsewhere (Arr Anab III.29,7). So it may well be that in fact the detachment was a fraction of *one* chiliarchy: the third of the Royal Hypaspists (300 men) and not the third of the Hypaspist Corps.

If the Hypaspist Corps, which had been a standing army (Kambouris et al 2019) was the equivalent of the Achaemenid Kinsmen or Immortals, one can be bold in some deductions. The Hypaspists accounted for 10 per cent of the Macedonian infantry levy, the ideal conscript to elite ratio (**Figure 2.2**). If there is a parallel, the Persian national infantry levy must have been 100,000 at the very least, forming the backbone of the *kara* and supported by 10,000 national cavalry levy (Her VII.41,3), totalling, if the various guards are included, approximately 120,000 Persian troops, as reported by Xenophon (Cyr I.2,15), the guards not included. Perhaps this national cavalry draft, diminished to 6,000, were the white-clad 'guard' cavalry of Artaxerxes II mentioned by Xenophon in Cunaxa (Xen Anab I.7,11). Most probably it was not a guard, but the national Persian cavalry draft outfitted according to the personal beliefs of the then sovereign. A totally different proposal is that at some point the Imperial standard had been one cavalryman per five infantrymen (Xen Cyr VIII.6,19), but this may be Xenophon's suggestion for a cavalry-heavy force rather than the actual Achaemenid practice. Later writers proposed one per six (Arr Tact 11 & 14,2 & 18.1).

(Royal) Bodyguards

The view of *Somatophylakes* ('bodyguards') and *Basilikoi Somatophylakes* ('royal bodyguards') being one and the same (Bosworth 1997) is ill-substantiated. The Royal Bodyguards of the Argeads were seven (Arr Anab VI.28,3), ostensibly one on duty next to the king per weekday, although the number of days in an Ancient Greek week remains controversial. They might have been an echo of the Seven Conspirators in the Achaemenid court. There are some missing details, like the total number (the Seven Conspirators included Darius I, while the bodyguards of Alexander were Seven without counting the Person of the King) but similarities are perhaps more important. Peucestas became the eighth bodyguard by exception, as an honour for saving Alexander's life in the citadel of Malli (Arr Anab VI.28.3). Peucestas must – or might – have been a Hypaspist.*

---

* In I. 11,8 Arrian says that the sacred arms taken from Troy were borne by the Hypaspists before Alexander in battles, and in VI. 28, 3–4 Peucestas is supposed to have assisted Alexander in Malli citadel bearing the shield taken from Troy, which makes him very probably a Hypaspist. Moreover in VI. 9,4 Arrian specifically states that the Hypaspists were following Alexander in his assault to the walls and Diodorus in XVII. 99,4 calls Peucestas a Hypaspist.

On the other hand, the bodyguard follows Alexander in a special mission, against the Uxians, along with some Hypaspists and '8,000 of the other infantry' (Arr Anab III.17,2). This means that the bodyguard was a (guard) unit by itself, for there would have been no reason for Arrian to enumerate just seven bodyguards along with other units (Hypaspists and other types of infantry). Furthermore, Alexander took the 'Bodyguards and Hypaspists up to 700' to storm a fortified place (Arr Anab IV.30,3). If a standard unit of the Hypaspists (500, since their major unit was the chiliarchy) is subtracted from the total (700), the difference is the strength of the Bodyguard, i.e. 200, most probably two subunits of 100 men each. This is similar to the Achaemenid structure of two guard units of 1,000 as described by Herodotus (VII.40,2 & 41.2), one for commoners and another for aristocracy, a symbolism of the divine duality, the binary universe of Mithraism (Soudavar 2012). The primary function of the bodyguard would have been to attend to a variety of duties, such as the guarding of the palace in peacetime or the lodgings of the king in general, plus secret police or military police functions. It is very tempting, almost ccompulsory to identify them with the Royal Pages, one more institution possibly copied from the Persians (Keinast 1973), and described as such by Xenophon (Xen Anab I.9,3–4). The pages are mentioned as bodyguards (Arr Anab IV.13,1), and their duties fall squarely into the jurisdiction of a bodyguard. The bodyguards are mentioned by Arrian as an elite infantry force, but since the pages had horses, they would be able to fight mounted as a unit. They might have been the elusive heavy cavalry unit mentioned in Diodorus (Diod XVII.57,1) but not by Arrian at Gaugamela, but has never been mentioned before, neither at the Granicus nor at Issus; in both cases though the cavalry line-up is not particularly detailed. But it remains plausible that they were established after the Battle of Issus and Alexander's claim to the Crown of Asia. Before this time the King's entourage in battle was the Royal Squadron and the Hypaspists – most probably the *Agema*.

Chapter 5

Innovating and Conserving

A pivotal issue is the idea of Macedonian frontline main units being of tertiary structure. Even outside Thebes, the Hypaspist Corps may be seen with three units (see above). Is this so with the phalanx and the Companion Cavalry? The Macedonian army follows, for the most, the southern Greek golden rule of a 1:10 ratio between cavalry and infantry (Plut Vit Aris 21,1) which also seems to apply with the ratio between special or standing units and full levies (Rzepka 2008), insinuating a double balance of 10 to 1 of regular infantry to foot elites and to regular Cavalry (**Figure 2.2**). Thus the regular phalanx *taxeis* must be 10 times larger than the *ilae*; following the same structure, the Hypaspists must be ten times the Royal Squadron and the cavalry must be equal to the Hypaspists. Although this is difficult to prove, as half the army stayed in Macedon with Antipater, the basic idea remains valid: it is no coincidence that at Gordium (Arr Anab I.29.4) the ratio of Macedonian cavalry and infantry reinforcements is 1:10. The notion of *ilae* being 150-strong comes from the Battle of Issus (Arr Anab II.9.4 & II.9.3). Before that, both at Pelion (Arr Anab I.6.1) and in western Asia Minor, after Granicus (Arr Anab I.18.1) the number 200 for detachments of Companions is reported. This cannot accord with 150-strong *ilae*; they are obviously 100-strong and of binary structure as standard Greek practice. The key are the reinforcements arriving at Gordium (Arr Anab I.29.4): the 300 new cavalry are enough for one more fifty-horse subunit for each of the six Companion *ilae*, and the same goes with the 3,000 fresh phalanx troops: one more 500-strong subunit for each of the six *taxeis*. It is at this point, before the obvious showdown with Darius III and the imperial Persian Army, that Alexander changes the structure of his army, to enhance tactical flexibility; he will do so once more after Gaugamela, again after receiving massive reinforcements under Amyntas in Susa (Arr Anab III.16, 10; Curt V.1,40), returning to binary structure, better suited to the upcoming mountain and irregular warfare and dispersed campaigning following multiple axes. And this time it will remain thus to the end of the Macedonian state, almost two centuries later.

For the cavalry Arrian is solid; Companion *ilae* were augmented from 150 to 200 horse and divided to two *lochoi* (Arr Anab III.6, 11), supposedly

100-strong (Tarn 1948); for this, the 500 cavalry brought by Amyntas (Curt V.1,41) were more than enough. For the infantry conjecture is needed: the existing six *taxeis* were augmented from 1,500 to 2,000 by one more 500-man *lochos* (Curt V.2,3) and divided to two 1,000-strong *chiliarchies* each; this transformation required at least 3,000 phalangites, the product of six by 500 men. The Taxiarchs would have been automatically assigned one of the two chiliarchies of their respective *taxeis*. As a result, six new commanders (*chiliarches*) were required, who were *elected* by the army, not selected by the leadership, as described (Curt V.2, 3–5). Another two were needed for the command of the two *chiliarchies* of the newly established seventh *taxis* which must have taken place at Susa (Milns 1966a), as at the Hydaspes there are seven *taxeis* (Arr Anab V.11,3–12,2). Its establishment required another 2,000 troops, bringing the total needed to 5,000 phalangites, whereas 6,000 had been brought by Amyntas (Curt V.1, 40).

Macedonian conscription

The formal military institutions of Macedon are assigned to an enigmatic King Alexander (Matthew 2015), who created a decent military instead of a horde. The two basic foundations were the Companion Cavalry, raised among the aristocracy and considered, as the name implies, comrades of the King, and the conscription of infantry to standard units and also standard deployment depth and formation. Instead of an unruly mass, companies (*Lochoi*) and other units were created and manned and a standard deployment system, with fixed file depth and positions within a file, created. The name of this file, *dekas*, meaning ten in Greek, not only shows early Greek used in the military – and thus no such thing as a Macedonian language – but also a distinctive Achaemenid influence. The model must have been the *dathabam*, the ten-man file (Sekunda 1992), completely different a concept from the southern, urbanized Greeks' file of eight men (Connolly 1981). If this fact is combined to the possible, not to say obvious, relation of the term 'companions' to the Achaemenid term *Anusiya*, later translated as 'Kinsmen' and perhaps mistranslated by early Greek writers and wanderers as Immortals (Kambouris 2022a,b) a strong influence of Achaemenid practice in the military institutions of Macedon is implied and this makes Alexander I, King of a realm recently annexed by the King of Kings and thus his subject or *bandaka* (early fifth century BC) the perfect candidate. After all, a part of the expansion of the state under his rule was accomplished dynamically, and not only diplomatically (Matthew 2015) and this corroborates the previous associations. This conscript infantry was of two kinds, at least since King Archelaus started his own reforms – but possibly much earlier: the light, peltast model, possibly the *only* troop type of infantry before said reforms, and the line infantry, meaning *some* attempt, obviously of debatable success, to produce hoplites. No matter the social mechanism this second body required to come into being, they were named Foot Companions, the middle to low class Macedonian regulars. The rabble were, as in southern Greece and Thessaly, peltasts or even lighter, and they were many. So many that Philip was able in twenty years to triple the strength of his infantry to 30,000 *despite* sustaining massive casualties in battle against the Illyrians in 359 BC. Thus, instead of a few, less than 10,000 and possibly 6 to 8,000 Foot Companions in 359 BC, possibly a 1,000-strong *taxis* from each conscription region, as the six territories of Lower Macedon (Hammond 1990) Philip produces in *one* year, in 358 BC, 10,000 line infantry and twenty years later, in Chaeronea in 338 BC, up to 30,000 (Diod XVI.85,5), while Alexander, when crossing the Hellespont, had a total muster of at least 24,000 phalanx-grade infantry (the Hypaspists included).

A massive increase of Foot Companions was enacted, achieved by conscripting *everybody* into the line infantry (Randall 2012) and outfitting them as pikemen (Hanson 1999; Anson 2010), is the simplest way to overcome the sources' contradictory evidence, namely between Theopompus, maintaining that the Foot Companions were the elite of the draft and Anaximenes who implies they were the sum of the line infantry (English 2002). They were the elite part of the draft (not the standing guard unit) similar to the hoplite-gentlemen of the Southerners, while line duty was limited to a small part of the citizenry, as were the hoplites of Athens, hardly the ⅓rd of the citizenry at Marathon (Kambouris 2022a). When the line infantry was recast as pikemen, almost everybody was meeting the conditions – especially when partly subsidized – and became Foot Companions.

There are two different theories regarding the Macedonian recruitment system under Philip and Alexander. One is followed more or less unanimously and was proposed at its best long ago (Hammond 1990). It envisions a regional conscription system, similar to the one used possibly in Sparta and definitely in Boeotia (Bonner 1910; Buck 1972) and Thessaly (Strootman 2012), with specific quota for each administrative unit. Whether the idea was in the spirit of federal formations of southern Greece, such as the Boeotian league that Philip had the opportunity to study from close by, which could be copied in a monarchical version by Macedon (Rzepka 2008), or in that of the national tribal states as was Thrace under Sitalces (Diod XII.50,1) and Cotys (Diod XVI.2,6) can be debated. The bottom line is that the conscription was by territory, not on a tribal basis, although territories of tribes tended to be identified as regions and thus be homogeneous in population.

This regional hypothesis is supported by the use of territorial or ethnic names for units, both of infantry (Diod XVII.57,2) and of cavalry (Arr Anab II.9,3; I.12,7). A local aristocrat or member of the local dynasty was appointed commander in a most feudalistic manner (Tarn 1948). The succession in the command of at least two phalanx *taxeis* (**Table 5.1**) being among members of the same family (Heckel 1992) corroborates this line of thought. All such territories should contribute something; infantry or cavalry or light cavalry (**Figure 5.1**) or any combination (**Figure 5.2**).

As mentioned above, the Macedonian line infantry under Philip was what in southern Greek (city-) states would be considered light infantry in social terms (Randall 2012), as they lacked the means to equip themselves as line infantry (Hanson 1999; Anson 2010). Though, mimicking Athens, with state sponsorship of cavalry and hoplite infantry by issuing shields and spears and financing cavalry mounts and remunerating the fodder, Philip did the same. He issued the basic gear to his peasants, farmers or shepherds, and created with lower costs a massive line infantry arm by his national levy instead of keeping them as skirmishers of dubious quality (Thuc IV.126,5–6). In doing that he far exceeded in numbers – and eventually in quality – the hoplite arm improvised, with little success, by his predecessors; and this *despite* the massive casualties in 359 BC (Hammond 1994).

But it is important to note that of the army of his late brother, less than 10,000, Philip inherited the survivors who were hoplites, or at least a proportion of them, and thus a nucleus of his pikemen was adept with hoplite gear and methodology. One should not be surprised if these troops retained a secondary ability to engage in hoplite warfare throughout the campaigns of Alexander. This would make them the heaviest-armed, in contrary to the usual remark of Arrian concerning the lightest-armed of the phalanx *taxeis*. This ability was obviously restricted to infantry from Lower Macedon, as the far less urbanized conscripts from the Upper Macedon cantons were drafted into the national army by Philip and were from the outset trained as pikemen, and issued with the basic gear on public expenses. As a result, there was possibly a differentiation amongst the Foot Companions regarding the kit: the light kit must have been issued to younger recruits, but also to recruits of Upper Macedon possibly without age distinction. The veterans of Lower Macedon experienced in hoplite warfare must have been promoted gradually to the Hypaspists and/or used with heavier kit, even within their native *taxeis* regiments – kit possibly acquired by their own means.

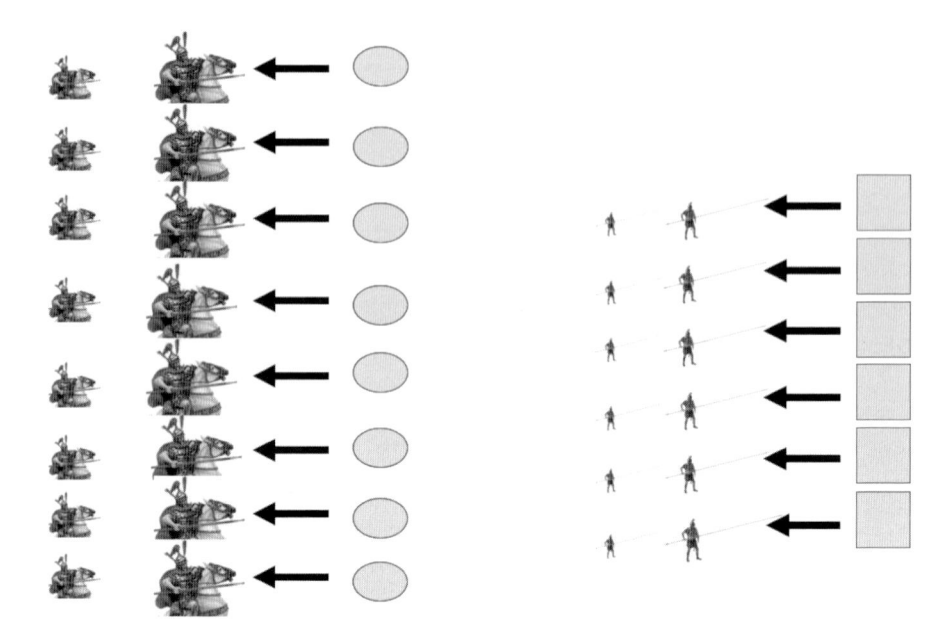

Figure 5.1: The Macedonian conscription system by Sarantis, 1977.
Conscription units equal to tribal districts, possibly eight from Lower and six from Upper Macedonia. Each of the former raising two Companion Cavalry *ilae* or squadrons and each of the latter two phalanx *taxeis* or regiments. One of the two units was available for expeditionary duty and one remained at home, similarly to Achaemenid practice (Xen Cyr I.2,9, 12).

The extensive and very productive Macedonian plain(s) – plus the reforms of some kings including Archelaus at the end of the fifth century – imply a farmer population (Fuller 1958) and allegations that a proper middle class did not exist in the social structure of Macedon (Markle 1978), and thus most of the population were shepherds of some kind, read a bit unconvincing; at least for the older part of the Kingdom, the Lower Macedon. The speech

Table 5.1: The *taxeis* commanders in different battles and campaigns. The number in parenthesis indicates the order of precedence in the respective battle.

Granicus	Issus	Gaugamela	India
Coenus (2)	Coenus (1)	Coenus (1)	Python
Amyntas (4)	Amyntas (5)	Simmias (Amyntas) (5)	*Attalus*
Meleager (6)	Meleager (3)	Meleager (3)	*Meleager*
Perdikkas (1)	Perdikkas (2)	Perdikkas (2)	*Alcetas*
Philip (5)	Ptolemy (4)	Polysperchon (4)	*Polysperchon*
Craterus (3)	Craterus (6)	Craterus (6)	Gorgias

of Alexander at Opis (Arr VII.9,2) that corroborates such a pastoralist view of Macedon was exaggerated and highly biased due to the bitter emotions of the moment and overstated, amplified and generalized diminishing or outright offensive realities – still, realities regarding mostly *Upper* Macedon, a rather unruly and backward area (Hammond 1990). The said speech does not provide an objective and accurate description of the *status quo ante*. True, before Philip the urbanization in Macedon was limited (Heckel & Jones 2006) and especially in Upper Macedon, where a significant percentage of the population were indeed shepherds and goatherds (Hammond 1994) but this says little; the middle-class which produced the hoplites of the south were not city folk, but peasantry to a great degree, in most Greek *poleis*. The association of hoplite warfare with the city should be understood in the context of the city-state, not the city-urban centre, and in the former the pastoralists, especially the small farmers, held sway (Hanson 1999).

The only true skirmishers, the archers, might have been raised centrally as specialist troops and the same goes for elite units. For his Asian campaign Alexander selected units of some particular administrative entities and left the troops raised from others back with Antipater. Yearly recruits, as teenagers were coming to age, were either incorporated into the home army or dispatched to the expeditionary army, once more by the assignment of their units. This scheme is simple, straightforward and can accommodate any number of Macedonian commands one could deliberate upon, and any

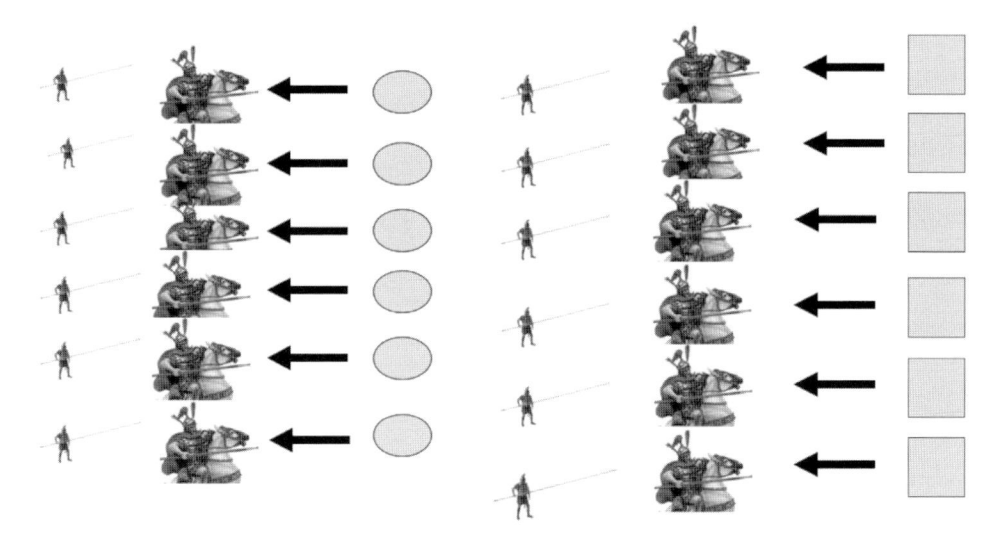

Figure 5.2: The Macedonian conscription system by Hammond, 1988.
Conscription units equal to tribal districts, possibly six from Lower (ovoid) and six from Upper Macedonia (square), each raising one phalanx *taxis* regiment and one Companion Cavalry *Ila* squadron. Selected units form the expeditionary army as ordered.

number of subunits at any given time, as the organization of the army was transforming, for example from binary to tertiary, to adapt to the changing conditions of the terrain and the enemy.

The contribution of heavy cavalry, light cavalry or infantry or any combination according to the population and economic realities of any region is realistic and flexible and recalls Persian practices: in the army of Xerxes there were infantry-only national contributions (Her VII.84) and also some cavalry only, as were the Sagarteans (Her VII.85) and then some contributing both (Her VII.84–86). The system is adaptable to the realities of the land and allows leeway for any kind of change at will. Under this model the new recruits when arriving, as happened at Susa, were assigned to the *taxeis* of their place of origin, quite corroborating the Greek used by the narrator (Arr III.16,11).

The alternative theory proposes a more standardized and elaborate system (Rzepka 2008), made possible by measures and executive actions fulfilling this very purpose. Such measures included, without being restricted to, massive population movement within the limits of the realm and the introduction of new administrative internal borderlines for jurisdiction. It was modelled on the Athenian arrangement (Her V.66,2 & 69,1), possibly due to the influence of Iphicrates who had been employed in the royal house and actually adopted by the Argead king Amyntas III in the early fourth century (Nepos Iph 3.2). It was based on a federalist notion and similar to the Athenian civic tribes. Each of the latter was made up by three regions in three different locations and actually in three different territorial zones. Philip's version resulted in six different conscription areas (**Figure 5.3**), not ten as with the Athenians. Given that each conscription area of the Macedonian state under Philip is understood to have produced units raised from three different regions with different tribal associations, this was an effort to weaken such affiliations for the sake of the central state, as happened in Cleisthenic Athens (Her V.69,1).

Each conscription area was not homogenous and comprised regions from three territorial zones: Upper Macedon, Lower Macedon and the Eastern territories, fairly recently included in the hard core of the Macedonian state. Each of the six conscription areas provided infantry and cavalry, possibly light cavalry, too. Half of its resources was expeditionary-grade, and on short notice it would go on far-off campaigns, a very Persian arrangement (Xen Cyr I.2,9), both cavalry and infantry. As a result, half the troops and units from each conscription area followed Alexander and the other half remained with Antipater in 334 BC.

This arrangement would be best implemented if every region was raising one binary territorial unit of infantry and cavalry, as was the standard Greek practice. By contributing one of the two to the expeditionary army, the three units of the same arm of one conscription area would group together into tertiary divisions (cavalry *ilae* or squadrons, infantry *taxeis* or regiments), a fact that would have facilitated enormously the creation of multi-arm standard commands (corps-level in today's parlance) at the later stages of the campaigns of Alexander (Arr IV.16,2 & 17,3) by simply assigning the units of both arms of one conscription unit to one CO (Commanding Officer).

This scheme allows for a rigid number of 6 units that correspond to the 10 Athenian Tribes and were commanded, similarly to the latter, by a General (*Strategos*) each. It also explains the naming of divisions by their commander in infantry (i.e. Arr Anab III.11,9) but also cavalry (i.e. Arr Anab III.11,8). Under this scheme the reinforcements, as the ones arriving at Susa, were assigned not to *taxeis*, but to the specific *lochoi* of their place of origin, something as compatible with Arrian's report (Arr III.16,11).

The commanders here are no princelings, but professional specialists and occasionally the unit is known by the place of residence or origin of the commander. Since the highlanders were better in raising infantry and the lowlanders in cavalry, cavalry units frequently used the names of the eastern territories or from Lower Macedon and infantry from Upper Macedon, but this was actually coincidental. Still, the commanders were residents within the recruitment unit. Thus one phalanx *taxis* was commanded by a series of non-related commanders, something out of the context of territorial bonds. There were exceptions, when a brother replaced another brother in a certain command, or the son the father, as in a given case in phalanx *taxis* (Arr Anab III.11,9) but this case was special; the commander had not to be replaced, but temporarily surrogated as he was away in a mission.

Since the events at Tyre, a part of the phalanx is referred to as the *Asthetairoi*. Initially it is identified with the *taxis* led by Coenus (Arr Anab II.23,2), but eventually no less than four phalanx *taxeis* are considered as such (Kleymeonov 2015). There is the notion that this refers to phalanx *taxeis* recruited from a certain location, namely Upper Macedon, and the name indicating some quality or other, such as recruitment from urban populations or a special relationship with the King (Bosworth 1973). On the other hand, the name might have been a title and thus earned on merit (Kleymeonov 2015). This would explain how it has not been reported before a certain time, and how, subsequently, more units are seen to be so designated reaching a staggering four out of six brigades of the Foot Companions (Griffith 1979).

It is obvious that such an honourary title, name, or status is not extended to units of the home army, but the privilege is reserved for the ones

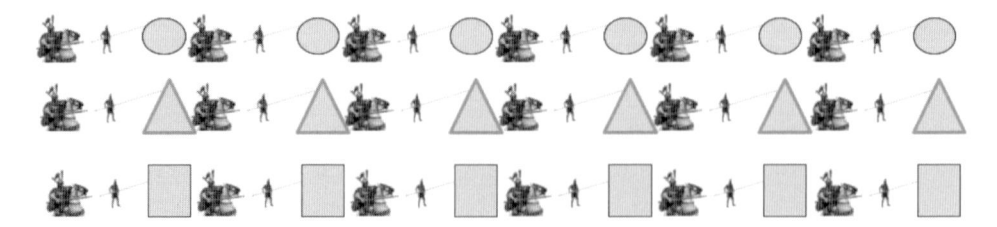

Figure 5.3: The Macedonian conscription system by Rzepka, 2008.
Six conscription zones – represented in columns – not corresponding to tribal districts, as was the Athenian and the Spartan practices. Incidentally, under Xerxes the Achaemenid empire had just as many (Kambouris 2022b). Each zone is comprised by one territory of Lower Macedon (circle), one of Upper Macedon (square) and one of the new lands to the east, Chalcidice included (triangle). Each territory furnishes one 1,000-strong *taxis* or regiment of phalanx infantry and one 100-strong ila or squadron of Companion Cavalry, both of binary structure. One half of such units (500- and 50-strong, respectively) formed the expeditionary army under Alexander, and the other remained with Antipater, following the Achaemenid practice (Xen Cyr I.2,9, 12) to the letter.

participating in the Eastern Campaign under Alexander, when they meet some criteria. And this explains also why at Issus and Gaugamela the order of precedence of the phalanx *taxeis* is identical, but different to the one at the Granicus. Once the order is not pre-ordained, and changes by the day (Bosworth 1980a), as was the case with the Athenian *taxeis* (Her VI.110) this identity may be something else and not a coincidence. It may reflect the rating of the different phalanx units during previous actions, a kind of battle charts (Milns 1976).

Hoplites and phalangites

At the beginning of the Persian Wars the Greek hoplite was not a citizen soldier, but a dismounted knight. A small percentage of his society (in Athens almost 10,000 of 30,000 in 490 BC, but this was due to the massive upgrade of status of 4,000 lot-holders given lots at Chalkis after a resounding Athenian victory sometime after 510 BC and at a similar or worse ratio in Lacedaimon), they were less of a rarity compared to the Knights of Christendom but a rarity nonetheless. Thus Delbruck's view that in Marathon the Greek citizens took on the Persian knights is off the mark. Whether the *sparabara* were also knights is debatable: the Persians had the *asabara* cavalry for their stratum of knights, and the shock infantry may well have been ballooned by the subsidy of the King due to the imperial income, both loot from campaigns and taxes from everyday life – although Xenophon mentions nothing of the kind *for his time*; it seems that it is a social Darwinism for Persians able to partake in the warrior and administrative class. Both Sparta and Athens at their imperial phases forgot the class-war-centric prerogative of the hoplite and subsidized unprivileged folk; the former *helot*-slaves, the latter poor citizens, to swell the numbers and fill the ranks.

In this view, one must first acknowledge that the status of the Boeotian hoplites of Epaminondas is lost to us; but it seems it is still the upper tier of the Theban citizenry in a deeply conservative state. He may have started expanding the recruitment base, but this is debatable. Jason of Pherrae, on the other hand could never have raised the necessary numbers without actively subsidizing local levies; still, this is also debatable. Philip II and Alexander, on the other hand, were definitely using a fully 'democratized', or rather class-agnostic shock infantry force. Lighter and cheaper, at least originally, than the hoplites, and funded by imperial expansion and especially the goldmines of Pangaeum, the full levy of the Macedonians filled the phalanx ranks, with the aristocrats joining the cavalry – similarly to the Persians. The phalanx of Alexander had never been mercenary. It was the conscript Macedonian army, with men doing their duty to king and country and properly remunerated by the state. They were called to arms, thus the conscript reinforcements were heading to Asia regularly, when their class was called, and some – many – of them had served long and were veterans. But they were NOT professionals and were decommissioned as veterans having performed their due. This is similar to the long-term campaigning required by Roman citizens, joining a certain number of yearly deployments up to a certain age. They were called to arms and remunerated for it, they were not career soldiers.

Siege engines and artillery

Among the siegetrain and the engineer component in general – an ancient element, in both oriental and Greek Bronze-Age traditions, but nurtured through the hoplite era especially by the Spartans) (Xen Lak Pol XI,2) – the artillery element was to prove an innovation of crucial importance. Possibly introduced from the source of this discovery, Syracuse under Dionysius I, either directly or indirectly through networks of alliances, the artillery thrived in the Macedonian arsenal, in contrast to other Greek states. This development was due to the combination of three factors. First was the innovative thought on military matters in Macedon – an involuntary gift of Epaminondas and his crew, since Sparta and Athens were introduced to artillery but partially or wholly disdained to use it. The second factor was the bitter experience of Philip at the hands of the vagabond Phocian chieftain Onomarchus who used catapults in field artillery mode, becoming the inventor of the discipline. And the third factor was the ample funds (after Philip II acquired the goldmines of Pangeum) and was vital. Under Alexander the standard catapult, launching bolts/arrows (*oxybeles*) is used for suppressive, area fire and is coupled to more accurate and amenable to fine-tuning torsion systems, but also to stone-thrower models (*lithoboloi*) (Campbell 2003). Whether the latter could already shatter point targets, possibly but not necessarily including fortifications, is controversial. Still they could be used for area suppression, destruction of soft targets as were rural or urban lodgings and possibly with incendiary charges, as were ignited containers filled with flammables (Campbell 2011). Whether the bolt-shooters could snipe against individual targets or this was a later development is also debatable (Heliopoulos 2002, Keyser 1994).

It is important that the arch-enemy, the Achaemenid empire, had acquired the same technology (possibly by the reverse way, through Carthage, once the Syracusan secret was sold out) and deployed it in western Asia Minor, in Greek cities and massively so in the Phoenician Metropoleis such as Tyre and occasionally in the deep of Asia, at the Persian Gates, within the hardest core of the empire; but not further to the East, nor in more backward and/or mutinous and indomitable western areas (Keyser 1994).

Chapter 6

Phalanx Warfare

At the time of Alexander, hoplite warfare was the standard throughout the Mediterranean. The great tacticians Agesilaus and Epaminondas used cavalry but had the phalanx as their main instrument and exploited different aspects of it. The hoplite had been exported to Carthage and Etruria (D'Amato & Salimbeti 2018; Salimbeti & D'Amato 2014) and also Latium/Rome (Sekunda 1995). The Balkans were using it; as hoplites since 385 BC, by Syracusan sponsorship, the Illyrians became a regional power and formidable enemies of the Macedonians a generation before Philip (Hammond 1966 & 1994), and the Persian throne recruited masses of Greek hoplites, while also trying to raise home-grown ones, as already mentioned. The Macedonian pike phalanx was designed to tackle a hoplite phalanx since the days Macedon could not afford a proper one of the latter. Although changing their point of gravity, from protection and shock by shoving to lethality and shock by thrusting, it is the same principle and the same mechanics.

The word 'phalanx' is first met in Homer's Iliad. Although its precise meaning is hazy, it went on being used for Greek battle orders for almost a millennium, with the hoplite, classical phalanx and then the Macedonian pike phalanx. The definition seems vague as well throughout that millennium, but a useful one might be 'a closely knit line abreast with the depth of the files being used as force multiplier and not only to replenish first lines' casualties with troops moving up along the files'.

A phalanx is much more than a number – or a mass – of soldiers in close formation. Close formations were not infrequent in ancient history, wherever spears, or pikes or other thrusting weapons were favoured. The 'Stele of the Vultures' shows a Sumerian formation with rectangular shields and thrusting spears that is interpreted as a proto-phalanx. It might be so; the rectangular, most probably flat shields, do fit well with one another to produce a protective barrier, but this is no phalanx. Had it been so, Persian *sparabara* and Roman legionaries in *testudos* would qualify as phalanxes. A close-packed formation of line infantry is a prerequisite for a phalanx, not a proof of it.

(Proto)phalanx and Homer

Some Mycenaean formations, on the other hand, are specifically if loosely termed 'phalanxes' in Homer. The Lion Hunt Dagger shows Mycenaean warriors wearing figure-of-eight and tower bodyshields, both of them hollow, and wielding two-handed lances and being supported by embedded archer. The other representation, the fresco of Akrotiri, is less straightforward: the troopers carry swords and are helmeted, but their shields might be either hollow or flat, and the warriors themselves might be either parading in single file or advancing as an open line. Should the latter be the case, it is no phalanx: the long, two-handed pikes allow countering chariotry and mutual support against light infantry incursions for close-quarters sword strikes.

Despite these facts, which present an important artistic convention issue, the epics present a fully compliant picture, but much more detailed. In the *Odyssey*, the battlekit is explicitly minimalistic, with bodyshield, helmet and a pair of javelins, which must have replaced the lance, or could substitute it in cases (Hom Od xxii-101102). The sword is a plus, but not necessary. The difference with the fully armoured warriors in the *Iliad* (Hom Il III-329/36) is marked. Still, it is in the Iliad that the extreme density of the phalanx is first described (Hom Il XIII-129–131) and the kit defined: big shield, stout spear (not javelin) 'helmet' and dense concentrated action (Hom Il XIII-145). The latter is more important than it seems: Trojan warriors have bodyshields as well, but throughout the epic they are never mentioned as forming dense phalanxes; neither did their allies. Hector and Aeneas are mentioned with bodyshields (Hom Il VI-118); doubtless the rank and file would own a number, as well, to form a line firm enough to withstand an exchange of missiles as a prelude in battle (Hom Il XV-710), much in the Roman way. But they could not form a close phalanx *sensu stricto*. The Homeric term used in the plural, *phalanxes*, for both contenders, means a line-abreast formation, contrary to the line-ahead ones (much like the Napoleonic assault columns) the *towers* (Hom Il IV-334).

The concave shape of both bodyshields was essential for a phalanx. It deflected blows and missiles, it provided protection over a wide angle and allowed the bearer to change front and direction in shoving, as well as to apply and focus his shoving energy better. Tower shields in contact, with pikes projecting over their rims were a solid defence wall. In the Iliad the dense Greek phalanx is a static defensive formation, neither advancing nor retreating. It receives and withstands enemy assaults. It does not even repel them. If the main defensive position is the one depicted in some representations, that is a semi-kneeling position with the shield resting on the ground, inclined to fully cover the bearer from missiles and thrusts, and the lance held over-rim, or on-rim, this is easily understandable. But, other than covering with the long reach of the lance from the subsequent lines the lines in front, the depth does not seem to be of any practical use.

On the other hand, the ridges of the respective models of the figure-of-eight shields (D'Amato & Salimbeti 2011) were ideal to shove and create a breech in a shieldwall and in this context the depth, both as a reinforcing factor behind the assaulting shield-bearer, and as an interception precaution behind the assaulted individuals, steadying them and not leaving them to falter or break, comes into play. For a shoving match, with or without hacking and thrusting of opportunity, the semi-kneeling position is suicidal; one has to stand, either crouched or upright. In such a position the lance protruding through the narrows formed by 4 cycles (two on each of two successive, almost overlapping figure-of-eight shields) is a serious advantage. Thus, instead of spearing over the shield rim, fully using the upper protrusion of the tower shield (D'Amato & Salimbeti 2011) to cover one's face, the figure-of-eight allowed spearing almost *through* the shield, while advancing or retreating. A measure of mobility might have been restored, which allowed manoeuvring and, much more important, slow, ordered, disciplined and massive offence during advance.

The importance of the figure-of-eight shield is underlined by its appearance alone, as a symbol in frescoes. It must have been a game-changer and many warriors seemed to have retained it at least in its improved iteration, the Dipylon shield (D'Amato & Salimbeti 2017; D'Amato & Salimbeti 2011), even when higher technology round shields, concave and made of metal, were made available. As the tower shield was just as good if not better in deflecting missiles and blows (Hom Il VII-219/23) and surviving through a rain of missiles the true value and the reason of the popularity of the figure-of-eight shield must have been the enhanced offensive utility. The newer, much easier to handle circular shields as the Herzsprung model (Hencken 1950; D'Amato & Salimbeti 2017), with their superior resistance to penetration and slashing (Hom Il XX-265/72), did not allow any offensive use in condensed, close quarters fighting – at least not till the invention of the Argive *hoplon*.

It cannot be assessed if a dense and well-disciplined phalanx of this era could stop in its tracks a chariotry assault by providing enough interception, by successive lines of lances, against a charging chariot team. But it certainly could keep the heavy armoured warrior, a perfectly trained aristocrat, at a safe distance from the unarmoured rank and file (Hom Il XIII-145), who would be slaughtered massively should the former approach to spear or sword range, as is vividly described (Hom Il XI-309). Moreover, a great deal of hand weapons such as swords and warheads of lances and spears display characteristics compatible with a role of piercing bodyshields (especially if not copper-faced) and striking the target behind them; another category, such as axes and cleavers (D'Amato & Salimbeti 2011), show a preferential suitability for hacking, possibly targeting the upper rim so as to destroy the integrity of the shield and perhaps what lies just beneath – a crouched head in a helmet or headgear.

Hoplite Phalanx

The primary characteristics of a phalanx formation are its width, its depth and its density. There are many other secondary ones and of extreme importance nonetheless: weaponry, shock or striking weight, flexibility, mobility, coherence, durability, collective protection and … cost. The interaction among all these features produced the winner in symmetric confrontations (phalanx against phalanx, similar or different) and the verdict in asymmetric ones (like hoplites against tribal warriors). The most important characteristic of hoplite phalanx is that the main feature in its formation is the shield (Plut Moral 220a), a defensive weapon which can be used offensively in both technique and tactics.

Creation and formation

The equipment used within the hoplite phalanx clearly predates it and was never designed for such a role, but once used in such a way it evolved and adapted. Its basic attribute was the double-grip, rimmed and concave (**Plate 2C,D**) Argive shield (*hoplon*), which named the respective warriors, the hoplites, and ultimately the formation.

The *hoplon* shield and the hoplite panoply were not intended for close-packed warfare. Providing excellent all-round protection, freedom of movement and much room for expertise in handling, contrary to the bodyshields or the central-grip shields of previous dates, they were meant for wealthy, excellently trained aristocrats who would master their secrets, potential and weight with uninterrupted, continuous training. It was not a common amenity, neither the shield nor the panoply (Thuc VIII.97,1). The analogy with medieval knights is absolute.

Still, as the defensive power of the panoply outdid the offensive, a densely packed group could sweep its opponents rather easily, maximizing the protection by the coordinated, combined action. The ability of more troopers to engage at the same time one opponent, thus overpowering or saturating his defence, was important; but, the most important thing was that in close proximity much of the expertise in weapons handling was inapplicable. This allowed later for savings in both equipment and training. All these facts together brought a wealthy, non-noble class into play, as they could afford the new weaponry and became tactically efficient rather fast. This was the birth of the hoplite phalanx.

Although at later dates the panoply was discarded except the shield and perhaps the helmet, this must be put into context: it was not due to physical or tactical restrictions but to economic ones. For a hoplite phalanx a *hoplon* shield was necessary, no doubt. Cuirass and greaves were very advantageous but not necessary (Plut Moral 220a). In broken ground, they were a liability, but this is overrated: in broken ground phalanx could not be formed and thus the hoplites were very vulnerable, but for their panoplies. Thus, in the Greek colonization, where small detachments were fighting against enemy colonials or unfriendly natives, the hoplite panoply was never questioned despite its cost in the seventh[s] and sixth centuries. The reason for the lighter phalanx, which evolved in the relatively more wealthy states of the late fifth century, was socio-mechanical: it allowed the arming of more low-income dwellers, an event rather unwelcome in aristocratic societies. And the numbers were all important in phalanx versus phalanx, as was the case in the civil wars which caused this shedding of armour. This importance of the numbers deployed is the reason for never keeping real reserves, nor evolving the respective tactics.

The three primary attributes of the phalanx interact in a temporal dimension: in a phalanx engagement if one of the opposing phalanxes is wider than the other, it can achieve a flanking. Flanking at the unshielded, right side will immediately destroy the enemy by spearing straight at the bodies, and, if some troops turn there to present shields, the creation of weak points in the phalanx structure both in the ranks in contact with the enemy and in the depth of the phalanx will make the collapse total. No decent general would allow this, which means that a flanking at the left was perhaps easier. There the flank is shielded and spearing, shoving and psychology take some time to decide the issue. During that time the extended phalanx must hold and not disintegrate, nor break frontally. Usually by extending its width a phalanx either decreases its density, allowing the enemy front-line troops multiple concentrated engagements against smaller numbers of own file-leaders, or, in order to sustain the density, decreases the depth (**Figures 6.1 & 6.2**). After the initial exchange of spear-thrusts while approaching to each other, where the depth is good only for providing prompt replacements as gaps appear in the front lines due to casualties, it is possible to come

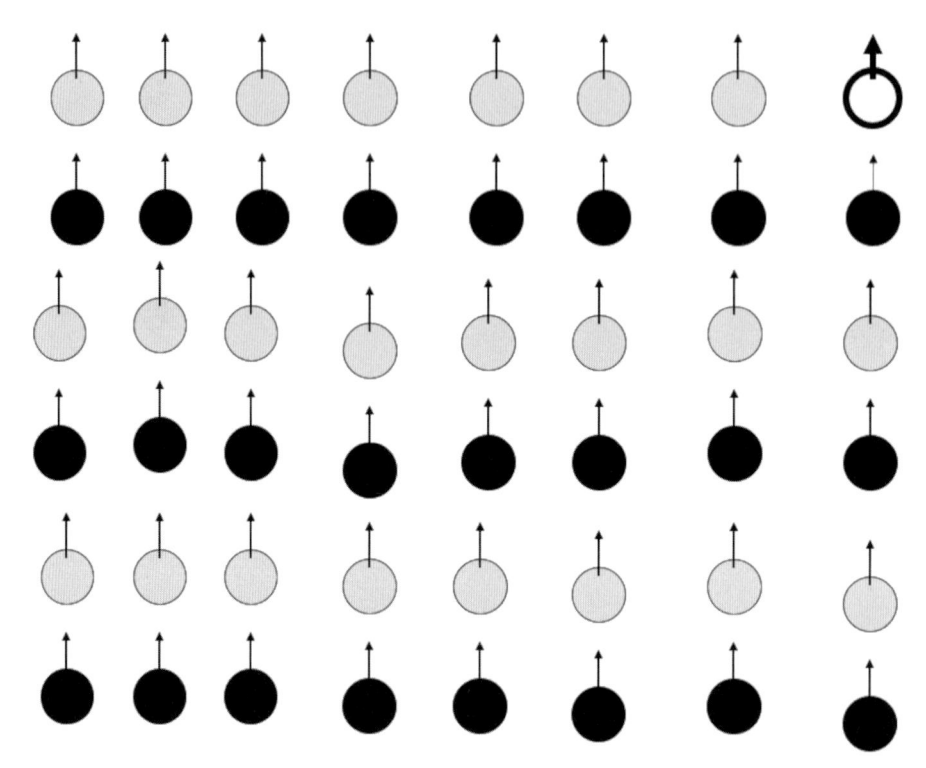

Figure 6.1: The basic layout of the unit.
A detail of a phalanx unit (sixteen files) in standard depth (sixteen ranks) and density.

into closer contact and start shoving (*othismos*). Shoving might also happen earlier, if the approach of at least one of the two opponents is at the double, crossing fast the verge of the spear points and coming into shoving. In the shoving match, depth is the most important attribute, as it provides both durability and assault mass.

Thus, if by spearing and/or shoving the flanking phalanx is disintegrated frontally before the flanking move has taken its full effect on the opposing phalanx, the battle is lost. This is why the numbers have exceptional importance in phalanx versus phalanx warfare. And it is also the reason for testing other approaches, so as to tackle this issue. For example, with good collective training, as was the Spartan practice, men of a rather shallow phalanx may coordinate efficiently to produce the same pressure and shoving power as a less cohesive and coordinated, even if deeper, force. Alternatively, by charging at a run, a less dense formation can overrun by sheer impact a denser one, or at least the two or three front lines where the best troops are posted.

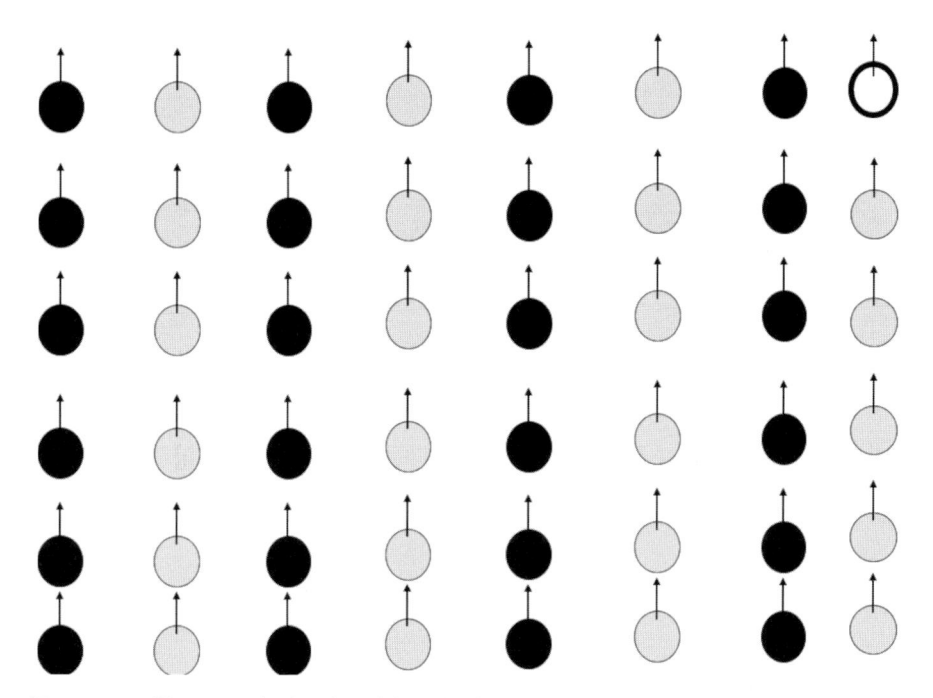

Figure 6.2: Changing the depth and front by file.
By projecting the even numbers of a file to the left of the preceding odd numbers, the front may be doubled for half the depth, keeping the density unchanged if the original order has expanded laterally, to cover – and create – space. The drill allows instant transformation from sixteen to eight ranks (*paragogi kat epistati*) and vice versa.

Phalanx Dynamics

The most logical presumption is for three possible density levels for the hoplite phalanx. The densest option, with overlapping, 'locked' shields (*synaspismos*), was a purely defensive formation, where the phalanx received an enemy attack, including massive archery or cavalry charges, under maximum protection, mutual and collective support, stability and ease of coordination; manoeuvring, attacking or retreating, in fact most individual moves like turn, half-turn, about-face are virtually impossible (Arr. Tact II.3) but offensive push forward, to literally 'push back' the enemy is feasible and actually *sine qua non*. Such order has its best effect against an aggressive enemy who shall engage and perhaps at a favourable position (Xen Hell VII.4,23; Thuc IV.93,3).

The locked shields are a very tricky issue: Pictures in pottery and sculpture show a rightward shields' rack, with the left part of a shield under the right half of the next leftward shield. Field experiments conducted by the *Koryvantes Association of Historical Studies* have shown, though, that a leftward rack (right half of the shield under or behind the left part of the next at its right) is more solid to uphold the shield-wall integrity when clashing with opponents who try to smash it by impact and momentum, such as Achaemenid infantry in Plataea (Her IX.62,3).

The second option is the usual battle-order density (closed ranks), when a hoplite is protected by the collective formation but has space to use his weaponry and dress his posture. Arrian uses the term '*Pyknosis*' (condensation) but he may refer to the Macedonian phalanx only (Arr Tact II.3). The collective mobility is not unlimited, but allows the usual brisk-paced advance ('*Ephodos*') to thrust, clash and shove. It is not clear whether moves like turn, about-face etc. were possible; but they should have been, if for nothing else than to permit transformation to open ranks.

The third option is an open rank format, used for manoeuvring, dressing, transforming, advancing in column, approaching and/or charging at a run or any other movement of a deployed phalanx, thus allowing maximum flexibility. As noted by Xenophon, the open format combines low density with increased depth (Xen Const Lac XI.6). It allows carefree personal movement, even on uneven ground, without too much danger from the butt-spikes of other hoplites' spears, but there is no collective action and concerted effect, nor immediate side cover.

The necessity of body armour for the first rank, exposed not only to shoving but to clashing, spearing, direct and indirect missile fire, sword stabbing and hacking by dirk and sabre and to violent blows by obtuse instruments (like nearby shields, both friendly and enemy) during the clash, poses another problem: where to field the fleetest and youngest and lightly clad hoplites, tasked to pursuit of enemy light troops who might harass their phalanx; such skirmisher hoplites (*ekdromoi*) are attested in the early fourth century (Xen Hell IV.5,16 & 4,16) but might have been present at least since the Battle of Marathon, at 490 BC or even since the introduction of the *hoplitodromos* (race under arms) in the late sixth century BC to the programme of the Olympic Games (Paus V.8,10). It is obvious that these troops, stripped of armour for the sake of mobility, could not be positioned at the first rank(s). The first ranks were for the best and steadiest troops: the Spartans would post there the winners of Olympic Games (Plut Lyc 22,4), the Thebans the Sacred Band (Plut Pelop 19,3). These troops were most reliable, valuable and motivated; not the best choice for mobile action and light gear. Consequently, there should be enough space between neighbouring files for the *ekdromoi* to spring out of order, emerge before the phalanx and conduct pursuit and skirmishing. This, in turn, leads us to assume open order for much of the advance of the phalanx(es) into contact. The same open order allowed light troops, skirmishing before the clash of the heavy infantry, to retire among the files of the phalanx (Thuc. VI.69,2). After such transformation of the battle

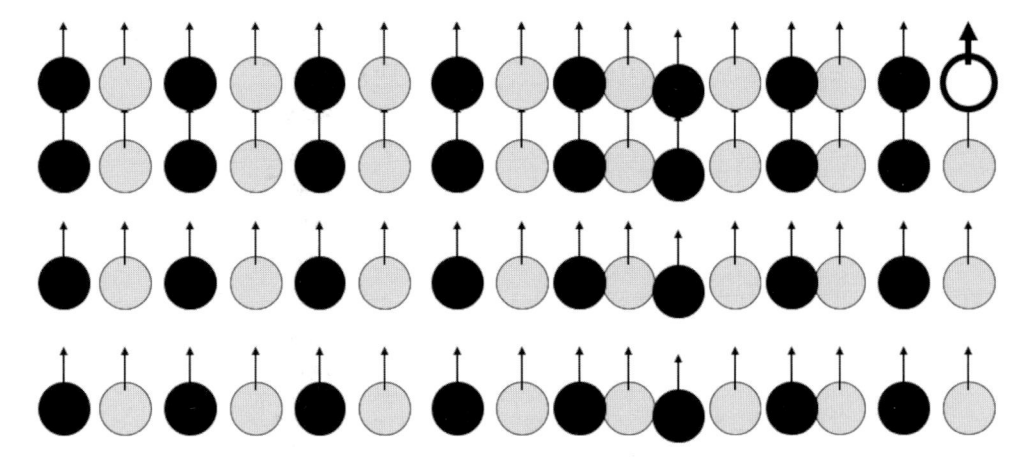

Figure 6.3: Changing the depth and density by file.
By projecting the even numbers of a file to the left of the respective odd numbers, the density may be doubled for half the depth, keeping the front unchanged. The drill allows instant transformation from sixteen to eight ranks (*paragoge kat'epistaton*) and vice versa.

order, the phalanx could adopt closed ranks by the even-number troopers of each file coming fore and left of their preceding odd numbers (**Figures 6.1 & 6.3**), doubling the density and halving the depth (*paragoge kat' epistaten*), or by simple *paragoge* (deployment); the latter refers to the back half of a file coming forward and left, aligned with the first half (**Figure 6.4**). In both cases the width of the front remains, the depth decreases, the density increases. If a general were confident for the drill level of his phalanx, he would wait until the last possible moment before closing the ranks, in order to keep his options open for any eventuality; perhaps he might have kept them open even *after* the last moment (Kambouris et al 2014).

The first ranks need armour more than any other, but they also have to execute the running charge to engage the opponent, an interesting solution developed from the end of the fifth century: the running charge was performed by a part of the phalanx, which would engage the enemy and deny missile fire with free field of view, but would be content just to clash and then fight by spear-thrusts The rest, slower part, with heavier troops – in arms and in years – approached at a slower pace (Xen Ages I.31) and only after its arrival and incorporation did the phalanx proceed to shoving, should the need be. This is most probably what happened at Marathon (490 BC) and the logical apex of the running charge is reached by and with the creation of the *ekdromoi*, trained to skirmish, pursue and charge but also to follow a cavalry charge at a run to provide support in combined arms fashion, as *hamippoi*.

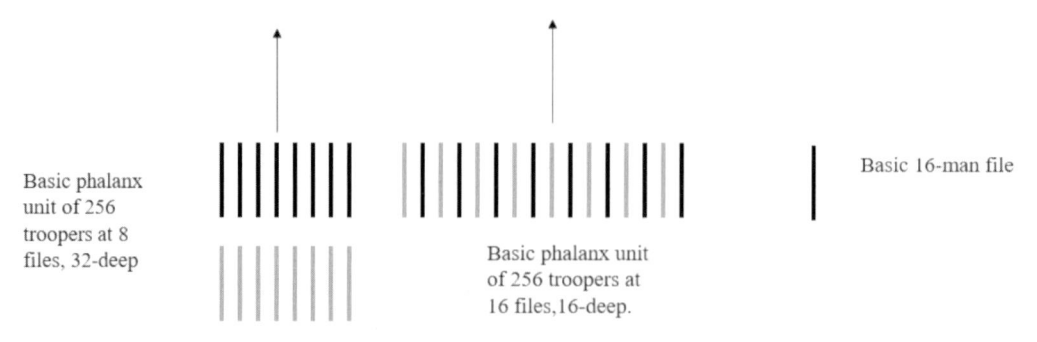

Figure 6.4: Unit deployment.
To change depth and front beyond the scope of a file, i.e. beyond the eight-to-sixteen depth range, the even files of a unit may drop behind their respective odd numbers at their right (*epagoge*), thus halving the front (or the density) and doubling the depth indefinitely. Conceivably a 256-strong unit may form two long, 128-man files or even one 256-long. The drill is valuable in defiles, was perhaps used at Pelion by Alexander and allows, in reverse (*paragoge*) phased extension of a column down to the standard depth of 16 men. It must have been used at Issus. For further reducing the depth to eight, the drill changes to *paragoge* or *epagoge kat' epistaton*.

At least from the end of the fifth century Xenophon reports that phalanxes deployed in line abreast are not the only way for a hoplite force to advance, nor to attack. In many cases the assault was carried out in great depth, where units were deeper than they were wide and formed columns. These columns are either posted side by side to form a much more adaptable line, as when on the march (Xen Anab III.4,21–23), or detached from each other, with wide gaps between them, to storm uphill against strongholds (Xen Anab. IV.8,9). In the latter case, where the main weapon is still the spear, it becomes obvious that the hoplite kit was not invented for phalanx warfare, as this kind of engagement hardly qualifies as such. It was, though, within the troopers' skills, drill and practice. The formation and order are a bit tricky, and there might lie the quintessence of Xenophon's statement that the *Myrioi* organized ad hoc six 100-strong *lochoi*, each divided to *pentekostyes* and *enomoties* (Xen Anab III.4,21) – clearly following the Spartan binary standard (Xen Const Lac XI.4), as the force included a whole regiment of Lacedaimonian regulars (Xen Anab I.4,3). Each echelon was divisible to two lower ones. Moreover, these *lochoi* could be formed up, according to the tactical situation, by *lochoi* proper in narrow areas, by *penetkostyes* in wider areas and by *enomotiae* in open terrain (Xen Anab III.4,22). As each echelon comprises two of the lower ones, if all the *enomotiae* are in line-abreast, the formation is 'by *enomotiae*'. If the two *enomotiae* of each *Pentekostys* are in line-ahead but the *pentekostyes* of a *lochos* in line abreast, it must be 'by *pentekostyes*', and if all *enomotiae* are in line-ahead, it must be 'by *lochoi*'. The term '*lochoi orthioi*' (Xen Anab IV.3,17) meaning 'battalions in column' most probably implies the last of the above deployments; thus a *lochos* covers the front of an *enomotia*. This successive transformation from line-ahead to line-abreast is the '*paragoge*' (Arr Tact XXVIII.1–3; Xen Const Lac XI.6).

It is unclear whether these formations took into consideration the arrangements within the *enomotiai*; in Spartan armies of the day of Xenophon *enomotiai* could have a front of one, three or six men (Xen Const Lac XI.4). Whether a 'battalion in column' had a standard front, or if this differed and was at the discretion of the commander, is unknown, but the second, more adaptable and less standardized option sounds preferable. This 'battalions in column' deployment, with the *enomotia* deployed at its maximum width and minimum depth is peculiarly similar to a Roman Manipular Legion. In reality, the only difference is that the Roman battalion, the *cohort*, had three, not two sub-units (maniples); this tertiary structure, possibly attributable to Alexander the Great (Arr Anab V.23,7 & I.6,1 & II.9,3–4), permitted posting one of the three maniples out-of-axis, producing the quincunx looks of the Roman army (Polyb XV.8).

The charging columns, becoming renowned by Napoleonic infantry, were not new: a similar formation, the tower, is known to the Greeks of Homer (Hom Il IV-334). It is anyone's guess whether Epaminondas' charging columns were in similar disposition, with deployed sub-units arranged in line-ahead, or, as indicated by the number 50 of the Theban ranks in Leuctra (Xen Hell VI.4,12), he used sub-units in marching order (single file) arranged in line-abreast, i.e. next to each other.

Collision Kinetics
The main point of phalanx kinetics is to attain favourable dynamics at specific spatial and temporal parametres, especially if it found itself at a disadvantage or at a close match. The focal point was to exchange depth, density and length. Very deep formations, used for marching, should be able to transform to match ground and tactical conditions, or even weather. To deploy, meaning from a deep formation to transform to a wide one, there were three main ways:

First way: To have each subunit formed at the minimal front in terms of number of men/files. Making the files as deep as possible, the front was shrunk and the density kept almost steady, thus allowing the troops to negotiate straights and passages. This formation allowed prompt movement to change the front and/or the face of deployment and is similar to later column formations. It also keeps a first line of the very best troops, which is advantageous for assaults. It is, on both these grounds, the format used by

Epaminondas at Leuctra (Xen Hell VI.4,12) and perhaps at Mantinea and it could have been used in Tegyra also. In such occasion, a Spartan *enomotia* of the time of Xenophon would have a front of one man and a depth of 36 in normal conditions, producing a *lochos* with a front of four men (Xen Const Lac XI.4; Xen Hell VI.4,12). This approach might be the key for the Spartan flanking move at Nemea, 394 BC (Xen Hell IV.2,22) and perhaps the move intended by the Spartans for achieving a flanking at Leuctra also (Plut Pelop 23,2) – although there is another possibility, see the Third way.

To deploy, the commanders of the subdivisions of the files, which are in line-ahead within a single file, bring their men left and fore, in line-abreast, thus increasing the width and/or the density and decreasing the depth. The Spartan *enomotia* of our example now has a front of 3 men and a depth of 12. This case favours transformation from very long columns, as in marching order, to order of battle and the term might have been *Paragoge*. It allows either widening or condensing the formation and also managing the vector of the front. The disadvantage is that it takes some time and dressing for the units to form to battle order, thus presenting a window of vulnerability.

Second way: A unit having its subunits arranged in line-ahead or *epagoge* (Arr Tact XXVIII.2). Each subunit could be at any stage of deployment. In this way, fully deployed and ordered subunits (**Figure 6.5**) could step off the rear and emerge at the sides of the leading one, to cover an increase of the battle front as in the Battle of Issus in Chapter 11, or to engage in a threatened sector. The term might be *paragoge* by units (**Figure 6.6**). In this way, a Spartan *lochos* of the time of Xenophon (Xen Const Lac XI.4) could have the front of a deployed *enomotia* (three or six men) and be formed in four echelons, each being an *enomotia*. It is probably the deployment method of the six ad hoc formed *lochoi* during the march of the 10,000 (Xen Anab III.4,22). This is also the usual idea of Epaminondas' formation at Mantinea (362 BC) and of the format of the republican Roman maniples, the centuries of which are thought to have been formed in

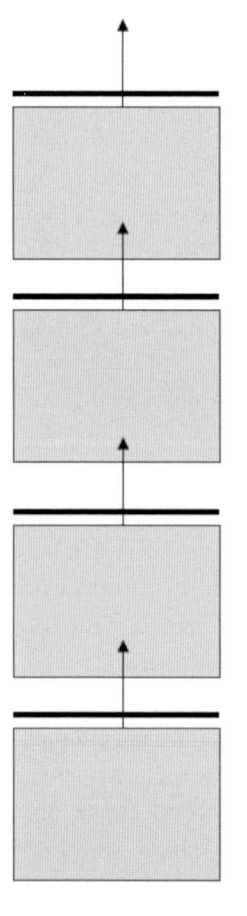

Figure 6.5: **Army in marching order.**
Large units (in here the *tetrarchiai* of 256 men of a binary, 1000-men *taxis*) in line-ahead (*epagoge*) with the file leaders of each unit following the file closers of the preceding one.

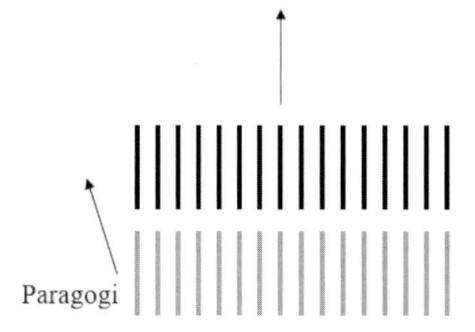

Two basic phalanx units of 256 troopers at 16 ranks and 16 files each in tandem

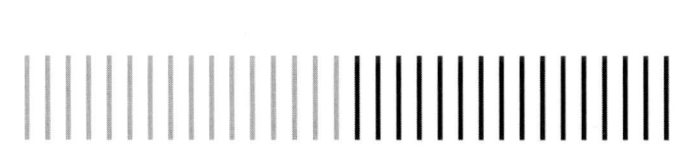

Paragogi

Two basic phalanx units of 256 troopers at 16 ranks and 16 files each side-by-side after Paragogi

Figure 6.6: Army deployment.
Separate units arranged in line-ahead may come to form line-abreast (*paragoge*), thus extending the front. Such drill allows a marching column to form a battle line.

line-ahead and transformed to line-abreast for the formation of a continuous line (Kambouris et al 2015).

The front of each subunit was the normal one for set-piece battle, and, being already deployed, it could turn to face frontal threats at minimal notice and without window of vulnerability while forming up, as in the first case. Of course this approach could be combined with the previous, to allow for extra thin and deep deployment, as in the marching line in friendly territory, along roads. Tactically, though, they were mutually exclusive as they addressed different needs: the first the need to change front fast, move fast and then deploy, while the second to the need to engage at an extended – although defined – front at a moment's notice with maximum security during the transformation, i.e. in conditions where the engagement could have been imminent. Moreover, the first case allows either widening the front or making denser the battle order, while the second allows only widening the front, specifically by means of forming a continuous front from a discontinuous one, a very useful drill when emerging from straights to wider terrain with the enemy in proximity.

Third way: to put whole parts of a deployed phalanx – not mere units, as in the second way – in successive echelons, in *Epagoge* (Arr Tact XXVIII.2). It is somewhat similar to the previous case, in that the following echelons are already deployed, but with two extremely important differences. First, the units found in line-ahead are not organically related – any two units could be found in tandem, according to the width and depth of the formation chosen by the general. Second, the following echelons can only be deployed to the flanks of the entire first line, thus extending an already fully formed and continuous line, not a discontinuous one as in the second way.

This approach was followed to suddenly extend the front to envelop the enemy, possibly at both wings (Pol Strat II.10,4) by diminishing depth and keeping the density steady; its opposite, the *Anastrophe*, was used either to drastically shorten the front (Xen Hell VI.5,19) or, more typically, to augment the depth and thus the solidity of the phalanx (Xen. Hell VI.2,21). It is possible that this was the transformation attempted by the Spartans in the Battle of Leuctra, to no avail (Plut Pelop 23,2).

Aside from changes in depth, width, or density, it was essential to reverse front. None of the abovementioned methods could promptly about-face an army for dealing with an enemy emerging from the rear. About-facing each troop individually was easy when in open order, but this left the phalanx order inverted, with the ablest fighters last and the most experienced but not top performers, the veterans, first and exposed. A proper inversion of the phalanx was done by the countermarch (*exeligmos)*, which presented the best troops against the new-found enemy, while keeping the same space or moving forward or backwards (Arr Tact XXIII.1–4). *Exeligmoi* though need open order and reverse the order of the files from left to right; this can also be fixed, but it is much more complicated (Arr Tact XXIII.5).

Seizing the initiative
Once a phalanx army is deployed and set for battle, the usual approach is to advance to make contact with the enemy. Another is to stay put and await the enemy advance. The usual choice was to advance, though, due to the beneficial psychological effect and to the momentum to the collision. While on the move, the troops of a file cannot be in contact and shove in a coordinated manner, as is dictated by the principles of *othismos*. Moreover, the ranks cannot be well-dressed. Thus, the least the number of files, the easier is the dressing of the ranks, which implies a deep deployment is preferable to maintain order. At the contact point, the first, or the first two

ranks will eventually come to spear-thrust distance from the enemy and will attempt to fall their opposite numbers, using their momentum to add to the penetrative power of the spear and to the collision efficiency, as they literally smash onto the enemy line.

Although the approach was at a fast pace but more or less leisurely, over the last few metres the attacker might charge at a run, to add momentum to their charge. The distance of such charge varied, but standard training at the *hoplitodromos* indicated a stadium (between 150–210m) or so, to avoid massive archery, and this is the distance reported for the Theban charge at the double at the Battle of Coronea, 394 BC (Xen Hell VII.2,22). Still, depending on the tactical situation and the field, the run might initiate at once, upon sight, or evolve after proper advance at the moment thought opportune by the general, to achieve surprise or to save the stamina and endurance of his men.

This 'charge at a run' was very demanding for the front rank, as it destroyed dressing, cohesion and thus any notion of collective action and support (Xen Hell VII.2,22), while physically exhausting if executed in full armour. It did provide increased momentum to the clash and thus would rupture the enemy formation by sheer impetus, or at least achieve penetration of armour and shield with the spear extended and secured underarm – at the last moment. The momentum was aimed at falling the leading enemy ranks by spear-thrust or by physical impact through the shield and thus throwing the following ranks into confusion fast enough that the subsequent shoving or hand-to-hand fighting might start with an advantage and promptly disorganize and shatter any resistance. It also allowed crossing fast the field of fire of massed archery and made difficult the aiming in precision bow-shots.

Once shield contact is made, if one of the two opposing file leaders does not fall due to the collision or spearing, shoving would ensue. The hoplite has the rim of the shield firmly on his left shoulder, to take most of the weight and the porpax arm-grip at his lower arm to adjust the direction of the push. He leans forward on the left leg, right leg straight at the aft, thus presenting as small a target to his opposite number as possible and focusing the power with great efficiency. The next rank, upon arrival, put the convex of their shields in the curves of the backs of the front rankers, adjust the concave and their posture similarly, and add to the push; and this happens with successive ranks arriving. The pacing, which decides how fast they will be in pushing position, the ability to combine, coordinate and synchronize so as to produce the optimum focusing of the collective weight, the number and the physical strength of the file members are all-important factors; as is the valour, the resilience and endurance, in order to stay concentrated in the shoving instead of minding the random stabs and hacks of the enemy, especially in the first two or three ranks.

Obviously, if shoving develops, the side which first achieves concentration of all its weight, from combining all the ranks, has a decisive advantage as it can break the enemy phalanx while the latter is still assembling its depth. In any case, if both sides were dense, one eventually gave way, perhaps at a single file's front, and this rupture quickly shattered the whole phalanx. The winning phalanx could shove and push to the ground the beaten hoplites and then finish off the rest of the broken phalanx, or spear and hack the broken troops as a moving juggernaut, with impunity – if only it did not lose its own cohesion. In this way, it cannot give proper chase afterwards, which is the reason for the notorious hoplite flights. If a hoplite turned and fled, the chances for escape were very good. To properly give chase, the winning phalanx had to break ranks too, but doing this, the fleeing enemy might decide, individually or collectively (Spartans used fake flights) to rally, turn and fight at close quarters (Her VII.211). If this happened, it was down to personal equipment and prowess, coupled with the psychology and the numbers. The latter two favour the winning side, as the retreating troops move away from the fray, whereas winners were coming towards the fray and accumulate spontaneously. Casualties or even reversal of the verdict of the battle might ensue, and the Spartans did not give proper chase (Plut Lyc 22,5) to avoid breaking their formation and expose their men to the random hack.

But a conclusive shoving was not the only reason for CQC. If the clashing phalanxes were not dense enough, collective shoving could not develop and after the clash and some pushing hand-to hand combat would ensue to decide the outcome, as the front troops of the opposing armies intermingled, as at Nemea between the Thespians and Palleneans in 394 BC, (Xen. Hell IV.2,20). In this case training, morale and equipment rule supreme.

A third option to the two mentioned above was the slow Spartan advance (Plut Lyc 22,3), something in between the former two options. It added no momentum to the stabbing or clashing but retained the initiative and allowed very prompt concentration of the collective pressure to the first-rankers, thus giving an instant shoving over-push, similar to the one of static formations. This immediate shoving was able to break at once the advancing or charging enemy, far before they become coordinated and set for shoving – and this if they had endured the Spartan thrusting, which was much more effective, as the troops were well-dressed by rank, near to each other by file and slow moving, thus being able to aim better.

Forfeiting or having lost the initiative

If a deployed phalanx perceives its opponent incoming, there are two choices: remaining still, to receive the attack as a solid body, immobile and well-dressed (Xen Hell VII.4,22) as mentioned above, or counter-charging to meet the enemy head-on (Xen Hell IV.3,17). The first option should, but not necessarily must, be coupled with a strong position, and/or maximum density. A 'strong position' may simply imply the inability of the adversary to flank or outmanoeuvre the defensive force, or to bypass it towards access to vulnerable areas of the defended territory (Thuc V.65,1); or it may account for degrading the enemy aggressiveness by uphill or other contested approach parametres. But this choice means forfeiting the initiative and also being deprived of the momentum (élan) of the forward motion, which renders the first spear-thrust upon contact most powerful and penetrative. It also gives up any psychological impetus inherent in the aggressiveness and action for a passive, solid mode. So why choose it? Being firmly positioned on the ground, a phalanx could produce maximum density between files, with shields overlapping as there is no need for space for moving. The ranks could also be perfectly dressed and very close to each other, ready to shove promptly. In this way the phalanx presented a metal fortress, impervious to missile fire, undaunted by cavalry and well-protected from stabbing, as the shields were in the best possible formation and angle. Enemies may be impaled by their own momentum onto the projecting spears. And, most important, this rock-dense phalanx was ready to shove at once at full power, against an enemy who would be arriving piecemeal, thus creating an over-push which could decide the encounter at once (Xen Hell VII.4,22–23). Even the best hoplite armies refused to advance against a competently set solid phalanx (Thuc V.65,2–3). The Athenians who, full of fervour, *did* engage uphill at Delium in 424 BC, suffered a catastrophic loss (Thuc V.96,1–8).

Moreover, it is possible that a general would not trust his troops' drill or mettle. The static defence is best for low morale, as it discourages desertion and needs not the same level of determination and resolve. Furthermore, the dynamics of collision are complicated by definition. Thus, by doing away with all need for transformations, timing, issuing orders and execution, the commander might use some strengths of his host, such as numbers or resilience and endurance, or even good equipment and carefully selected positions, to wrestle a victory from more capable opponents (Diod. XV.32,5–6). At least two occasions are known where Spartans, under very competent generals, refused contact with immobile, static opponents set in advantageous ground (Thuc V.65,2–3; Diod XV.32,5–6).

The counter-charge is the usual response though. It is the most difficult to execute properly, and this is the reason for the continuous strings of victories of better trained, or better motivated troops: that it negates any advantage to the weak. The counter-charge means that all issues described herein interplay with the mind game of the opposing generals. If a counter-charge is at a pace whereas the enemy charge is at the double, it is very likely the counter-charging phalanx intends to stop to a stand, at the last minute, transforming to higher density in order to augment its stability and cohesion and increase its advantage when the enemy would be too committed to counteract. Or it may burst at the double as well, to catch the enemy out of breath (Xen. Hell VII.2,22).

In the latter case if the signal is not perfectly timed so as to allow space and time to build momentum, it will clash with the utter disadvantage: open, unsteady and low on impetus. Similar issues plight all other combinations of actions and reactions. The former case is also tricky: if the transformation is not complete before contact, that is if not perfectly executed and timed, disaster follows, as might have happened in Leuctra 371 BC (Xen. Hell VI.4,13).

On the other hand, if the enemy charge is at the usual, brisk pace, it is open to debate whether it will continue so all the way to contact. It may well end with a running charge, to build momentum and stagger the enemy. Of course this undermines order and dressing of the phalanx and offers an opening to an opponent able to couple good order with resilience.

Phases of the struggle

The collective phases were practically two: the spearing and stabbing over and under the shields, upon contact, where the sword was mostly a thrusting substitute for a broken spear, and, subsequently, the collective shoving. It was not necessary to have both in any given battle, but the spearing was perhaps indispensable. If a shoving match developed, the use of offensive arms would become problematic due to spatial constraints. But it was also decisive, since the best troops of the enemy were within range and losses destabilized the whole phalanx, which literally leans on them: thus the Spartans shrank their swords to dirks for this specific reason at the end of the fifth century, electing only a brisk thrusting phase with spear and going quickly to shoving where their training was most telling, but also their dirks offered unfair advantage. As the shoving needs a coordinated effort, stabbing some of the foremost opponents – even if not mortally – throws the rest out of focus and may bring a decisive result, quite out of proportion to the body-count.

Still, shoving might have not occurred. The stabbing phase might have decided the issue at once or become prolonged. Even if the two sides had come into close quarters, either by executing a proper charge or progressively by spearing and advancing, the exchange of blows between opposing phalanxes could devolve to individual fighting with broken ranks instead of shoving. This phase was most probable if the clash happened in open order mode and favours the sword (Plut Tim 28) and the best armoured and more extensively trained troops. If the best equipment does not lie with the best trained side, things get unpredictable.

It is clear that a phalanx well-dressed, coordinated and cohesive had a decisive advantage in shoving and might make up for disadvantages in numbers, weaponry and even individual training and valour. To achieve this, the rank and file should be dense and break the enemy not only before the opposite happens, but also before any asymmetrical counteraction could be implemented, such as – but not restricted to – some flanking attack. Reverting to single combat also needed to be avoided.

Training for the shoving match could be provided in the form of festivities and public events promoting rhythm and dance, team-building activities promoting collectiveness and coordination (Xen Const Lac IX.5), gymnastics, hunting and every stamina and strength-building exercise or work. It is understandable, though, that the first rank of a phalanx shoving brilliantly as it might, the collective potential was fully developed when all ranks were in contact and pushed together and achieved focus of their effort to the shields of the file leaders. Thus, if a phalanx reached shoving distance after an advance, its full potential would take some time to develop, as successive ranks arrived and had the backs (literally) of their previous numbers and started shoving them with the shields.

This is the critical point; when two phalanxes were clashing (if it had come to the clash) all previous results were null: the side winning the shoving is the victor, no matter what happened in missile and thrust exchanges. And the winner of the shoving would be the one who would be the first to bring the most of the pressure to focus on the shields of the first rank.

This simple fact means that the file leaders were the neediest for armour, so as to survive and allow the phalanx to enter the shoving phase with integrity, i.e. without weak points where troops had been killed or stabbed. It also means a densely packed phalanx had an advantage, as its first rank was better covered with the shield-wall and more survivable and brought on more pressure. But it also becomes evident that the final advantage lay with the side able to muster speedily all its ranks to produce maximum pressure. Troops being able to coordinate with each other increased the pressure exercised by a given depth and density, and this is the reason for the laborious, protracted, continuous collective Spartan training and rehearsals:

to enable optimum participation of every hoplite. It is also the reason for the – largely ignored – necessity in hoplite armies to find oneself in one's *assigned* position, with his assigned comrades. They were trained together and had learnt to cooperate and coordinate optimally. The Spartans, on the other hand, could coordinate and produce the optimal result even if posted near complete strangers, provided only they were Spartans as well (Xen Const Lac XI.7; Plut Pelop 23,2–3; Xen Hell VI.4,15).

Spartan reflections

The Sparta projected by Thucydides and Xenophon was a shade of the Glory of the Persian Wars. This decline was mainly due to the massive loss of life during the earthquake of 464 BC and the resulting Helot insurgency (Diod XV.66,4; Plut Lyc 29,6). With not enough regular troops, other parts of the population were armed, trained and drafted into the phalanx. The distrust towards them, along with a financial decline due to a prolonged and destructive state of war, had reduced the available armour and diminished the individual training for CQC, both issues prone to misuse by the less trustworthy elements of the new military. Thus, decision of a battle at the phases where exchange tells and numbers, weaponry and personal virtue decide the issue should have been avoided. The solution was to go for a decision by shoving, thus avoiding casualties before and uncertainty after. The whole training scheme of *agoge* instilled discipline, cooperation, coordination, every possible skill and attribute to allow maximization of the pressure the limited manpower of Sparta could bring down on the enemy. The effort was by no means straightforward: the new, very short sword (Plut Lyc 19,2) allowed expertise in stabbing within the constraints of the shoving, thus undermining the shoving effort of the enemy first rank. Although whatever had happened before the shoving had no direct impact on it, it did have indirect: the loss of file leaders caused confusion, drop of morale and order, and creation of weak spots in the phalanx. Moreover, once shoving had begun, any mishap such as the destabilization and repulse of some enemy ranks and/or files impaired the concerted effort of the phalanx and spelled defeat.

Consequently, the Spartans advanced intentionally slowly, orderly, perfectly dressed and to the tune of flutes so as to maintain order and advance coordinately, as one solid body (Plut Lyc 22,3), with minimal distance needed between successive ranks. In this way they could move and manoeuvre, so as to engage the enemy in the way they judged suitable, in order to achieve an advantage (such as a flanking opportunity), but they could also consolidate fast into a single body for effective shoving. This consolidation was way faster than their opponent's, no matter whether the latter simply advanced or charged at the double. The Spartan motion would enforce shoving over thrusting and the Spartans would consolidate much faster, dislodging the first or even the first few ranks of the enemy as they come into contact by shoving them out of balance before the enemy phalanx is amassed. Thus a speedy decision is achieved locally, but the tear is transmitted throughout the enemy phalanx, resulting in final victory – with one exception. A phalanx big enough, and/or diverse enough, might not shatter all at once and the destabilization due to a local break might be contained (Xen Hell IV.3.18). In such cases, manoeuvring can press decisive advantages home, such as flanking positions (Xen Hell IV.2,20–21).

It is clear that a balance of different factors should be achieved so as to ensure the success of a phalanx army in a symmetric battle; similar or different considerations apply in asymmetric confrontations, too. The abilities to come to grips fast and with good order and to transform for maximizing density or depth was crucial: if both phalanxes advance against each other, maximum density gives an advantage at thrusting and at the shoving between the first few ranks at most. Great depth decides the issue if things go to fully developed shoving. A longer line, of course, offers the opportunity to outflank an opponent. All these are dynamic issues in a spatio-temporal context; the rapidity and extend of a local success and its impact may nullify a reverse at a different point (Xen Hell IV.2,20–21). This is why in phalanx warfare numbers were of essence and no reserves were kept: they were needed to deepen or widen the phalanx, which, if broken, or turned, could not be restored by reserves.

The pike phalanx of Macedon

The Macedonian phalanx was modelled upon the hoplite phalanx. No matter the origin, lineage and pedigree of troops, organization and weaponry, the tactical context was securely based there. The revolutionary issue was the use of pikes which exerted the mechanical effect instead of the shields. The small buckler (**Plate 2A,B**) of the Macedonian pikeman allowed denser formation than the hoplite phalanx, perhaps as close as one cubit per file; the other two density settings could have been two and four cubits, as with the hoplites (Taylor 2021).

The accumulative weight of a file could not add to a thrust as it did to the shove, but it could implement three collective performance parametres: firstly, push the file leader so as to exert much greater pressure if the latter was keeping his weapon steady and stable, couched underarm or planted at a slant to the ground, thus increasing stopping power and penetration. This was important against beserk opponents and large-animal cavalry. Secondly, provide follow-on lethal effectors (warheads) to deliver killing blows to any weak points or vulnerabilities exposed or created by the *sarissa* of the first-rankers, as a pinned or dislocated shield or an enemy trooper exposing body parts by parrying the weapon of the first rank. This was also better effected by the linear density of the phalanx, not only by its depth. And thirdly, against non-yielding targets, further pressure could be applied, thus preventing the shearing and even more the splintering of the shaft of the first trooper; even pike shafts are not as unyielding and robust as were shields in shoving actions.

Wielded by both hands, the *sarissa* was usually couched underarm as a medieval lance to spare the left hand and allow better use of the shield. To maximize the penetrative power and the aiming and range of the thrust, though, the left hand had to be employed and the thrust was level or slightly upward, with some help for the upper body.

Whether the front – left – hand was used to guide the thrust of the right, as in shooting pool (sliding thrust), or was used to add to the propellant force (stabbing thrust), cannot be deduced; the latter seems well-substantiated by the sources (Plut Aem 20,2) but this does not exclude the former in some cases, where accuracy rather than force would be needed. Similarly, it must be taken for granted that the weapon was made as rigid as possible and not as the Chinese and Japanese pikes, which were flexible and such flexibility was used to develop skill and disarm the enemy, or circumvent protective equipment and fortifications. Such attitude would have been invaluable to actively counter incoming missiles, too, especially at an angle, and this use of the *sarissa* is explicitly reported, although a passive, barrier-like function is understood (Polyb XVIII.30,3). Wobbling pikes do not stand impact well and are not penetrative. Thus, flexible and bending examples, occasionally wobbling (Toohey 2020), in a Macedonian context, should be considered as failed experiments; no European pike of the Pike Era, sixteenth to eighteenth centuries was flexible.

Furthermore, the wielding of the *sarissa* with force from both hands in stabbing thrusts accounts for low, not underarm thrusts in spearfight parlance. It is an interesting question whether higher positions, such as the high guard, shoulder-level use of the Mycenaean pike (Dahm 2019) was ever employed massively. To assault superimposed positions on the battlefield one would expect the troops to adopt every posture they could, including the 'double overhead', the equivalent of the reverse overhead of the regular spearfighting syllabus: hand and shaft simply rise from the low position over the head, without any change in the positioning of the hands on the weapon. But these postures would be unsuitable for battle for many reasons. The Mycenaeans had bodyshields (**Plate 3D**) and closely packed files, but their ranks were less closely packed. The Macedonian pikemen were too closely packed in files and thus the buttspikes were a problem if held at shoulder level. The bucklers were small and strapped to the left forearm; thus wild movement of the left arm would expose the fighter and present openings in his protection. To fight superimposed enemies it was acceptable, as the shield was automatically raised to offer coverage from missiles shot downwards. But in level fights, such a posture only exposed the wielder. True, for very dense formations with interlocked shields (*synaspismos*) the high guard, shoulder-level position, seen in Mycenaean and medieval representations was the only way to produce effective thrusting, or even intercepting effect while interlocking shields as the low guard would entail suboptimal biomechanics for thrusting (Du Plessis 2019).

The pike thrust from the low position could aim by depression at an opponent's thighs and perhaps legs, and when kept level at the abdomen. In slight elevation the target area of the pike moved to torso and higher up to face. Thigh wounds would be perfect for small-shield infantry, leg wounds for hoplites, and face wounds against everybody, with the added advantages of easy warhead extraction, assured target neutralization and immense psychological impact. The torso was an easy and preferred target when facing functionally unshielded infantry (Diod XVII.84,4). Additional elevation would aim higher targets such as cavalry, but there the couching underarm would provide better elevation and stability. Underarm thrusts were aimed by the elevation of the front – left – hand, both in sliding and stabbing thrusts.

The coordination of the thrusts in a phalanx is unknown and has not been examined. It may have existed, and it may not. It applies, once more, in both sliding and stabbing thrusts, delivered from any position. It is not known whether the position of the *sarissa* for thrusting and the aiming was a matter of individual choice or directed by command by the CO. But the coordination could be crucial, and it could refer to ranks or files. In the former case, coordinated thrusting could produce volleys. More elaborate combinations can be thought of, as alternate thrusting by file, so as to keep at any time half the points of the phalanx front at a specific target distance, thus discouraging any approach of the enemy timed upon the recoil. Coordination by ranks would allow the optimum cover of the front rankers while they were recoiling their weapons for a new thrust by the respective following numbers within each file.

A 4.5m *sarissa* implies holding it a minimum of 3m in reach (front-hand to point) to passive, interceptive mode, to which 0.5m should be added for a two-hand, stabbing thrust and a maximum of 1m for sliding thrust for offensive action. Sarissas of a unit were uniform in length (Nefedkin 2011); only between different arms (cavalry-infantry) or armies or eras there were differences in length. Otherwise a replacement would not be able to advance when a man in front of him was incapacitated.

On the other hand, the recoil is more or less the same with the thrust, although for sliding some more recoil from the static position may be used to add momentum to the next thrust. A tall man has an extended arm range of 0.5m for the two-hand thrust, plus 10–20 cm if tilting the upper torso. To this functional figures, one should add 2m for a hoplite spear held at ⅔ of its length in low or underarm position, and 50–70cm for a sword or sabre, resulting in a 1.5m of range for the sword and 2.7–3m for the spear against 3.5–3.8 for the *sarissa* in stabbing mode (the most plausible use). This means that the spearman must approach the pikeman to make up the difference in order to get him into range, and this means one or maximum two paces, easily taken during the recoil of the *sarissa* (after a par or an evasion) if executed without backstepping. For the swordsman it is perhaps two unsuccessful *sarissa* thrusts to get into range, and the pikeman cannot regulate the distance by backstepping himself; his next number in the file pushes him forward. Thus, it is imperative for the latter to thrust when the first ranker recoils his weapon, to inhibit the opposing spearman or swordsman to approach the first pikeman within range.

Different types of thrust can also be identified: pushing, to exert pressure to a well-shielded enemy to push them back and ideally out of balance so as to expose themselves. High-velocity stabbing, for penetration, or to exploit an opportunity at an exposed bodypart. Intensive persistent pushing to drive the warhead through (perforation) soft protection, to the like of wickerwork oriental shields, as the *taka* and *spara*, but also the European pelte. Then there is the steady, unmovable, wall of spearpoints to intercept enemy onslaughts. And finally, the static use, when carried at a slant or planted on the ground. The latter would be to repel cavalry, or a violent enemy charge and would be perfectly matched to dense and static locked shields or *synaspismos* format (Du Plessis 2019); the former so as the hind ranks would divert enemy missiles (Polyb XVIII.30,3). This effect could be maximized by waving the weapon sideways, even to a very limited angle.

The first four or five ranks, depending on the length of the weapon at different eras and armies, had it levelled to assault or threaten the approaching enemy (Polyb XVIII.29,7). The rest had it at a slant; in this case it could be supported by the hind arm only, if the weapon was couched underarm, thus allowing the left hand to handle the shield properly, as when under an enemy missile barrage; or even in this case the *sarissa* might be brandished with both hands, in underarm or low holding positions. To exert massive pressure, similarly to hoplites, each rank could rest the weapon at the shoulder of the previous rank, thus supporting its weight, adding to the impetus of the charge and also restricting – or rather denying – any backward move, such as backstepping, retreating, turning and fleeing (Polyb XVIII.30,4).

Although the cumbersomeness of the *sarissa* is overrated, and its use from elephants or fortifications (Matthew 2015) implies probable applications in every kind of non-pitched battle, it is true that for many missions it is less than practical, and this occasionally holds true for the hoplite spear. Whenever the enemy could dictate fighting at a range longer than its reach (Randall 2012), the hoplites were in dire straits, as in some confrontations with light troops, including, but not limited to Sphacteria in 425 BC and Lechaion in 394 BC. In pitched battle, fought in close-order, well-drilled infantry with shafted weapons was unbeatable; there are tricks and methods to use its assets in complex conditions without forfeiting the range advantage. For example the unsuitability of the *sarissa* for a measured, orderly retreat (Markle 1978) is simply a misconception. The range advantage, coupled to its persistence (it is not expended, as with the magazine of missile weapons) allows for holding back the assailant while stepping back, as happened at Marathon (Her VI.113,1) and Chaeronea (Pol Strat IV.2,2). Not being able to hold out is due to the troops or officers, not to the weapon.

It is more than probable that, similarly to the Companions fighting occasionally with the javelin, so did the Macedonian infantry. Especially for the buckler-issued Foot Companions and even more the conscripts that joined lately, without following the syllabus of hoplite warfare, the javelin would have been a much handier alternative main weapon than the hoplite spear (Connolly 1981; Ashley 1998; Matthew 2015), since it was the national standard. The truth is that the two are not mutually exclusive. In any case, if the Greek is to be taken verbatim the Macedonian veteran Coragus who fought a duel with the Athenian Dexippus was armed with his usual weapons, the javelin, the *sarissa* and the sword (Diod XVII.100,6,7), making him a standard infantryman. Although occasionally a spear may be understood instead of *sarissa*, it is not a plausible, nor a warranted amendment of the text. It was much easier to break a *sarissa* with a club as Dexippus reportedly did (Diod XVII.100,6) than a hoplite spear, which was a much more flexible weapon and offering less of a target. Thus, javelins are a most probable main weapon for the phalanx, used alternatively and not in combination with the *sarissa* when conditions demand it. There is no way to handle both, even if used serially, as did the Achaemenid *sparabara* with their own ranged and shafted weapons. Such concepts would emerge with the hybrid phalanx tested by Alexander before, and possibly developed for, the Arabian campaign (Nefedkin 2011) but scrapped by his Successors. The hybrid phalanx integrated organically light and line troops instead of the occasional tactical integration in the form of *parentaxis* in hoplite armies (Kambouris & Bakas 2021). It will be left to the Romans to change the weapons at the depth of a phalanx, with javelins arming most but spears the rear ranks (Humble 1980; Connolly 1981; Warry 1980). The Byzantines continued the practice and evolved it further, with archer ranks included in the line-up (Nefedkin 2011).

Part II

The Campaign

Macedon during the times of Alexander the Great was a rapidly modernizing kingdom with two different external sources of influence: it was in the Achaemenid sphere for the last twenty years of the sixth century and directly incorporated in the empire between 490 and 480 BC, at least according to Herodotus. If so, it must have copied, willingly or not, some administrative and customary practices.

The other pedigree is the southern Greeks. The Macedonian court was open and contracted many artists, sages and generals especially at the sunset of their lives – which was also the ripest period. Euripides the tragic poet and Iphicrates the general were only two (Athenians) of a wide collection. Culture and military matters (methodology, organization, know-how and perhaps technology) were imported regularly.

One such practice of Achaemenid origin may have been the guard of the Satrap, an image in scale of the one of the King (Xen Cyr VIII.6,10). Although guards are common to all monarchies and autocracies, here there might have been more intriguing similarities implying a transformation or transplantation of the practice. The Satrap (and the Macedonian ruler might have not attained the status of a satrap) had a unit of Spearbearers for his personal security. The King of Kings had two, one of Spearbearers and one of Applebearers, the former recruited from the scions of the nobility, each 1,000-strong (Her VII.40,2–31,1–2). The Satrap did not have enough nobles to acquire such a unit, but protocol might have been more restrictive than reality had ever been. This practice, infused with the southern Greek formation of the Elites (*epilektoi*), especially as introduced since the late fifth century – although widely used before, as in the Persian Wars (i.e. Her IX.21,3) – might have spawned the Hypaspist Corps.

Another case is the aggregation of aristocrats in the court of the King, who at war were fighting as a fully-fledged and thoroughly organized field unit but were also trained and always available for military and administrative commissions. These were the Kinsmen or Friends of the Achaemenid King (Arrian III.11,5) and of the Successors of Alexander who copied such institutions. This aggregation, irrespective of being associated with the elite combat unit of the Immortals (the name might be a mistranslation of some Iranian word meaning friends, relatives or any other with intimate association with the king), might have been the origin of the Companions of the king, seen at the latest under Philip II but possibly existing for quite some time; possibly since Alexander I, a true servant of Xerxes.

And then there is the expeditionary practice. Composite armies containing national troops, subjects or allies and mercenaries were standard in the Achaemenids and in the Athenians during their experiment with Empire, but Spartans had some experience on the subject before coming in contact with the Persians; thus in principle this is not an adoption of Achaemenid practice (the details might be another issue). Still, contrary to the allied practices used in the Great Persian War, where the C-in-C assigned by the League commanded national contributions of whatever arm under their own chains of command, in Alexander's army all regiments were under Macedonian commanders – something reminiscent of the *Achaemenid* practice (Her VII.81). This allowed a far greater degree of integration and control, the lack of which was obvious in the defeat of Thermopylae, as the Phocians were not attuned to the needs and priorities of the C-in-C Leonidas (Kambouris 2022b). But this does not make the practice Persian: in the armies of Agesilaus, Spartans were always commanding mercenary and allied units (Xen Ages II.10).

But if Xenophon's two statements in the *Cyropaedia* are taken together, that the fully enfranchised Persian males were 120,000 in number (whether this was the available manpower in the case of a general mobilization or the sum, including the elders, remains unclear) and that an expedition included half the standing army, one may draw some conclusions. That the Persian expeditionary forces had a 50 per cent quota (Xenophon states this quota for the *standing* army not for the reserves, so there is an extrapolation here), and that Alexander's expeditionary quota were similar. If one compares the numbers of the Macedonian troops Alexander led to Asia and the ones left behind with Antipater (Diod XVII.17,3–5) an almost exact 1:1 ratio is evident, similar to the Achaemenid as deduced above and definitely different from the southern Greek practice of ⅔ (Thuc II.10,2).

Chapter 7

Before Alexander: 200 Years of Greek Efforts to Neutralize the Asian threat(s)

The Greco-Persian antagonism took the best part of two centuries. Since the time of the Lydian kingdom, the Greek colonies in Asia Minor were under pressure from the force located in the centre of the peninsula. The metropolitan forces did not get involved and the result was the submission of said thriving colonies, initially to the Lydian Kings (Her I.6,2). The political situation, under Croesus, had become rather smooth; the Persian threat from the east, under Cyrus the Great, caused no uprising of the Greek subjects of the Lydians. Croesus' good relations with metropolitan Greece and especially with the very powerful Sparta clearly played a role in this.

Croesus' clever hybrid war, with dummies of Greek armour and rumors of Spartan aid (Pol Strat VII.8,1), as well as Spartan ultimatums, created some expectation of a vivid antagonism between mainland Greece and ascending Persia. However, the resistance offered against the onslaught of the latter was eventually weak, as the Ionians preferred to accept the new regime and the opportunities it provided (penetration of a vast and politically unified market) and the Spartans were busy building their own base of power, especially to curb the Persian influence.

Things changed with the enthronement of Darius I. The heavy taxation, the clear racial and cultural preference towards the Phoenicians, the control of the two granaries (Egypt, by occupation, and the Black Sea, by holding the straits) brought despair to the Ionians but also rang the bell to the metropolitan Greeks. With the Persian intentions reaching Italy and the Carthaginian intrusion at the gates of their Sicilian brethren, many in mainland Greece began to worry seriously due to the two-front pressure (**Map 1**). Darius' I Persia also showed a religious intolerance that Cyrus' had never done (Farahmand 2015).

After suppressing – bloodily – the Ionian revolt (~499–493 BC), which had been encouraged by two mainland powers of the day, Eretria and Athens, dispatching minuscule naval *escadras* with token amphibious elements to assist the rebels, the Persians returned the favour. The three Persian attempts within 12 years to conquer mainland Greece (492, 490, 480 BC) failed and in 479 the Greeks were again on the offensive. Once again the Greek axis of attack was through the Aegean, with bridgeheads in Ionia and a radial expansion of their sphere of influence. Within the Greek operational plan the provision for sealing the passage of the Straits was focal, a move that on the one hand opened the access to the Black Sea with its Greek colonies, after decades of separation, for importing cereals and trading with the metropolitan Greeks, and on the other hand denied Persian incursions to Europe, or rather to mainland Greece, by land. This measure of security was magnified by the total destruction of the Persian navy in two phases: in Salamis in 480 BC and then Mycale in 479 BC (Kambouris 2022c). At this point, however, the Athenians, under the leadership of Aristides, changed their priorities by promoting the building of an Athenian power base and a hegemony – a.k.a. empire – rather than conclude the ousting of the Persians.

In this context, the Persian threat was useful if it kept on being intimidating, to align the subjects spontaneously while the Spartans had to be marginalized. The collaboration of the expansionist Athenian faction with the super-conservative Spartan one led to the recall, slander and eventual execution of the only Spartan who drastically pursued the completion of the ousting and neutralization of the Achaemenids: Pausanias, the victor of the Battle of Plataea (Thuc I.128,3). The anti-Persian campaign then took on the character of small-scale operations, mainly amphibious, reducing the operational tempo to levels manageable for the Persian Empire. Despite some Athenian successes, the conduct of operations were restricted in scope and methodology and thus allowed the Persians to regroup, especially once the Athenian effort focused on the establishment of Athenian hegemony. The campaign in Egypt in 453 BC, an endeavor that (some) Athenian leaders probably did not wish to prosper, was the final failure. The continuous exploitation, the strategic over-expansion and the constant revolts of the wildly oppressed 'allies' of Athens allowed the Persian restoration, which stopped only thanks to Cimon in Cyrus in 449 BC. The Peace of Callias followed. Athens now, under Pericles, turned against Sparta to fight the two Peloponnesian Wars and left the Persian Empire alone.

From the Peace of Callias to the Decelean War (413–404 BC) small-scale ventures in cities in Asia Minor were the only type of conflict that occurred in Asia Minor; the paradigm of low intensity war. By the prerogatives of the Peace of Callias, Imperial Persian forces should not cross the Halys River. It was left to the local satraps to conduct a frontier, limited war.

But in the Decelean War, the Persians tried to use the Spartans to regain possession of Asia Minor and the whole system of balances changed. At first, various, mainly Athenian detachments, confronted Persian forces with rather encouraging results, which showed that the Greek tactical superiority was still a fact. Then, the policy – courtesy of Alcibiades the Elder (Thuc VIII.46,1–2) – of both Tissaphernes the Satrap and King Darius II himself to exhaust the two antagonists, Sparta and Athens, with selective and interchanging support, infuriated the Spartans who read the ultimate Persian purpose. After trying to develop a more sincere relationship with the Persian throne by sponsoring unofficially but not so secretly, the coup of Cyrus the Younger with the expedition of the 10,000 (Xen Anab I.4,2–3), the Spartans realized that their failure left them with one choice: direct confrontation with the Persians, before the – established – Artaxerxes II Mnemon could counterattack to get rid of his father's former allies (Xen Hell III.4,1–2).

At this point begins the last phase of the Greco-Persian conflict in Asia Minor, between Spartan hegemonic forces and royal and satrapal Persian forces (400–395 BC); a war sealed by the personalities of Agesilaus and Xenophon. The Spartan epic of the first decade of the fourth century will be the last direct Greek attempt in Asia Minor before Philip II of Macedon, although sometimes Greek troops would reinforce local satrapal uprisings for many years to come, frustrating the royal troops sent for suppression (Diod XVI.22,1).

The campaign of Agesilaus

Agesilaus was the last great Spartan King, and actually proved fatal. A military genius, at the beginning of his reign Sparta was a superpower and at his death it was small and insignificant, fighting for survival. Nevertheless, he was clearly the most capable soldier of ancient Greece, until the arrival of Alexander, although he did not have the flare of Epaminondas' innovation, nor the admiration of the Muse the latter enjoyed for centuries. His only admirer and apologist was his friend Xenophon, who saved him from obscurity.

In 399 BC it was clear that once Cyrus the Younger was dead, so did the Spartan attempt to become a factor in Persian affairs. It was also clear that the Greek military system of the time was superior to the Persian. Sparta would begin full-scale hostilities before the Persian royal army could move west of the Halys River, to retaliate for the Spartan support to the pretender. With the whole of the Greek world (**Map 1**) including Sicily under its leadership, with the best warriors in the Mediterranean under its command, with a victorious and experienced fleet backed by the resources of all Greece and with a multitude of well-trained commanders, the Spartans believed that they could wage the war Pausanias was unable to, eighty years earlier.

Central in the Spartan plan were the survivors of the 10,000, the living knowledge of the Asian hinterland and the facts of the war against the Asia Minor minions of the King on their own ground. Nevertheless, the operations conducted by the feeble army entrusted to King Agesilaus, a mere 8,000 troops (Xen Ages I.7) – plus local reinforcements – were at a pace similar to the Athenians' of the previous century, and the successes even smaller, since the strategic goals were not clear and the competent captains he employed were rather few. It was a troublesome incursion, nothing more.

Few Greeks had joined the Spartan crusade and some, such as the Thebans, were openly opposed (Xen Hell III.4,4). During the second year of his campaign, Agesilaus had reason to be optimistic: he enjoyed the support of all the Greeks in the region, he had commanded respect from the locals and he had established an admirable recruitment – mobilization – training system that provided quality local soldiers and mercenaries. An army fully capable of manoeuvre warfare and extended operations. Thanks to Xenophon, Agesilaus was able to organize and equip a decent cavalry corps, which would increase the effectiveness of his force: long-range reconnaissance, dealing with anti-access missions of the enemy light troops and cavalry, foraging and pursuit to efficiency levels unattainable by the lightest infantry.

The infantry of Agesilaus, with hoplites, peltasts and lights (*Psiloi*) was the best of his times. Capable of manoeuvre warfare, territorial warfare but also unsurpassed in set-piece battles, these troops were expected to sweep the enemy from the countryside on all terrains, at least as long as they remained adequately equipped, supplied and led. His only weakness was scattering on flat ground for looting, and that until he formed a cavalry. The glorious success, especially the victory in the Battle of the Pactolus near Sardis in 396 BC (Xen Hell III.4,24), underlined the Persian impotence on the field. But not everything was rosy, and some factors were important enough to lead to his ultimate failure without being defeated even once in a major action.

First of all, Agesilaus' army was way deficient: it was to a great extent mercenary. This means low motivation, mediocre performance as it was lacking the best of the best (the citizen troops of Sparta proper and of other Greek states) and, as a result, unimpressive in numbers. Sparta was the only superpower in the Greek world, but this world was wrecked from a century of civil wars, low on resources and cash-stripped. And the mercenaries – there were many and very good ones – demanded cash.

The Spartans had not taken the field themselves because they were few; too few compared to the days of Leonidas and Pausanias, mostly due to the devastating earthquake of 460s but also due to the war and to the rigid social structure that did not provide for the citizen status of those socioeconomically destroyed by the war. This lack of human resources, combined with the dispatch of negligible state forces by the other Greeks, created a liability: their rear. If their dominant fleet was somehow bypassed, they were in trouble – much to the like of their Athenian frenemies of 480s.

Second, a purely military drawback was that the total force, with all the reinforcements and on-site recruitment, remained tragically small. And slow. Agesilaus could sweep off the fields of Asia Minor any organized Persian force that would dare to line up, but he could not undertake separate operational axes for strategic pursuits in any depth to prevent reinforcements pouring in. That is, if the Persians did not oblige the Spartans by lining up on the field, the latter had no way of forcing them by threatening strategically critical entities.

It is at this point that other weaknesses are identified. Agesilaus' army was basically infantry, with a small proportion of cavalry, and therefore with reduced strategic and operational agility. The new types of infantry had sufficient mobility for the small and very rugged fields of Greece, but in the vast areas of Asia Minor they were very slow. His infantry could take on and route enemy cavalry, but could not pursue and exterminate it. The *asabara* would retire for a distance from the pursuit of the infantry, regroup and return. The cavalry of Agesilaus was too weak and few, even to properly pursue the *asabara* after a hoplite decision – as in Pactolus (Xen Hell III.4,24). Thus, the enemy power base, the cavalry, was beaten, dispirited but virtually intact and developing a feeling of security despite failure. It was obvious that without siegecraft one had to challenge and defeat the most mobile arm of the enemy. With Athens it was the fleet; Persian gold and Syracusan crews took care of the issue. With Persia it was the cavalry; the one put up by Xenophon and Agesilaus was Greek-grade, a support arm. The Achaemenid cavalry was the decision arm.

He also lacked any worthwhile siege park that would allow him to conquer resisting or unyielding cities and forts, which would encourage still others to surrender. In short, he was unable to take the strategic initiative and conquer territory – he could just march through it. Catapults and sophisticated siege engines were invented at that very time in Sicily, by Dionysius, and it would take some decades to become common in mainland Greece, as happened by the time of Philip and Alexander.

Agesilaus' poor finances and the mercenary composition of the army meant that, among other things, he had to operate with the forced priority for producing supplies and income for the mercenaries. Lacking in siegecraft he could not tap into the urban resources, especially the treasure accumulated by the Achaemenid authorities. He had to plunder the country. The practice was obviously a failure in Greece proper, as it infuriated the local populations, who – when they were hostile – were transformed from civilians into professional soldiers for the sake of survival! The wealth of Asia did not make this practice any less burdensome for its inhabitants, nor did they turn less hostile. They were aligned with the Achaemenid administration. Last, but not least, despite having a mercenary army, Agesilaus was conducting seasonal campaigns, as did most Greek generals and armies.

Finally, Agesilaus suffered from precarious communication lines. The distance between Sparta and Ephesus, his base of operations in Asia (Xen Hell III.4,4), was interspersed with the whole of the mainland Greek states, of a disposition hardly cordial, and the shore line of Macedon and Thrace, potentially hostile. The distance was also disheartening. Agesilaus had to rely on his fleet, and he was a Spartan, he knew few things about fleets. Should he lose the naval superiority, his position was untenable; and naval superiority was a matter of resources, material resources he did not have. When the Persians helped Sparta, the latter absorbed and made good repeatedly the heaviest of casualties in a war of attrition, where it finally emerged victorious. Now, the Persian gold was an enemy; it would creep into Sparta's naval superiority and would undermine it.

It did not need to; a resounding naval victory of an anti-Spartan coalition of Phoenicia, Cyprus, Athens and many Greek states at Cnidus shattered Agesilaus' naval support. A flood of Persian gold raised mainland hoplites by the thousands against Sparta; and they were next to its door. Agesilaus realized, too late, what the Persians were faster to note, and the Greeks were not, due to denial: trans-Aegean invasions were not practical. Raids yes, massive invasions no. After Marathon the Persians assimilated the lesson. The Greeks, after an impressive success in 479 BC thought they could do it. For decades the Athenians dismantled the Achaemenid network in the north Aegean shore and replaced it with their own. Their numbers and size made naval campaigning more appealing. But not as effective as it should. They occupied the shores of the 'Aegean Lake', a *Mare Nostrum*, but made no progress to the hinterland. The same was true for the Spartans; and the latter, contrary to the former, *were* trying to venture further inland.

When the Perso-Athenian fleet won the naval Battle of Cnidus, the consequences in the strategic plane were incalculable. It was not only the recall of Agesilaus to rescue Sparta from the massive onslaught of its Greek enemies. Agesilaus promised the Ionian Greeks he would be back once the issues at home were settled. He died 35 years later without fulfilling his promise; he could not pierce the barrier installed by Persia in Greece, between Sparta and Asia, nor could he settle the said affairs. Sparta was a world power with the Persian gold. Without it, it was a strong, powerful state. With the said gold against it, its position was unsustainable.

It is clear that Agesilaus' weaknesses deprived him of the possibility of a decisive victory, although his optimism included reaching Susa and Ecbatana (Plut Pelop 30,2). Given this, the Persians could simply delay him and overthrow him, until the gold and a fleet made all of Greece (*almost* all of Greece) revolt against Sparta and side with the Orientals. The Persians assimilated this lesson well. Agesilaus caused trouble in Asia Minor and could have done worse; he did not show any sign of being able to penetrate beyond Asia Minor, by any of the itineraries leading from the west to the east (**Map 5**). Still, the Achaemenids took precautions and preventive action. In the next half-century, and more, they thwarted repeated attempts of major Greek campaigns against them with assassination and regime change being the primary means. In early 360s Jason of Pherae, a most charismatic warrior king was murdered before initiating a panhellenic campaign (Xen Hell VI.4,31). The same happened to Philip II, Alexander was to survive several coups and attempts. But this was not all. The reformer Macedonian king Archelaus was also slain in 399 BC during a royal hunt (Ael Var Hist 8.9). At least three kings in Greece were liquidated by assassination or accidents just before invading Persia. No dangers, no battles, no destruction, no unreliable subjects. Just some treasure for assassins. The most affordable waging of war was the use of the Assassins' Creed.

Philip

Philip's strategy against the Persians was implemented to the fullest and then expanded manifold by Alexander. The important thing is that he laid a series of solid foundations, on which his son built, which shows the differentiation from the previous Greek efforts. It is doubtful whether Philip considered any advance past Asia Minor, much less beyond the Euphrates (Green 2007).

The conquest of these areas by Alexander showed that it could be done, but a look at the skills of the Macedonian war machine says precious little. It was designed to rectify the weaknesses and liabilities of the army of Agesilaus so as to enact the conquest of Persian lands as far as Cilicia. That would have liberated all Greeks on Asian soil, and would have offered some geostrategic safety margin – hitherto unimaginable – thanks to the enormous territorial depth. Just what the sage (Isocrates) ordered (Isocr Philipp 120). The strategic principles of Philip's campaign can be summarized as:

a) Full pacification of Greece, so as not to suffer distractions (as happened with Agesilaus) while in Asia.
b) Creation of a tight alliance between Macedon and southern Greek states, so that even if clause a) failed, a failsafe would exist that would prevent the development of dangers at the rear of Macedon. Any unrest in Greece had to be contained south and west of the Macedonian borders.
c) To achieve b) it was necessary to devise and build a security system that basically would prevent the unification of the most dangerous forces of southern and central Greece. Thus, with the victory of Chaeronea, the two closest opponents, the Athenians and the Thebans, were defeated (Diod XVI.89,1), while the occupation of Corinth, together with the fidelity of staunch Arcadian allies (Diod XVI.89,3), kept the Spartans isolated, far south of Macedon and out of contact with the other troublemakers. In this respect, the Thessalians were attached to the Macedonian state as equal participants and were thus an operational and geographical buffer, as they had been for the Achaemenid estates in Macedon and Thrace after the Battle of Plataea.
d) An efficient, in security and flow, approach to the realm of the Achaemenids that could be secured by and matched the character of the Macedonian army. The land route through Thrace and the straits

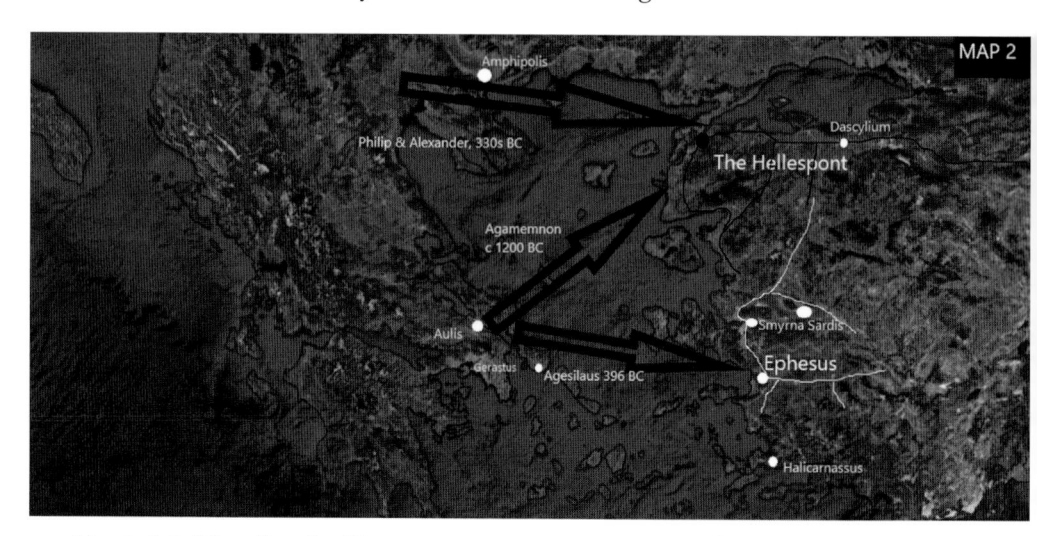

Map 2: Asia Minor Invasion Vectors.

was chosen, and the natural position of Macedon contributed to this. Philip kept the land arms of his antagonists (main southern states and the Empire) separate and by controlling the Dardanelles he achieved different goals at once. First, an easy route or supplies and reinforcements, overland, with minimal exposure to the elements and to sea denial efforts. And second, a stopgap position allowing isolation of the home territory if things turned sour and, just as important, the seizing of initiative. This position offered a choice of south (to Smyrna), southeast (to Sardis) or east (to Dascylium) directions of attack in Asia Minor (black, thin lines in **Map 2**).

e) An early dispatch of assault troops to establish a bridgehead for the main invasion. This was the most important element of the project. The strength of the first wave was about 10,000 men (Pol Strat V.44,4), roughly the same as the *total* power of Agesilaus that stood at 8,000 (Xen Hell III.4,2) and meant to exploit the turmoil after the string of assassinations that destabilized the empire, at least momentarily (Kholod 2018). In addition, the bridgehead would provide greater freedom of movement, a source of uncertainty for the opponent due to different options for advancing further and resources (food, fodder, fuel, raw materials) to host the main army until follow-on conquests were achieved to properly supply and support it.

Chapter 8

The Invasion of Alexander

Prospects and hot (bridge)head(s)

The existence of a Macedonian bridgehead at the Dardanelles in Asia Minor since 336 BC is indicative of the strategic thinking of Philip and Alexander. Agesilaus, in 398 BC, sailing from Gerastus at the southern tip of Euboea, chose for his bridgehead the cities of the Ionian coast that had been liberated from the Athenian yoke, and more specifically Ephesus (Xen Hell III.4,4), the ancient *Apasa*, capital of the asian *Arzawa* confederacy, possibly ruled by his Argive/Mycenaean ancestors (Kambouris 2023). The city was a recurring choice, as in the Ionian Revolt in 499 BC (Her V.100) it was instrumental for the offensive plans of the insurgents. It allowed a number of choices for further advancing and manoeuvring (**Map 2**), keeping the enemy guessing (Xen Hell III.4,11–13) and provided enough means for sustenance. Landing at the Dardanelles, on the other hand, offered a mostly overland route through conquered and recently (re)pacified areas of the realm in Thrace, and, in case sustenance could not be commandeered *in situ*, ample resources from said European territories.

The force structure of the first wave that invaded in spring 336 BC under Parmenio and Attalus remains a mystery, although it was comprised of Macedonian and mercenary elements (Diod XVII.17,10) and of cavalry and infantry arms (Milns 1966b); but whether both elements contained contingents of both arms is doubtful (Diod XVI.91,2). Initially it scored quite some progress, wresting the whole of Northwest Asia Minor from the Kyzicus peninsula in the Propontis to the Erythrean Peninsula opposite Chios (Kholod 2002; Panovski & Sarakinski 2011). If one follows some geographers, such as Strabo, it was the realm of King Priam of Troy (Kambouris 2023).

But the 10,000 men (Pol Strat V.44,4) of this advance force were clearly inadequate to defend, expand and maintain such strategic positions for any length of time; the idea was to establish a safe base of operations, that could billet and feed the army that Philip was to lead after 6 months at the most – just to conclude the festivities initiating such a campaign of epic proportions and symbolism. Staying there, engaging an enemy more and more aware while back home hell broke loose, with the assassination of Philip and the revolts in Illyria, Thrace and the insurgencies in southern Greece, as north as Thessaly, was not part of the plan. Perhaps some units were recalled, morale plummeted and the senior commander, Parmenio, was found back in Macedon for the succession (Green 2007), the preparation of the invasion (Tarn 1948), and the crisis management processes. On top of these, the second commander, Attalus, was assassinated by the order of the new king, Alexander III, with the accusation of high treason (Diod XVII.5,1–2).

Thus when a – nominally – smaller force of Greek professionals, under Memnon, just 5,000 (Pol Strat V.44,4; Diod XVII.7,3) carried out, without any worthwhile siege equipment, a mobile and imaginative manoeuvre campaign against Calas, who was standing in for Parmenio, the bridgehead shrank (Panovski & Sarakinski 2011). So much so that it could only be used to disembark the invasion force safely in Asia Minor (Diod XVII.7,10), not to support and sustain it independently of sea transportation once the Persian navy as mobilized. And in there the war may have been lost for the Empire. Darius III thought Game Over and made no preparations against the incoming invasion of Alexander; neither recruitment, nor mobilization of troops and fleet, not even appointment of a theatre commander (*karana*), who would have been of course Memnon (Tarn 1948). The latter is a key issue; this would have been an extremely unpopular measure with the Persian satraps in the vicinity.

The tidying up of the successful Persian strategic distraction through the insurgencies in Europe took two years (Arr Anab I.1,4–6,11), but built a reputation for Alexander (Arr Anab I.4,6); an excellent investment as he was dashing to glory. The men he was leading had bled and triumphed under him, and some had followed due to his personal achievements and mystique, as had the Thessalians, who originally had rebelled and, shocked by his speed and prowess, then realigned (Lane Fox 1980). The truth is that the Persian delay to respond with a move similar to the campaign of Memnon looked like paralysis or advanced sepsis. If the strategic distraction and the campaign of Memnon, the first directly or indirectly and the second directly, were conceived or authorized by Darius III, one may understand the paralysis brought about by the Persian dynastic upheavals before his establishment.

The successes of Memnon deprived Alexander in 334 BC of the safe base he needed and exposed him to enormous danger in case scorched earth strategy was to be implemented; the very proposal of the architect of the opportunity, Memnon (Arr Anab I.12,9). In addition, it became clear that the conduct of operations would be prolonged if some significant Persian army was nowhere to be found concentrated in one area to be swiftly crushed in decisive battle. A war of attrition would occur, favouring the vast resources and slow reflexes of the Persian Empire. One can hear the echo of the words of Pericles in 431 BC (Thuc II.13,2). Alexander's force, infinitely more powerful technically, qualitatively and quantitatively than that of Agesilaus, could deliver only after a decisive field victory. Against city guards and local detachments, tribes and national guards, the main invading force of 334 BC could have operated successfully (which it proved, in stark contrast to Agesilaus' force), but not decisively.

This important condition was clear to Alexander and Memnon. Therefore, Alexander's first concern was not the successful conduct of territorial warfare, but the crushing defeat of the enemy in order to indulge in territorial warfare and position operations with better options and shrouded in an aura of dashing and terror. Memnon wanted to deny Alexander a decisive battle (Arr Anab I.12,9), but the Persian aristocrats commanding the concentrated satrapal forces plus royal reinforcements (Diod XVII.19,4) would have nothing to do with such Greek niceties (Arr Anab I.12,10) that would result in prolonged hostilities, loss of income, possibly of some satrapal heads and might culminate in Memnon being appointed *karana*. The course, for the above reasons, was set for a face-off by decision of the C-in-C, the *spadapatish* (since there was no Supreme Commander or *karana* appointed by the throne). The *spadapatish* was by feudal right the local satrap; in this case, though, a viceroy; Arsites was *not* a satrap (Arr Anab I.12,8).

On Asia Minor

Alexander led his army from the coastal road from Macedon to Amphipolis and then to the Dardanelles (**Map 2**); this was one of the three routes Xerxes' host had followed back in 480 BC (Her VII.121,2–3). He crossed to Asia, more specifically into his residual bridgehead, by means of the mediocre allied fleet of 160 warships (Arr Anab I.11,6), and did so at the location of Xerxes' bridges (Arr Anab I.11,6; Her VII.33). He disembarked first (Arr Anab I.11,7) and when approaching the Asian shore he cast his spear to the beach to signal the onset of the – formal – invasion (Diod XVII.17,2). This ritual duly performed, he took some time to visit Troy (Arr Anab I.11,7–12,1). Alexander studied the epics and his role model was Achilles, but the visit to Troy echoes the opposite process than that of Xerxes in 480 BC (Green 2007) as described by Herodotus (Her VII.43). At the same time, his army was ferried across, which would take several trips as the 160 triremes could ferry a minimum of 8,000 troops but definitely not more than double that; which means anything from two to four trips for the entire infantry force. Once in Asian soil, the troops guarding the bridgehead would have been absorbed into the army, by territorial affiliation. Then, the tally would have been taken and the final arrangements made regarding the commands. This is similar to Xerxes' practice in 480 BC, when the final arrangements were carried out at Doriscus (Kambouris 2022b). This explains how the commander of the – residual – bridgehead, Callas, became the CO of the Thessalian horse (Diod XVII.17,4) that had just arrived.

Contrary to Agesilaus, Alexander's rear (politically and militarily) was much more stable, for various reasons. Philip had played the underdog card and the minor states and leagues of Greece, brutalized to the extreme by any of the three major states (Sparta, Athens and Thebes) were very loyal to him and his son. Although small states were more easily and cheaply toppled in their deliberations by some Persian gold, the example of Thebes, razed to the ground, by the very vote of some such states (Hammond 1997) was discouragement enough to these states and Athens. Destroying the city most loyal to the Persian cause since at least 480 BC, the only one which publicly and openly proclaimed its allegiance to the King-of-Kings (Diod XVII.9 5) while a member of the new League (Green 2007), which meant oath-breaking (among many other grievous offences including treason) was the single best investment of Alexander for the security of his rear. Claims that the (southern) Greeks hated him for that (Hanson 1999; Green 2007) are unsubstantiated: they hated him and his father anyway, as they hated each other and their own guts for centuries. Thebes had brutalized and bullied many cities, especially symbolic cities in the anti-Persian struggle. Spartans were to turn pro-Persian, and the Athenian crimes during the empire were a very long list. Thebes wanted Athens razed by Sparta in 404 BC, and tried to do this to Sparta in 369 BC and 362 BC, and Sparta had also tried to obliterate Thebes *circa* 377 BC. The fact that Alexander did it, simply secured the fearful cooperation of Athens and the gratitude of all the victims of the Theban aggression, such as the Thespians and the Orchomenians that were now vindicated (Hammond 1997).

And the invading force of Alexander was better suited to the task at hand than Agesilaus' hastily assembled expendables. It was, at first, larger, had better logistics and was more mobile and of top quality. Alexander was followed by the elite units of the Macedonian army, while Agesilaus by the most expendable parts of the army of Lacedaemon: only thirty Spartan Peers served with him (Xen Hell III.4,2). Alexander's troops were faster moving, the proportion of cavalry was very high and, most importantly, there was the most advanced and quite numerous – and effective – engineer corps, allowing successful siege operations to completely remove enemy control from the axes of advance and the rear. In addition, it allowed the prompt negotiation of all kinds of obstacles, such as rivers or steep mountain faces (Arr Anab I.26,1). This combination of troop mobility and efficient corps of Engineers excelling in siegecraft and artillery (Campbell 2003) resulted in an incredible strategic mobility that toppled the planning of the enemy; only the steppe nomads would achieve similar or better such performance. In addition, the better organization of the army and the existence of what would account for a formal officer corps, combined with the size of the army, allowed for the conduct of multiple and independent operations. But Alexander had to face something Agesilaus had never had: a decent Persian infantry, comprising tens of thousands of dependable Greek mercenaries.

The large proportion of cavalry, combined with the organization and training of the infantry for regular and forced marches, produced an unprecedented degree of mobility; but actually, only little use was made of this advantage while in Asia Minor. In battle, the cavalry manoeuvre contributed significantly to the victory at the Granicus – or brought it about almost single-handedly (Arr Anab IV.8,6); but similar battles were won by the previous model armies of Greeks under Agesilaus (Xen Hell III.4,22–24) and Chares (Diod XVI.22,1). Most of the sudden, short campaigns, as in Pamphylia and Pisidia, were carried out by infantry, and the cavalry was used in an independent reconnaissance or interdiction role as the scouting missions were an integral part of Alexander's intelligence establishment (Engels 1980a). Occasionally, a more decisive role could be assigned to – predominantly – cavalry forces as when dispatched to prevent the Persian fleet's resupply with water near Miletus (Arr Anab I.19,8).

Similarly, the 30–40,000 men of the invading army were many more than those of Agesilaus, a mere 8,000-strong (Xen Ages I.7). More than four times the size of the original, first-wave force of the bridgehead, it was larger than any previous Greek land expeditionary force, and well-balanced. In addition to siege equipment and engineers, Alexander's army also featured a financial service and staff and a competent operational plan. The vast territory and economic magnitude of Macedon – despite the temporary cash shortages – allowed Alexander not simply to understand the economic dimension of the war at least as accurately as earlier generals and captains did, but to employ it to his advantage.

The occupation of Thrace and Illyria provided raw materials, cash and supplies in larger quantities than the ones available to any previous Greek autocrats. Nevertheless, a significant cash injection was needed promptly to develop operations to spatiotemporal depth and improve the credit. From the first moment of the invasion, Alexander's goal was to seize a Persian vault that would alleviate his dire lack of funds in hard cash, so as to allow the operations to develop smoothly, while at the same time preventing the financing of the pro-Persian factions in Greece. But the greatest significance of this aim, which was implemented after quite some time with the capture of Darius' war chest in Damascus by Parmenio, after the Battle of Issus in 333 BC (Arr Anab I I.11,10) was the luxury to sustain the army without looting and pillaging the occupied lands (Fuller 1958, Green 2007), resulting in a favourable mood of the population and, in cases, his reception as a liberator even from non-Greeks.

Despite this ingenious policy and overwhelming victories, Central and Eastern Asia Minor showed devotion and loyalty to the Persian throne, surrendering only in appearance, as did Cappadocia, Paphlagonia and Armenia. The first two joined the Persian survivors of Issus in their quest to reclaim Asia Minor (Curt IV.1,35); the trek of the 10,000 and the invasion of Agesilaus were fresh in the memory. Armenia supplied massive cavalry forces to Darius III for the Battle of Gaugamela all the way to 331 BC (Arr Anab III.11,7) as it was the Satrapy of Codomannus before his enthronement as Darius III (Badian 2000).

A conquest, in these conditions, had little chance of success, as opposed to large-scale plundering raids. The social fabric of Imperial Persia had diversified in Asia Minor and acquired a local identity, rooted in local societies and made them susceptible to autonomy projects, as the ones led by many local satraps; or loyal to the Achaemenid order. The resilience shown by the Persian administration in the region even after the Battle of Issus is astonishing and was by no means predicted by the previous generations of Panhellenist scholars and statesmen. But such issues were fully predicted by Alexander, who was descending upon the reorganized Persian state with a completely novel mix of Greek prowess, military and intellectual – the latter being a combination of military intellectualism, political philosophy and intelligence gathering (Russell 1999; Engels 1980a).

Every bit as important was the possibility of tapping the huge pool of human resources of the Greek mercenary market, with the means offered by the Persian fund. The 200,000 unemployed soldiers estimated by the Panhellenists (Just IX.5,6), without funds to hire them for the Greek Cause, were immediately becoming candidates for the armies of the Great King.

A key element is that while prestige was an important liability for the Persian Empire of the fifth century BC, this was not so in the late fourth. Everyone had witnessed Persian humiliations and plights by satrapal uprisings, dynastic claims and coups. The empire had learned to deal with such reverses, as well as catastrophic battle outcomes, without losing its cohesion. What had been a valid choice for Aristides and Cimon around 470–460 BC, and was not put to good effect due to Themistocles and Pericles, had ceased to be a prospect for Agesilaus in 396 BC or Philip in 338 BC. Alexander had to beat Persia to death literally, not just shatter its image.

According to Diodorus (XVII.17,3–5), the invading army included, infantry-wise, 12,000 Macedonian phalanx infantry under Parmenio (the *taxeis* of *Pezetairoi* or Foot Companions and the *chiliarchies* of the Hypaspists), 1,000 Agrianian peltasts or javelineers and as many archers, 7,000 southern Greek allies, 5,000 southern Greek mercenaries (possibly the ones in the bridgehead) plus Illyrian and Thracian units from the alliance and empire relations of Macedon proper amounting to 7,000. Cavalry-wise there were 1,800 Macedonian horse under Philotas, 1,800 Thessalian horse under Callas, 600 Southern Greek Allies under Erigius, 900 Thracians and Paeonians scouts under Cassander.

Diodorus sums them to 4,500 instead of the 5,100 that result from the addition of the parts, so he possibly overstates a contingent by 600, most probably the Thessalians due to his pro-Thessalian bias (Strootman 2012). The other possibility is that the difference is the cavalry detailed in the bridgehead (Milns 1966b), counted into the total tallies of mobilization. On the contrary, the infantry total matches to the number given by Diodorus (32,000). The above reports of Diodorus refer obviously to a date *after* the passage of Alexander to Asia, as the bridgehead during the crossing was under Callas of Harpalus (Diod XVII.7,10) who in Arrian's (Arr Anab I.14,3) and Diodorus' account (Diod XVII.17,4) leads the Thessalian cavalry contingent. Other sources increase the tally up to a maximum of 40,000 infantry (Plut Alex 15,1) and the inclusion or exclusion of the forces already at the bridgehead, estimated as mentioned before at some 10,000 (Pol Strat V.4,4) seems a valid way to bridge the differences (Green 1991).

The rear

During the invasion by Agesilaus, once Athens and Boeotia turned traitors Agesilaus was cut off from Sparta but for the naval route through the Aegean, and Sparta was limited to the Peloponnese and even more to the south, avoiding the hostile Argolid or Arcadia.

Alexander, due to geography, ran the danger of two fronts but his realm, both Macedon and the occupied territories was a continuous area allowing manoeuvres by internal lines. The chokepoint of the straits could not be reliably interrupted by the enemy navies, especially in winter. Sparta was cornered in the Peloponnese and had to strive to emerge from the Isthmus as Argos plus other Peloponnesians were pro-Macedonians and could choke the Isthmus. Athens was recalcitrant beyond the Isthmus and Thebes razed to the ground, leaving vacant the niche of the Viper's Nest in Greece. After the exemplary punishment of Thebes, the vacant seat was not appealing to any other state, in stark contrast to events before said destruction. After Xerxes' repulse, none of the three leading Medizer states suffered anything existential, for different reasons: Thebes payed a penalty and had some politicians executed in the blood of whom the treason was washed. Argos suffered nothing. And Thessaly, the mastermind, had only a regime change, the traitorous Aleuadae of Larissa losing the supreme leadership (Tageia) to the Echecratidae of Pharsalus, previous holders of the office and perhaps kingpins of the anti-Persian feeling in Thessaly.

Thus, when Alexander burned Thebes, it was a shock for the Medizers in the Greek world: the first time a whole city was brought to pay for the whole city's crime of treachery against the Panhellenic ideal. Thebes was third offender, after the Persian War and its role against Agesilaus. Thus Sparta was in a very good bargaining position towards Darius III, with Athens' opportunism simply underlining the Spartan determination, which proved unfaltering for two gruesome years, to the Final Day in Megalopolis, 331 BC, where Agis III perished, true to his treacherous beliefs and stance.

The summer of 333 BC that Sparta allied with Persia was a veritable turning point in world history; the Spartans turned traitors against a fellow Greek for the first time. In the 450s Artaxerxes I bribed them to attack the rear of the Athenians who were meddling in Egypt, once more bruising the empire. Although they were already fighting intermittently against Athens, they flatly refused to embrace the imperial cause. In 412 BC the King of Kings saw an opening due to the Athenian disaster in Sicily to rebound in the Aegean, through the local satraps. It was an indirect move against Athens, flatly terminating the Peace of Callias but not erupting in a state of war. Alcibiades, triumphant in Sparta but wanted for High Treason (his impregnating a queen meant tampering with the bloodline) escaped to the court of Tissaphernes, one of the two satraps near the Aegean and enforcers of the new Persian policy. He turned the directly anti-Athenian mandate to a balanced playing both sides. A win-win. The Athenians, weakened but not defeated, avoided total capitulation as a second opponent, most likely the Persians, was not forthcoming. The empire had both its western enemies bleeding each other dry instead of one being triumphant. Alcibiades would be avenged against Sparta and gain credit with the Athenians. Only the Spartans were losing and reciprocated by befriending the princeling Cyrus the Younger, the *karana* sent by the King to supervise a front again turning sore and not concluding business against Athens. And then, they assisted Cyrus against the new King in 400 BC, fought against the empire for a decade and were finally brought to terms in 387 BC as a defeated party and a member of a new status quo by the King's Peace. In 333 BC, half a century later, they concluded the transformation and became not simply accomplices but pawns – and voluntarily and spontaneously so. They simply allied to the empire to help it survive an assault threatening at that point to throw the Imperial standards back to central Asia and liberate an enormous area in Asia, twice Agesilaus' wildest dreams.

Chapter 9

Granicus: The Battle for Asia Minor

As soon as Alexander crossed into Asia, he was confronted with the bulk of the forces of Asia Minor. All the satrapal forces plus royal reinforcements were mobilized against him. Darius III and his satraps were tired of the Greek invasions. Agesilaus had invaded 52 years earlier, Philip two years earlier, and now it was Alexander's turn. These invasions resulted in huge economic costs, unbearable loss of prestige and great political, social and economic consequences as the western border was in turmoil, and this favoured other centrifugal processes. Therefore, they decided to solve the problem promptly, as 35,000 Greeks posed a real threat, given that the 10,000 of Parmenio and Attalus had occupied Northwest Asia Minor for two years (Pol Strat V.4,4). Thus, they were assembling their forces at Zeleia, very near the major satrapal capital of Dascylium, where support and supplies would abound. They were also covering the said capital should the Macedonian brat felt like dashing east, as he had already a reputation for lightning action and prompt advance.

Once at his secure bridgehead Alexander had to expand it. He could go south (**Map 2**), as mentioned, to the rather friendly Greek cities of the coast, many of them just subjugated anew by Memnon and in part anxious for reacquiring their freedom. He could also turn to the east. There, the satrapal capital of Dascylium would provide interesting loot and plunder and a great psychological bonanza, to occupy in the first days a major administrative centre; doing almost that had been a significant propaganda and morale boost for the insurgents at the beginning of the Ionian Revolt (Her V.100 &103,2). To date, Agesilaus had not succeeded in doing so in some 2 years of successful campaigning.

If going east, Alexander could also hope to find a worthwhile Achaemenid field army to crush, thus gaining a free hand for further operations and demolishing the morale of the enemy, while further enhancing that of his troops, his allies and his own reputation. After all, leaving an enemy army to his rear was not a good idea no matter the aspect: it would give the Orientals and the Medizers confidence and could undo his conquests. Field action was the highest priority, especially before the current opponent had gained

116   Alexander the Great Avenger

first-hand intelligence on the Macedonian prowess and before the war of attrition could wear down the Macedonians. Surprise would be at their side, in technical terms.

After Alexander's landing in Asia Minor, the assembled Persian commanders had an operational problem (**Map 4**): most probably Alexander would move south, to occupy the coast, dotted with Greek cities and rich enough to sustain his troops. There he could also be supplied and transported, whenever needed, by his allied fleet – a sorry excuse for one, actually, numbering 160 war galleys (Arr Anab I.18,4). They, in their turn, could try to block his advance by using imaginatively a series of successive locations suitable for defence and fortified strongholds. However, many cities were hostile to the Persians, having only recently been reconquered by Memnon and at that time the Persian fleet had not been mobilized. Alexander's fleet had a free hand, allowing amphibious operations that would bypass the Persian defensive lines.

Therefore, they kept their position east of the crossing of the Macedonians, in an area least accessible by sea, contemplating two possibilities. If Alexander was to follow the indirect approach and head south, to the defenceless coasts, they would rush west to cut off his land communications and flank him, or undo his conquests by taking back the cities and forts going over to him. They knew that Alexander needed to extend his foothold to obtain on-site sustenance resources for the army. But due to his ambition and character he could opt for direct confrontation and seek battle. If so, he would be forced to fight over terrain of their choice; namely, the banks of the Granicus, as in

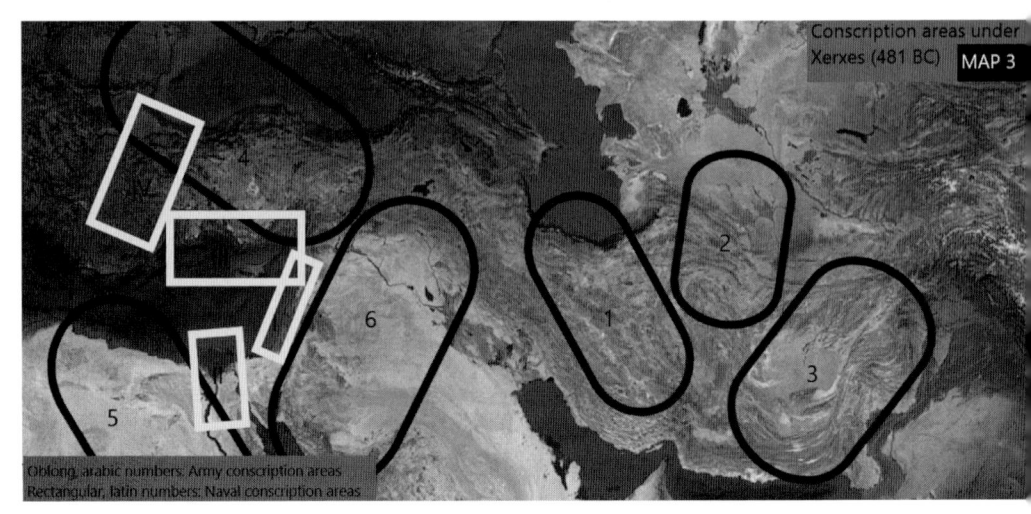

Map 3: Recruitment Areas.

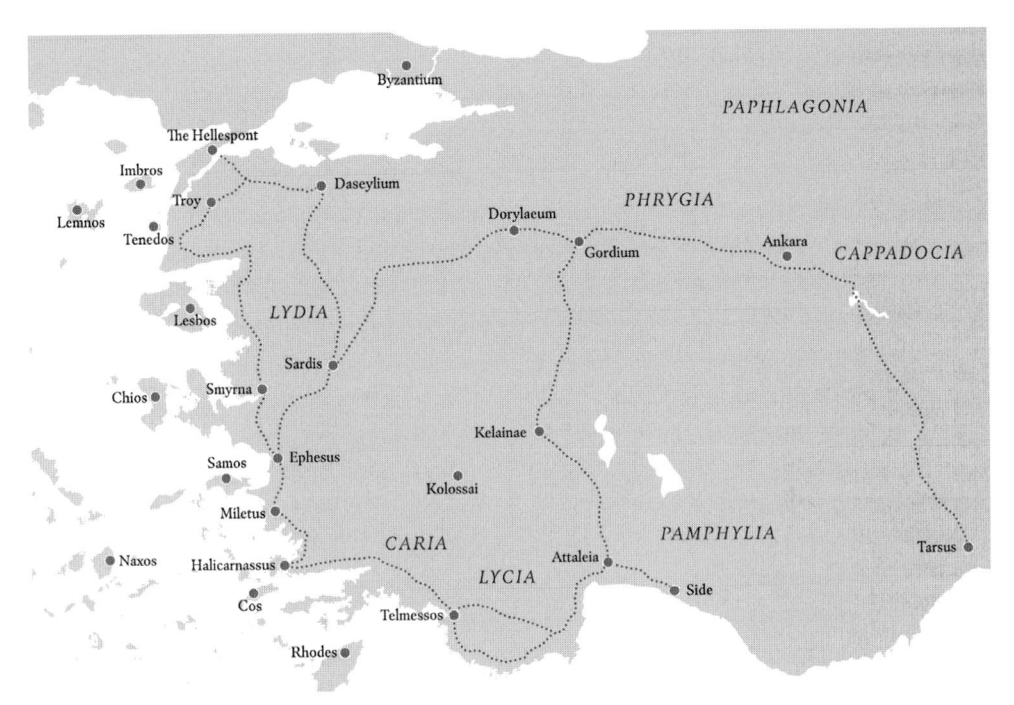

Map 4: Campaign in Asia Minor.

that position they could block his possible eastward advance, if he felt like being unpredictable, as he had shown he could be during the last two years.

This means that Memnon's plan for an indirect approach was shelved. It was based on the elaborate combination of the results of the shrunk bridgehead with an actively pursued scorched-earth campaign (Arr Anab I.12,9), possibly enhanced by guerilla operations by the mercenary contingent, well-versed in devastation warfare and mobile operations, and possibly assisted by an Achaemenid fleet to interrupt or ideally sever Alexander's communications and supply lines to Europe across the Hellespont. True, after the Battle of the Granicus Darius III named Memnon *karana* in the west, in order to implement it (Arr Anab I.20,3), but it was too little too late.

The plan was valid indeed, but only Memnon could implement and execute it as it needed Generals, not leaders or heroes.

The Achaemenid aristocrats had no wish to serve under Memnon's command, and the local viceroy had no wish to see his estates ruined, his reputation with the locals and his colleagues tarnished and his income reduced. Satraps were both civil and military administrators in the current Persian system and the algorithms for their decisions were at times dominated by civil concerns and their social status as *azata* aristocrats (Sekunda & Chew 1992). They really felt obliged to protect their subjects by their martial prowess. In the fourth century the Achaemenids thought they had found the antidote to the Greek field supremacy: the combination of armoured shock cavalry and Greek mercenary infantry troops. At the Granicus they had the good judgment to deploy to the east bank of the Granicus, behind a water barrier, in contrast to their confident but destructive practice in Pactolus 50 years earlier against Agesilaus (Xen Hell III.4,22–24).

The Achaemenid cavalry comprised local mounted draftees and royal forces sent as reinforcements. The former were mostly Persians, settled on manors in the respective satrapies, but probably also native aristocrats and other fief-holders of the king, with their household troops, such as Memnon (Arr Anab I.15,3). In 396 BC the Satrap of Dascylium fielded about 600 such household horsemen (Xen Hell III.4,13) while in 401 BC Cyrus the Younger, the *karana* of the whole of Asia Minor, had just as many at Cunaxa (Xen Anab I.8,21). Which means that the balance towards the Imperial mounted force at the Granicus, anything between 10,000 (Diod XVII.19,4) and 20,000 (Arr Anab I.14,4), were royal reinforcements from the equestrian nations of the empire, as cavalry could be dispatched fast over very long distances following the Royal Road and its branches.

The royal forces consisted of standing cavalry units from the heart of the empire; one of the nobles at the Granicus commanded Bactrian and Hyrcanian cavalry (Diod XVII.19,4) and there is no need to consider them local fief-holders of Bactrian origin planted in Asia Minor. They may have been royal dispatches to reinforce the local satraps (Thompson 2007). They could have been true Bactria-raised cavalry serving its standard tour of duty and dispatched to the west. After all, in the invasion of Agesilaus, sixty-two years earlier, Artaxerxes II had also urgently sent royal troops, especially cavalry, to reinforce Tissaphernes (Xen Ages I.13).

One has to contemplate the timelines and this is not very easy. The mobilization of Macedon to launch the campaign was no secret, as the southerners had to mobilize and send their contributions under the league terms. If the official onset is taken, an informer could rent a fast boat with Persian gold and reach Persian soil in western Asia Minor in just three days. Two days would be needed for the cavalry dispatch to reach Dascylium or Sardis, and nine more for the mounted courier to reach the King at Susa (Her VIII.98). The units were standing army, thus in a day or two after the deliberation (taking another day or two) the cavalry would be on its way, this accounting for less than three weeks. From Susa to Sardis Herodotus estimates three months (Her V.54,1), but this is a journey on foot or by wagon or cart. Cavalry on forced deployment could do less than a month, which makes the reaction time for cavalry-only reinforcements 50 days, or less.

Arrian reports 20,000 cavalry and the same number of Greek mercenaries (Arr Anab I.14,4). This is a weird ratio and composition, indeed. But it is reasonable. Any foot levies would be slow to raise and move; cavalry was swift and the Greek mercenaries were accustomed to forced marches and perhaps recruited from close-by or assembled from nearby deployments.

Additionally, this 1:1 ratio was typical for Greek cavalry and accompanying *hamippoi* mobile infantry; the Elites in many cities had played this role very successfully (Xen Hell VII.2,10). Thus, this ratio was operationally justified and tactically sound. The fact that this cooperation never took place must be attributed to Achaemenid arrogance but also to their being unaccustomed to fight in this way; at Gaugamela Darius would field mixed cavalry-infantry formations for the first time in Persian practice, possibly to implement this kind of synergy but without our knowledge of the results (Arr Anab III.11,3). Equally unhelpful, the equipment of the Persian infantry deployed with the cavalry in that battle is not described: hoplite equipment, as at Issus (Arr Anab II.8,6) or the national attire, excellent for mobile warfare?

Diodorus' account has half the cavalry and 100,000 infantry levy (Diod XVII.19,4–5), including the Greek mercenaries. As usual, the scholarly effort to reconcile is to take the lower numbers from both accounts, and perhaps further trim them down. True, inflated numbers are usual, but not standard practice in ancient (and modern) historiography, but trimming as SOP is not a scientific approach, either. For example, this massive infantry levy could have been correct, but most probably it was not present for lack of time to be assembled, organized and dispatched. But it is ridiculous to consider it unduly large: Xenophon operated with the army of Cyrus and the part of Asia Minor under the latter's command furnished a massive infantry levy: (Xen Anab I.7,10). This levy did not include the Greek and assorted mercenaries, or any loyalists who had escaped to the King, such as Tissaphernes. To corroborate that, one may notice that an important number of Xerxes' recruitment units or Corps back in 480 BC was from Asia Minor, which may have furnished one of his six main recruiting areas (**Map 3**), each under a Field Marshal (Her VII.82).

And then there is pure logic: a look at the map and a comparison between the geographical footprint of the mostly mountainous and arid Hellas that fielded the 100,000-plus infantry army of heavies and lights at Plataea in 480 BC (Her IX.30) and Asia Minor, even west of the Halys, much more fertile and extended, shows that 100,000 infantry mobilized to defend, not campaign abroad, would be a low figure, not an unbelievably high one.

What advises against this 100,000 draft host being employed in any way in the battle is that it is not mentioned in the account of the battle by Arrian. His is the account of an unorthodox battle and many would rather follow the more conventional one of Diodorus (Green 1991), but more conventional means conformation rather than reality. The battle as described by Arrian matches the Achaemenid knightly philosophy of the era, as seen time and again, as in the Battle of the Pactolus (Xen Hell III.4,22). The reverse then was pinned on the *karana*, Tissaphernes, who was executed (Xen Hell III.4,25), and not to the Persian fighting style; after all, the invasion was ultimately repulsed and the Persian aristocracy saw no need to effect any changes to its practices and privileges.

Moreover, the ratio of infantry to cavalry in Diodorus' account is 10:1. This is suspect by definition, as it is a Greek standard (Plut Aris 21,1), not an Achaemenid. It must be an extrapolation of a Greek writer, or his source. This was most probably the notorious Cleitarchus, a mercenary in the army of Alexander and a resident of Alexandria, and thus under the good graces of Ptolemy I, whose propaganda he served by belittling and besmirching Alexander, especially in comparison to southern Greeks that Ptolemy wanted to align with him against the other Hellenistic kings, his antagonists, in Asia and Macedon.

The Persians were copying *some* Greek military practices, and this with great reluctance, as the latter were demonstrably superior. They had no reason whatsoever to copy administrative practices; quite the opposite. Achaemenid administration was able, especially at this particular timeframe, to keep the empire together and reacquire considerable lost territory in the west and southwest, such as Ionia and Egypt. Their procedures and processes needed amendment, but they could do it themselves, and did, without following any Greek example or practice. After all, the Greeks, winning most battles and still being existentially threatened and much weakened after 150 years of friction with the empire, were hardly the raw model for anyone to copy in terms of administration. And drafting quota is an administrative, not a tactical consideration.

Equally interesting is the disposition of Alexander's forces. He left much of his heavy infantry (and light) to guard the bridgehead and the nearby occupied area from any manoeuvres by Memnon at his rear; this is the only logical explanation for the total lack of Greek infantry, both mercenary and League contributions, in the description of the formation of the order of battle (Arr Anab I.14,1–3). His move was not short-range, to pin and fight the Persian army assembled nearby. He was initiating his invasion, and this can be deduced by the fact that he had his baggage train with him (Arr

Anab I.13,1), while for a short-term operation he could have advanced on short-term rations carried by the troops and thus unburdened by the baggage train. Thus, his concern for his rear is most understandable. Incidentally, these forces included most of the southern Greek infantry groups (allied and mercenary) that were not particularly politically reliable to fight against their mercenary brethren for a northern king (Devine 1986). Such sensitivities were not very probable, especially for the mercenaries, but Alexander in many cases took every precaution and felt that he was better safe than sorry.

An alternative explanation could have been that all such troops were used, in unspecified manner, but their use was suppressed by the sources of Arrian, who were a bit unfriendly to the southern element of Alexander's army. This hostility does not seem to apply to the cavalry (Arr Anab I.14,3), raised from the pro-Macedonian upper classes of pro-Macedonian southern states, such as Achaea and other states of Peloponnese, Locris, Malis and other states of central Greece (Diod XVII.57,3).

Alexander's basic tactics against a superior enemy do not centre on flanking, which cannot be achieved by a smaller force against a larger one, especially if the larger one has better or larger mobile elements at its disposal as is the mobile arm *par exellence*, the cavalry. Despite scholars insisting on Alexander using flanking manoeuvre at the Granicus (Dahm 2019; Warry 1991; Thompson 2007), the obvious interpretation of Arrian's account is the frontal split and creation of internal flanks, at which he then unleashes flanking attacks by reorientating his own, much more manoeuvrable cavalry, due to the wedge (trans)formation (Hanson 1999). This follow-on exploitation of the rupture of the enemy linear deployment by attacking the exposed internal flanks is based on Theban practice as exemplified by Pelopidas in 377 BC at the Battle of Tegyra (Plut Pelop 17,4) and by Epaminondas in 362 BC at the second Battle of Mantinea (Xen Hell VII.5,25). Both cases are developments of the Spartan practice to turn their phalanx perpendicularly to the opponent's so as to take it by flank, as in the first Battle of Mantinea in 418 BC (Thuc V.73) and in Nemea (Xen Hell IV.2,21).

The proceedings of the battle

The deployment of the two opponents showed their intentions and was most representative of the two military systems. The Persians left the Greek mercenary infantry behind, well behind the bank, so as not to mess with the Persians and their glory, and lined all their heavy cavalry to the eastern bank, a typical case of *protaxis*, and actually independent employment of cavalry, seen in Malene, 493 BC, Plataea 479 BC, Pactolus 396 BC. The infantry was to provide a safe base for retreat, rallying and regrouping should the need be, as standard in their SOPs at least since the Scythian campaign (Her IV.128,3). They were not going to use the Greek mercenaries as *hamippoi*, as they had no such training, nor to risk a sentimental change of mood of said infantry towards their opposite brethren. Despite the loyalty of Greek mercenaries, the Persians had been taught about Greek betrayals: the Ionian revolt, the line-up behind the pretender Cyrus the Younger, the support of rebellious satraps throughout the fourth century and, of course, the massive rebellion during the Battle of Mycale in 479 BC and the instigation of Egyptian rebellions, or, at least, the assistance to them.

Alexander, on the other hand, presented a classical Greek order of battle with the limited numbers of his cavalry divided almost equally between the flanks of the heavy infantry line-up (*parataxis*). The transformation of his order of march to the order of battle is described in detail (Arr Anab I.13,1) and is exemplary, as it provides maximum security during the approach and the deployment. This is a cumulative cognitive inheritance from the Persian Wars to the bitter clashes of the late-fifth to the mid-fourth centuries. It is also a perfect example of adaptation to the terrain, which must have been well-known from intelligence gathered from his vanguard, as the area was at some time under their control. This intimate knowledge of the terrain by the Macedonian staff is seldom appreciated or taken into account. To top up such residual knowledge, Alexander had sent a powerful reconnaissance group under a certain Amyntas (not to be confused with the Commander of a *taxis* of the phalanx): four squadrons of mounted Scouts supported by one squadron of heavy Companion Cavalry (Arr Anab I.12,7). Arrian's mention of the former *may* suggest that there were more such squadrons, probably six in total. The Companions' squadron was supposed to provide protection and support to the Scouts should there be any clash with Achaemenid cavalry scouting, counter-scouting or surveying, as had happened near Dascylium in 396 BC with tragic results for the Greek cavalry doing the scouting (Xen Hell III.4,14).

A screen under Hegelochus, made of 500 light infantry and the whole of the Macedonian Scouts (**Figure 9.1**), armed with lances, was thrown to cover the transformation of the main army (Arr Anab I.13,1); Darius III would act similarly, although holding a fixed position, at Issus (Arr Anab II.8,5). Alexander transformed the army at least twice as he approached the river bank: from parallel columns of march to a formation of advance in line, with the heavy infantry in two parallel lines, the support train and baggage carriers at the tail and the cavalry at the sides in deep formation, and then to

Granicus: The Battle for Asia Minor   123

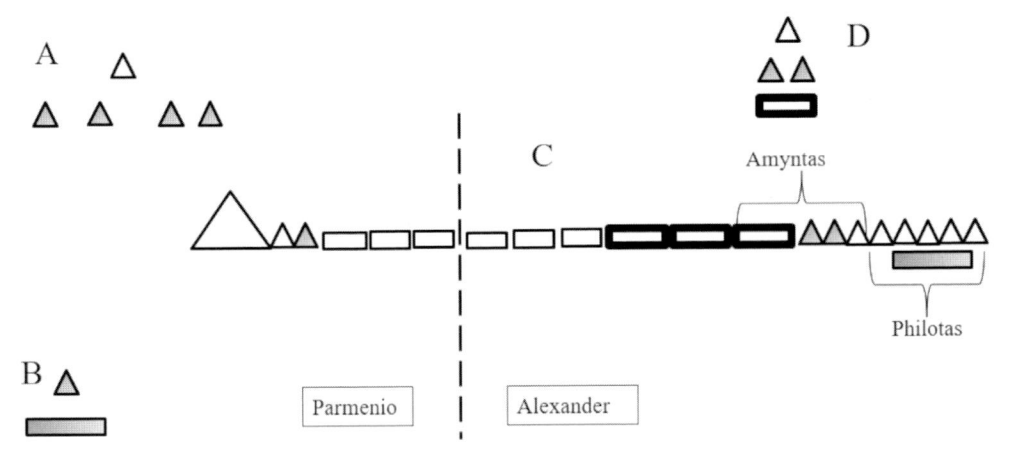

Figure 9.1: The campaign of Granicus.
A. Long-range reconnaissance by Amyntas' task group. One squadron of heavy cavalry to support four squadrons of mounted Scouts.
B. Short-range scouting by mounted Scouts and light infantry, to secure the approach and deployment of the army.
C. The deployment of the army of Alexander at Granicus, in two wings (left under Parmenio, right under Alexander), as per Arrian. The strike group of Amyntas is made of successively deployed units, as the light cavalry is linking the heavy cavalry with the heavy infantry.
D. Amyntas' strike group of a heavy cavalry squadron, the light cavalry and a heavy infantry unit, most probably deployed next to each other, form up in depth to rupture the enemy by the heavy cavalry, extend and enlarge the breach by the light cavalry and secure the ground by the infantry, which is to support the mounted troops directly as *hamippoi*, thus securing solid ground for Alexander's assault force.

Triangle: cavalry (dashed: light, hollow: heavy). Rectangle: infantry (dashed: light, hollow: heavy, thick line: elite/Hypaspists). The Companion heavy cavalry under Philotas is directly supported by light infantry fighting as *hamippoi*.

the final order of battle; a single line (Arr Anab I.14,1–3) that incorporated the forces which were previously screening the deployment.

On the left the Thessalian cavalry under Callas was followed by the allied, southern Greek cavalry under (one) Philip. These were followed by a mounted force of Thracians under Agathon (Arr Anab I.14,3) who commanded the Odryssian horsemen (the *Odryssai* were a Thracian tribe) at Gaugamela. It can be concluded that this was his command at the Granicus as well, being unarmoured light cavalry (Webber 2003) functioning as a link between the heavy cavalry and the line infantry. In the middle, the Macedonian phalanx was deployed, six *taxeis* plus the Hypaspist Corps under Nicanor, the son of elderly Parmenio at their right, the position of honour. The phalanx *taxeis* from left to right were those of Meleager, then of (another) Philip, recruited from the district of Tymphaea, then of (another) Amyntas, then of Craterus, then of Coenus, recruited from the district of Elymiaea, and then of Perdikkas, recruited from the districts of Orestis and Lyngistis (Arr Anab I.14,2; Diod XVII.57,2). To their right the Hypaspists were lined up, linked by more light cavalry, i.e. the Lancers and the Paeonian light horse, brigaded under Amyntas (Arr Anab I.14,1), the same man that had commanded the reconnaissance mission while approaching (**Figure 9.1**) the Companion Cavalry. The latter was positioned to the extreme right and commanded by another son of Parmenio, Philotas (Arr Anab I.14,1).

The light cavalry was posted at the inner flanks, to act as junction with the infantry. It is not clear from the Greek of Arrian whether the same deployment was followed for both the flanks; but it is reasonable to present symmetry in a battle. The use of light cavalry as a junction means that the external flanks of the heavy cavalry are left hanging, but the clearly defensive Persian deployment, in some cases over precipitous parts of the banks, made very clear the Achaemenids were not going to charge across the stream. Last, but not least, is the issue of light infantry, archers and Agrianian peltasts or javelineers: they are mentioned as being under the command of Philotas, the commander of the Companion Cavalry (Arr Anab I.14,1), but without specifying if they are deployed to their left, right, front or interspersed among them.

Arrian is a bit confusing in this battle, and not at his best; he reports, however, the creation of a task force that opened the battle. Alexander wanted to attack immediately, despite the troops being tired by the march throughout the day, and the few hours of daylight. The latter was advantageous, should he be defeated, as the enemy would have to pause any pursuit, but perhaps Alexander was too confident to see that. He knew well that he had the sun to his back, possibly marring the enemies' vision, but not his, as would have happened early in the morning. Now his vision was clear and the enemy, reflecting the sunlight, most observable, contrary to his own troops casting and hiding into the shadows. Moreover, an immediate charge would take the Persians unawares; they were posted to deter, not to receive an attack. Possibly to gain time for infantry levies to arrive, or for any other reason; the Persians had no reason to hurry, believing that the Macedonians had limited supplies. But Alexander had no reason to let the Persians, and especially the Greek strategists amongst them, to contemplate overnight over his deployment, strengths and liabilities. He had information dominance as his scouts had made the enemy order of battle known to him, he had arranged his forces accordingly, and he had no reason to allow the Persians to reciprocate by adapting – something they occasionally were good at, as Mardonius had done at Plataea in 479 BC, ominously under Medizer Greeks' advice (Her IX.47).

This is not the first time Alexander opens the battle by sending a contingent to provoke the enemy into a mistake. He did something similar during the Balkan campaign against the Triballi (Arr Anab I.2,4–6); in that case his troops were more of a bait. At the Granicus, although they were tasked with an impossible mission, they were a rupture force, to create the conditions that would allow the tactical plan to fall into order where there were not suitable conditions. This detachment, in this battle, was based on the reconnaissance detachment of Amyntas (**Figure 9.1**); a squadron of heavy cavalry (the very same), the sum of lancers and the Paeonians, who were under his direct command, plus an infantry regiment (Arr Anab I.14,6). The parlance of Arrian implies a *taxis* of Foot Companions, but he fails to name it. A chiliarchy of Hypaspists would fit the bill better, as they were more mobile, highly trained in different scenarios, one being to intermingle in cavalry formations and fight as *hamippoi*.

The key to the identification is the elusive officer Ptolemy, a very common name in Macedon, who is not properly identified by Arrian, perhaps because his sources fail to do so. He is presented as the commander of the Companion squadron for that day, as the usual commander was absent (Arr Anab I.14,6). But he must have been the commander of the infantry regiment; an officer of the Hypaspist Corps.

In consequence of the above, a detachment of heavy and light cavalry and heavy infantry effected the first assault (**Figure 9.2**). The Companion squadron, better armoured and protected, was the rupture force against their Persian opposite numbers, hoping to cut through their line with their robust spears; the lights, more mobile but less well-protected would follow suit, armed for the battle not with javelins but with their extra-long lances and using their superior agility, to dislodge the heavy *asabara* as they would be distorted by the assault of the Companions, and the heavy infantry would secure the foothold and support the cavalrymen in close engagement, as the fight would be in congested space and the enemy would have trouble to parry blows coming from below to their horses, especially if the latter are immobilized by being engaged in CQB. Alexander's idea was tactically sound, but the storm of *palta* double-purpose spears hurled in masses from the Persian cavalry to the attackers took a toll and distorted the formation of the Macedonians. Following their SOPs, the *asabara*, after hurling one spear as a javelin, closed in (Arr Anab I.15,1) with the second to use it as a thrusting weapon (Xen On Hors 12,12) and to physically push with their

126   Alexander the Great Avenger

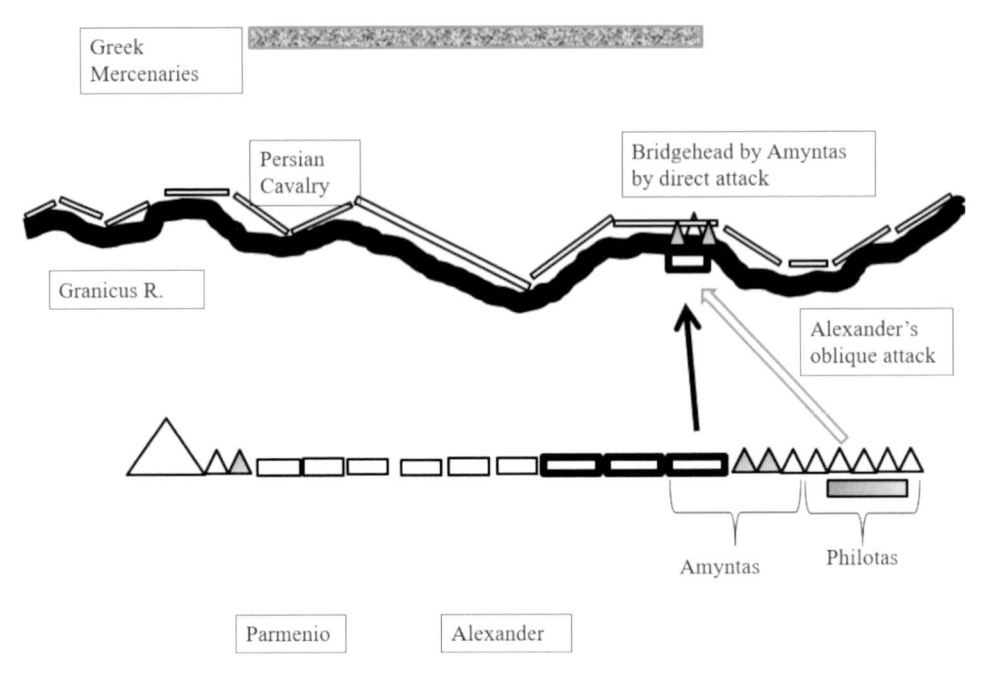

Figure 9.2: The battle of the Granicus.
The Persian cavalry invests the bank, with the Greek mercenary hoplites being at no great distance, at a strong position on a height. Supposedly they form a defensive barrier for the cavalry to find refuge and rally behind, but this is not the proper position for this purpose, for whatever the reason.

Alexander opens the battle with a direct charge of Amyntas' task group, the units of which, being initially deployed in line, converge to make rather an assault column. Although met with stout resistance and taking many casualties, they occupy some ground for some time. Alexander leads his cavalry in oblique order into the river, instead of straight ahead. Thus he suffers fewer missiles, especially as Amyntas' men have taken a great many projectiles and now form a protective barrier between Alexander and the defenders. Thus, the Companions and the supporting light infantry easily gain dry, solid ground and strike at the flanks of the Persian line which has precious little room to manoeuvre and counterattack, thus giving way and forfeiting the day.

horses' mass the Macedonians down the slippery bank to the even more slippery riverbed (Arr Anab I.15,2).

And there the Macedonian shafts, both the *xysta* spears of the Companions and the *sarissa* lances of the Lancers began taking their toll, longer and sturdier as they were than the Achaemenid weapons. This explains why in impossible odds and under a hail of missiles, the leading formation, the decimated Companion squadron that lost 25 men out of 150 or, most probably, 100, was not swept away and secured a foothold (Arr Anab I.15,3) for just the time it was needed; of course with the help of their friends, the lights and the infantry.

The time needed for what? For the main attack wave, under Alexander, to arrive without the threat of being physically pushed back into the river bed, with the slippery and precarious footing and the current dislodging them, depriving them of mobility, averting them from coming to spear range, blunting their momentum and making them sitting ducks for the volleys that kept pouring in. And this is not all; the wave of Alexander faces much fewer missiles flying its way, from greater distance and with worse aiming. The Achaemenids nearby had hurled their weapons and were down to the spares, to use for CQB. Additionally, the first wave was between them and the wave of Alexander. Thus, the latter came to the shore actually in assault formation, probably wedge, gained solid ground, closed to thrusting distance without interventions and engaged, assisted by the light infantry (Arr Anab I.16,1), definitely the ones placed under the command of Philotas (Arr Anab I.14,1) obviously intended from the beginning to be interspersed among the mounts and fight as *hamippoi* (Xen Hippar V.13).

This lethal combination decided the engagement there and then (Arr Anab I.16,1). The Achaemenids tried to move squadrons from other points of their line, but this caused great consternation and chaos, as the phalanx crossed and, taking the javelins on their shields, thrust the *sarissai* to the arrayed and immobile standing targets, the *asabara* and their mounts, especially the bellies of these mounts as they were positioned, supposedly advantageously, on higher ground.

The proceedings of the left part of the army under Parmenio are not recorded by Arrian, as he follows sources hostile to the old-timer; not once are the achievements of his sons, Philotas, CO of the Companions and Nicanor, CO of the Hypaspists, mentioned in Arrian's account; they cannot have been so unimportant. At Gaugamela the old-timer is criticized as incompetent. This amounts to true malice; the signature quality of Ptolemy I. But still, it is entirely possible that once the cavalry centre was put to flight by Alexander's final onslaught, both wings collapsed and fled (Arr Anab I.16,1) before the phalanx or anyone else, the Thessalian cavalry included, had time – and opportunity – to cross and engage.

Diodorus follows sources hostile to Alexander and very friendly to the Thessalians and the southerners, namely Cleitarchus, and thus eulogizes the Thessalians (Diod XVII. 21,4). In any case, the Macedonians under Alexander had cut through the Persian line and then broke the reinforcements that came their way. A wedge of Achaemenid knights engaged one under Alexander. A leadership contest developed in physical terms; Alexander, using the standard skills of the Companion horseman delivered a spear-thrust to the chest, and when his lance broke, reverted to the butt-spike with which he struck the enemy in the face, mortally. Obviously the first thrust was from underhand or underarm to the chest, and once the shaft splintered, Alexander raised his hand to the overhead position thus projecting the buttspike with which he delivered a lethal, face blow to his opponent (Diod XVII.20,5). Thus engaged he was attacked by the following Persian trooper in the wedge, who was reportedly coming to his flank (Plut Alex 16,5) but he was covered by one of his own wedge, Cleitus the Black who chopped the arm off the assaulting enemy (Arr Anab I.15,8), meaning that he had lost his spear, too. The same happened with another cavalryman, Aretes, a Royal Esquire, who obviously was fighting mounted in the direct vicinity of the king; he was also fighting with his broken spear (Arr Anab I.15,6), most probably using the butt-spike as a warhead. A Corinthian Companion, one of the southerners installed into Macedonian estates after the expansion of Philip's realm, Demaratus, a mature if not outright aged gentleman, passed his own weapon to the King (Arr Anab I.15,6) to keep him fighting without a disadvantage to enemies still brandishing their spare *palton*. Demaratus, having played the intermediate to mend a quarrel between Philip and Alexander (Plut Alex 9,6), must have occupied an honourary position very near the King, to be positioned so as to make this move – something natural for the man who had gifted to Alexander the steed Bucephalus (Diod XVII.76,6).

The violent cavalry duel finished abruptly as the Achaemenids took to flight. Having lost many of their commanders they suffered shock and awe due to the efficiency of the Macedonian novel weapon, the long and sturdy *xyston* thrust at the face of *asabara* knight and Nyssaean mount (Arr Anab I.16,1). Their dispersion limited their casualties to 5 per cent fatalities of their initial number, a mere thousand horsemen (Arr Anab I.16,2), but left exposed the mercenaries who were flabbergasted by the rapidity and magnitude of the disaster. This is somewhat strange; the victory of Agesilaus at Pactolus should have been common knowledge, but then, age must have blunted memory: this had taken place sixty years previously, two generations. Thus stunned, the mercenaries remained where they had deployed (Arr Anab I.16,2). This might have been due to something more serious than the result of being stunned. The enemy had a most lethal cavalry arm, as was obvious from the proceedings, and retreating on open ground before a heavy infantry phalanx and a massive cavalry assault would have been suicidal.

Alexander fixed his attention on them, and after rallying his forces turned against them. Pursuing the fleeing cavalry could be fruitless and expose his pursuers to counterattacks, while his infantry could be facing trouble from the mercenaries. The latter were the most capable troops in Achaemenid service, invaluable for the defence of fortified cities and for manoeuvre warfare. Taking them out with little fuss by his combined arms and with the morale of his troops being sky-high and of the enemy having plummeted, Alexander was to deprive the Achaemenids of a large number of top fighters and also sow terror to their kin still in Persian service. If the terror was to work, the Persian field armies would be for naught.

Their surrender was not accepted, to make an example. Stunned and encircled they tried to use the high ground where they were posted by choice, but *sarissai* greatly undermined this advantage, and the cavalry striking their flanks and rear could not be properly averted as they were frontally committed. It was a slaughter (Arr Anab I.16,6). Very few survived and escaped, playing dead (Arr Anab I.16,2).

Memnon was fighting with his sons with the cavalry (Arr Anab I.15,2) like a true Persian feudal lord, as his estates were in Troad (Kholod 2002). Nothing is heard about his sons; they must have perished, as they are never spoken of, and this could explain his grim determination against the son of the man who had extended refuge to him (Diod XVI.52,3).

Many mercenaries were slain, or rather slaughtered, and the rest thrown in bondage as traitors since their cities were formally allied to Macedon against Persia (Arr Anab I.16,6). He could have killed them for treason, especially since he had refused their surrender, but found a useful leverage in them for the goodwill of their cities; a flexible lever, applicable on a city-by-city basis. Some cities would like to have their human capital restored to them, some others could be made looking guilty, and others still may feel better if they were to hear nothing of such vermin (traitorous vermin) in the future; some factions would have loved to see them vanish.

Thus, these traitors of Greece were given life sentences and sent to the mines of Pangeum, where Philip and Alexander mined the gold used to finance their endeavours but also to inflate the international exchange rate so as to diminish the Persian ability to finance mercenaries, fleets, traitors, assassins and insurgents (Heliopoulos 2019).

The battle sequence: the report of Arrian

Alexander was posted on the extreme right of his line, and had under his immediate control the right half of the entire line (Arr Anab I.13). The Persian leadership was posted to the centre (Arr Anab I.15,2), as was customary (Xen Anab I.8,22). Arrian makes very clear that Alexander's attack struck the centre of the Persian line and its collapse resulted in the wings, less heavily committed or virtually uncommitted, breaking and fleeing (Arr Anab I.16,1) – which explains well the very low number of Persian fatalities, only 1,000 out of between 10,000 and 20,000 horse (Arr Anab I.16,2) pinned onto a riverbank. This means that Alexander and his wave could advance and attack obliquely, from the right wing of their line to the centre of the Persian. There were three problems: the first is that during this oblique advance, in the riverbed (there was no other space) the Persian left wing could charge downriver at the exposed flank of the advancing column and engage with advantage of position, momentum, concentration and formation. The second problem was that even if the Persians would not, or could not charge to contact, the advancing column would be moving under their javelin volleys, into a veritable shooting gallery, with the flanks of the men exposed – and, especially, those of the horses, being juicy, large targets, inadequately armoured. And the third problem was that when gaining the opposite bank, the Persian cavalry stationed there could still javelin them down from close range and attack to literally shove them back to the river, as they would be exhausted, out of formation and on slippery ground, while the Persians would operate from solid ground.

The first wave did much to tackle all these issues. The Persian left wing could charge to contact only at a limited length of smooth land, as the banks were precipitous for much of their length. The first wave proactively intercepted such a move by putting a Greek force into such an access point, thus averting a Persian charge to the river; they had first to overcome the resistance of said advance force, and this force included the ultimate defensive weapon, a brigade of heavy infantry, which, once on land, would provide a defensive barrier for friendly horsemen to retire and regroup, and a definite obstacle to enemy onslaughts towards the river. Additionally, said force made it much more difficult for the Persians to javelin down the second wave, by being placed between them, by pushing them some tens of metres away from the bank at its most level point, and, to a great extent, by enticing them to expend their missiles on this advance force and thus having nothing left with which to engage the second wave.

It is important to notice that once Alexander was through, a formation of Persian cavalry, with the one-third of the high command at its point, came to intercept (Arr Anab I.15,7). This means that they were not in position, they had to move from where they were posted to reinforce and engage. A further point is that in the engagement the Persian leaders attacked with sidearms. There is not a mention of hurling missiles, and thus they received the Macedonian countercharge at a distinct disadvantage. The *xysta* lances of the Companions, by Arrian's account scored a couple of casualties, one with a chest wound through the cuirass (Arr Anab I.15,8) – an homage to the penetrability and sturdiness of the weapon – another to the face (Arr Anab I.15,7) – an homage to its accuracy and to the training of the bearer – the third Imperial being dispatched by sidearm (Arr Anab I.15,8). But both the dangerous Persian attacks on the person of Alexander were by slashing swords (Arr Anab I.15,7–8), meaning the culprits had spent both *palta* javelins, not just the one as was SOP, obviously due to the fervour and to the extraordinary development of the situation. Other accounts differ on the details and succession of the kills but the lack of thrusting shafted weapons for the Persian nobles is still noticeable (Diod XVII.20,5–6).

Alexander's wave galloped, as a result, into the riverbed *following* the current; Arrian's Greek is compatible with this version (Arr Anab I.14,7), although the whole account occasionally is problematic. Additionally, Alexander seems to deploy his squadrons linearly, so they form a cordon in the river, a long line, to offer no vulnerable collective flank. If charged, they can always turn 90 degrees and transform to a line from a column. This is the most logical and plausible interpretation for Arrian's description (Arr Anab I.14,7). When they started getting to the opposite bank, one by one (probably this is meant by the expression 'successive *taxeis*' of Arrian), they attacked the pinned and engaged Persians, and flanked the Persian centre. When they repulsed the reinforcements and decimated the Persian leadership (Thompson 2007), the whole centre collapsed, creating internal flanks to the wings, which followed suit in the flight (Arr Anab I.15,1). Central to the above is the understanding that the term *taxeis* is occasionally used by Arrian *sensu lato* and not as the strict term for the Foot Companion brigades (English 2002), something observed also in Xenophon (Xen Anab IV.3,17); similar to the current use of the word 'unit'.

The battle sequence: the report of Diodorus

Diodorus reports the battle as it would have happened if Alexander had taken Parmenio's advice: camp on the western bank and, as the Persian cavalry had withdrawn to retire in safety as per procedure (Xen Anab III.4,34–5), the Macedonians cross unopposed by dawn, before the Imperials had time to resume their defensive position on the eastern bank and deploy for battle. Then a conventional battle is fought on the east side the next day (Diod XVII.19,3). Of course there is a slight problem: with Alexander sporting only 5,000 horse and the Persians 10,000 (Diod XVII.19,4), as Diodorus reports their mounted arm much smaller than Arrian, how did Alexander's cavalry win in a conventional, level fight? In Arrian's account, the Persian horse is pinned on the riverbank, unable to manoeuvre but little and it disintegrates once broken and its leadership, posted in the centre, decimated. The easily read version of a conventional battle as reported by Diodorus rather than the complicated and innovative one as described by Arrian is by no means more plausible, despite the opinion of esteemed scholars (Green 1991) who paste the reports of Plutarch and Diodorus to invent a bloody failure of Alexander's evening whirlwind attack. Neither Diodorus nor Plutarch suggest a repulse of the first Macedonian onslaught.

In any case, the details of Arrian are unlikely to have been made up, in contrast to Diodorus' version where Alexander, while on horseback bears a shield (Diod XVII.20,3), something completely out of date and army, showcasing a merging of historical Homeric and almost current southern Greek fighting practices, as is the use of javelin from horseback (Arr Anab I.2,6). Plutarch reports that Alexander led 13 squadrons to a successful, though bloody, attack (Plut Alex 16,2). It reads as a slightly distorted version of Arrian's account, the vanguard and the Companion waves being considered as one incident; which it was, at some time they were all fighting simultaneously. The light infantry is missing, but the rest of the account corroborates Arrian.

Unfortunately the above-mentioned excerpts are consistent with a wide variety of theories about the numbers and organization of the three regiments, the Companions, the Lancers or Scouts and the Paeonians. For starters, at the Granicus there is no mention of the Royal Squadron, destined to become famous in later operations. It is reported for the first time during the operations off Miletus (Arr Anab I.18,3) the same year. It might have been created after the Battle of the Granicus, to accommodate select cavalrymen on merit and/or loyalty, and Cleitus the Black was appointed commander as a recognition for saving Alexander's life in the Battle of the Granicus (Arr Anab I.15,8). Thus, the easy conclusion of a seven-squadron Companion Corps, and a possible two-squadron Paeonian and four-squadron Scout light cavalry arm remains debatable, as are other proposals (Rzepka 2008).

Afterthoughts and impact

The Battle of the Granicus is mentioned by Arrian as a cavalry battle or *hippomachia* (Arr Anab IV.8,6). This is important. Strictly it is incorrect; in nothing else, infantry participated from both sides in the slaughter of the Greek Mercenaries, an event that would have infuriated their kin in Achaemenid service and also would have encouraged the Achaemenid High Command to make tactical amends, as was to happen at Issus. But the mercenaries were an expendable body that both sides could well overlook

Granicus: The Battle for Asia Minor   133

in their storytelling and propaganda: the Persians so as not to partake in the disaster of their employees, and also not to cast doubts on their wonder weapon; the Macedonians in order to hush the fact that too many southerners were eagerly taking the field against them, some for pay, some under the pretext of pay.

But the most important thing is the verdict of the cavalry duel. If Arrian has it right, it was a change in history; despite their martial prowess, the Greeks had never conquered the Imperials in cavalry duels. Against the Imperials, Greek cavalry forces could – and did – intercept skirmishers or give pursuit to broken enemies, infantry or cavalry. They could also provide non-battle functions, such as security and reconnaissance. What they could not do was face the *asabara*. There the verdict was ominously unanimous. The Greeks stood a chance only if assisted by combined arms, as in Pactolus. At the Granicus the unthinkable happened: the Greek-type Macedonian Companion cavalry had beaten the Imperial *asabara* single-handedly *and* at a numerical disadvantage. The only assistance were light infantry dispersed among the horses fighting as *hamippoi*, a practice actually going back to the Bronze Age and the chariot-runners (Kambouris 2023). Knight to knight, the tactics and weapons of the Companions prevailed clearly; as they were using javelins in a campaign one short year before (Arr Anab I.2,6) the existence and the performance of the *xyston* lance, as well as the murderous way it was used, may have been a nasty surprise for the Imperials.

Was it a cavalry battle? Scholars who do not think so refer to Arrian's own account (Arr Anab I.15,4) where he explicitly states that 'the successive *taxeis* were gaining ground'. The word *taxis* means, mostly, the infantry regiment in Macedonian and southern military terminology, especially the regiment conscripted locally, a large territorial unit. In Alexander's Army it is the word for the Foot Companion regiments of the phalanx. Still, the word has another meaning, the generic meaning of 'unit', and 'large unit' at that. So, if Arrian uses it in this way, *sensu lato*, he might imply the successive squadrons (*ilae*) of the Companions that Alexander had deployed linearly to avert a flanking from the Persian left wing and then turned them to column, in order to obliquely cross the river to the area of the Persian centre. As a result, the squadrons were arriving at the scene serially, one after the other, gaining the bank and thrusting into battle, a very matching reading of Arrian and one that both shows how the Persian cavalry defeat happened fast and by cavalry only. This reading explains also why the Greek mercenaries of the Imperials were astounded by the rapidity of the events. After some brief engagement, in a matter of minutes, the whole cavalry in front of them just vanished, most of it without engaging. Arrian makes no mention of any engagement by the left wing cavalry, nor by the phalanx. The mercenaries were so astounded they failed to rush in to deny the foothold to the Macedonians, their only chance not to have the phalanx at their front and heavy cavalry deployed over open ground, taking their rear.

Which brings the question: why were the Imperials deployed as they were? Memnon had advised a scorched earth policy (Arr Anab I.12,9) and also to avoid the risk of a fight as they were inferior in infantry. The 20,000 or so mercenaries were top quality, but the foot element of Alexander's army was at least 32,000 and in phalanx warfare numbers matter. But Alexander had not all his infantry with him; with the exception of some skirmishers, it was only the Macedonian heavies; thus the Persians had rather an advantage in infantry. Alexander knew that many allies and perhaps mercenaries were not staunch supporters of his masterplan and his prerogative. Additionally, they had not trained with his phalanx and his cavalry to attune to the great orchestra of the Macedonian army; especially the allies might have been wanting in training. The allied cavalry could be used fairly conventionally to bolster his plans; thus it participated in the Granicus. The infantry, however, did not participate.

Alexander enacted counter-intelligence, especially with the deployment of counter-reconnaissance patrols of his light cavalry. Had the Imperials caught word despite such measures, then they thought they had a chance and surged to the Granicus, a nice obstacle made by Mother Nature. Thus it is possible that their cavalry was deployed because it arrived first, to deny the Macedonians an immediate crossing; Alexander had already a reputation for swift advance and lightning action. But suppose they had all the time in the world, what troops would they entrust with the defence of the bank? They only had the Greek mercenaries; conscript infantry hosts had not been there, or perhaps were not even mobilized.

The *asabara* were decently armoured and equipped with both ranged and close-quarters weapons. They were shock troops; shock depends on momentum and awe. Momentum on speed and mass. By putting them there, in a static capacity, the Persians were wasting their mobility and their ability for shock action. But this is half the story. Mobility is not everything, at least not always. The commanding mass of mount and rider, both armed, would be excellent to physically push tired and half-drowned enemies, with slippery, unsecure footing, back to the river while delivering blows from a superimposed position and on steady footing. Before that, before the enemy ever came into contact, javelin volleys during his crossing would decimate troops and mounts and destroy the formations even more than did the current and the slippery riverbed. And then, wounded, suffering casualties, dispirited and out of breath and formation would be met by huge man-animal complexes, armoured, steady and well-armed. This picture seems very logical; if the Greek mercenaries were the only infantry present, the *asabara* were the only missile troops available to allow the full exploitation of the obstacle presented by the Granicus.

Alexander from this battle kept two interesting undernotes: he had a very successful chemistry in the combination of one squadron of Companions with the Lancers or Scouts and a heavy infantry unit. The concept was used at Gaugamela with similar results; highly successfully but with considerable casualties. Alexander was innovative in using task groups but rather conservative in forming such assets. Once a good combination and a working chemistry were identified, he did not change the synthesis if he had not to; actually, he tried to change as little as possible. So, the formation may be somewhat changed (as at Issus as well) but at Gaugamela, much enhanced and with considerable substitutes, its use is evident; although operating in the extreme right, off the front of the Companions. At the Granicus, as already mentioned, they were at the junction of heavy cavalry and line infantry to include units from both (**Fig 9.1**).

Alexander at the Granicus played a number of cards. Some may have been surprises, others less so. For example the smart and elaborate tactics, as with the task group that opened the battle, should have been a surprise and an indication of an advancement of warfare. The Greeks used tactics and combined arms for quite some time, but this particular hand was something rather novel, especially against the Persians. Though the nobles that fled the field may have not been explicit on the subject, the other most probable novelty, the use of the *xyston* that gave the advantage to the Greeks must have been focal in their recounts during reporting and debriefing. With this weapon, something very different from the flimsy *kamax* spear of conventional southern cavalry, the standard throughout the fifth and early fourth century (Xen On Hors 12,12), the Greek cavalry had a distinct advantage in shock action against the *asabara* horsemen. In reach and sturdiness it was superior to double-use *palta*. Not the heavy armour, nor the mass and strength of their mounts changed that. They had to avoid contact fight at *xyston* range.

Whether the Companions used wedge formations when deployed to the far bank cannot be surmised (the engagement of Alexander, Aretes, Demaratus, etc. reads like if a wedge was formed, however), and thus nor can it be whether the Persians were now informed of this trick, or not, or had already known it. The same goes for the phalanx. Arrian never says explicitly that the *sarissa* pikes were used in this battle. For the river crossing their long reach offered some advantages, especially against higher-placed enemy and charging cavalry, both conditions present at the Granicus. But there were some liabilities too, due to its cumbersomeness; if a melee was to happen it was next to useless, as the Romans showed some centuries later, and a melee could well occur due to the detrimental effect of the river crossing on the formation, even had the current been weak and the banks less precipitous and slippery. Thus, there is some controversy on the issue (Markle 1978). In previous operations it had been used at least once (Arr Anab I.4,1), in the crossing of the Danube (Ister). Whether it had been used at Chaeronea, or was eventually taken into action during the many confrontations of the next year in Asia Minor one may not be certain, but the possibilities are for its use to have been known to the Persian High Command by mid-333 BC, before the Battle of Issus.

Chapter 10

Asia Minor: A Year-long Campaign

The geostrategic reality

In Asia Minor there are two key areas: Celaenae and Sardis. Imperial forces could cross using any of the three available East-West axes, although there were more. First was the northern road of Armenia through Pteria, the road of the invasion of Cyrus the Great and Croesus to each other's territory (Her I.76) and the favourite of the Byzantines and the Sassanid Persians in the conflicts of the fifth century AD. From Dascylium/ Ergili in the southern coast of Propontis it proceeds East-Southeast to Dorylaeum/Eskisehir – Gordium/Polatli – Ankara – Sebasteia – Erzurum – Tarbriz – Ecbatana/Hamadan. Two secondary itineraries to the north also converge there, just before Erzurum: the coastal (Dascylium/Ergili – Sinope – Trebizond/Trabzon), north of the Pontic Mountains and the road of Amasya (Dascylium/Ergili – Amasya – Erzurum), just south of the Pontic Mountains (dotted lines in **Map 5**).

The second and main choice would be, of course, the Royal Road (Her V.52–53). From Sardis/ Salihli, lying due east of Smyrna/Izmir the trek goes

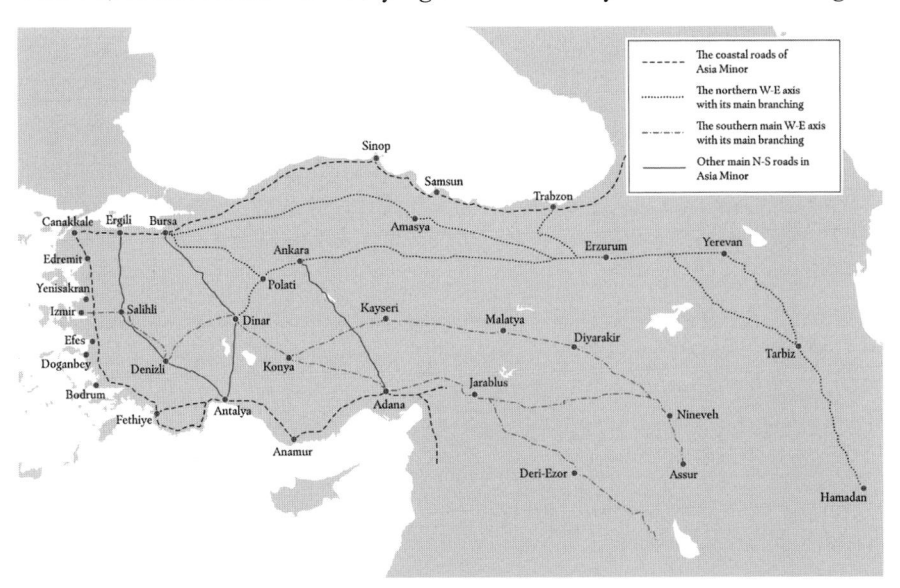

Map 5: The road system (two axes) in Asia Minor – Armenia Asia Minor options from the Hellespont.

East-Southeast to the hub of Colossae/Denizli (where the roads from Aydin/Tralleis-Efes/Ephesus and from Caria converge as well) and then to the hub of Celaenae/Dinar (where the roads from Attaleia/Antalya and Perga in Pamphylia and from Gordium/Polatli converge) to Iconium/Konya and through the Cilician Gates, to Tarsus and then, through the Amanic Gates to the Euphrates, where the Middle Road to Mesopotamia starts, and then to the Tigris, and Southeast to Susa, which is the Upper Road (part of the Royal Road). This road offers an interesting option: from Iconium/Konya a branch goes East-Northeast, without entering Cilicia, to Kayseri, Malatya and all the way to Diyarbakir and from there converges to the Royal Road into the valley of Tigris, at ancient Nineveh (intermittent line in **Map 5**), and then follows the Upper Road to Mesopotamia as above. This option, the third main East-West Axis, allows bypassing Cilicia should the need be. And there was the southern coastal road of Cilicia, starting from Halicarnassus (modern Bodrum) in Caria to Telmessus (modern-day Fethiye) and then Habesus (modern-day Kas) in Lycia, Attaleia (modern-day Antalya) and then Side and Syedra in Pamphylia and entering Cilicia at the environs of Anemourion (modern-day Anamur), reaching the main Cilician coast at modern-day Silifke (Seleuceia) and ultimately ending in Tarsus.

There were also North-South roads that unified this system, such as the one from Dascylium through Sardis to Smyrna and then, along the coast to Caria; to Smyrna converges also the coastal road from the Hellespont to Troad, Atarneus and down the coast of Aeolis. The second, more to the east is the road from Gordium to Celaenae to Perga or Attaleia in Pamphylia and

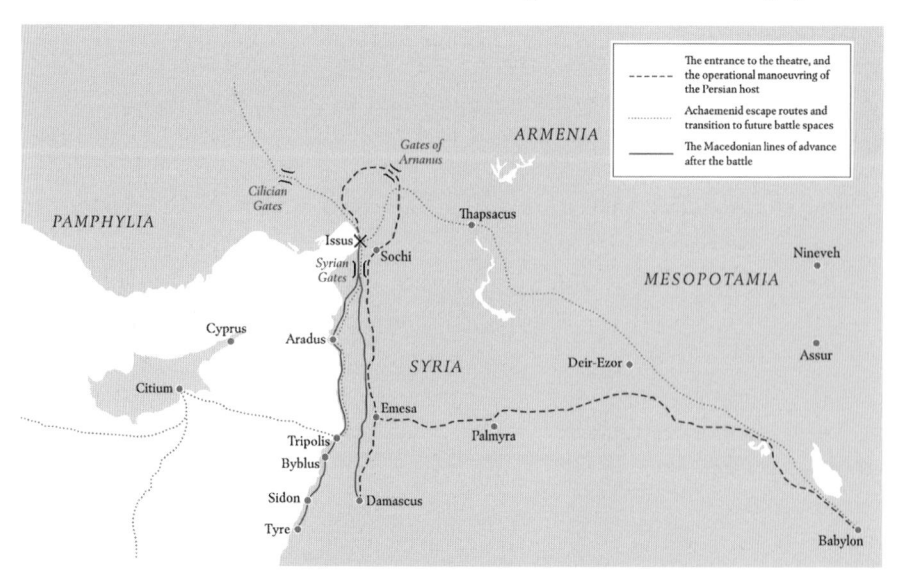

Map 6: South-East Asia Minor – Cilicia – Mesopotamia – Issus Campaign.

Lycia. And then the road from the coast of the Euxine to Ankara to Tarsus. But Sardis was the final centre for the concentration of land forces, as with the campaign of Xerxes (Her VII.26,1). Sardis was not seriously threatened either by Agesilaus or the Athenians before him; it had been torched, though, during the Ionian revolution in 499 BC (Her V.101–102). After Salamis, Xerxes settled there for some time (Her VIII.117,2 & IX.3,1), like his father after the Scythian campaign (Her IV.11). The fact that Sardis was not threatened for more than 100 years shows the operational limitations of Greek military thought and/or machine.

After Sardis, Celaenae was the second key to Asia Minor, located on the Royal Road (Her VII.26,3) and allowing access to the central plateau from the SE areas of the Asia Minor peninsula. Whoever owned it, controlled the movement on three axes. Immediately after Salamis, Xerxes had it fortified because he was expecting a Greek invasion to destroy his empire (Xen Anab I.2,9). He did not care about the small provinces in the West, but the central plateau that unlocked the three roads to the heart of the empire (especially the Royal Road and the Road of Pteria, to the north). But no Greek army had negotiated the double obstacle of the heavily fortified Sardis (Arr Anab I.17,5) and the network of fortified coastal cities such as Halicarnassus and Miletus to even threaten Celaenae. And there was no reason to believe that would change now.

And then, there was Cilicia. Persian forces often passed through there heading west, as did Mardonius in 492 BC and Datis in 490 BC (Her VI.43,2 & 95,1 respectively). A large fleet could set off from Cilicia and transport large amphibious forces to the Aegean theatre. This happened in 490 BC with Datis, and this is exactly what troubled Alexander in 333–332 BC. Thus the occupation of Cilicia was an unyielding necessity, and the same went with the entire southern coast of Asia Minor including the coasts of Pamphylia and Lycia, given that they could accommodate fleets (Arr Anab I.24,4).

The Persian navy that appeared in early summer of 334 BC, hoping to find and beat the 160-strong allied navy (Arr Anab I.18,4), is reported as 400-strong (Arr Anab I.18,5). There are no Ionian Greek squadrons or Egyptian ones reported at any time; although both areas had been realigned with the Throne, they were too volatile and unreliable to raise navy; or, concerning Ionia, Alexander's advance too swift. The two triremes of Ephesus were commandeered by its mercenary garrison and joined the Imperials (Arr Anab I.17,9). The navy, with its massive crews, demanded a great degree of trust to operate; real or imagined lack of trust could be devastating to a cause, as happened at Myous, in 500 BC (Her V.36,4–37,1) and at Salamis, in 480 BC (Her VIII.90,1–3) respectively.

This means that Darius III was down to two naval conscription areas from the four (**Map 3**) under Xerxes (Her VII.97). Actually, only Cypriot and Phoenician squadrons are mentioned for 334 BC (Arr Anab I.18,7), which begs the question what happened with the ones of southern Asia Minor, securely in Persian hands at the time, which produced in 480 BC, some 150 vessels (Her VII.91–92). At that time Phoenicia had contributed 300 vessels and Cyprus 150 (Her VII.89,1 and VII.90 respectively). It is notable that Phoenicia and Cyprus provided 400 ships in 334–333 BC (Arr Anab I.18,5), after they had revolted and been suppressed most brutally not so many years before (Diod XVI.45,4–6).

It is so favourable, that one tends to believe that southern Asia Minor squadrons may have been included in this total, with the only indication to this being that the local petty king of Cilicia, under the throne name Syenessis, never appears during the operations of Alexander in his home territories during 333 BC; an indication that he is away with the fleet, something allowing the local satrap Arsames to consider reducing the area to implement scorched earth policy (Arr Anab II.4,5; Curt III.4,3). Additionally, vessels from Asia Minor are reported during the fighting (Arr Anab I.19,11) and also reinforcing Alexander at Tyre (Arr Anab II.20,2); meaning that before they were earmarked for the Imperial navy.

The trek of Alexander for eighteen months after his resounding victory at the Granicus shows exactly the scant imperial forces in Asia Minor. After the battle, where a couple of thousand Persians perished, the satrapal seat of Northwest Asia Minor (i.e. Hellespontine Phrygia and Aeolis), the city of Dascylium was defenceless; the garrison had vanished (Arr Anab I.17,2) and the city passed without any trouble to the detachment of Parmenio sent by Alexander. Had its garrison all been mercenaries, who perished in the battle? It seems that the Persian military colonies in Asia Minor produced no infantry any longer. In the Battle of the Pactolus, 396 BC Agesilaus had scored a similar or greater victory against the *asabara*, but there was no such collapse, perhaps as there was no extermination of the leadership.

Alexander took Dascylium by a detachment of Parmenio (Arr Anab I.17,2) and Callas did the same with Troad (**Map 4**), without any resistance (Arr Anab I.16,8), possibly using the troops not committed at the Granicus. Callas was appointed satrap in Dascylium as he was the commander of the bridgehead (Diod XVII.7,10) after Parmenio returned and Attalus was executed (Diod XVII.5,1–2); thus he was in contact with many locals and all the area, even south of the Troad and opposite the island of Lesbos.

Alexander himself took the third possible route from the bridgehead; he went down to Sardis (**Map 4**), situated South-Southeast inland, at a breakneck speed, and not along the coast. Sardis – actually its citadel – was a nest,

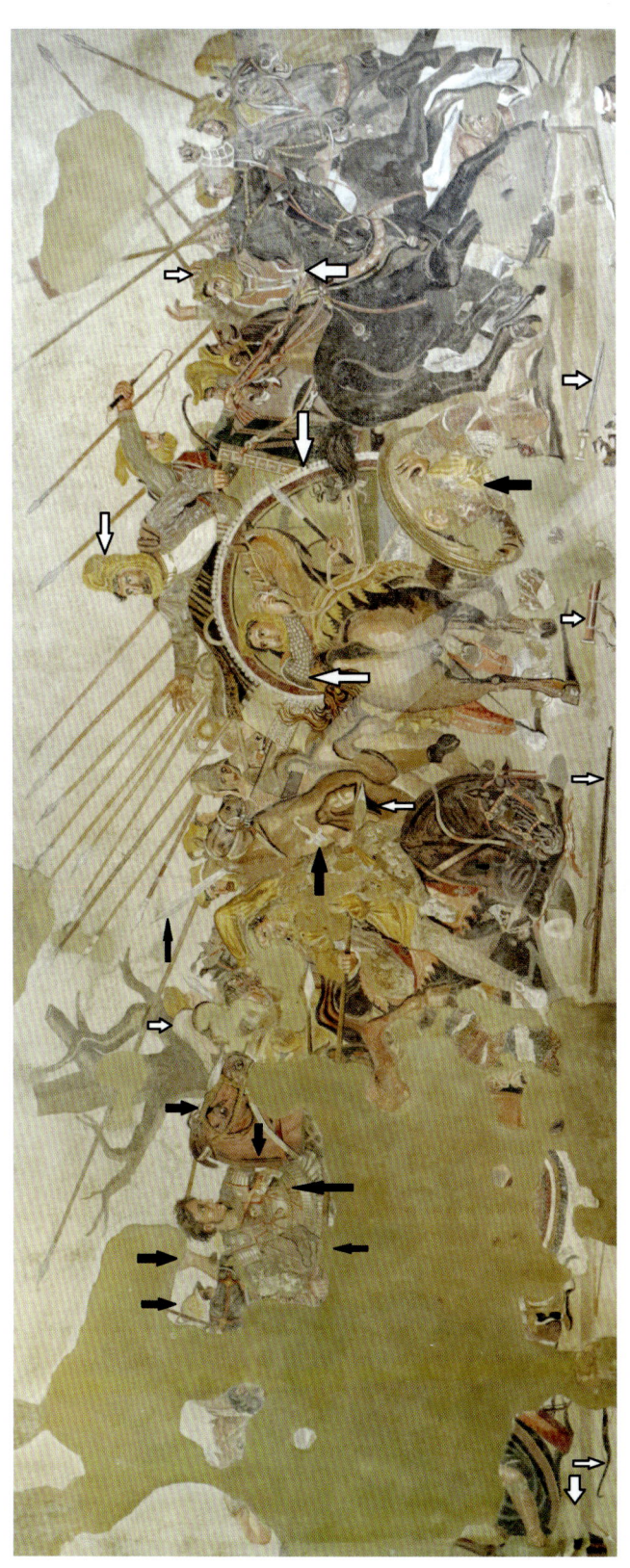

The mosaic from Pompeii shows a confrontation between Alexander and Darius and is supposedly a snapshot of the Battle of Issus, or of Gaugamela. Important details are annotated with arrows, with a full explanation for each given in the List of Plates. (*Courtesy of Brigadier General B. Papathanasiou, Hellenic Army-Ret*)

Greek shields of line infantry at the age of Alexander III. Compared to the Argive *hoplon* shield (C–D) the Macedonian (front (A) and back (B) views) buckler has a baldric for hanging from the shoulder; it is shallower and rimless (thus occasionally called *pelte*, and in this case the armband or *porpax* is off from the centre. Front (C) and back (D) views of the Argive *hoplon* shield of the southern Greek allies and mercenaries outfitted as hoplites. The armband or *porpax* is a bit off, as it should be placed squarely on the diameter, to allow optimal coverage. The handle *antilabe* is also seen, along with the inner aspect of the rim and the internal suspension cord for carrying the shield hanging at the back and packing stores in it. (*Courtesy of Brigadier General B. Papathanasiou, Hellenic Army-Ret*)

(A) The underhand use of the *xyston*. The prominent butt point plus the moderate length identify the weapon. The helmet is a crested version of the standard-issue *konos*. (B) A popular interpretation of the Macedonian Phalanx shows the bucklers hanging like talismans, from the neck and the arms extending, uncovered, around the bucklers' rims to brandish the *sarissa* pike to waist or chest level. (C) The fresco of the very renowned Macedonian tomb of Lyson and Callicles shows different painted items of weaponry. (D) The Mycenaean line infantry use body shields hanging from shoulder straps and handle their *egxeia* pikes with both hands to shoulder level. (*Courtesy of Brigadier General B. Papathanasiou, Hellenic Army-Ret*)

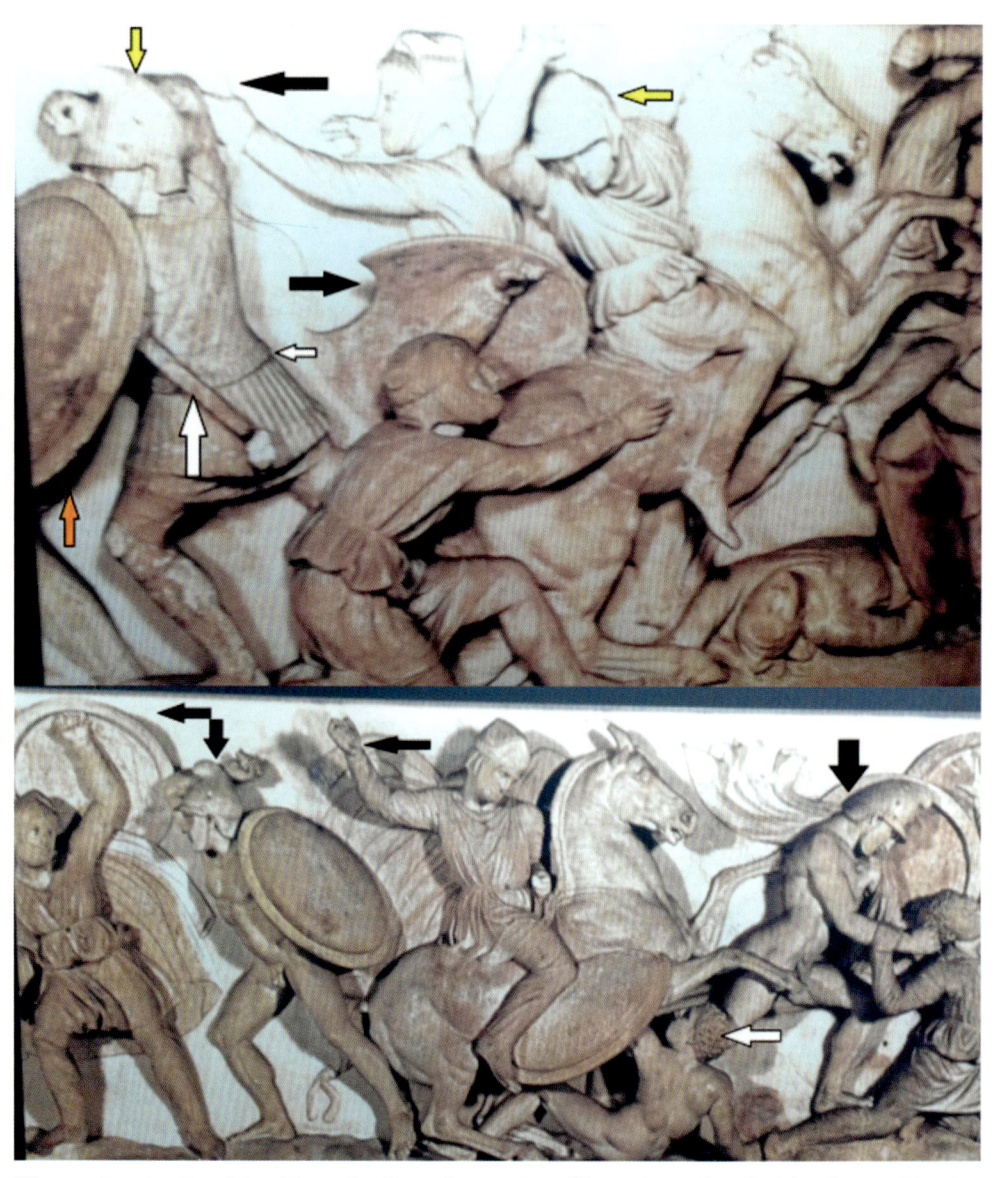

The varying details of the Alexander Sarcophagus show Hypaspists, identified by the combination of Argive shields plus Phrygian helmets. They are presented both in nudity, for mobile missions, and with body armor with flaps and obviously flexible materials, with or without metal inserts between the layers of the leather or the fabric. The difference in armor may reflect different chiliarchies, or missions. The Macedonian cavalry are Companions with Boeotian helmets, while Alexander has the signature one recreating the lion's head insinuating Hercules' lion skin. Oriental infantry can be seen using Argive shields, implying *kardaka* hoplites, and scalloped shields, definitely *takabara* plus the Persian headgear. Greek cavalry brandish, according to the position of the arm, shafted weapons or sidearms, the latter possibly including *kopis* sabres. The fallen hoplite under an Achaemenid cavalryman may be a Hypaspist operating as *hamippos*, trying to disembowel the enemy mount. (*Courtesy of Brigadier General B. Papathanasiou, Hellenic Army-Ret*)

Greek *kopis* sabre reconstructed to the right along with *pelte* crescent moon shield, typical for Thracian troops of the fourth century and signature of peltasts. The spear is most probably the Persian infantry model, with spherical butt, while there are two axes, a Scythian-type straight one (*sagaris*) and a conventional *pelekys* possibly used by Persian infantry, especially veterans, as a CQB item. (*Courtesy of Brigadier General B. Papathanasiou, Hellenic Army-Ret*)

The reconstruction (A) refers to the linothorax of Alexander, enhanced with metal foils, interpreting the famous mosaic. The cuirass of Callicles (B) interprets the fresco from the Tomb of Lyson and Callicles, in here made by leather and reinforced in select areas. The cuirass of Vergina (C) is represented as a composite design, formed to the lines of usual linothorax but containing metal plates sandwiched between the layers of fabric. (*The recreated cuirasses, displayed at the Museum of Ancient Greek Technology in Athens, were created by the professional armourer D. Katsikis (www.hellenicarmors.gr) and photographed by D. Karvountzis*)

Native infantry of the larger Macedonian Kingdom. They sport different types of helmet, the one on the top left being a later, more exquisite model of the Phrygian lineage. The small buckler has no rim and is tidy to allow the left hand to support the pike at the assault position (bottom left), the length of which and its small penetrating warhead are well-attested at the standing position (right). (*Re-enactment photographs courtesy of Koryvantes Association of Historical Studies*)

The plain attire of this hoplite showing conical Laconian *pilos* helmet, argive *hoplon* shield, spear and sidearm, probably a *kopis*-type sabre. This would be the standard attire for mercenary hoplites fighting both for and against Alexander. (*Re-enactment photograph courtesy of Koryvantes Association of Historical Studies*)

strongly fortified, only in 499 BC threatened by the Greeks due to the surprise of the eruption of the ionic Revolt. It had to be conquered at once, as the shock of the victory and the physical extermination of most of the Achaemenid leadership of Asia Minor would at some point ebb. It was the position, as it controlled the crossroads to western Asia Minor and the western end of the King's Road. It was the prestige, the seat of the King when venturing at the West or any assigned *karana*. It was the money, the treasury of western Asia Minor (Arr Anab I.17,3). Such funds would make less mercenaries available to the King of Kings, and would definitely take care of Alexander's needs of cash – especially for the sustainment of the allied fleet.

This meant the detachment of a huge area, five times as large as Greece (for the pacification of which Philip II needed some 20 years) from Persia. A vast area, with many cities and relatively few Greeks and other peoples who were really hostile to the Persians. It was the hostility of the locals that was instrumental for the success of Alexander; it had brought Agesilaus' failure. The spontaneous surrender of the keeper, Mithrenes, a Persian, for unknown reasons (Arr Anab I.17,3) resulted in special honours paid by Alexander to Mithrenes for life, although he was a Persian aristocrat who changed liege, nothing more. By having the funds and the position of Sardis, Alexander could spare the locals. He continued taxation but let them do as they please in every other case, with special care to their traditions (Arr Anab I.17,4). He even conscripted Lydian youths, a very sensitive issue in their *psyche* as the nation had been denied proper training in arms as a deliberate demilitarization and effemination policy was put in place by Cyrus the Great to discourage future risings (Her I.155,4). It was a policy of resounding success, as the Lydians did not side with the revolted Greeks in 499 BC, but with the Imperials ever since, and never revolted. They did provide troops for Xerxes, and for the suppression of the Ionic revolt (Kambouris 2022a,b,c) but their bellicosity was a thing of the past.

Additionally, it is evident that the coastal cities of the Northwest needed no action to align with the invader. After all, they had been under Philip's control for a couple of years and social realities had no time to change since Memnon's *Reconquista*. Alexander wanted to align all populations against the Achaemenid rule, and his benevolence, natural as it was, became a realistic policy option by the treasure of Sardis, and allowed a nice play. He would make the Imperials become the villain and alienate themselves even from loyal subjects.

The importance of the coasts, ports and other areas of amphibious operations and the whole planning of Alexander for the denial of such moves to the Persians are a whole chapter of multi-domain/cross-domain warfare. It must be emphasized that, coming from a continental empire and knowing the meaning of the in-depth operations, Alexander attached great importance to the occupation, stable occupation and securing not only of the coasts, but also of the hinterland. This persistence of his was to bear fruit in all the cases in which rival detachments would attempt to retaliate. Unlike the classical Greek armies (especially invading armies), the Macedonians did not feel uncomfortable when they left the coast. Theirs was a land force, not an amphibious force and felt perfectly comfortable far from the coast; even safe.

From Sardis Alexander went to the coast (**Map 4**); the carefree excursion of his secondary detachments that roamed southwards was over, and there were important assets in the coastline, where the action was to develop; the Achaemenids had lost one army, but had a fleet and a very good general. Memnon was appointed *karana* (Arr Anab I.20,3), the previous C-in-C (*spadapatish*), Arsites, who survived Granicus, was decent enough to commit suicide (Arr Anab I.16,3) to avoid the disgrace of Tissaphernes (Xen Hell III.4, 25). Memnon assumed control and would try to salvage the assets needed to fully exploit the one arm he would have at his disposal, the fleet.

Halicarnassus, Miletus and other coastal cities, especially the major centres to the southern edge of the bridgehead of Parmenio and Attalus (Ephesus), were adequately garrisoned by natives and mercenary Greeks, possibly satrapal contractors. Persians are not explicitly reported, nor other Asiatics, permanently transplanted or transferred but for Halicarnassus (Arr Anab I.20,2). Ephesus, as it was previously held by the Macedonians, had a pro-Macedonian faction that sprang to action and exacted terrible revenge (Arr Anab I.17,11–12), obviously after some years of bloody retributions from the pro-Achaemenid faction (Arr Anab I.17,11). This was very Greek and totally justified, but Alexander thought it would be even more productive if he discouraged the infinite continuation of the atrocities or the mass extermination of the opposing factions. By showing leniency there would be room for reaching understandings in other cities – a most wise decision as in this way the factions were not pushed to fight for the Imperials. A carrot-and-stick policy at its best: the pacifier of Greece and the destroyer of Thebes, with his siege engineers and the fame of dashing action, faced little opposition.

Miletus had not been included in the bridgehead and was well-guarded and with an excellent set of port facilities, the ideal base for the Achaemenid fleet. Memnon wanted to make it the apex of his operations, but Alexander found a use for the allied fleet for the first and last time. It arrived first (Arr Anab I.18,4), blockaded the city and, due to its advantageous position and the support of the army from the land, intercepted the approach of the Achaemenid navy, which entered the theatre a few days later and cast anchor across the bay (Arr Anab I.18,5).

Alexander's reputation was true, and vindicated. His speed had given him the possession of the two-thirds of the coastline before the Persian navy even appeared in the theatre. The Macedonian cavalry raids from the mainland to the nearby coasts forced the Imperials to cast anchor at some distance, at the island of Samos, to gain access to water and provisions (Arr Anab I.19,8), and thus could not interfere with siege operations. The city fell with some fuss but in an exemplary assault with the aid of Alexander's siege engines, giving a chance to the siege equipment of the Macedonian army, probably conveyed in the ships of the allied fleet, to increase the uncertainty of loyalist cities. The assault of the Macedonian infantry with Alexander at its apex carried everything before it, with some support from naval infantry (Arr Anab I.19,2–3). The resilient Greek mercenaries of the garrison who were swimming on their shields (Arr Anab I.19,4.) to escape the fate of the survivors from Granicus (Arr Anab I.16,6) were also offered quarters and employment (Arr Anab I.19,6), which would sap the determination and resilience of their ilk in Achaemenid service. No desperate courage any more, not to mention the updates in intelligence from their debriefing regarding the whereabouts and resources, if not intentions also, of Memnon (Russell 1999; Engels 1980a).

The next step, Memnon's main base, was Halicarnassus. With a chequered history and being some years earlier a principality semi-autonomous if not totally autonomous under the despot Pixodarus (340–334 BC) who had made away with Queen Ada, his sister, (Arr Anab I.23,7), the city was now a reliable Achaemenid asset as it was by royal mandate under the control of Orontobates, a Persian, who was married to the family of Pixodarus (Arr Anab I.23,8); and a very important asset. It was the entrance into the Aegean for fleets raised in the south. With Miletus gone, it was the only suitable base and Herodotus' silence, as he was a national, implies that Halicarnassus played some important role in the operational scheme of the imperial navy sent to suppress the Ionian revolt in 494 BC (Her VI.6). Without Halicarnassus there would have been no such campaign.

Alexander had declined a seafight outside Miletus. It was a brilliant opportunity to wipe out the Persian forces in theatre and conquer Asia Minor unopposed. But, contrary to his usual rashness, he proved a general, not a hero (Fuller 1958). He declined as he lacked the capabilities to bring a favourable outcome (Arr Anab I.18,8–9). He had no experience, nor numbers; his captains were the best, but not the most reliable. There is no issue of Phoenician superiority over Athenian seamen, but the numbers of 160 versus 400 were a grim reality. Fighting a boarders' fight meant his army would be decimated in defeat. Fighting a ramming fight meant he could lose to enemy numbers and give them a satisfaction. He prudently and politely denied the offer and kept doing so for the next years but for the direst need. He actually decommissioned the allied fleet then and there (Arr Anab I.20,1).

With no fleet Alexander accepted the risk of a massive amphibious assault of the Achaemenid navy at Miletus, which could undo his work. The lack of supplies, the time that was ticking against the naval arm due to the end of the sailing season and his thrust towards Halicarnassus persuaded the Imperial fleet to retire to defend their base. Alexander invested and besieged it; hemmed there to support and protect it, the Persian fleet would do no damage to his rear in mainland Greece, the Aegean or the Straits.

Orontobates was the head of the city and satrap or regent of Caria, son-in-law of Pixodarus, the somewhat rebellious late dynast who had serious dealings with Philip II (Plut Alex 10,1–2). Together with Memnon, the *karana*, they had concentrated not only mercenaries but also Persians to beef up their defences (Arr Anab I.20,3); the only city garrison in the coast explicitly mentioned to have included Persian troops. The city was very strong as a position, with three fortress-citadels. The circuit was rather easy work for the Macedonian siegecraft, thus the defenders, greatly enhanced by the crews of the fleet (Arr Anab I.20,3), who amounted to 80,000 for 400 triremes, more for other types of vessels, and some part of loyal citizenry tried to dispute the approaches and, when defeated on the field (Arr Anab I.20,4) they reverted to trying to incinerate the deployed siege equipment by surprise attacks and sorties by elite units, with feints and diversions (Arr Anab I.20,9 & 22,1–2). They had some spectacular successes, but little effect overall (Arr Anab I.21,5; Diod XVII.25,6 & 26,3).

It is possible that the most part of the non-combatants had left the city before its investment, at least to save supplies. The stockpiling of the latter means that Alexander's success in arriving there first and establishing a siege camp would have been anticipated by the local Achaemenid High Command, probably before Memnon took command (Panovski & Sarakinski 2011). The citizenry could have assisted as both fighting and support personnel, and once the outcome seemed inescapable they were evacuated by the Achaemenid navy to the island of Cos (Diod XVII.27,5; Arr Anab II.5,7). The failed sorties depleted the garrison (Arr Anab I.23,1) and being hemmed in Halicarnassus the navy could not execute the plan of Memnon for a strategic counterattack at the rear of the Macedonians. Both antagonists decided to disengage: Memnon took his fleet to fight elsewhere and Alexander did the same; they both left proxies, the former select troops to garrison the fortresses (Arr Anab I.23,3) and to explore any opportunities, and the latter troops to invest the fortresses (Arr Anab I.23,6).

The naval dimension

Both the Persians and the Greeks (all the Greeks) remembered that Agesilaus' demise was due to the instigation of an anti-Spartan front, actually a coalition in mainland Greece that resulted in the Corinthian War and culminated in the loss of Spartan naval dominance (Xen Hell IV.3,10). Alexander, therefore, tried not to suffer the same. The political and military situation he left at his rear was more stable. Antipater, his Regent in Macedon, had troops sufficient in number, quality and force structure (Diod XVII.17,5) to an extent the Spartans never had.

Macedon's location and its new borders made it basically invulnerable to amphibious attack. Throughout the campaign Macedon was under no threat from the Achaemenid navy; once the coastal cities were not allied or friendly, but integrated parts of the realm, no enemy amphibious force could establish a bridgehead to cause anything but fuss with some raiding and devastation. Invasions needed bases and supplies, and the structure of the Macedonian state allowed neither. Beyond the borders, the system of international alliances was solid. In the land sector, the stable occupation of the Isthmus by the Macedonians meant that even if Sparta and Athens were to align, they could not unite, while the Macedonians had the gate of the Peloponnese open. The destruction of Thebes meant that there was only one notable city north of the Isthmus, Athens; a neighbour of Thebes, the plight of which would encourage Athens to think seriously before making any hasty moves. Thus the West-Southwest border of Macedon was secure. Its direct proximity to the Achaemenid empire meant that the flow of supplies, reinforcements and communications were very difficult to sever by diplomacy and diversion; campaigns were needed, but, as mentioned, the home guard was powerful and up to the task. Armies, not detachments, were needed.

The Aegean was the soft belly of the Macedonians. On the other hand, with sufficient depth to the mainland of Asia Minor, even if the Hellespont and the Aegean were lost, only the rapid flow of reinforcements and the communications were endangered. Supplies would come from the Asia Minor possessions, while there were also the itineraries from Macedon through Thrace to Byzantium and Propontis and then to Asia Minor. Not safe, not short, but they were there, difficult to interfere with.

Therefore, Alexander sought to neutralize, first of all, the Persian navy, the only intact arm of the enemy. Since he had decided not to fight, an indirect approach was needed. After conquering Miletus, and thus confining the Achaemenids to Halicarnassus, he decided to save the huge expenses his fleet cost by disbanding it (Arr Anab I.20,1), and also to deny the enemy a target and a possible victory, which would be extremely important in the psychological and propaganda plane.

By dissolving his fleet, Alexander did not give the Persians the opportunity to acquire naval dominance. In no case, however, did Alexander dismantle his naval arm. He simply dispersed it, safeguarded it and left the responsibility of its maintenance to the other allies by deactivating it. Few ships were kept, while most were sent back to Greece, where their maintenance would be the responsibility of the allied cities that owned them. At the same time, in this way it was ready to deploy to points where it would be needed to counter Memnon's naval offensive, although the concept was not very responsive; the readiness level was to be dismal. The existence of small allied naval detachments-to-be in the western and northern Aegean simply meant that the Persians could not launch the major strategically important attacks they had planned, without securing safe and adequate basing facilities.

The one reverse with the disbanding of the navy so as not to present a target, was that the siege equipment had to be transported by land, making dashing advances a difficult proposition. Security and escort details would be needed from this time on, and also relatively comfortable roads, enlarging the footprint of the army and either restricting its mobility or degrading its cohesion and compactness; or even reducing its overall effectiveness, as would be painfully obvious during the winter campaigning of 334–3 BC in Lycia, Pamphylia and Pisidia.

Even for small-scale operations, the Achaemenid fleet had to operate in a centralized manner, coordinated if not concentrated, to be able to fend off possible sea guerilla operations by the dispersed divisions of the allied navy. Many vessels of the latter would have been decommissioned, but others not. This created a huge problem of uncertainty and need for naval intelligence, both of which would slow the tempo and drain the war chest of Memnon. The efficiency would be greatly diminished and the logistics complicated. The sheer size of the Persian navy made it impossible for some logistics functions to occur without large nearby bases, and plentiful supplies. The Persian Naval High Command became more enterprising after the death of Memnon and executed deep movements with small squadrons (Parpas 2013; Ruzicka 1988). This led to important reverses, since the latter were similar in size to allied squadrons, more or less. For example a small squadron was taken by surprise in Siphnos and was all but eliminated (Arr Anab II,5).

The existence of an allied navy in dispersion put heart and sinew into the coastal cities and islands (Parpas 2013; Ruzicka 1988) not to side with their previous tormentors and masters of decades past (Arr Anab II.2,3); a choice inescapable should the allied navy have been defeated in a major engagement. In such a case these cities would have had no choice but to surrender immediately. Their resistance led to prolonged sieges to secure the required bases, resulting in the procrastination and wear and tear of the Persian fleet in its effort to wrest naval dominance.

The first aspect was the story of the ensuing possible naval battle. The time of Alexander had seen quadriremes and quinqiremes built in large numbers, vessels much larger than the triremes, with four and five rowers respectively in every file instead of three. Prior to their appearance, much of the tactics had reverted to boarding engagements, after the ramming spree in Salamis in 480 BC (Aesc Persai 279–81). Ramming could take out a gallant boarding party without giving them an opportunity to engage. Afterwards the Athenians advanced this kind of naval manoeuvring into real art. But as early as 413 BC, tactics reverted. Under certain conditions, the boarding battle overturned the Athenian propulsive superiority (a lesson that the Romans fully assimilated) and the new, larger and heavier ships were much harder to sink by ramming, due to their solid construction. Accommodating more infantry and being more stable, they allowed even better use of missile troops, including catapults with their crews. We know precious little about naval tactics in the time of Alexander, but it is clear that naval battles did take place by boarding (Arr Anab I.19,11). This kind of battle left little room for manoeuvring and in the open sea gave a huge advantage to the side with numerical superiority. This is a bit complicated, by default. Superiority in the number of ships, or the size of the boarders' group or the total number of boarders available to a fleet were producing different combinations of prospects, liabilities and advantages that allowed various tactical brains of the time to set rules of engagement and develop their art.

Alexander, a brilliant tactician, knew that things were tragically simple. In the open sea he enjoyed no advantage. In Miletus, the straits between the shoreline of the city and Lade island (perhaps the very position of the rebel fleet in 494 BC) allowed his ships to face the Persians on equal footing (Arr Anab I.19,3), but this could not play out in the open sea. Moreover, although there is no reason to consider the Achaemenid Cypriot and Phoenician crews any better than the allied ones, it was true that the allied fleet was heterogeneous, had not been trained together to reach the performance standards of the Macedonian forces, nor had any training that would have allowed it to build cohesion and coordination. Furthermore, its assets in many cases were politically unreliable, as were the Athenians, and/or lacking in discipline compared with the Macedonian land forces. But it would be these Macedonian land forces who would provide missile fire in many capacities (interceptive, direct support, incendiary) and elite infantry, including the Hypaspists (Arr Anab II.20,4) for the actual boarding fight, that would have to attune and coordinate with such seamen and crews of the Allies.

Alexander was reluctant to risk dozens of his best fighters in literally every turn of an allied helmsman, whose value he did not know (as opposed to the value of ALL his officers and troopers). Here, it must be emphasized that it was not the complete and utter lack of Macedonian seamanship that advised for large boarding parties; as mentioned before, it was the naval tactics of the time, most probably. The Persian fleet had a huge number of boarders, especially Greek mercenaries – whom Darius recalled before the Battle of Issus to use them on land. This means, in absolute and relative terms, a very large number of men. And the Tyrians, when they sailed to fight against Alexander's hastily assembled fleet before they realized that he enjoyed a decisive numerical advantage of 2.5:1 also had their ships outfitted with large numbers of boarders.

After Miletus, Alexander had to cope with the city and harbour of Halicarnassus, the ancient capital of Caria, residence of the regent and the only remaining naval base for the Achaemenid fleet on the Asian shore of the Aegean. Taking this city was a quantum leap. Excellently fortified, with three citadels, some years previously it had been the seat of the local dynast Pixodarus (Arr Anab I.23,7), now succeeded by a Persian regent, Orontobates, his son-in-law, (Arr Anab I.23,8). To keep appearances the widow and sister of the previous dynast Hidrieus (Arr Anab I.23,7), the 'queen' Ada, originally deposed by her younger brother Pixodarus, was not apprehended but lived in relative isolation and relative luxury if in public obscurity (Arr Anab I.23,8). The title 'Queen' was not vainglorious: Artemisia was queen in 480s and the Persian emperor was for good reason called the King of Kings (Shah-an-Shah). Other kings, of conquered states and nations, were his *bandaka* (subjects) but occasionally retained their titles and remained Kings.

Thus the conduct of a siege by Alexander was politically sensitive. He could not level the city that represented the recently aggrandized Carian state. He should not leave it under Achaemenid rule; it was a matter of symbols, prestige and of relations and relationships. Carians were fighting for Darius; their current dynasty had been instrumental in suppressing the Cypriot insurgency that followed the revolt of Sidon between 351–344 BC (Parpas 2013) and a large garrison in Celaenae was mostly provided by them (Arr Anab I.29,1). Many Carians had relatives in the capital, they could not remain hostages in the hands of the Imperials. And it was the dimension of military strategy, pure and simple: a thorn in his side, and a base for a meddlesome if not dangerous fleet. Memnon had retrieved most troops from other city garrisons to turn Halicarnassus into a tough nut to crack.

These conditions may account for what is considered the worst conduct of a siege operation in Alexander's career (Ashley 1998). The classical view, on the other hand, does not share this opinion and in cases such as the loss of two opportunities to storm the city attributes the proceedings to Alexander's wish not to conquer the city by assault (Arr Anab I.22,7), which would mean great casualties for its civilian population and a public relations disaster, showing that he treated the city as an enemy. Alexander, after the destruction of Thebes, wanted to avoid razing one more great and ancient urban centre affiliated with an extended area that could willingly participate in the crusade against the Achaemenids, with troops but mostly with capital. He let the Achaemenids take the blame. Memnon evacuated the citizens to Cos, the island just across a swath of sea, and tried to burn the city. Alexander attacked just in time to curtail the fire. The proceedings are a bit hazy; he took no revenge on the remaining, non-evacuated citizens who had assisted the Persians, even passively, or at least the ones who had not been arrested while torching the city. And then, Arrian says he destroyed and razed it to the ground, something logical if the city had been evacuated. In this context the Persians evacuated the city, deported the population and torched the city. Alexander just made sure there would be nothing for the Persians to reconquer, and left them to their fortresses. The problem is that this story is not convincing: the historic Halicarnassus, with its marvels, most probably was not razed to oblivion just then.

Also, the classical view holds that the investment by Alexander of the three fortress-citadels, after the fall of the main city, which remained under Achaemenid control (Panovski & Sarakinski 2011), was a clear case of economy of power and precious time, time essential to conquer as much of Asia Minor as possible before the depleted garrisons were manned again by royal or local recruits; not a token of military inadequacy and failure, as is the opposite view (Ashley 1998). But there is another possible aspect. Alexander occupied the port and the residential sector of the city. This fact completely neutralized it as a large naval base, as there was no place to service the vessels, nor the possibility to bring in and load supplies, not in any scale needed for such a navy. Although they had the three fortresses in their possession, the Persians could not dock a large fleet and maintain it, let alone use the city as a base for naval and amphibious operations. If the Persians wanted to storm the city from the sea, with a massive amphibious assault – a prerequisite to using it as a major naval base – they would have to undergo the same hardships as if they had not retained their presence in said fortresses. These were supposed to control and protect the city and its harbour; not to facilitate the storming of the city by invaders. They were to be the last places to fall, not the first, to create a path for ingress. Therefore, Alexander, who controlled the city, basically had no reason to waste time, lives and effort on the fortresses. This would probably have been the wish of the Persians, to slow and wear him down.

On the contrary, the three fortresses in Persian hands were a liability for the Imperials. They had to keep replenishing them with supplies the fleet itself had difficulty in obtaining; thus Alexander indirectly reduced the mobility and increased the wear and tear of the Persian fleet. Moreover, with the progress in the hinterland, in a winter campaign, Alexander made any possible reverse in the coast inconsequential. His communications in Asia Minor would pass through the interior and any losses in the coast would not compromise them, as the troops assigned to the fleet were insufficient for major campaigns inland, to penetrate deep and maintain the conquest, as the history of the Greek incursions against the Empire amply showed.

The Persian fleet in the eastern Aegean could not have any strategic effect, even in full force. Its ultimate targets would be mainland Greece and the Straits. The first target, however, was defended by the squadrons of the disbanded allied fleet that had returned home. The second seemed more vulnerable and also vital, the more so as the campaign progressed. It did have a standing guard of Macedonian and allied ships; a token force, but to sever the lines of communication and cut off the Macedonian expeditionary force, semi-permanent occupation of forts, cities and strongholds in the region, were essential in order to exclude or repel a Macedonian countermove. Halicarnassus was not available as a large base. Memnon's option was to occupy a number of Greek islands, preferably of some size and safe from Macedonian field armies; from there he would entice reinforcements, if not sedition in Greece. The reinforcements from anti-Macedonian factions could reach a level adequate for a campaign in the straits, even if his own force was not enough for any credible threat in Macedon directly or indirectly, through mainland Greece,

Memnon, besieging Mytilene (Arr Anab II.1,2), was trying to achieve just that, but the whole project was clearly beyond the capabilities of the Persian fleet in terms of numbers of men and force structure. With up to forty boarders per vessel (Kambouris 2022) there were 16,000 troops with the fleet, half the army of Alexander. But these had limited mobility in every sense other than on deck. They had no cavalry, no wagons for siege equipment to be brought inland. They were a coastal raiding force, nothing more.

Inland advance

With this in mind, Alexander moved in two directions from Halicarnassus and without having totally pacified Caria, where pockets of resistance, in strong and fortified cities answered to Orontobates, perched in the citadels of Halicarnassus (Arr Anab II.5,7). He sent, after the fall of the city of Halicarnassus, his newlywed troops back, to winter with their spouses and raise new recruits from Macedon and mercenaries from Greece (Arr Anab I.24,1–2), obviously with the funds from the vault of Sardis. The rest of the army remained assembled and gained a whole campaigning period in terms of time; a winter campaign. Alexander wanted to settle the geostrategic issues with the occupation of the plateau of Asia Minor.

He himself followed the coastal road, first to Lycia (partly annexed by Caria during the reign of Pixodarus (Arr Anab I.24,5)) and Pamphylia, to lock the usual entry of the Persian fleet into the Aegean. It is a masterstroke of indirect approach, to counter the enemy fleet from the land, by depriving it of bases, friendly shores in general and harbours (Arr Anab I.24,3). In order to enter or exit the Aegean, the Persian fleet had to sail directly to the Levantine coast (Syria-Phoenicia), a gruelling journey that exhausts crews and supplies (especially water) and wears out the ships. The further he could extend his coastal occupation zone, the less available such facilities became for the Persian fleet.

Simultaneously Alexander dispatched to Sardis (present-day Salihli), obviously by the main road followed by Daurices in 498 BC in the opposite way, the heavy and allied forces, under Parmenio, and ordered them from there to invade Phrygia to the east at a set time, possibly arranging for a rendezvous at Gordium (Arr Anab I.24,3), near present-day Polatli, where he was planning to arrive from the south, moving from present-day Antalya (Attaleia) in Pamphylia to Celaenae (present-day Dinar) and from there to Gordium (**Map 4**). This put him squarely on the northern major East-West axis in Asia Minor, roughly Ergili/Dascylium – EskiSehir/ Dorylaeum – Polatli/Gordium – Ankara – Sebasteia – Erzurum – Yerevan/Erebuni – Tabriz/Tauris and from there either to Hamadan/Ecbatana or to Tehran/Rhages (dotted line in **Map 5**). This saved time by simultaneous, converging approaches from different axes, which also covers more ground. He acted similarly after the Granicus by sending three detachments in three directions (to Dascylium, Sardis and the Troad) and he did it here as well, covering a lot of space in a short period of time, increasing the opponent's uncertainty and adapting the type of his forces to the ground. A payback to Xerxes who must have taught the idea to the Greeks (Kambouris 2022b).

His detachment was insufficient for serious operations and meant to take advantage of the power vacuum caused by the Battle of the Granicus and the successful extermination of most of the Persian garrisons on the coast. His winter campaign, at a time when the typical Greek armies were rushing home, took the Persians unawares. The Achaemenid army never conducted extensive operations and strategic concentration in the winter, and the navy was retreating to safe bases. Initially, Alexander moved to Lycia, after occupying the last forts and cities of Caria to the Southwest, on the axis of advance. Alexander enjoyed a healthy stroll to Lycia, which was mostly empty of any Imperial garrisons and reached the river Xanthus, while subjugating the area of Mylias, which was mountainous. He also secured the area of Phasilis from Pisidian incursions (Arr Anab I.24,6) and then invaded Pamphylia by two routes: a detachment moved by the mainland road, ascending from the west of Mount Climax, as his engineers cut a road through the mountain – or rather widened the existing one – and reached the bay of Pamphylia and the city of Perga (Arr Anab I.26,1). Another force, under Alexander followed the precipitous coastal road, almost half-submerged at that time of year. Alexander's good fortune saw to a change in the wind so the road became accessible and the sea receded so as to have the army through to Perga (Arr Anab I.26,2) fairly close to later Attaleia (modern day Antalya) (**Map 4**).

This was a hub, with a road to the north, to the heart of Asia Minor through Celaenae. Alexander first moved east of Perga, until he met the sheer face of Mt Taurus (the border of Cilicia and Pamphylia), subjugating all the cities and strongholds east of Perga and west of Taurus (Arr Anab I.26,2–27,5) and then recoiled to Perga, to ascend to the north, in order to secure the central plateau of Asia Minor (**Map 4**).

Although Alexander was in no immediate danger from Memnon and his fleet, he did not enjoy the possibility of chaos and insurgency at his rear. If he could venture near the sea, not so near as to be himself really exposed and susceptible, but enough to entice Darius to recall his fleet for such tactical and operational use to the defence of Asia, he could relax the pressure to his rear and possibly defeat the Persian navy on the land, in a land battle.

Alexander understood that the southern route was not suitable for any invasion army; any Achaemenid army venturing to wrest Asia Minor from his control could not flow through Pamphylia and Lycia to Caria. Nor could it follow the coastal northern route (roughly running from Ecbatana/Hamadan – Tauris/Tabriz – Erebuni/Yerevan – Erzurum – Trabzon/Trebizond – Samsun – Dascylium/Erigli) along the Euxine (**Map 5**), as had the 10,000 of Xenophon. There was no navy there, a major Persian asset. The game was focused on the two central East-West axes: the northern, through Gordium and Pteria, followed by the Lydians and the Medes during their conflict, and the southern, the Royal Road, through Celaenae and Cilicia.

As it was, he expected that his approach from the south, while Parmenio would move from the west (**Map 4**), from Sardis (Arr Anab I.24,3) would throw off balance any possible Achaemenid forces assembled to intercept. True, there were not many Imperials, but Alexander did not know that for sure. After all, there were the locals, who might have felt like being loyalists.

The area that Alexander entered to the north of Perga was Pisidia, with fortified strongholds, precipitous mountain passages, and a detestation for rule and lieges. Because Alexander had attacked some of their countrymen on behalf of Phasilis (Arr Anab I.24,6) the Pisidians were aroused and Alexander had to eagerly engage in the storming of strong positions without siege equipment (Arr Anab I.24,4 & 26,5 & 28,8), as that was left in Sardis, but with the help of some locals whose city had been long at loggerheads with its neighbours (Arr Anab I.28,1). By defeating the locals in open battle he secured a carefree passage, but nothing else. Other fortified cities he passed by, unable to properly besiege them, (Arr Anab I.28,2) as he had done occasionally in Pamphylia as well (Arr Anab I.26,5).

Entering Phrygia he reached Celaenae (**Map 4**), a major city in a commanding position, which was defended by a small guard, about 1,100 men; one tenth Greeks and the rest Carians (Arr Anab I.29,1). There the policy followed towards Caria paid dividends. They promised to surrender if reinforcements did not come from the satrap of Phrygia on the appointed time and thus kept their honour when they did surrender the city (Arr Anab I.29,2). Alexander did not have to attack an excellently fortified position while without his engines. The satrapal detachments did not appear, possibly due to the shock of the Granicus and the decapitation of the Achaemenid rural aristocracy; or because in mid-winter they did not expect an invasion and were stunned, possibly due to the invasion of Parmenio.

From Celaenae, Alexander moved to Gordium (Arr Anab I.29,3) that surrendered; it was the ancient capital of Phrygia. Now Alexander had interrupted the northern route, bifurcating to end in Propontis and Sardis. Alexander could now strike from Gordium to Ankara, Cilicia and the Euphrates; or from Ankara via Cappadocia and Armenia, along the northern road of Pteria, towards Ecbatana; or, by the road passing just north of Cilicia, to Tigris (**Map 5**). He held the central position. He rested his army in the area, waiting for the spring, his reinforcements and the absentees who were on leave (Arr Anab I.29,4) and tackled the Gordian knot, a huge propaganda boost (Arr Anab II.3,8) while his heavy formations under

Parmenio found him there (Arr Anab I.29,4). When, in early spring, the newlyweds arrived, headed by three (newlywed) generals, Meleager, Coenus and Ptolemy, a massive instalment of Macedonian infantry and cavalry and Thracian cavalry was at his disposal, plus mercenaries and allies (Arr Anab I.29,4).

The occupation of western Asia Minor brought into Alexander's hands huge resources to sustain his existing army and then some. His position was more stable than any general who had conducted operations in the last 150 years in Asia Minor. The Greek cities were safe. The dispatch of the newlyweds to Macedon was joyous for the families and the soldiers (Arr Anab I.24,1–2). The latter disseminated the news of Alexander's victories, their first-hand accounts being an excellent measure to keep the morale high, raise enthusiastic conscripts and volunteers, stabilize the home front, discourage southern dissention and in general promote the campaign. Moreover, such a move would have been interpreted by the Imperial High Command and local commanders alike as a safe indication for a winter lull in the operations, as standard. The cost of this error was two-thirds of Asia Minor. Alexander's PsyOps (psychological operations) and hybrid operations in all the affected domains proved highly effective.

After Gordium, Alexander, with his rested, reshuffled and possibly reorganized but definitely reinforced army went on the offensive in central Asia Minor. He went on following the northern central axis, invaded and/or accepted the surrender of Paphlagonia and Cappadocia (Arr Anab II.4,1–2) with relative ease as he trekked to Ankara; it was almost certain that these areas jockeyed for time and were less than sincere as they were to declare for Darius some months later. Their Armenian neighbours to the east did not trouble to negotiate, as Alexander turned sharp to the south, to the King's Road and Cilicia (Arr Anab II.4,3). Alexander avoided an invasion of Paphlagonia not only as standard policy when an area surrendered – so as to entice others to do the same (Anson 2015) – but not to be drawn too north, away from the probable site of action; this meant he did not visit and liberate from the Achaemenid yoke the Greek colonies of the southern Euxine, as was his duty by the provisions of the (second) League of Corinth.

Alexander seems to take every precaution to keep a central position, able to turn anywhere, including his rear. His assessments are simple: if Darius leads a massive host and he beats Darius, everything else is inconsequential. The same happens if he is defeated; all other efforts are in vain. The point is that Darius may *not* lead a royal host himself. He is known to delegate authority, he did that at the Granicus and this time he may appoint somebody of decent abilities. Even worse, maybe Darius is not to dispatch a royal host, but an expeditionary force under a commander who knows how to conduct manoeuvre and territorial warfare. This is the case of Memnon but also of Charidemus, the Athenian mercenary commander who proposed exactly that and then became arrogant, lost his life and the Achaemenid empire (Diod XVII.30, 2–5). His idea was for an expeditionary army of 100,000 (Diod XVII.30,3), thrice the size of the army of Alexander (Arr Anab I.11,3), under his personal command, to carry out territorial warfare.

Destination: Issus

Alexander's estimate is correct. Whether he is tipped off regarding Darius' mobilization and plans or not, we can draw no conclusion. But after roaming Asia Minor for months himself, he evidently has deliberated on his enemy's most probable course of action, once a royal host is the choice of said enemy, for a decisive battle. And he has decided that the game will be played in Cilicia. He knows that if Darius, leading a massive host, appears in the north, the newly subjugated areas, especially Cappadocia and Paphlagonia will change sides and rally under the achaemenid standards. But he reckons this will not happen. He believes that Darius will listen to the experienced mercenaries he has in his employment and will try to repeat the strategy of Artaxerxes II who defeated Agesilaus with an indirect approach: with a navy and attacks in his rear, in Greece (Xen Hell IV.2,1–8). Therefore, the Persians in the next campaigning period will continue to use their strong naval arm. This, in combination with the occupation of Lycia and Pamphylia by the Greco-Macedonian forces, means that the Persian fleet desperately needs Cilicia as an intermediate base. A most valuable area when sailing from Phoenicia to Aegean, as evident by the proceedings of Mardonius in 492 BC and Datis in 490 BC (Kambouris 2022a), with the loss of Lycia and Caria it became vital. And Darius will move his host preferably through the wide and comfortable Royal Road, which enters Cilicia by the straits in the eastern mountain range, the Amanus (the Gates of Amanus) and exits in the west, through the Cilician Gates in the range of Taurus. Alexander's uncertainty was over; he knew that from the six possible routes, Darius would follow the obvious, the Royal Road (dotted and dashed line in **Map 5**).

And so, pre-dating the maxims of Napoleon, namely to interfere with anything one's opponent does, Alexander descended from the general direction of Ankara and entered the mountain-locked plain of Cilicia with a lightning operation against the garrison of the Cilician Gates, without striking a blow, and reached Tarsus (**Map 4**), thus establishing presence in Cilicia first. As Xenophon said of Jason of Pherae, 'he conquered by speed'

(Xen Hell VI.4,21); Alexander, at this point, by dashness and reputation (Arr Anab II.4,4).

Cilicia was by nature a supersized fort and the only possible mainland station left in the Persian navy between the Levant and the Aegean. It is unclear why the Satrap Arsames decided to apply Memnon's advice for scorched earth policy (Arr Anab II.4,5); it was too little too late (Curt III.4,3). The occupied portion of Asia Minor probably made this policy ineffectual if there was no bigger plan to deprive Alexander from supplies brought through the Cilician Gates. One should remember that an important part of the Achaemenid fleet had set sail 'for Lycia' (Arr Anab II.2,1) *before* being recalled by Darius to land the mercenary Greeks serving as boarders to the Levant, so as to be used by the sovereign on land. Why was a sizeable squadron going to Lycia? Was it going *to* Lycia or *towards* Lycia? Could the destination be Pamphylia, to skirt the Taurus range all the way to the Cilician Gates to seal Alexander in a thoroughly devastated Cilicia? If this was the idea, it explains why the garrison at the Cilician Gates left (Arr Anab II.4,4); it could have been a bait to lure Alexander in, only to trap him in a devastated area, with the amphibious force sealing the Cilician Gates at his rear and Darius' army sealing the gates of Amanus and the Syrian Gates in front.

In any case, Alexander was at his best. His lightning speed brought him to Cilicia without a loss, allowed the swift conquest of a large footprint and many cities, and thwarted the plan of Arsames to devastate the area (Curt III.4,3); the area remained intact (Arr Anab II.4,6) and available for despoiling or commandeering. Such sparing of a city meant to be razed by its Imperial protector bought Alexander the goodwill of the locals.

The satrap took everything and everyone he had, especially local Persians but also loyalist natives and left, after a token resistance, to meet Darius' army outside Cilicia (Arr Anab II.4,6). This implies that Darius had been nearby or approaching and Alexander got wind (Just XI.3,1–2); this explains his sudden dash for Cilicia. It must be stressed that up to a point Alexander would not have any idea of the whereabouts of Darius as the King's location was kept secret by the Persians (Curt IV.6,5–6), at least before he set his insignia and royal splendour wherever he chose to. Alexander's rapid entry into the region, though, did not automatically bring him definite control of it. Extensive and long campaigns were needed, in contrast to the rather carefree though not leisurely roaming in central Asia Minor.

As the devastation or starvation plan did not play out well due to the speed of Alexander, Darius asked the fleet to disembark the mercenary troops to assist the land engagement he was contemplating (Arr Anab II.2,1).

Alexander, if he settled defensively in Cilicia, could keep Darius out and away from his fleet. He wedged himself between them and he himself had no supply problem as he could live off the land, and he had the supplies of the whole of Asia Minor. Darius' large host could not get to the sea virtually anywhere and could not remain in the field indefinitely; such a large army absorbed enormous quantities of food and fodder and also water; it would need to bring in supplies from further and further away.

If Darius, exasperated, decided to change the axis of his attack and transfer the operations to the north, either towards Iconium or Ankara, Alexander was swifter and he could intercept or flank him. Such smart manoeuvring is not incompatible with Alexander's character (**Maps 4–5**). He was dashing and daring but with some deliberation. As evident by his refusal to engage in naval battle off Miletus (Arr Anab I.18,9), he was not to be drawn by his temper to rash moves. After the entrapment plan – if there was one such – failed, the Imperials perhaps tried to keep footings in Cilicia either to facilitate the ingress of the royal host, or to prevent the army of Alexander from making sorties.

It is no coincidence that Darius was waiting for him at Sochi, located in Syria, two days walk from the Syrian Gates (Arr Anab II.6,1). The position allowed contact with the shoreline, from where the boarders of the fleet approached from the Aegean – actually they disembarked in Tripolis in today's Lebanon (Arr Anab II.13,3). This interpretation of the motive for the selection of Sochi stands if the common assumption, that Darius moved from Babylon to Sochi by the Middle Road, is correct. If he took the Lower Road (Monerie 2019), through Palmyra (dashed line in **Map 6**), it becomes evident that Sochi was selected due to its features but also due to being close to both exits from Cilicia, a central position.

Why Tripolis? Sidon was the foremost Phoenician city, especially under the Achaemenids, and this is more than obvious in Herodotus, where its King is the senior naval commander in the fleet council (Her VIII.67,2). But after the revolt of King Tennes in 351 BC, it was trusted no more. Savagely reconquered and subjugated, the prestigious status of the king's favourite was now bestowed upon Tyre, which was much to the south. Moreover, establishing the Persian administrative centre in a great city would burden it in many ways, would hurt the pride of the inhabitants, might have resulted in counter-productive high-handedness, such as the one that triggered the revolt in 351 BC (Parpas 2013) and would also expose the crucial staff and resources to the insurgents for an easy decapitation strike. Thus, the centre of operations was at the time the more cooperative Tripolis, to the north (**Map 6**).

Although Arrian is very clear that the fleet brought to Darius the Greek hoplites serving as boarders (Arr Anab II.13,3), this would – but for the native marines – denude it of its main weapon for the kind of campaign it had originally embarked upon. And the proceedings of the royal fleet after the Battle of Issus do not suggest, at least not with certainty, that they were not well-outfitted in terms of boarders. It is much more logical to suggest that the fleet took to Darius a fresh batch of mercenaries recruited from different places but especially from the mercenary market at Taenarum, near Sparta and transported to Asia, to join the royal army (or undertake some other task), in a standard mission to strategically move reinforcements to the theatre where the clash will be decisive.

The intended battlefield at Sochi was a nice wide plain, allowing deployment and cavalry manoeuvres (Arr Anab II. 7,3) – obviously a rationalization over the static deployment at the Granicus, where the Achaemenid cavalry could neither charge properly, nor manoeuvre, nor control the range of the engagement but fought statically in CQB conditions (Arr Anab I.15,4–5). The position also protected the approach of units coming from Egypt, as the ones following the satrap (Arr Anab II.11,8). Last but not least, it was positioned so as to allow responsive measures in case Alexander would opt to egress from the Gates of Amanus, as will become obvious. Thus, Darius held as central a position as he could, regarding the two exits from Cilicia, and over advantageous terrain.

Still, he was there partly intentionally, but also out of necessity. He cannot enter Cilicia. Alexander controls the Syrian Gates with the detachment of Parmenio, which is roughly half the army (Arr Anab II.5,1). Darius did not intend to assault Greeks positioned in the narrows; Thermopylae was too painful a lesson.

Darius knew full well that in strategic terms Alexander was immensely more mobile and manoeuvrable. To be able to adapt he had left (or dispatched) the War Chest and the heavy support items, including the Royal Household and the families of the nobles at Damascus (Arr Anab II.11,9). In true Achaemenid silence, he must have approached from an unexpected and short direction: the Lower Road (**Map 6**). Starting from Babylon he passed through today's Bagdad, crossed to Palmyra and from there reached Emesa (today's Homs). Once there, he sent his burdensome baggage train to Damascus, to the south, to establish an expeditionary capital adequate for governing the empire and befitting the Royal Dignity, while he himself continued with the army units and the most basic support elements to Sochi, to the north.

Darius probably was not concerned that Alexander would go out into the Syrian expanses. After all, he later tried to challenge him to leave the Cilician Gates and proceed to Sochi unhindered to confront him. But Alexander did not oblige. Under the pretext of illness, he secured Cilicia and stayed put at Tarsus (Arr Anab II.6,4) to frustrate the King and strain the treasury, but mostly the seasonal provisions – something perhaps reminiscent of Leonidas' thoughts back in 480 BC (Kambouris 2022b). If the season advanced any further, the weather would be unfavourable for naval operations and the Persian fleet would have to pause operations before a decision was reached, an even more expensive and risky proposition with the enormous enemy territories keeping the sovereign away from his fleet.

Once supplies and/or treasure were exhausted, the Royal Host would have to retire and Alexander could strike wherever he pleased. Alexander could stabilize Northeast Asia Minor and better establish himself there, or invade Media from there. Another option would be to invade Syria and then to advance to Mesopotamia or Phoenicia. Disbanding an army while the enemy was in the field led to the demise of Croesus in the past (Her I.79). Trying to avoid it led Xerxes to fight it out eagerly in 480 BC at Salamis (Kambouris 2022c). Darius needed a decision during this campaigning season; Alexander did not. This is why Parmenio was at the Syrian Gates, to keep Darius out of Cilicia. Alexander locked Darius out to exhaust him.

The difference in mobility and the season would not allow Darius to think of bypassing Alexander (e.g. by skirting Cilicia via Kayseri-Konya, (**Map 5**) to reconquer Asia Minor and perhaps campaign against Macedon and southern Greece with his host and fleet. His baggage train, with the valuable human possessions was a major liability, but not the biggest.

In the game of chess, the Macedonian knight beat the Persian rook. When the Macedonian deserters stated that Alexander would eventually come to meet the royal host (Arr Anab II.6,6), Darius understood that the latter was actively cultivating a reputation for boldness and swift decisions, which he wanted to preserve – and thus the story of his illness was invented (Arr Anab II.6,4), to avoid any detrimental effect of the waiting game on the morale of the army. The Macedonian deserters were telling half the truth to Darius. Alexander would attack the Persians very quickly, but when he thought it wise, and not so as to oblige the Persians longing it. These and other thoughts led Darius to manoeuvre through the Gates of Amanus to recapture Cilicia and secure the use of its shoreline for the fleet (Arr Anab II.7,1).

Darius had left his treasury and heavy support or non-combatant formations in Damascus (Arr Anab II.11,9) as already mentioned. One should remember that the non-combatants included all the regal retinue with its pompousness and lavishness, including the families of the dignitaries and the whole royal household. In the latter were included the families of assigned generals kept there for safekeeping but mostly as hostages to ensure the good behaviour of important commanders, and their conduct before and during the fighting.

This fact creates two queries: why did he do so? Perhaps to be able to engage in manoeuvre warfare and a speedy campaign? His army was enormous, by definition it could not move as fast as Alexander, but, if one keeps the difference in size and context, it became instantly lighter; true it is the difference of a whale and an elephant, but said difference is very important when one contemplates upon moving such animals in a four-wheel truck. The second query is whether Alexander knew that Darius had lightened his army by leaving/sending most of his baggage to Damascus; in this one cannot be sure. Nor of whether Darius knew what Alexander knew or not. It is also not well-understood when exactly Alexander got news from the Aegean that his proxies in Halicarnassus had defeated Orontobates (Arr Anab II.5,7) who had patiently and systematically enlarged his enclave in the last months; he could enlarge it no more.

Alexander had sent Parmenio with most of the non-Macedonian part of the army, something like half of the total, to occupy and guard the southern, Syrian Gates (Arr Anab II.5,1). He clearly wanted to deny them to Darius. He did nothing of the kind with the Gates of Amanus; no way did he not know about them, they were the eastern exit of the Royal Road. So, he left them unguarded intentionally, almost inviting Darius in. He spent much time waiting, either at Tarsus under the pretext of illness (Arr Anab II.6,4), or in the area of Soloi to wage suppressive campaigns (Arr Anab II.6,4) and other operations of minimal importance, given the pockets of resistance he had left behind in Caria and Pisidia. Cilicia was more vital, but still the time spent was just to spend it. By pushing Darius through the Gates of Amanus, he could attack from two sides, himself from the west, Parmenio from the south and southeast; even if he was not able to do so, he would have Darius in very restrictive terrain, emerging from the narrows. This thought implies that he considered the royal army capable of such a manoeuvre. But at some point he decided he was waiting in vain and the Persians were not going to oblige him. Either they grew sense, or they were not as mobile as he thought. In any case, he thought that their advance through Amanus was not going to happen, thus it was safe to leave his invalids behind at Issus and move through the Syrian Gates to fight it out. Why he decided to do so is unfathomable. He did want to face the royal army, no doubt about that; he simply preferred to do it on his terms. Why he decided to break off the waiting game at that point cannot be explained. He might have limitations, too. Any bad news from the coast, depletion of supplies and treasure, no more excuses for not engaging for an army half-new, sustained with stories of previous valour and glory, all these were issues. Or he believed that it was time, as Darius' time and patience was running thin and the psychology of his army would be shaken if the enemy appeared, after so long, in front of them.

Most importantly, Darius had made contact with his fleet south, to Phoenicia, which meant that he could load expeditionary forces and land them to Alexander's rear at will. Not just Greek mercenaries any longer, but diverse forces that could flank him, transfer the war to Greece, or undo his work of conquest at his trail. So, Alexander moved south to the Syrian Gates to meet his destiny at Sochi (Arr Anab II.6,2). The battle that would eventually take place was to be the first in which a Greek army faced in battle a Persian royal army led by the Persian King himself on Asian soil. The disastrous Persian defeats on land had occurred against generals and satraps of the Great King, even in the days of Xerxes (but for the Battle of Thermopylae, where the Imperials had won decisively). Therefore, a defeat in this battle would erode the prestige of the divine Royal Person among the peoples of the Empire, and would show that Zeus was more powerful than Ahura-Mazda in Asian soil.

Darius was also on a timetable; his resources were not unlimited. He had no intention of walking in the trap; he was a good general and he must have seen it. He could force his way from the south. He had Greek mercenary hoplites aplenty, good for such kinds of warfare and he stood good chances of succeeding. The memory of Thermopylae though was too painful for the Persians, and, additionally, their Greek mercenaries may have loathed such a plan as it was a meat-grinder. Alexander must have counted on both these factors. So, Darius did take his army to the Gates of Amanus (Arr Anab II.7,1). It was an easy going, by the Royal Road, and he could expect to capture the enemy by surprise and divided. Thus he could hold one half of the enemy with a pinning force while he eradicated the second. If it was for him to choose, his choice must have been to assault first the weaker part of the enemy; Parmenio with less troops, lower quality and less politically reliable units (Arr Anab II.5,1) and deployed facing the wrong direction. Subsequently, he would turn to the first half to destroy it in detail, enjoying a huge advantage in morale, after a field victory. He could have opted to pass through Cilicia to Asia Minor to win it back, and/or contact his fleet for an amphibious campaign. He had enough forces to pursue both approaches. But it is very probable that he did want to crush the Macedonians to make an example out of them. His preparations, especially the recall of his mercenaries from the Aegean, suggest this line of thought.

Darius, once leaving Sochi, advanced fast through the Amanus range and positioned himself right on the tail of Alexander, who had moved south to meet him. He found his invalids at Issus and had them tortured and then butchered (Arr Anab II.7,1) to satisfy his army and create some terror. It was a perfectly logical and utterly stupid move, instilling grim determination and vindictive aggression to an army much more seasoned, much more homogenous and up to the point wildly victorious.

Alexander was startled; he about-faced and rushed to engage (Arr Anab II.8,1). Darius *was* holding a passage to his rear, unobstructed. This was not a disaster; his army was agile and resilient. In theory he could go for the treasures in Damascus, had he known that these were there; or go on adding conquests. But then Darius, especially once in contact with his fleet, could follow any number of options – except chasing Alexander, whose army was way faster and more mobile in general. Things were not rosy for Alexander, who decided that he had to resolve things by fighting, even in territory carefully chosen and perhaps improved by his opponent, near the sea, with his back to the wall in case of defeat, and against huge numerical superiority. Basically his main advantage was his speed, which could give him the initiative.

His second advantage was that Darius did not wholeheartedly want to engage in a war of deep manoeuvres. Its purpose was to neutralize the Macedonian army. If this was achieved by manoeuvring, it was ideal. Otherwise, it had to be achieved by battle. It must be underlined that the cramping of the Persians was not an advantage per se for Alexander. Alexander had the tactics against wide and against deep opponents. What was important was to understand the whereabouts of the enemy with some reliability. He dispatched a reconnaissance mission sending in a small, thirty-oar skiff, some Companions of his staff (Arr Anab II.7,2), a very dangerous proposition as the Persian fleet could have been anywhere once the coast of Cilicia was under Achaemenid control, and indicative of the need for many different functionaries in the staff of Alexander to get a correct impression, by their own eyes, on the size, location and moves of the enemy. It was vital to estimate the size and composition, and whether it was there in a body or only a part of the host, with the difference to be sought for elsewhere, perhaps on the road to the west.

It is interesting to consider how things might have developed if the two opponents had not decided to face each other. Actually, Alexander was much faster and could catch the Persian host before it exited Cilicia, but rearguards could be deployed to forestall him while Darius advanced on the Royal Road to Asia Minor to reconquer it and perhaps invade Macedon or Greece, with the help of his Medizer friends and his navy. This is why Alexander reversed. If he continued, he could select any number of targets, such as Phoenicia, Syria and perhaps Mesopotamia or any other direction; but he would be a roving host, a horde, while Darius would undo his conquests and his power base.

Still, this prospect must have given Darius cause for concern. With his army intact and advancing, the massive wave of surrender in Phoenicia would not have happened; but there were many areas that did not like the Achaemenids, or not any longer – and Phoenicia was amongst them after the bloody suppression of the Sidonian rebellion in the mid-fourth century (351–344 BC) under King Tennes (Parpas 2013). The Babylonians were always incensed, the Egyptians more so. While Darius would attempt a replay of Cyrus the Great's campaign in Lower Asia, meaning especially Asia Minor, and then imitate Darius and Xerxes – the fate of whom was common knowledge – Asia and Africa could well raise the standards of rebellion. It was a very moderate and cautious idea not to embark on such adventures and fight it out.

As long as Alexander occupied Cilicia, the operations of the Persian navy in the Aegean did not prick him to the point of seeking resolution through a decisive battle. The season was advanced and the naval operational period in the Aegean was coming to an end. As the weather deteriorated, and with secure bases only in Phoenicia, Cyprus and within the Aegean the Persian fleet was too exposed to the weather and to the unfriendly Greeks of the maritime states. Alexander had won time; any major naval offensive, or amphibious one, would occur in spring 332 BC at the earliest. Massive armies, and navies, do not campaign in winter.

But why was Alexander surprised by Darius' move? It was an obvious one, he had been expecting it for quite some time if not inviting it. Had he been so frustrated by the King's refusal to attack so as to become careless? It is rather improbable that Alexander, a commander always giving priority to intelligence and reconnaissance lost a gigantic army, pinned for months at a given location. And, without any idea of what was going on, to pass through the very straits he had kept defended, without leaving any kind of garrison for some unexpected occasion – as implied by his haste to send a flying detachment to recapture it once returning to Issus; namely archers, for ranged firepower, and cavalry – of unknown type but probably Scouts – for the swiftness of the advance (Arr Anab II.8,1). It is possible that, given his much higher mobility, he set out after Darius had struck camp and moved to the north. His surprise indicates that he simply did not expect Darius there, back in Cilicia, by the Gates of Amanus, a move he declined for months. Where would he expect to find him? Obviously he was expected to retire east either to winter or to gain the road to Nineveh (see **Map 5**) which would bring him into the Asia Minor plateau north of Cilicia through

Diyarbakir-Malatya-Kayseri-Konya. Central Asia Minor was loosely held by the Macedonians – and far from his fleet and any prospect for a massive, strategic amphibious counterstrike in Greece. From Cilicia, Alexander, as the fastest, could overtake Darius anywhere in Asia Minor. With this estimation in mind, learning that Darius had moved, and supposing that he was probably going to Nineveh, Alexander decided to give chase and inflict some significant blows on the Persian rearguards that were now exposed, in northern Syria or Damascus. His mobility advantage allowed him to pursue Darius at will and engage him at discretion. His guards and garrisons in various areas of Asia Minor would hinder the movements of the imperial host. In other words, Alexander may have hoped to lead Darius in the network of *his* fortified positions in Asia Minor, by presenting him with a nice bait: the opportunity to undo Alexander's conquests and to reclaim the area for the empire. His Greek advisers, versed in territorial warfare, would assuredly counsel the King accordingly; Memnon had done exactly that some years before, and efficiently so. But this time this approach would only shake the balance of the royal army, perhaps divide it to smaller units to move and be sustained locally, as it was now in enemy territory. This would allow Alexander to beat it in detail one part at a time, in a winter action over itineraries and landscapes known to him, his staff and many of his men from the previous year, with friendly (more or less spontaneously) locals and good possibilities to cut the escape routes and thus exterminate the royal army, capture Darius himself and win the throne of Persia.

A major issue is the role of the expanded family in this war. On the Persian side, the figure of the Rhodian mercenary Memnon is prominent, and he is not alone. His brother Mentor, a mercenary also, had found refuge at the court of Philip, along with Artabazus, their former employer and father-in-law (Diod XVI.52). The son of Mentor, Thymondas, is one of the mercenary commanders at Issus (Arr Anab II.2,1 & 13,2). Memnon was the *karana* in the west (Arr Anab I.20,3) and once he died the command went to his brother-in-law Pharnabazus (Arr Anab II.2,1). Memnon's sons were with him at the Granicus (Arr Anab I.15,2) and we hear of them no more. They were grandchildren to Artabazus, sire of Pharnabazus (Arr Anab II.2,1) and Barsine. The latter was the spouse of Mentor, after his demise of Memnon and then would become lover of Alexander as she was captured at Damascus, after the Battle of Issus (Curt III.13,14; Plut Alex 21,4), to whom she bore a male child, Hercules, in line for the throne of Macedon until murdered (Just XV.2,3). This stalwart family survived four sovereigns of two dynasties and made the war of the Achaemenids against Alexander a family project, only to finally succumb and serve him with dedication.

Chapter 11

The Battle of Issus

Line-up and approach of the Opponents

During the sea reconnaissance Alexander had his men rest and dine, until the situation was clarified, as the tempo of the operations seemed to accelerate. Cavalry (apparently light) and archers were dispatched in a hurry to re-secure the Syrian Gates (Arr Anab II.7,2). Being actually shut out of Cilicia in an area denuded by the imperial host, Alexander would have to pay in blood to conquer any small town or village. The reconnaissance mission returns with details and with reassuring news: Darius is there, with a most massive army, possibly his entire host. Alexander does not have to trouble with anything like soviet-era Operational Manoeuvre Groups going deep to his rear; nor is there any indication of the massive enemy host attempting anything threatening, such as trailing or pursuing the Macedonian army. And no trace of the fleet! Darius is there, and there only.

Alexander about-faced and conducted his approach in maximum security once more (Arr Anab II.8,1), passing the Gates under the eyes of his guards and then resting his troops on the spot under sentinels and pickets (Arr Anab II.8,2). The next morning, by dawn, he initiated his approach gradually deploying his phalanx as the space between the mountains and the sea opened; the infantry units approaching in the open deployed alternatively right and left (Arr Anab II.8,2) while the cavalry remains at the rear (Arr Anab II.8,3) until the whole line is deployed. This gradual deployment kept his flanks anchored on the seaside and the mountains, preventing any enemy unit slipping to his rear (Boardman 1999), a thought entertained by Darius, as evidently shown by the late disposition of his light infantry at the summit of Amanus, as mentioned later.

The infantry of the phalanx deployed initially 32-deep, then 16 – the normal assault depth (Polyb XVIII.30,1) – and then 8 (Polyb XII.19) to extend as much as possible. At this depth and mass it seems fragile, as will be discussed next, to the depth of the enemy phalanx of hoplites and 'hoplitized' *kardaka*. This suggests three things. First, that there is no indication of alternating Greek hoplite phalanx units among the *taxeis* of the Macedonian phalanx. Second, that the only way to sustain the frontal impact of the enemy, cavalry or infantry, may that remain static or deliver a charge, is by an asymmetric advantage and this can only be the use of the *sarissa*, thus ending all discussion on its use in this battle (Markle 1978) – a discussion erroneously starting in the first place as shown convincingly (Matthew 2015). Without the *sarissa* the battle would not have started, at least for the deployments and numbers reported by Arrian. And third, that only by assault could Alexander hope to deliver a decisive blow to the enemy, hoping by shock and momentum to shatter the determination and courage of less competent and confident enemy troops, especially the novice *kardaka* hoplites.

Alexander advanced slowly, to have time to observe and adapt, but also to enervate the opponent and let the terror from the flawless drill sink in. The size of the Persian army and its position, hemmed in narrows behind a river, means that there can be few amendments by Darius, and thus when he adapted his own deployment to that of Darius he would have won half the battle. He also wanted to save the strength and stamina of his troops (Arr Anab II.10,1); they would need top endurance.

The Imperials

He is right; Darius was well-informed. He surprised everybody by using entirely new elements in his battle scheme; surprise in weapons and deployment – his numbers were huge anyway, it was the Royal Host. He must have fully mobilized the central and western satrapies. This means from the Iranian plateau to the loyalists in Asia Minor including Arsames, the fugitive satrap of Cilicia (Arr Anab II.4,7) and Egyptian and Levantine forces; the Satrap of Egypt perished in the battle, leading Persian elements raised in his satrapy (Arr Anab II.11,8). He might have also collected standing forces from the eastern satrapies, but not properly mobilized quota, as he had only one winter to prepare, compared to four years for Xerxes' full-state mobilization. Being informed of the approach of Alexander he threw a screen of cavalry and light infantry (Arr Anab II.8,5). This was to block the view of his enemies and to avoid any dashing attack while still forming up, as reported by Arrian (ibid.), but it may well have been intended to exploit any laxness of the Macedonians to throw them into confusion, delay them, cause attrition and possibly flank them as they emerge (Boardman 1999). Why Darius was concerned that the Macedonians may interfere with his deployment is dubious. It may have something to do with the thought that the Persian deployment at the Granicus was not the intended, but a preliminary one to buy time. Or it may have been the case of Darius being a very watchful, prudent and competent commander, with good counsellors and tacticians on his staff and thus leaving nothing to chance, especially against a daring, dashing opponent.

The screen before deployment was not a Persian SOP; Epaminondas was doing such proactive moves at Leuctra (Xen Hell VI.4,10–12), and Alexander at the Granicus (Arr Anab I.13,1). Nor was it in any case a Persian SOP to mix, in any way, light infantry and cavalry; the Persians used the *asabara* independently, while the Greeks used light troops to support heavy cavalry directly. It was a standard practice (Xen Hippar V.13), Alexander did it at the Granicus by assigning light infantry directly to the commander of the Companion Cavalry (Arr Anab I.14,1). Only in one case did Persians use cavalry and light infantry in combination: it was after the Battle of Cunaxa where the presence of Phalinus the Thessalian in the service of the Imperials (Xen Anab III.3,6–10) makes the origin of the method difficult to establish (Russell 1999). Why this novelty? Because Darius was sick and tired of the attacks of Greek cavalry supported by light infantry against *asabara* who were operating alone. At the Granicus the latter suffered to no small degree because of the Greek combination (Arr Anab I.16,1) and the disaster at Pactolus, in 395 BC was similarly attributable to Greek combined arms (Xen Hell III.4,23–24). Some of his advisors must have tipped him off to deploy light infantry, if for no other reason than to discourage their Greco-Macedonian opposite numbers.

Of course this novelty was ad hoc. Once the screening mission was over, the *asabara* would assemble separately, all equals; they hated low-lifes and were not trained to operate in combination. The light infantry would be used somewhere as expendables and unreliable – they proved both.

This time there was no nonsense about the superiority of cavalry over infantry ingrained in the Persian masterplan. The line of the river Pinarus would be bristling with heavy infantry. The centre, before the King, was made up of 30,000 Greek mercenaries under Thymondas, Aristomedes of Pherae and Bianor of Acarnania; it is tempting to assign 10,000 to each of them, as *baivaraba* (divisions of 10,000) the standard operational unit in Achaemenid armies. To their flanks, two corps of *kardaka* hoplites were posted, each of 30,000, a total of 90,000 hoplites (Arr Anab II.8,6). On the more accessible parts of the bank, these hoplites were augmented by the un-Persian practice of fieldworks, palisades and trenches (Arr Anab II.10,1). This was Greek practice, mostly Theban (Xen Hell V.4,38) and advised by the events of the Battle of the Granicus; Darius did not want a Macedonian assault bringing full momentum. He expected to stop the enemy horse with stakes and spears.

The massive number of hoplite troops could be accommodated only in following every turn of the river bank, to leave no vacant space for the opponent (**Figure 11.1**), and by a Theban-type phalanx at that, 50-deep (Xen Hell VI.4,12) and most dense, static and meant to dull phalanx and cavalry alike in *synaspismos* (interlocked shields) mode (Kambouris & Bakas 2021). This depth accounts for six times the depth of the Macedonian pike phalanx, which fought 8-deep to deploy properly (Polyb XII.19,6). It was a repeat of the Battle of Leuctra, 371 BC. This depth, which was applicable also to cavalry (Xen Hell III.4,13) was the response to the doubts raised by Polybius regarding the numbers involved. Polybius assumed 'normal deployment depth of 8 ranks' for the cavalry (Polyb XII.18).

Once the deployment of the first line was complete, Darius took his position behind it with the usual entourage; Arrian (II.8,11) gives no detail whatsoever, simply referencing Xenophon. The mass of conscript infantry deployed behind the first line, in great depth, as the total strength of his host was something like 600,000 (Arr Anab II.8,8), something compatible with Xenophon's report of four 300,000-strong Persian armies forming the Royal Host (Xen Anab I.7,12) corrected for the available time and resources and also Artaxerxes III Ochus' army prepared for the invasion of Egypt (Diod XVI.40,6).

This was not a mistake, or an unfortunate event caused by the narrow battlefield. The narrow battlefield did dictate it, but this was hardly a mistake. The great depth could dull any onslaught, instead of a shallower deployment that may break (as at Granicus) and expose the rear. At Issus there was no way to create an internal flank, to get to the rear or outmanoeuvre the Imperial host; Alexander had to fight it out with a meatgrinder. There was no chance that the deeply arranged imperial infantry was meant to emerge and give relentless chase (Ashley 1998). It had to pass over mercenary Greeks and *kardaka* phalanx, densely and deeply packed as it was, then the obstacles,

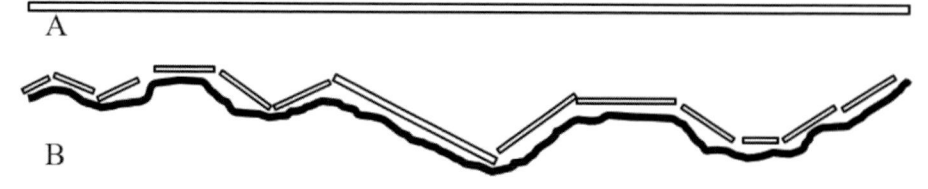

Figure 11.1: Riverine deployments.
A linear deployment following the banks of a river (B), such as the Pinarus at Issus, requires many more troops in standard density than a straight line-up at the projection of the bank (A).

both natural and man-made, and cross the river. By the time all this was done, the much faster Macedonians would have escaped.

Additionally, Darius deployed light troops in a U-arrangement to find themselves at the back of Alexander's army when it approached to engage (Arr Anab II.8,7). These must be the lights deployed in the screening action with the *asabara*, as they were the same in number and in favourable position, close-by, to move to the foot of Amanus and wait. At the same time, Darius recalled his heavy cavalry to position it at the flanks of his main line, by the seaside and to the summit of Amanus (Arr Anab II.8,10). It is a most Greek *parataxis*, cavalry at the flanks. Darius and his *asabara* are unfamiliar with the scheme and make a mistake; there was no room at the left to accommodate the designated cavalry squadrons, so he sent most of them, in full view of Alexander, to the right (Arr Anab II.8,11 & 9,1).

It was not as bad as it seems. Darius was deployed in great depth, and he could not change sides to his cavalry except by sending them in front of his deployment. There was no room behind the battle line. The Persian cavalry wanted to fight concentrated in a body. It changed its position from standard Achaemenid *protaxis* to *parataxis*, but they preferred to enact no more novelties. All massed together to create an irresistible hammer, along with all their peers, this was the *asabara* ideal. And this took them away from the murderous cavalry spears of the Macedonian horse, posted in the right. At the Macedonian left, there were only a few southern allied squadrons (Arr Anab II.9,1), armed with javelins, most probably, making it a better hunting ground. This cavalry hammer was supposed to demolish the Macedonian left.

And do what? The Persian mass could not easily change vector, it needed much space, and especially when formed in deep and dense formation. This became evident at Gaugamela (Arr Anab III.14,5), but also much earlier at Cunaxa, when Tissaphernes' cavalry passed through the Greek peltasts but then did not take the rear of the Greek order of battle (Xen Anab I.10,7–8). Most probably they were to gallop almost to the end of the plain, perhaps engage with the guards at the narrows had there been any (Alexander probably used his very last man in this battle), to regroup and attack from the rear against the phalanx; not any more in deep formation, but roaming the field, in pursuit mode. They had not the drill nor the fast reflexes of Greek units that promptly changed direction to flank an opponent after breaching the enemy line, as at Marathon, 490 BC (Her VI.113); or manoeuvring to position, as in the Battle of Mantinea 418 BC (Thuc V.73).

The Greeks

Alexander lined up his army (Arr Anab II.8,3–4) in a similar manner to his previous deployment at the Granicus (Arr Anab I.14,1–3), with some adjustments. Having received ample reinforcements at Gordium, he had developed tertiary units, with three subunits each, and had enough mercenaries to use them for his task groups (Arr Anab II.9,4) and for combat support missions (Arr Anab II.9,3), thus saving every last Macedonian for the vital missions, especially strike. There was no joint between heavy cavalry and infantry; his light cavalry, Scouts and Paeonians (Arr Anab II.9,2) either formed a vanguard before the Companions (**Figure 11.2A**), or was tasked to extend the right wing of his deployment (**Figure 11.2B**), as the danger there was the encirclement; the Greek is ambivalent, unfortunately, and Arrian seems to paste two different accounts of the same event or fact. There was no light cavalry at the left wing, since its mission was to pursue

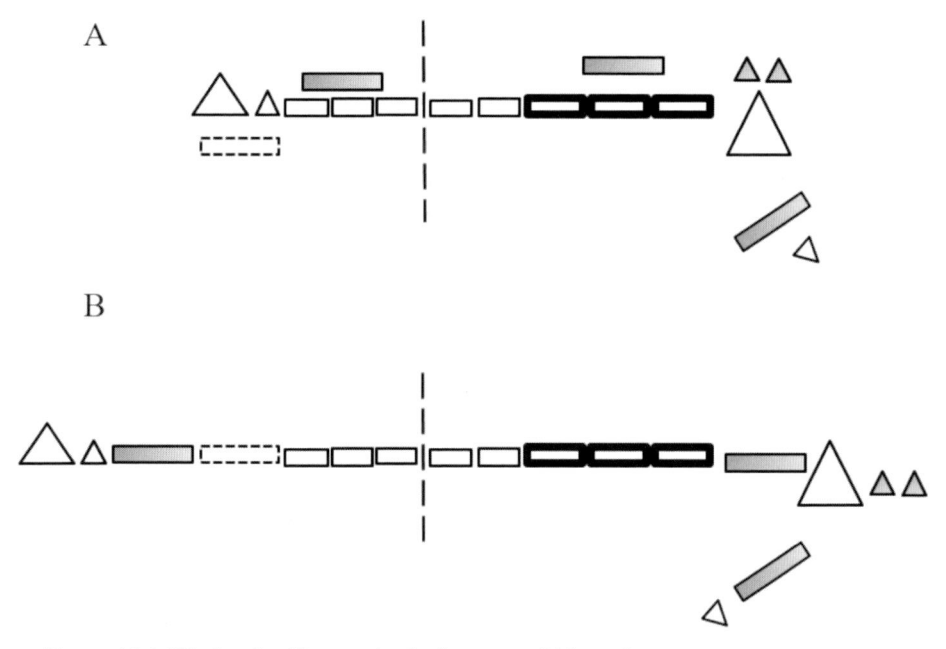

Figure 11.2: The battle of Issus – the deployment of Alexander.
There are two different interpretations of Arrian's description of Alexander's deployment:

A. Disposition in several echelons, with light units as vanguards and a heavy/medium infantry unit as rearguard to support the cavalry of the left, so as to allow it rallying if bested and stem the enemy cavalry onslaught.
B. Conventional, linear disposition, with light cavalry at the exposed inland flank. Upon attack deeper formations may develop, as in Granicus. The reversed rearguard on the right faces the imperial force posted to the summit to threaten the Macedonian flak and rear.

Triangle: cavalry (dashed: light, hollow: heavy, thick line: elite/Royal Squadron). Rectangle: infantry (dashed: light, hollow: heavy, thick line: elite/Hypaspists, dotted line: non-phalanx heavy or medium mercenary infantry). The Companion heavy cavalry under Philotas is directly supported by light infantry fighting as *hamippoi*.

broken and fleeing enemies so as to allow the Companions to regroup and redirect to new targets after a breach.

On the contrary, in both wings there were light infantry flank guards or vanguards, ready to assist heavy and light cavalry or support the infantry. Once more, whether these units are set as vanguards – skirmisher lines before the main battle line – or are integrated within one battle line is subject to controversy due to the ambivalent narrative. On the left the Cretan archers and the Thracian javelineers were posted (Arr Anab II.9,3); on the right, archers (obviously Macedonians, see in the Battle of Gaugamela later) and Agrianian javelineers (Arr Anab II.9,2). A heavy infantry unit (dashed rectangle in **Figure 11.2**), seems to be posted as a reserve behind faster, more mobile units such as the allied cavalry of the left (Arr Anab II.9,3); or the task force of Companions and light infantry on the right (Arrian II.9,4), thus standing in for the Macedonian heavy infantry used in this capacity at the Granicus (Arr Anab I.14,6).

Alexander understood that this was a meat grinder kind of fighting and he had to penetrate and then turn, within the enemy mass, to dislodge the rest of the enemy first line and perhaps kill the king and end it. If this could not be achieved, he somehow needed to make the deep enemy line shallow, so as to flank the best troops, the hoplites, without going through the entire depth of the enemy mass; this could be achieved by creating confusion and panic that may collapse the enemy deployment throughout its depth and leave exposed the already frontally engaged hoplites, both mercenary Greek and *kardaka*. Thus, he had all his strike cavalry with him, Macedonians and Thessalians, and left a token force of southern squadrons (Arr Anab II.8,9) to take on the *asabara* at the left. When he saw that almost *all* the *asabara* were posted to his left, he sent almost half his shock cavalry, the Thessalians, *behind* the line, unobserved, to stiffen the left flank (Arr Anab II.9,1). They were regularly used on the left, as at the Granicus (Arr Anab I.14,3; Diod XVII.19,6) contrary to the Companions – a most vital issue of unit precedence – and they had the skill, with their rhomboid formation, to break the deep cavalry columns of the Persians, who up to then had not faced this Greek formation. The Companions were the only unit that could cut with impunity a hoplite phalanx, combining wedge formation and *xyston* lance (Markle 1977; Samuels 1997); the Thessalians were not that well prepared for the task. Possibly they brandished standard *palta*.

Arrian gives only five infantry *taxeis* for the phalanx, from right to left: Coenus', Perdikkas', Meleager's, Ptolemy's and Amyntas' (Arr Anab II.8,3–4); one more may have been left in some vital garrison in Asia Minor, possibly with Antigonus the One-eyed in Celaenae (Arr Anab I.29,3). Or

Arrian may have it wrong and Alexander deployed all his six *taxeis*. The missing *taxis* from the account of Arrian is that of Craterus. Craterus himself did participate in the battle and was responsible for the whole infantry of the left wing (Arr Anab II.8,4). As at the Granicus (Arr Anab I.14,1) and Gaugamela (Arr Anab III.11,10), Alexander at Issus divided the whole order of battle into two operational commands (Arr Anab II.8,4), left and right, with himself commanding the latter and Parmenio the former, but the infantry of each operational command had its own commander. Based on the fact that at Gaugamela Craterus commanded the infantry of the left (Arr Anab III.11,10), consisting possibly of two of the six available *taxeis* (Arr Anab III.11,9–10) and positioned next to the Thessalian cavalry, he could have been doing exactly the same at Issus: that is, heading his own *taxis*, a fact compatible with the wording of Curtius (Curt III.9,7) although not stated explicitly. The *order* of the *taxeis* at Issus (Arr Anab II.8,3–4; Curt III.9,7–8) is identical in Arrian and Curtius and differs from the one at the Granicus (Arr Anab I.14,2–3) and this is highly probable if the deployment follows the Order of the Day, as with the Athenian *taxeis*. However, the *taxeis*' deployment at Gaugamela as given by Arrian (Arr Anab III.11,9) is identical to the one at Issus (but for the addition of the *taxis* of Craterus to the extreme left). This may be a coincidence of calendar, but most probably a change of practice, with a more standardized order of battle due to the good chemistry exhibited at Issus.

The battle

And then, it is the Persian lights at his rear. They are many, 20,000 (Arr Anab II.8,7) half his own force, they threaten his rear, and, what is immensely important, they are the eyes of their Commander-in-Chief, seeing his line-up, his force structure and its evolutions and transformations. Both functions are annoying, although the command reflexes of the Persian High Command are dubious. Still, Alexander takes no risks when he does not have to. The first move is to chase them away with a task force formed ad hoc by brigading some Agrianian javelineers, some archers (obviously Macedonians, as the Cretans are on the left wing) and cavalry (**Figure 11.3**), two squadrons of the Companions, for providing support on the level ground (Arr Anab II.9,2). The assault sends the unenthusiastic Imperial light infantry running up-mountain (Arr Anab II.9,4), so as to neutralize them for the duration of the decisive part of the battle both as a force and threat and as a sensor, an ISR (Intelligence-Surveillance-Reconnaissance)/HUMINT (Human Intelligence) asset. To discourage their return Alexander leaves

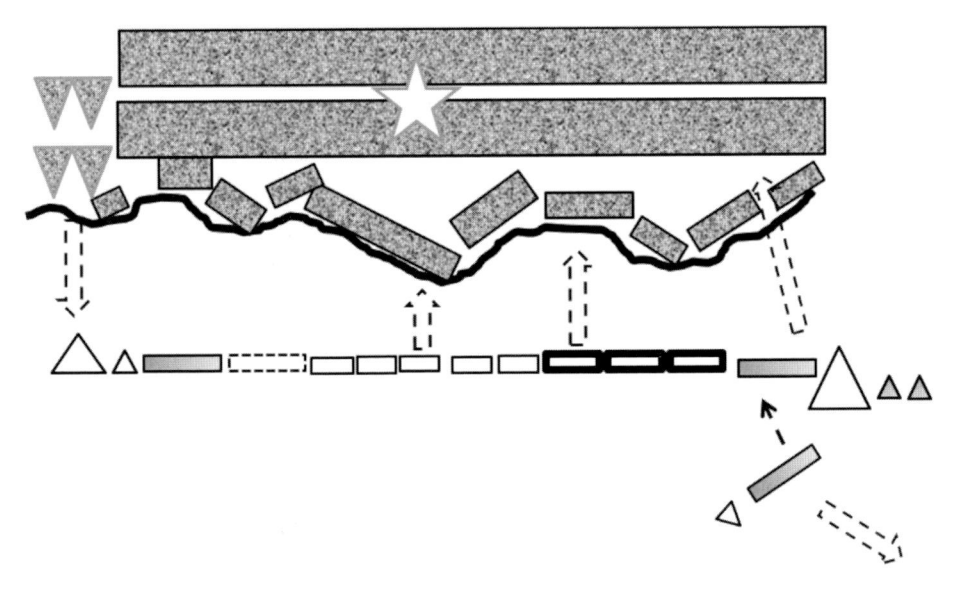

Figure 11.3: The battle of Issus Phase I.
After the extreme right flank guard pursues the Imperial lights from their flanking position to an upmountain irrelevant one, the infantry returns to join the main line of battle while the heavy cavalry, two squadrons, remains on the spot to discourage possible rally and return. Alexander's wing (as per interpretation B) storms through the river against the hoplite phalanx positioned on the far bank in-depth, following its course. The target is the left *kardaka* wing, where the inexperienced and hastily organized Persian hoplites do not stand their ground. The rest of the phalanx advances as well into the river, but the Persian cavalry near the seashore reciprocates by crossing the river to attack the left wing Greek cavalry.

two squadrons of the Companions (Arr Anab II.9,3), amounting to 300 cavalrymen (Arr Anab II.9,4) implying squadrons of 150 horse each. It is a terrible waste of heavy cavalry, but Alexander seems to value more, for his attack, the elite light infantry he tasked with the dislodging and initial pursuit of this enemy group. He recalls them (Arr Anab II.9,4) to support the main event leaving the two cavalry squadrons (Arr Anab II.9,3) bereft of light infantry support, a most uncharacteristic risk for Alexander.

Thus, Alexander in his three great battles, but in these only, follows a pattern: he decides the issue with a lightning charge that ruptures the battle order of the Imperials and allows access to the physical command of the enemy so as to degrade, physically exterminate or functionally neutralize it. Before this decisive charge he opens the battle by a preparative action by a special ad hoc formed task group, which either secures the charge, as at Issus, or enables it, as at the Granicus, or both, as at Gaugamela. At Issus the enabling move was to repulse the enemy light infantry positioned at his back (Arr Anab II.9,4 & 10,3).

The established opinion is that it was a typical attack of the Companion Cavalry, although Arrian does not explicitly mention cavalry; thus there is the suspicion that in this case it was an infantry assault, by the Hypaspist Corps, as the verb used by Arrian suggests men running rather than horses galloping (Hammond 1992), though Arrian demonstrably uses the same verb for horses galloping in other cases (Arr Anab III.14,2 & 15,1). The original view has some irrefutable pros: since the Battle of Mantinea at the latest (362 BC) Greek cavalry in wedge formation charged intact hoplite phalanxes with the hope of cutting through (Xen Hell VII.5,24). The addition of the *xyston*, which outreaches the hoplite spear, delivers the momentum of the charge while being more robust and accurate; it was used to strike facial blows and one may entertain the possibility that the murderous effect was not witnessed by the Persian infantry, which if so, would have made a lethal psychological combination. The details of the Battle of Chaeronea 338 BC (Plut Pelop 27,3 & Alex 9,2; Diod XVI.86.2–4) are hazy and thus whether the weapon had been used there, and the geometry of the charge, are not solidly established (Rahe 1981; Markle 1977). At the Granicus the *xyston* was used against the mercenaries but few survivors may have relayed their impression, as it was a battle of annihilation at this stage; and, additionally, the Companions charged flanks and rear, as the pike phalanx was engaging the hoplites head-on (Arr Anab I.16,2).

The charge – the description of the Battle of Issus is the poorest in Arrian's work – poses another issue: Darius' front line are hoplites. This means that the Persian national weapon, archery, is not used where it would have performed miracles. Having targets plunging in disarray due to the stream and riverbed and not shooting them down is moronic at the very least; at the Granicus, if nothing else, there were the javelins of the Imperial cavalry that exacted a toll at the crossing (Arr Anab I.15,1–2). At Issus, Arrian mentions no Persian archers, and only casually any missiles falling on the attackers; as if a rhetorical device and not an established event (Arr Anab II.10,3). At Gaugamela, where Arrian is at his best, there is a unit of archers, the Mardians (Arr Anab III.11,5), who come from the outskirts of the Persian hinterland (Her I.125,4). Arrian does not mention them at Issus, but this might be one more of his lapses in performance for this battle. It makes no sense that Darius had no archers, especially against the position of Alexander and his cavalry, where they would have abundant, sizeable and not fully protected targets, the mounts. Which brings us back to the possibility of an infantry assault, proven since Marathon to be able to take the attacker through an arrowstorm, by the competent use of the hoplite shield. And the Hypaspists, as evident on the Sidon Sarcophagus, could fight outfitted as hoplites, with Argive shields and body armour, and perform dashing attacks and mobile missions. Alexander is reported time and again to lead on foot task groups formed around the Hypaspists in such endeavours (Arr Anab IV.3,2).

The above poses the question of the whereabouts of these archers. They were opposite to Alexander, but since there were Imperial hoplites all the length of the front inland and to a great depth, where were the archers posted? The great depth of the Imperial front line means that an *epitaxis*, being positioned behind the phalanx so as to shoot over the hoplites; this is out of the question. It is an inefficient and awkward way, to shoot without seeing the target, no matter what the trajectory of the arrows may be. One could suggest that at some curve of the river the hoplites were not lining the bank but were kept some metres back, in relatively straight line, to allow these troops a foothold to stand and shoot. The *kardaka*, who were positioned against Alexander, were newly outfitted as hoplites, meaning that probably they were not well-drilled in transforming their formation to allow the lights to retire through their lines, nor to shoot in *Parentaxis*, integrated in the mass of the phalanx and protected by the shields of the hoplites.

Alexander's violent charge breached the opposing *kardaka* phalanx (Arr Anab II.10,4), possibly after putting (some) archers to flight and driving them onto the phalanx of the *kardaka*, thus causing some disorder if not chaos. His troops turned left (**Figure 11.4**) and started to flank the phalanx of the *kardaka* and then of the Greek mercenaries (Arr Anab II.11,1). Alexander either went on heading the Companions, or, by Hammond (1992), mounted his horse at this point and led the Companions, who followed behind the Hypaspists to the gained foothold so as to develop momentum. The general disorder by the breaching and collapse of the first line would degrade the following units set in successive lines in the Imperial battle order, evidently conscripts from the subject populations. To see the collapse and then a cavalry charge head-on would have shaken these troops to flight, and this opened the way for Alexander to also turn left, not at the flank, but behind the enemy hoplite phalanx so as to take out Darius in his central position. Whether lights and Hypaspists followed the cavalry charge is not attested, but it was SOP. Stricken from the side the Persian command centre was at a tactical disadvantage. The nobles protected their king (Curt III.11,8; Diod XVII.34,2–5) but the geometry, not to mention psychology, did not help and Darius seeing an imminent danger took to flight (Arr Anab II.11,4). He did the right thing. Had he been slain it would have been Game Over. He was not a trooper, nor an officer, to show bravery, he was a sovereign and had to show responsibility (Badian 2000).

176 Alexander the Great Avenger

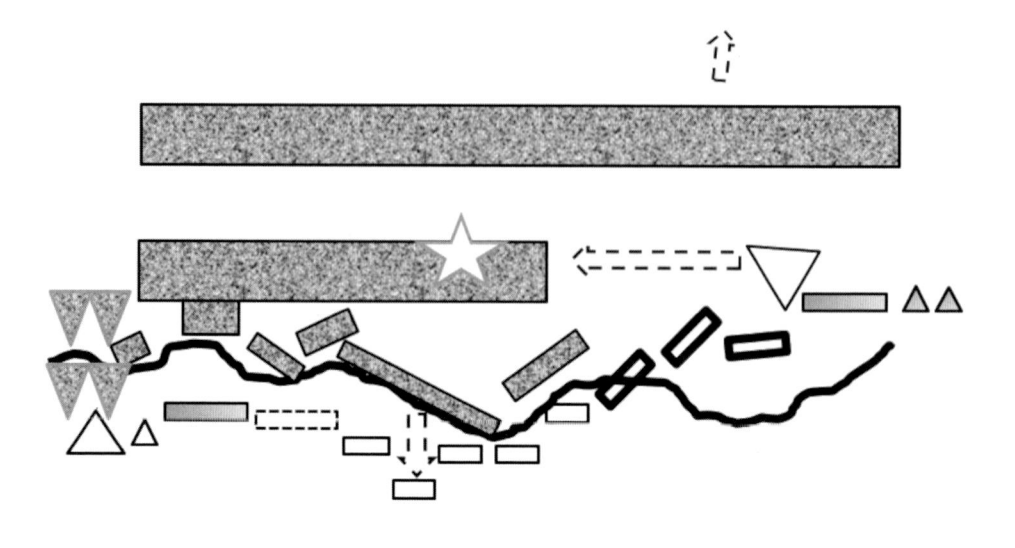

Figure 11.4: The battle of Issus Phase 2.
Both Companion Cavalry and phalanx units (especially the Hypaspists) turn leftwards to flank the Greek mercenaries who are much more resilient than the *kardaka* and also threaten the position of Darius. At the wing of Parmenio, the mass of Persian cavalry attacks with considerable *elan* and some initial success, but is intercepted by the Thessalian determination and innovation. The Greek mercenary hoplites at the centre perceive a breach in the Macedonian phalanx formation in front of them and seize the initiative. They emerge from their prepared position and surge there, giving a hell of a fight to the Foot Companions until they collapse like dominoes. The right *kardaka* wing remained put on the bank and passive till the time of the rout.

The Macedonian phalanx plunged into the river following the lead of Alexander. The *sarissai*, if used in this battle, would have been the only means to dislodge the hoplites from the bank and their fieldworks and to uphold the integrity of the phalanx, as formation and cohesion were gone with entry into the water. Thus, the pikemen dislodged the *kardaka* and engaged the mercenaries frontally, pinning them for the flanking forces. There was no need for the flight of Darius to disintegrate frontally engaged men stricken from the side. But further to the Macedonian left things were different.

The Persian cavalry was thirsty for revenge after the Granicus, as the numerous survivors of that humiliating encounter were present, perhaps to the last man. On the Persian right they were positioned on level ground

(Arr Anab II.8,10 &11,2), at the river delta, near the sea. The ground must have been soft and thus made the gallop somewhat of a problem, but they were facing opponents much fewer in number, similarly outfitted or worse, and with mounts of lower quality and size. They were also positioned to make their signature move, the sledgehammer attack, with their bigger and stronger mounts. When exactly they launched their attack, across the river (Arr Anab II.11,2), before or after Alexander launched his own upriver, is not mentioned. Hitting the Thessalians they smashed a squadron (**Figure 11.5**),

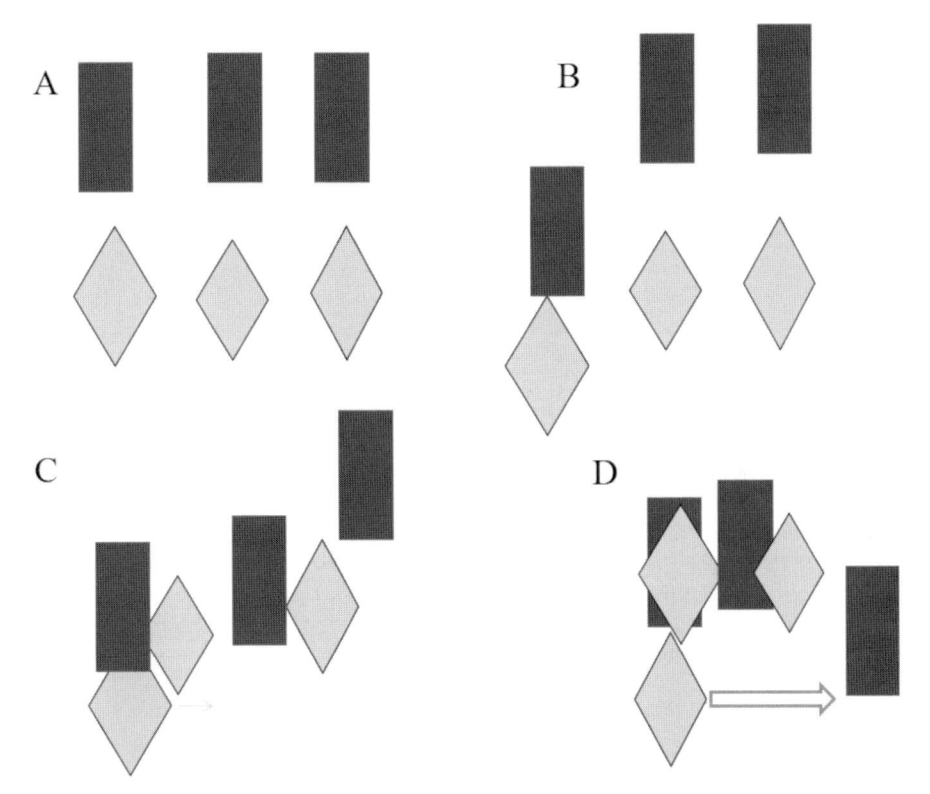

Figure 11.5: The battle of Issus – The Thessalian use of rhomboids.
A. The deep Achaemenid rectangular, hammer-like squadrons (Xen Hell III.4,13) charge into the Thessalians, who deploy rhomboids either from the beginning or by transforming while advancing.
B. A Thessalian squadron is smashed or gives way, allowing an Achaemenid rectangle to advance.
C. This way the Achaemenid flank is exposed to a neighbouring Thessalian rhomboid which turns each rider sharply 90 degrees and charges at the flank. This creates a serial, domino-effect, with the Achaemenid squadrons taken at their flanks and losing integrity and cohesion.
D. The first squadron that gave way, may rally and charge at the flank of any Imperial squadron who infiltrated through gaps created at the Greek line; the Greek mounts are smaller but less burdened and faster, the latter partly due to their more compact formation.

probably two rhomboids, and the casualties must have been high. But the other Thessalian rhomboids evaded the charge, by having each man turning his mount on the spot 90 degrees and moving out of the way, the Persian column unable to keep track. Once passing nearby, the Thessalian horsemen about-faced and charged to the side of the Persian column. It was a disaster, but the disproportional numbers must have protracted the fight. It is suggested that these violent charges by small groups would have been very brisk, leading to disengagement and another charge and not to entanglement with heavier mounts and more heavily armoured opponents (Burn 1965). This is directly reminiscent of the views of Frederick the Great (Sears & Willekes 2016) and sets the idea apart from the caracole and other cavalry skirmishes, as practised by the *asabara* especially in the Great Persian War of 480–479 BC (Kambouris 2022c). In these cases they had been dashing in, shooting arrows and hurling javelins and recycling without coming to grips. The Macedonians and the Thessalians and perhaps the Greeks in general, as the same practice was employed at Gaugamela against the heavy and numerous Bactrian and Scythian cavalry (see below) made physical contact with spear and perhaps sword and then retreated, a practice used *in extremis* by the Macedonian cavalry against the invading Thracians of Sitalces in 429 BC (Thuc II.100).

The Persian attack kept the Thessalians back. This may have been an excellent reason for the leftmost units of the phalanx to check their advance. Even if they were not suffering attack by some cavalry squadrons, they would not be detached from their flank support and expose their left flank to the Persian cavalry, nor leave their own cavalry unsupported; Alexander's orders were not to be detached from the sea and to avert encirclement (Arr Anab II.8,4), for which reason he deployed mercenary infantry behind the cavalry (Arr Anab II.9,3), indicated by dashed rectangle in **Figure 11.2**. An initial lack of momentum or some particularly difficult part of the river, with strong current, more precipitous banks and slippery riverbed (Arr Anab II.10,4–5) or any combination of the above contributed to losing pace and delaying – it was to happen again at Gaugamela (Arr Anab III.14,4–5). This created a breach in the front of the phalanx.

The Greek mercenaries just across the river left their position and surged into the breach (Arr Anab II.10,5). No phalanx, no formation, a surging attack, Roman-type. They knew well that pinned in the bank and behind their fortifications they were losing their mobility. They could not manoeuvre, nor shove phalanx-like, and this against an opponent with greater reach in shafted weapons. They could only move troops laterally, in small distances, to curtail a breach and replace casualties. This was their chance not to face the dreaded *sarissa* head-on, as had their hapless brothers-in-arms at the Granicus. They surged in, plunging somewhat laterally in the river, forgetting about front and position to exploit the breach and flank the phalanx units.

The straggling phalangites strove to keep them off the exposed flank of the taxis at their right and fore (Arr Anab II.10,6). A bitter fight developed; one Macedonian general, CO of one of the central divisions of the phalanx was slain while fighting with his men – it was the second division from the left in Arrian's account (Arr Anab II.8,4 & 10,7). But the flight of Darius, the collapse of the mercenary phalanx under the flank attack upriver and the defeat of the Persian cavalry, which exposed their right flank as well, spelled the end for the surging mercenaries. The confusion allowed many of them to infiltrate between the taxeis of the phalanx and escape to the south, along the coastal road to Phoenicia (Arr Anab II.13,2). Others fell back, passed outside the hook formed by Alexander's wing, gained the mountain and escaped by following it to the south. This means that Alexander, after crossing the Syrian Gates northwards to meet Darius, had left no guard there; he took the troops that had secured the passage (Arr Anab II.8,1) with him, to use them in the field.

The Macedonians gave headlong chase. Darius, under hot pursuit, escaped through the Gates of Amanus (dotted line in **Map 6**). Mounted, as his war-chariot could not manoeuvre properly in the midst of his fleeing subjects; the latter were a perfect buffer that delayed by their bulk the pursuit. Slaughtered and trampled they fell by the thousands, butchered by foot and horse, or perished in the crowded mountain passes; the Greek invalids were avenged and with an interest. The Persian horse took the other direction, through the unguarded Cilician Gates to the interior of Asia Minor (dotted line in **Map 6**), but the heavy panoplies of men and horse made them too heavy to run and their pursuers, Thessalians and light cavalry were able to catch and dispatch many of them and others fell in ravines (Arr Anab II.11,3 & 8). If it was not for the battle weariness of the Thessalians, in the precipitous mountain trek the *asabara* would have been exterminated. They were not, many escaped; too many for the taste of Alexander, as they could roam the length and width of Asia Minor, wreaking havoc. But little else; neither win battles, nor capture cities.

The aftermath

The escape of several mercenary Greeks is interesting (dotted line in **Map 6**). Some followed Darius on his flight, to Syria as far as Thapsacus and beyond the Euphrates (Arr Anab II.13,1). Others escaped otherwise and met him later; 3 to 4,000 of them accompanied him to Gaugamela and some served him until his death. But one unit, with the pretender of the throne of Macedon, outlaw and deserter Amyntas, escaped by sea to Egypt. With satrap Sabaces killed at Issus, they tried to seize it for their own benefit, but the locals (it is unknown if this refers to the remaining 50 per cent of the Persians of the local guards under the new satrap or regent of Egypt Mazaces or the natives) defeated them and exterminated them.

How did these troops get access to Persian ships? Arrian mentions that some 8,000 escaped through the mountains, but he does not specify which mountains and in which direction. Apparently they passed through – or beyond – the Macedonian formation, before the latter regrouped for pursuit, and they descended south at full speed, escaping through the Cilico-Syrian Gates (the northern of a pair of two tandem straits leading out of Cilicia to Syria) or through the ravines of the mountains that form said straits. This is much more logical than any suggestion they escaped through the Amanus range, when Alexander's pincer movement separated them from Darius and the access to Amanus.

However, as soon as they escaped from Cilicia and reached Syria, instead of turning immediately east and escaping, through the main Syrian Gates to the east, to follow Darius and where Alexander was supposed to turn after the battle, they continued straight south, on the coastal road that brought them to Phoenicia, and specifically to Tripolis from where they took vessels from the royal fleet, and in fact those that had ferried them from Greece. They boarded, and burned as many ships as they did not need. This excess capacity indicates that many more than the 8,000 survivors were transported by sea from Greece, even if it was not the entire force of 30,000. Their first destination was Cyprus (Arr Anab II.13,3), obviously because it now was the greatest secure base in the environs, since Alexander had no fleet at the moment (Parpas 2013). Most probably the actual base and headquarters were located at the very dependable city of Citium, a colony of Tyre (Parpas 2013) and always loyal to the Achaemenids (Kambouris 2022a), with good harbour and plenty of resources and high-echelon Achaemenid officials from whom to take further orders. From there Amyntas sailed to Egypt with half the force, while the other three leaders headed to the Aegean (dotted line in **Map 6**), obviously to the Persian fleet under Pharnabazus, the cousin of Thymondas (Parpas 2013).

Alexander chased Darius to the Gates of Amanus until dark, bypassing and leaving behind his flying force the wretched Persian fugitives, for other units to complete the pursuit (Arr Anab II.11,6 & 8). Parmenio captured the camp of Darius, and Alexander his war chariot with his bow, shield and cloak (Arr Anab II.11,4); in essence this was a platform reminiscent of today's armoured command vehicles of mechanized forces. But, as already mentioned, not Darius himself. The sovereign mounted a horse (Arr Anab II.11,5) to make good his escape, through the routes he had taken so majestically a few days ago, by the Gates of Amanus. Returning to the occupied Persian camp for rest, and to his victorious soldiers, Alexander knew that the Cilician Gates and all other routes and narrows were now wide open; not necessarily good news, as Imperial fugitives were escaping to all points of the compass (dotted line in **Map 6**). He also obtained some loot of incalculable moral value, found in the Persian camp: Darius's family, namely his wife, children and mother (Arr Anab II.11,9).

Other prominent officials' families, being practically hostages for the good behaviour of their sires, were captured at Damascus, along with the mobile treasury with the campaign fund, the mobile palace, and the households of the great Persians with their entourage, fortunes, and slaves (Arr Anab II.11,9–10) and thus allegiances of some feudal lords changed. Barsine, Memnon's wife and stepmother of Thymondas was amongst them (Plut Alex 21,4). Damascus was occupied by a task group under Parmenio (Arr Anab II.11,10), which moved southwards independently from the parallel southward march of Alexander (solid lines in **Map 6**).

Above all else, Alexander visited the wounded, he honoured the distinguished, buried his dead with honours (Arr Anab II.12,1), dedicated altars and shrines, probably founded one or two cities (Nicopolis and Alexandretta). And he decided to move south, from the coastal road to Phoenicia (coastal solid line in **Map 6**), and not from the Royal Road, or the road of Damascus – the Upper and Lower itineraries, respectively (Monerie 2019) – to the heart of the empire.

Conquering the Eastern Mediterranean basin

The situation and the prospects after Issus
Alexander now had two strategic choices: the first was to immediately pursue Darius to the heart of the Persian Empire, before the latter could raise another army. This way he could occupy the vital centres of the empire, the capitals (emphasis on the plural) to end the war at once. The course he would follow, from Syria, was to the east, along the Royal Road. But this would entail going back up north, once he was some distance to the south, to Damascus, to confiscate the Persian war chest. Thus he had the option of the Lower Road, from Damascus to Palmyra and Deir-Ezor (**Map 6**). And he would have made this choice if he was as much a fan of direct approach and an acolyte of dashing speed and headlong charge as usually supposed.

But he was neither (Fuller 1958; Green 2007). Alexander opted for a more arduous and much safer campaign. He turned south to clear the

Mediterranean of the Persian navy and subdue it. He knew that with the Persian field army destroyed, his flanks were relatively safe and he could never find a better opportunity to accomplish this task; just in case, he left a powerful force to cover his flank, with the entire allied cavalry in Northeast Syria (Arr Anab II.13,7) and perhaps other units in Damascus; it is possible that neither the family of Darius nor other allied units such as the Thessalians and the southerners' infantry participated in the campaign south, as they are not mentioned; also conspicuous in silence regarding his absence from the campaign to the south is Parmenio, the natural choice for keeping the rear, and Curtius' wording (Curt IV.1,4) corroborates such an arrangement, although it does not explicitly report it.

The prize was Phoenicia and Egypt. Phoenicia would furnish Alexander his very own, and sizeable, navy; the one of the Macedonian throne was rather a sorry pretext for a navy, especially in the scale he was operating now. His southern Greek allies that had navies, namely Athens, were the definition of frenemies (Arr Anab II.15,3). The idea here was not to dissolve the Persian fleet, but to own it. And then it was Egypt, the ancient land of wealth, wonders and mystery, with great semantics attached to it and even greater potential for international propaganda and prestige, not to mention the production of wheat. From the three major areas, it was the only one within reach to be directly controlled. He had opened the seaway to Scythia through the straits, and made it safe, but in a world changing that fast, one could never be sure of trade partnerships. The approaches to Sicily, the other major source, were even more precarious. Alexander did not have the mastery of the seas that would allow unconditional access to Sicily. And conditions, such as the goodwill of others, he didn't like a bit.

It was to be a fairly easy campaign. Many Phoenician cities had in the recent past revolted, and were brutally suppressed into the bosom of the Empire by Artaxerxes III Ochus in 344 BC and the same went for most Cyprians (Parpas 2013; Tarn 1948). They sought an opportunity to secede from the Persians, especially Sidon, and exact revenge for the cruelty of 344 BC. The same, of course, applied to the Egyptians, who had only recently re-submitted, definitely in 342 BC to Ochus but possibly once more in 336 BC to Darius III, after a new insurgency fostered by the Nubian King Khababash (Patchen 2014). If Alexander moved immediately, he would be accepted in both areas as a liberator; a local leader, Semtutefnakhte, was already conspiring with Alexander for the liberation of Egypt (Parpas 2013). If he did not do so and went on to dismantle the Persian Empire first, a proposition risky and uncertain, with a fleet still able to stir troubles at his rear, especially when he himself would have completely lost contact with the sea when entering the heart of Persia, things would change. The opportunity the aforementioned people were seeking would have appeared right before them, and they would have no reason afterwards to join the empire of Alexander, since they would have *de facto* gained their independence, which they were tasting until fairly recently; 10 years previously. Persia was a very lax empire, with enormous centrifugal forces and autonomy sought by local satraps and regents and whole tribes and nations.

Thus, moving towards them *before* the dissolution of the Persian state, Alexander offered them a pleasant change of sovereign. If he was to miss that opportunity in 333 BC, then, at a later date, when his eyes were to fall on them again, after many years as he would have aspired to reach the end of the world, he would be perceived as a new aspiring conqueror who would deprive them of their newly acquired freedom and independence. Not to mention that the resources of both areas would not have been available at will. Therefore, he moved south (**Map 7**) and occupied a very important area not only to finally clear his coastal rear from the amphibious Persian threat, but also to accept the voluntary submission of areas that would otherwise require very hard and time-consuming conquest campaigns. As it was, Alexander won a great geopolitical area by only two major siege operations, at Tyre against the Phoenicians of the city (Arr Anab II.17–24) and at Gaza against the Arabs subject to the Achaemenids (Arr Anab II.26–27). By the way, Curtius states that the Syrians were subjugated by force of arms (Curt IV.1,5), because the Persian defeat at Issus had not intimidated them enough. It is unknown whether this operation was carried out by Alexander himself or by some detachment under Parmenio, who specialized in such missions

Map 7: Phoenicia-Egypt.

of expedient mopping up; it might have been the operation mentioned in brief by Arrian as 'the money [in Damascus] was confiscated by Parmenio' (Arr Anab II.11,10). There is nothing to indicate it went as smoothly as implied, and both primary sources of Arrian, especially Ptolemy I of Egypt, are rather hostile to Parmenio and his family.

By moving south, Alexander seized the opportunity that was one-off; he did not *miss* the opportunity to disintegrate Persia. He thought the opportunity would present again later when he was likely to have enhanced loyalist forces, especially from the vehemently Mazdaic eastern satrapies with rugged terrain and exceptional cavalry. For years he had been meticulously studying the extent of Persian power, and the battles so far fought showed him that the military dissolution of Darius' armed forces on land could be achieved almost at will. Even if an extermination battle, a 'Battle without a Morrow' was not presented to him, he could defend adequately the routes leading from Syria to Phoenicia-Egypt and Asia Minor, keeping under his direct and complete control a vast and very rich realm. On the contrary, in the event of an accident when in the pursuit of Darius, with Phoenicia and Egypt at his rear he could not secure any conquered lands, not even in Asia Minor, since its coast would be vulnerable to any Phoenician and Egyptian fleets anyone could muster. Even if Darius were killed or captured at Issus, Alexander would be moving south rather than east. After all, one must remember that the Imperial casualties at Issus were crippling, but not destructive. The Imperials, caught in a trap themselves, in a rather narrow place, still had three exits and suffered a 15 per cent fatality rate in infantry, 100,000 out of some 600,000 (nothing *that* destructive) and an incapacitating 33 per cent in cavalry, 10,000 out of 30,000 (Arr Anab II.11,8). Still, this left two-thirds of their massive, 30,000-strong cavalry roaming wild in Asia Minor, at the rear of Alexander, under their commander at Issus, Nabarzanes (Green 1991; Burn 1952). So, their chain of command was rather intact. They were many, and they were mobile. Not particularly well-versed in territorial warfare, but with local insurgents and loyalists, or mercenary Greeks, they were a factor to take into consideration.

The – not really – soft underbelly
The Campaign

After the capture of the campaign treasury of the empire in Damascus, Alexander's cash issues were solved for good. He could finance the war, not just a campaign, and the running of his conquests. Thus fees and taxes could be reduced, an immensely popular measure at home and in the conquered lands (Arr Anab I.16,5 & II.12,2). And the first thing he needed was a navy. A dependable one, as the Athenian ambassador apprehended at Damascus (Arr Anab I.15,3) revealed the secret dealings of the city with the Achaemenids. He could raise some ships in southern Asia Minor, from Cilicia to Pamphylia. But the best would be to take the navy of his enemy which was currently now making waves in the Aegean. As he would thunder southwards, city after city, upon capitulation, would recall its naval contingent from the Imperial fleet, and put it in the hands of Alexander. It was not a fast procedure; messages should be sent, received and action prepared and taken. But numbers were all important: if this happened with several cities, and large numbers of vessels, loyalist officers and boarders would not be able to prevent such moves. Indeed, with Marathos being the first to welcome him (Arr Anab II.13,8), all the Phoenician coast, with the exception of Tyre, declared for Alexander.

In the most privileged position and the current darling of the Achaemenids as it betrayed the Phoenician revolt 14 years previously, Tyre wanted to keep its privileges and thus declared neutral (Arr Anab II.16,7). Possibly it was thought that presenting such a formidable opponent, Alexander, in a hurry to invade Egypt, would bypass it as he did with Halicarnassus, so as not to allow time for the Imperial administration in Egypt to consolidate after the disaster. After all, with the rest of Phoenicia under his sway, the Persian fleet in the Aegean was crippled (Freewalt 2014); but if he did attempt a siege, which was Darius's not-so-secret wish, the Tyrians were confident they could endure and buy valuable time for both Egypt and Darius in the east.

Alexander assessed the situation accurately and, contrary to what had happened in Pisidia and Caria, he refused to bypass Tyre (Arr Anab II.17). He had done so with Halicarnassus and, despite the sagacity of that decision, he was still paying a steep price. He was seeing things as they were; the defiance was meant to repeat, in a massive scale, the idea of the defence of Halicarnassus. One objective would be to pin him down at a region ill-supplied in grain (Parpas 2013) while Darius was afforded more time to collect forces (Diod XVII.40,3) as attacks at his rear developed. The other objective of the defiant Tyrian posture was to actively support the Imperial fleet operations all the way to Sparta. Without taking Tyre, the Imperial fleet could return, under certain conditions, and the existing fleet would use its facilities and support. Moreover, many fortified cities, especially Gaza and then Pelusium and Memphis in Egypt (**Map 7**) were to make ominous assumptions. With Tyre taken, a clear message to such forts and fortresses would be delivered, and the Imperial fleet would be no more, with no chance for resuscitation (Freewalt 2014). The Persians would have to procure another, altogether.

Thus Alexander spared no time and expense to conquer it. After all, he had time to spare. He could not invade Egypt without the support of a fleet, at least in logistics; and he had no fleet. He was to acquire one from the remnants of the Imperial one that was disintegrating, but for that, some time was needed. Time well-used to make Tyre capitulate and improve his prestige and aura.

The Tyrians' decision to resist Alexander was supposedly religious, as the sacrifice he insisted on offering to the city protector, Melcart, equivalent to Hercules and thus demonstrably Alexander's ancestor, during the spring festival, was the prerogative of the Tyrian royal family. It is highly improbable that the sacrifice was a pretext by Alexander to find an opportunity to storm the city (Freewalt 2014); he was pious and a man of his word, and this would have been not only sacrilege but awful precedence for negotiations in the future. Not even the Tyrians believed this was a possibility or a danger. The issue was elsewhere. By requesting to perform it he paid reverence to the deity, his standard practice, and this is irrelevant to his personal religiousness, contrary to some views (Freewalt 2014). But he demanded to be accepted as co-owner of the city; nothing peculiar, as the King of Kings had such privileges in all cities and realms under his sceptre. And this is where the issue turned geopolitical. The Tyrians were not inclined to do so and thus shed the Achaemenid overlordship; the governing body, the crown prince and the Senate (the King was away with the fleet of the city in the Aegean) were at ease with the Persian overlordship and confident they could endure the siege. Alexander had a chequered record in Miletus, Halicarnassus and Pisidia; they had an impeccable one. More important, they wholeheartedly believed that the Persians would prevail despite the reverses. Xerxes' army and fleet had been crushed, but nothing happened other than to some cities in the Aegean. Things were a bit more serious now, but the Greeks had no fleet in 480 BC; now the Athenians were a bit short – very short – of openly medizing (Parpas 2015).

The Imperial fleet in the Aegean was most aggressive, possibly implementing a carefully studied strategy combining the operations in Cilicia with a strategic offence in mainland Greece and especially the Aegean (Arr Anab II.13,4). When the news from Issus sank in, the commanders did whatever they could and, with their Spartan allies, tried to adapt, including the establishment of a base of operations in Crete (Arr Anab II.13,5–6). But the Phoenician and Cyprian squadrons mutinied and came to Alexander along with some small forces from Rhodes and southern Asia Minor (Arr

Anab II.19,1–3), as Alexander expected, once their states capitulated. The Tyrian ships, of course, went to reinforce the defiant city. But now the mastery of the sea had gone to Alexander and, suddenly, there was no Persian fleet.

Alexander had correctly understood that he needed a spectacular siege victory to stun enemy cities and awe them to surrender (Anson 2015); Memphis and other Egyptian fortresses were amongst these. Halicarnassus had tarnished his fame, and the triumph at Issus was irrelevant. He had an excellent corps of engineers and by a lightning, ten-day campaign, to Mt Antilebanon to suppress the Arab tribes there (Curt IV.3,1–4; Arr Anab II.20,4–5) that had raided and attacked some of his work parties (Curt IV.2,24) he secured a free supply of timber for his siege machines, and at the same time he freed access to grain-producing regions (Parpas 2013). Just as important, he brought under control the 'Lower Road' to Mesopotamia through Palmyra (Monerie 2019) from where some elite Imperial force might appear to surprise him (**Map 6**). Thus he was securing resources and his rear and it was not an idle or detrimental diversion from his main objective as occasionally maintained (Freewalt 2014).

Alexander had only a portion of his forces, nothing like the 40,000 estimated by some scholars (Freewalt 2014) as he had left sizeable rearguards to Syria, to protect his rear – for example the allied horse (Arr Anab II.13,7). After a bitter siege the city of Tyre fell, its savagery met with a retribution in kind by the conquerors (Arr Anab II.24,3; Diod XVII.46,4) with the surviving defenders, natives and strangers (whatever the latter were) sold into slavery. It was not any unwarranted cruelty (Freewalt 2014, Hanson 1999); these views

Boarders, vessels, crews and fleets

Alexander came from no maritime culture. His prerogative was the land army (Arr Anab I.18,8); still, he was not reluctant to fight when the conditions assured decent possibilities. He did offer, in permissible environment, naval battle at Miletus (Arr Anab I.19,10) and in Phoenicia but denied it off Halicarnassus. In Miletus and Halicarnassus he had the same fleet. What was the difference?

The allied fleet of 160 vessels was much smaller than the enemy, and it was a patchwork of vessels with no common service history, common background, nor cohesion. The enemy did have all that, and excellent quality. It is not that Alexander's fleet had inferior quality. The Athenians had 400 warships. They could, or could not man those (Parpas 2013); but they *would* not. Their twenty ships that were part of the allied navy were thus unreliable and few. They were the masters of the seas. They were beating the Phoenicians always and all over the sea. But, contrary to 480 BC, they were not fighting for the Greeks. Once they took to sea, strictly to ensure the grain supply of their city, the superb, almost revered navy of Pharnabazus tried nothing (Parpas 2013); the reasons may be debated, but not the facts.

Once in Sidon, where he established his base of operations due to the venomous anti-Persian feeling of the city thanks to the massacres of 344 BC, just 12 years previously, Alexander enjoyed numerical superiority with a fleet just as cohesive and competent as the enemy's, he had no reason not to offer battle. Many of his vessels were kin to the Tyrians, and all of them their comrades-in-arms until some weeks before. Thus, he loaded massive boarding parties to ensure the loyalty of the crews and marines and also to acquire an edge in boarder's fight, where the Macedonians were by definition better; the same was the Romans' choice (Polyb I.22,8–10). And in the conditions of that day he could dictate the terms of the battle: he had the larger fleet, meaning it was not easy to be outflanked and, if closely packed, no *diekplous* was an option. Brawling, head-on ramming exchanges would lead to boarding. The Tyrians, seeing exactly these dynamics did not accept the battle and retired in earnest. Alexander's massive parties made his fleet somewhat slower, thus the enemy made good their escape.

The battle plan of Alexander was similar to land battles: he led the right flank, using the Hypaspists as boarders (Arr Anab II.20,6), while Craterus had the left, obviously with his own *taxis* as boarders (Parpas 2013). The Tyrians would have loaded enough marines into their vessels, but they were no match for the professional Macedonian foot. How many took to sea? In 480 BC triremes had a minimum of 40 boarders (Kambouris 2022b), as in 494 off Lade (Kambouris 2022a). In 334 BC the triremes might have had greater capacity, but there were also quadriremes and quinqiremes (Arr Anab II.21,9), much larger vessels. The latter were the standard in the Carthaginian Wars of Rome and packed a maniple of 120 legionaries each (Polyb I.26,7). Assuming just 30 Macedonian boarders, on top of the native marines, in the 200-strong fleet of Alexander, a massive 6,000 troops, meaning perhaps the entire Hypaspist Corps and two taxeis of Foot Companions is implied. Allowance for missile troops might lower the number, but it was an all-out effort for Alexander.

are simple polemic against Alexander. The massacre of his troops (Arr Anab II.24,3), if not the public execution by drowning of his emissaries in plain sight of his army (Curt IV.2,15) was simply answered in kind, possibly with the crucifixion of 2,000 PoWs (Curt IV.4,17). Nothing more than retaliation for a war crime or, rather, a sacrilege, had his men been emissaries.

Further to the south, the city of Gaza also stood defiant. The city was rich, a commercial hub, especially for the incense trade, bringing in quite an income that was used imaginatively for security in the form of excellent fortification. A eunuch regent, Bagoas, using the lull due to the siege of Tyre prudently, was adequately prepared for a long siege in supplies and defenders, many of them local mercenaries and the rest citizens, all of them Arabs. The Arabs' loyalty to their Achaemenid overlord corroborates their fame, that they were truest to their word once they had given it (Her III.8). They honoured their allegiance valiantly and to the death, which came once the siege equipment used in Tyre arrived by sea and breached their walls. The city was depopulated of the surviving non-combatants and repopulated from the tribes nearby (Arr Anab II.27,7). And Alexander took a note not to forget to subjugate Arabia, a task unaccomplished due to his death.

Alexander really spent much valuable time in Tyre, and some more in Gaza, time Darius was using first to consolidate after the quake caused by his resounding defeat, and then to ponder and prepare for a rematch. He tried to avoid it by seceding to Alexander everything west of the Euphrates, but Alexander understood that he seceded nothing he had not practically lost already. The siege of Tyre was not time lost; it was time well-spent, an investment. The epic proportions of the siege, especially to raze a city that had endured two historical, multi-year sieges (Parpas 2015; Freewalt 2014) and enjoyed the support and alliance of the King-of-Kings was an enormous boost to his prestige. The navy Darius lost meant that it was Game Over in the west; he could never replace or rebuild it, and his semi-guerilla practices between the rallied survivors of Issus (Curt IV.1,36; Burn 1952) and the resilient powerbase built around the citadel in Halicarnassus (Arr Anab II.13,6) was inconsequential without a navy. Forfeiting everything west of Euphrates was a bargain, had Alexander accepted it. He did not.

The hostility of the natives against the Persians made him very welcome in Egypt; the ongoing war gave them the jitters and pushed them to Alexander for protection as well. It was little less than a year after the Battle of Issus and things were happening in Egypt, notionally under Achaemenid control, but hardy accessible by the Throne. Looking at the proceedings in Phoenicia, the Egyptians had to contemplate their future. The fall of Tyre made the Achaemenid administration conclude they could not hold the Egyptian fortresses given the hostility of the natives; they had to surrender to Alexander. The natives reached a similar conclusion; to get rid of the Persians without any bloodbaths, and for good, they needed Alexander. He was victorious everywhere, and without him chaos was certain, as in the case of the Greek mercenaries. Just 8,000 men surviving Issus sailed from Tripolis to Cyprus and then, some of them sailed back to Taenarum to find other employment (possibly with the Spartan enemies of Alexander) and others under the Macedonian renegade prince, Amyntas sailed to Egypt and attempted to commandeer it (Arr Anab II.13,3). These were wiped out, possibly by the residual Persian garrison (Curt IV.1,27–33), amounting to half of the grand total as standard Achaemenid SOP (Xen Cyr I.2,10 & 12); or, alternatively by the natives (Arr Anab II.13,3). Alexander, reaching Pelusium (**Map 7**), where he had a rendezvous with his fleet (Arr Anab III.1,1) seemed the only practicable choice, for both the natives and their oppressors.

Alexander in Egypt took special pains to be admitted and embraced by the locals and especially their clergy. This was the reason for his trip to Siwa (**Map 7**). He knew that the Egyptians had no particular disposition to be subjects of any foreigner, and the massacre of Darius' 4,000 Greek mercenaries under Amyntas fleeing from Issus was ample proof. The mercenaries supposedly attempted a coup in Egypt as the appointed satrap Sabaces had been killed at Issus. The men of Amyntas (or rather, under Amyntas) had driven the natives into rebellion and defeated the remnants of the Persian garrison under Mazaces (Curt IV.1,30), the viceroy and surrogate of Sabaces the Satrap (Arr Anab III.1,2), as the latter had been killed at Issus (Arr Anab II.11,8). Their arrogance and self-confidence after the battle exposed them to a decisive sally of the Persian garrison, possibly assisted by some of the locals whom they had plundered, and led to their total annihilation.

Or this is the story of Curtius (Curt IV.1,27–33). It is just as possible that Amyntas was not stupid enough to hijack a whole country with 4,000 battle-hardened veteran mercenaries. He may have gone there under orders to secure it for Darius (Parpas 2015) and not simply under such pretence. There are some indications that point in this direction. Arrian's version is different from that of Curtius in that the mercenaries surviving Issus are double the number, 8,000 and first go to Cyprus. Cyprus is the naval base in-theatre, once Cilicia had been invaded. Although a very short distance offshore from Cilicia, it was utterly inaccessible for the power that held sway over Cilicia for some 6 months, if the said power had no navy; therefore, it was the perfect choice. There, Amyntas devised operational plans, was assigned a portion of the mercenaries and written introduction as well as provisions and accepted his new commission; all these do not corroborate Curtius' version.

The objective of Darius would have been to secure Egypt from insurrection by bitter natives who would like to welcome Alexander. His mercenaries might have imposed loyalism and shut the country, possibly somewhat high-handedly – a good reason for Alexander to pass some time in Tyre while events were unfolding in Egypt. The fall of Tyre would have persuaded anyone, especially the acting/surrogate satrap and his men, that resisting Alexander would be unhealthy and a bad career move; after all Mithrenes, who had surrendered Sardis (Arr Anab I.17,3), prospered under the new sovereign (Arr Anab II.17,4 & III.16,5). Amyntas would have nothing of it. He was wanted, preferably dead, by the current king of Macedon and thus was betting his head for the Imperials and this made him the perfect choice for Darius' cause.

And bet it he did; and he lost it. It must have been the natives that eliminated Amyntas and his troops (Parpas 2013) – or they were instrumental in his demise possibly by cooperating with the Persians remaining in Egypt, in standard Achaemenid expeditionary practice (Xen Cyr I.2,10 & 12) although Arrian explicitly reports no Persians in any military capacity being present there (Arr Anab III.1,2). For the viceroy to be alive and well when Alexander came, one may conclude that (a) there were Persian troops, or the natives would have slaughtered him; (b) that the locals were instrumental in Amyntas' demise, after the Persian garrison had suffered a crushing blow from Amyntas' mercenaries in battle (Curt IV.1,31) and cooperated with the Persians in a one-off common goal, to receive Alexander amicably. These events must have evolved shortly before Alexander's arrival and were possibly triggered by the news that he was approaching.

Alexander from Pelusium followed the eastern bank of the Nile and crossed it when he reached Memphis, where he had sent his fleet to occupy and prepare the city (Arr Anab III.1,3–4). After establishing himself in the region, he went north with his fleet, following the river, to the west of the Delta where he founded Alexandria on the Mediterranean coast (Arr Anab III.1,5). His sojourn there, to found the city, and his meeting with his captains coming from Greece (Arr Anab III.2,3) says much for the warmth of the welcome he received in Memphis.

From the coast he ventured due west towards Libya, so as to approach the oasis of Siwa from the north (Arr Anab III.3,1–3), and turn south through as little space in the desert as possible, since he had reasons to mistrust his guides and remembering the Lost Army of Cambyses that started from Thebes through the desert to pillage the oracle and was simply lost in the sand (Her III.26).

Strong guards, flattery of the local element, respect and semi-adoption of their religion (the core of the Egyptian soul and ideology), new cities and institutions designed for a fusion of different ethnicities into multinational societies with segregated neighbourhoods as was Alexandria, made the establishment of Alexander in the land of the Nile stable. The endorsement of the Egyptian religion, a religious vogue in Greece for quite some time and thus totally acceptable to his troops and believable by the natives culminated in the pilgrimage at Siwa where he was recognized as Son of the God. This was a precondition for a Pharaoh, meaning he was legitimized as sovereign of Egypt and thus insurgencies against him were sacrilege. The clergy in the oracle of Siwa was renowned in Greece and exhibited the political correctness to call him 'son of Zeus', something the attitude and sensitivity of his troops would have found less difficult to swallow. For the Egyptians he was the Son of Amun, the patron deity of the great southern city of the (Egyptian) Thebes.

Alexander returned from this expedition in Siwa to Memphis definitely *not* the way he had gone (Arr Anab III.4,5), a standard procedure of his to keep his possible local enemies in uncertainty, but mainly to cover and directly subjugate more land. Now he had dependable guides, from Siwa, and wanted to reach Memphis as soon as possible since he had been confirmed as son of a major Egyptian God and thus could be proclaimed legitimate ruler – that is, Pharaoh. Returning the way he had come meant a vast semi-circle. He returned as soon as possible, and established himself regally there to make all further arrangements (Arr Anab III.4) as the new, confirmed and acknowledged Pharaoh, giving the local Medizers violent fits of impotent rage.

This means that given that the priesthood of Ptah at Memphis, the Persian seat of power and ancient capital for quite some time, had obviously refused to acknowledge his divine pedigree and earned speartip-acquired sovereignty, possibly due to good relations with the Persians, Alexander had to legitimize his claim without plunging the country to religious and civil

Son of Amun

The Greeks had long dealings with Egypt; mostly friendly and commercial, but the factor usually overlooked is *which* Egypt. Even after the unification of Lower and Upper Egypt the country was not very homogeneous especially due to local clergies that were especially powerful and vindictive. It was by their active support that the Pharaoh was able to rule and once this wavered, centrifugal movements became uncontrollable.

The heyday of the Mycenaeans, a special cultural background for all classical Greeks but especially for Alexander who took pains to ascertain that he was offspring of the lineage of Achilles, coincided, causally or not, with the ascendance of Thebes in Egypt, under the patronage of Amun-Ra. Achilles mentions the riches of Thebes (Hom Il IX-381/384), not of any other city; the Thebes that had headed the national counter-attack to expel Hyksos, the Asian invaders. This was sitting well with the Mycenaeans, who had similar problems with Asiatic Luwians as seen in the Trojan War. Thus, Alexander, all these years after, was somewhat better attuned to Ammon-Ra, already known and revered in Greece and identified with Zeus and Apollo. Thebes was too far to the south, whereas the abode of Siwa was very conveniently located for Alexander to make a show of force to the western extremities of his African estates (**Map 7**); an area many times veering to Libya and trying to shed Egyptian overlordship.

But it is much more important to understand the status of Memphis. From the days of Cambyses, Memphis was the seat of Achaemenid power (Her III.37,1 & 91,3); after the Battle of Issus Amyntas with his mercenaries sailed from Cyprus to Memphis (Arr Anab II.13,3), obviously under Darius' orders (Curt IV.1,29), to consolidate the Achaemenid hold there under the viceroy Mazaces, since the satrap Sabaces had perished at Issus, possibly with the Persians of the garrisons of Egypt (Parpas 2013); or, if there were Persians that exterminated Amyntas and his men by sallying from the fortress (Curt IV.1,33), and not disenchanted locals, they should have been the half of the garrison that remained back per Achaemenid SOP when the rest was rallied for campaigning abroad (Xen Cyr I.2,9 & 12). Memphis was the city of the god Ptah, not so revered by the Greeks, as he was identified with Hephaestus, the lame master of technology – something not really exciting or respectable in Ancient Greece. Whereas there were proper religious centres and establishments for Amun in Greece, as in southern Macedonia and (Boeotian) Thebes at the very least, Ptah had no worshippers in and thus no income from Greece. The Spartans had very close relations with the Siwa oracle, and Alexander, by acquiring the overlordship in a very reverend manner deprived his Spartan enemies of a cultural and intelligence weapon. And then, it was a matter of Medizers.

The Persian presence in Egypt was closely associated, through ups and downs, with the Egyptian theocracy. With the satrapy being governed from Memphis, it was a matter of fact that the clergy there had

> to be properly aligned with the secular Persian power and very tolerant of the Mazdaism it was bringing along. When the kings clashed with the Memphite priesthood, with the obsessive Xerxes being one example, hell broke loose. If not, there was some uneasy but mutually beneficial co-existence. This pro-Persianism in Memphis became evident in many levels under Alexander and his successors, the Ptolemies. It was Memphis that declined due to Alexandria (**Map 7**), and Ptolemy never felt at ease in the ancient city as he was waiting for the new city he had commandeered to be completed and occupied. He constructed no monument for the hijacked corpse of Alexander in Memphis; in all, the Macedonian sovereigns were subtly but definitely hostile to the city, and they must have had good reasons to be. The role of the city – and its clergy – in the abortive Athenian effort to help the Egyptians shed the Persian overlordship in late 450s BC is never examined, and the reconquista of Ochus that ended the last period of Egyptian independence in 342 BC is not more so.

wars. The time spent there and the elaborate arrangements, as well as the foundation of a coastal new capital directly open to Greeks from the sea and under the patronage of another deity, outside the existing Pantheon, show the brewing troubles in the ancient land and the care Alexander was taking not to share the fate of Cambyses (Kambouris 2022a). Flattery was mixed with solid measures of security by removing the secular administration from the religious centres.

Not just a sideshow. The Aegean war of the imperial fleet against Alexander's captains

The Persian naval operations initiated by summer 334 BC were intended to imitate once more the Greek practices of the Great Persian War (480–479 BC) and to repeat the extremely efficient defeat of the Spartan land offensive undertaken by Agesilaus in 395 BC by a strategic naval counteroffensive at his rear (Arslan 2019). Alexander, an accomplished scholar in historical and military matters, denied the Persian High Command and fleet a victory that would enhance their prestige and give them free ride in the Aegean. Having lost a cavalry engagement to a Greek army was nothing to the Persians; Agesilaus had done so with minimal impact in strategic terms. The massive loss of Greek mercenaries meant double nothing. Until the siege of Halicarnassus, the Persian High Command was perceiving the

The Battle of Issus 195

issue as 'business as always'; though, in this particular case there was a slight problem: their Greek opponents had taken Dascylium and Sardis. Never before had the empire lost a satrapal capital to the Greeks. Not burned or assaulted; fully occupied and integrated into the enemy administrative and command system.

The decommissioning of the League fleet just after the siege of Miletus saved Alexander much gold from the spoils of Sardis and Dascylium, and denied the Persians an easy victory plus a free hand from then on. They knew there was to be some opposition and were careful not to suffer nasty surprises. Their own arrival at the naval front was late and the rest of 334 BC they were pinned to support Halicarnassus and then had to suspend operations for the winter; their only success to date was the occupation of Cos, just across the narrows.

As a base Halicarnassus was greatly confined, but still the Persians created, under Memnon, a sizeable foothold in the area, in both mainland and islands in the next campaigning or sailing season. Next spring, their operations developed fully (**Map 8**), mostly northwards by capturing Chios and attacking Lesbos, but also to the west, to keep the enemy off balance and stir Greeks in the mainland; a free – or cheap – diversion. But Alexander's winter campaign had brought him mastery over Asia Minor and occupation of something like two-thirds of its expanse, meaning his difficulties with supplies were over; the areas under his sway could provide for much larger forces, since he was not devastating anything. It has been convincingly argued that Alexander's expeditionary schedule was adapted

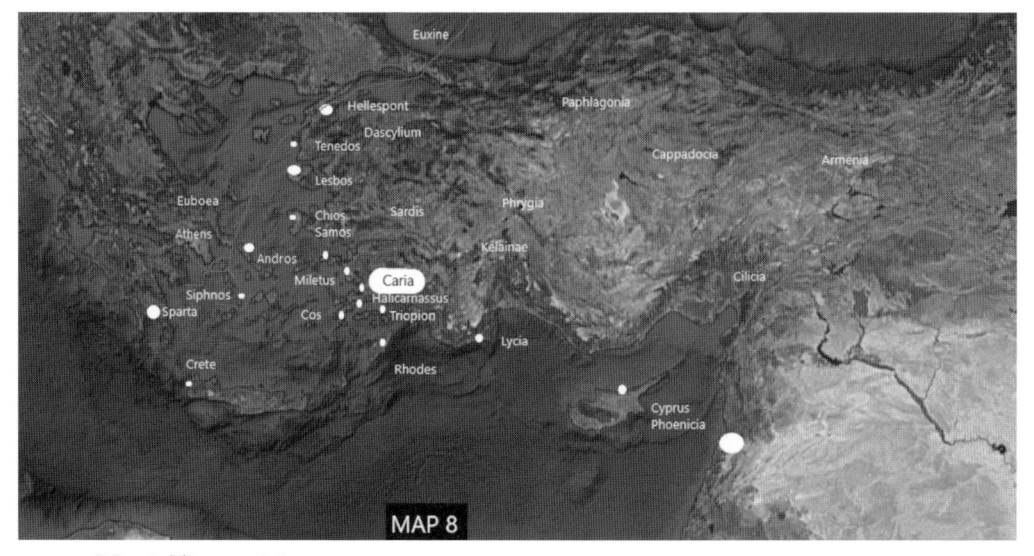

Map 8: The naval theatre.

to the agricultural calendar of the theatre of operations (Engels 1980b). By assuming a central position at Gordium and reducing cities to submission he was formally established all the way from the western coast to the river Halys in central Asia Minor, and notionally so even east of the Halys. He could invade 'Upper Asia' from Armenia or Cilicia, and both he and Darius decided upon Cilicia as the focal point of operations since it allowed combined action and mutual support of land and sea elements. Alexander moved there to prevent such synergies, Darius to ensure and enhance them.

The conduct of the winter campaign and the – pretended – surrender of Cappadocia, brought Alexander's authority near Armenia, the doorway to Media and Elam, and made Darius much more prudent. He was certain at that time, if not since the whirlwind campaign to the coast after the Granicus, that an Aegean counter-offensive had limited strategic potential. Alexander now controlled a part of Asia Minor larger than mainland Greece by a factor of more than two. Not all peoples of Asia Minor had the best opinion of the Persians and many needed a pretext to shake them off, as evident by the satrapal revolts. Alexander offered not just a pretext, but also good reasons. Darius had to intervene personally, not only to lead a massive army, but to show his revered face and royal presence. He assembled a royal army fast, very fast, in a matter of months compared to Xerxes' schedule. He had it assembled at Babylon and due to urgency it included only the western parts of the realm, from Persia to the west – the lands he still commanded (Badian 2000). He opted, correctly, for using as many of his massively recruited mercenaries by Memnon for the decisive action than to have them cruising the Aegean while the entry to Upper Asia was in dispute. A mass of mercenaries was transported by sea; his agents, both nephews of Memnon, shook hands in Lycia. If Darius was to be victorious, Alexander's conquests would be undone by him and his fleet in a matter of weeks and then Macedon would be invaded. Alexander's occupation of Cilicia deprived Darius of an extended campaigning season and brought the next winter lull of the naval operations very close to the date of the battle.

Thymondas was operating with Darius; he was the son of Mentor, the late brother to Memnon and a hero of the throne. Memnon, and now Pharnabazus were the *Karana*, the commander of the whole theatre. With Memnon dead, his other nephew Pharnabazus led the Aegean operations, with some success. He widened the foothold in Caria under Orontobates, sanctioned the latter's offensive at the near rear of Alexander in Lydia, to cause some real stress, and secured the whole of Lesbos and then Tenedos, just at the exit of the Hellespont (**Map 8**). Due to the latter success, he was able to leave a small naval task force to interrupt the flow of support elements in the

Hellespont, but this was a bit late, after the 333 BC wave of reinforcements had crossed from Europe to meet Alexander at Gordium. Still, he cut the itinerary of grain ships intended from the Black Sea to Greece, especially Athens, a development posing a real political problem for Alexander (Parpas 2013, Ruzicka 1988). The Persian offensive was expanding to his strategic rear in Greece by influence and proxies, and to his operational rear by the actions of Orontobates, satrap and defender of Caria and Halicarnassus. Only with the assumption that his operations had included Lycia (**Map 8**) can one understand Thymondas and Pharnabazus shaking hands there, as the region was conquered the previous autumn by Alexander. And if there is one thing that is certain, it is that the two Imperial commanders did not rendezvous and meet in the high seas, but on some beach.

Things seemed ominous for the Macedonians, if one resided in the Aegean, and thus the Spartans took the chance. They threw in their lot for the empire; Leonidas and Agesilaus would have found their graves uncomfortable and would think of rising, obviously. The Spartans could offer a land campaign from Greece northwards to the west of Macedon; from Tenedos the straits were within range. Moreover it is possible that a certain Memnon in Thrace, who revolted against Antipater (Diod XVII.62,6), was in talks with the Persian High Command in the Aegean and possibly relative to the Persian *generalissimo*, as the name is not that common.

It is not that the Persian strategy changed to direct land confrontation due to the demise of Memnon. There was no time for that, and Memnon *threatened* to cross to Greece, but prudently and conservatively developed his – direct – actions mostly to the north, to the straits. Greece would be stirred to fight, would not be invaded; Greek mercenaries made up most of his line troops. If there was a change in the Imperial Aegean strategy it would have occurred at the latest when Alexander took Celaenae and Gordium, not later, when Darius understood the true menace upon his empire and the serious measures it demanded. This is why Memnon was so conservative in his operations. He expected to see if Alexander decided to return near the Aegean. If not, Darius would face him in the east with a royal host and needed the mercenary hoplites massively recruited by Memnon. Pharnabazus continued the same family operation and along the same blueprint.

It is not clear how many of Darius' 30,000 mercenaries that were fielded at Issus (Arr Anab II.8,6) had been transferred from the Aegean. More than 8,000 for certain, as there were more ships than was needed for the escape of such a number after the battle (Arr Anab II.13,2–3). Once the mercenaries landed at Tripolis, in Phoenicia (**Map 6**), they advanced from the coastal road northwards, where Darius was expected coming from Babylon. It is understood that he followed the Middle Road along the Euphrates, in which case the rendezvous might have been just south of the Syrian Gates, the southern exit from Cilicia, near the royal road but not on it. If Darius took the Lower Road and emerged at Emesa, the rendezvous might have taken place exactly there.

With Alexander committed to Cilicia, the Persian fleet could intensify their activity in the Aegean without much fear, despite having sent many of the mercenaries to Darius. At this point, at the latest, the Imperial fleet subjugated Tenedos and a task force under Aristomenes plugged the Hellespont, while another under Datames expands to the west, to Siphnos, not only to exact funds from the rich island but also to establish an outpost to the Southwest Aegean, which would secure contact with the new proxies of the throne, the Spartans (Parpas 2013).

Actually, once the decisive action was to be fought in the east, between the kings, all these were superfluous for any sound strategic reason but for the promotion of the Persian commanders. The only sound reason for continuing such an expensive and universal, intercontinental plan of operations would be the decision of Darius not to win the war but to totally eliminate Macedon (Ruzicka 1988). Understandably so; Alexander was the third Macedonian King to engineer the demise of the empire, after Archelaus and Philip II. The other two had been assassinated; one of them, his father, *after* he had initiated hostilities.

And there, things started going south for the Persians. Halicarnassus was meant to be the base of operations in the west and increased its footprint to Caria and obviously Lycia, but the other, more ambitious effort, obviously to Lydia, which would threaten the main line of communications of Alexander with the Mediterranean world, failed. After a major defeat on land, by Ptolemy and Asander (Arr Anab II.5,7), the Imperial hold was curtailed and many parts of Caria recaptured by the Macedonians. Simultaneously, the Macedonian fleet was mobilized in the summer of 333 BC under Hegelochus to protect Euboea and reclaim the straits. A squadron eliminated the Imperial naval detachment at Siphnos, which was obviously feeling no danger whatsoever as it had not taken even standard security precautions, thus harassing the Imperial access to Sparta and southern Greece. The main effort of the Macedonian admirals, Hegelochus and Amphoterus (Parpas 2013) was towards the straits; they liberated Tenedos, always pro-Macedonian, and exterminated the naval contingent of Aristomenes in the Hellespont, thus allowing the grain ships into the Aegean and the flow of reinforcements to Asia.

Antipater resolved the Thracian rebellion and thus the communications were secure in Europe, the straits and Asia. The Athenians were convinced to man some of their fleet, perhaps 100 vessels (Parpas 2013) deactivated the previous year, to provide escort for the grain ships from Tenedos to Greece, as the small Macedonian fleet could not do so even if it left the straits and Tenedos totally unguarded, which they would not. It was a brilliant and wise decision. Pharnabazus insisted on countering the opening of the straits, at least regarding the supply of grain and thus the stability of Greece. This would be fulfilled by attacking the grain ships by his naval units of his and by enticing, organizing and perhaps financing pirate associates. He occupied Andros, to intercept inbound grainships for Athens in the strait between Andros and Euboea (**Map 8**), and financed pirates to cover other, longer routes. He also financed the Lacedaemonians, the only land diversion, as the Thracians had failed, the Imperial forces in Southwest Asia Minor were on the defensive and the northern seas were now under firm Macedonian control.

The Lacedaemonians had bet on Darius' victory at Issus – or wherever the battle was to be – and the whole set of the Persian operations. Alexander's victory must have left them flabbergasted. Their reply was to try to conquer or lure Crete to their common cause with the Persians by a new mercenary army raised by the Lacedaemonians from Taenarum with the gold of Pharnabazus and turn it into a secure and self-sufficient base to shelter the Imperial squadrons along the length of the Aegean during ominous times (Bosworth 1980a), especially in winter. Crete could provide the necessary grain and water supplies, which were in short supply in the islands (Parpas 2013), since more and more of them were falling to the Macedonians under Hegelochus. Phalassarna in the west side (**Map 8**) was rebuilt to become a major naval base (Hadjidaki 2012). Additionally, in this way the local archer resources that had been providing units for Alexander (Arr Anab II.9,3) would have been drained.

With the victory of Alexander, both Halicarnassus and the islands were deemed compromised, despite the decision to contest the Macedonians along every stride. Thus the two allies on the morrow of the battle had three objectives: the reversal of the sorry state of their condition at Halicarnassus, the stabilization of their hold on Cos, Samos, Chios and Lesbos and the conquest of Crete should the other two measures fail, in the middle or long term. A hefty force of 4,000 mercenaries, survivors of Issus, arrived to the Aegean under Thymondas and joined his cousin Pharnabazus, obviously in pursuit of the two first objectives, while their kin under Amyntas moved to Egypt possibly to guard it.

With the coming of the winter the opposing fleets retire; the Imperials and their Spartan allies operate in Crete and the centre of gravity of the operations moves to land. The gigantic Imperial army at Issus was defeated and dispersed but not exterminated. It did suffer appalling casualties, but it was so big that something like 30 per cent were killed in action. The remainder was still a formidable force, even with their shredded morale. Even the cavalry, which took more severe punishment with a third of its strength destroyed according to the worst case account, that of Arrian, had 20,000 survivors – that is as many as there were at the Granicus. Imperial troops had been escaping using all three exits from Cilicia (dotted lines in **Map 6**), namely the Gates of Amanus in the north east (along with Darius), the Syrian Gates to the south, at the rear of the Macedonian army (as did the Greek mercenaries) and the Cilician Gates west-north west, the furthest away but also the safest. As a result, Asia Minor was suddenly flooded with Imperial warriors. The fugitives from the Gates of Amanus could fall back east and then north, from Nineveh to Asia Minor (dashed and dotted line in **Map 5**).

From the Cilician Gates the survivors could follow the King's Road to the west, or move north to Paphlagonia; they opted for the latter course of action (Curt IV.1,34–35). As a result, Paphlagonia and Cappadocia, having only in pretence surrendered a year ago, once invaded (Arr Anab II.4,1–2), declared for the empire, while the mass of the mounted fugitives were heading for Lydia (Curt IV.1,34–35) and most probably the coast, perhaps to join the base at Halicarnassus. It is obvious that despite the disastrous defeat, the plan of Darius worked in operational terms; the army of Alexander was in Asia, although not at all destroyed, and masses of Imperial troops flooded his rear and instigated further rebellions, while the Imperial navy, despite some reverses, was in full force in Aegean waiting for the spring.

Both land attempts fail. Antigonus, satrap of Great Phrygia beats repeatedly, actually thrice, in the field (Curt IV.1,36) the rallied army of the survivors of Issus (Curt IV.1,36), while his colleague Callas, from Dascylium, disciplines the Paphlagonians (Curt IV.5,13). At the same time, Alexander descends upon Phoenicia, and most cities surrender. This means their squadrons, possibly low in loyalist mercenary marines for the winter, defect from the Imperial fleet and, even worse, declared for Alexander. The Cyprians did the same and the Tyrians also defected – to assist their city. It was the end of the Imperial fleet and the Macedonian one may have exterminated the remnants (Parpas 2013).

The Macedonians see no reason to mobilize another allied fleet in the spring; thus the Athenians stay put, and the Spartans find an excellent chance to try to lure them to the Imperial side; for a second time after Salamis, the Persians try to appropriate an Athenian fleet, the first being by Mardonius in 479 BC (Kambouris 2022c). The Athenians are not very enthusiastic and they do not oblige, although they would rather have. But they are realists. The Imperials seem to be in a steep decline. Now the former Imperial fleet squadrons follow Alexander, who, after invading Egypt, can spare it to send some lessons to treacherous Greeks. The Aegean is liberated from Imperial troops, all islands are free and the operations in Crete end with Persians and Spartans – and their mercenaries – flying the theatre of war. Now it is Alexander who hires mercs massively and with Crete in his hands, they sail from Taenarum south to join him in Egypt. With the allied Greek units in Syria to keep an eye to the crossing points of Euphrates for the next army of Darius, the mountains of Phoenicia purged so as to shut the 'Lower Road' from Mesopotamia to the Levant, and the Aegean clear, Alexander takes most of the troops of Macedon for his final match with Darius. This actually nullifies the last existential reason for the Spartan alliance with the Persians; not to allow massive reinforcements to flow to Alexander. But the latter dispatches fleets and money, which steady the Greek states and thus uses them as proxies against Sparta, the Persian proxy. Antipater would fight the Spartans enjoying crushing superiority despite sending massive reinforcements under Amyntas to Alexander.

Or did he? Alexander was expecting Amyntas for the final confrontation with Darius, but the latter arrived and met him at Susa. This was something like 2½ months after the battle, a most significant delay as from Sardis to Susa it was just three months' stroll (Her V.54). One could suggest that Antipater did not authorize the reinforcements eastwards before securing the situation back home. This could have been a thorn with Alexander afterwards, as to assure his victory and the security of Macedon the regent endangered the army of Alexander, the King's own security and the achievements up to that day.

Chapter 12

The Battle of Gaugamela

The strategic context

Alexander had secured the volatile Phoenicia and the potentially untrustworthy but invaluable Egypt (Anson 2013) and took his army leisurely from Memphis against the new Persian royal army (Arr Anab III.4,1 & 7,1). From Tyre (**Map 9**), he took the interior mainland itinerary to Thapsacus (Arr Anab III.7,1), striving both to pacify the interior and to use a road suitable for his baggage train, including the artillery and siege park (Engels 1980), which now could not be ferried by sea (Arr. Anab. II.27,2) and was expanded considerably after the siege operations of Tyre and Gaza. It was a hotter proposition in mid-summer, but took him to Damascus, to collect elements left there as discussed, while also it would create uncertainty for Darius: he could take the Lower Road (Damascus-Homs/Emesa-Palmyra, passing or bypassing today's Deir Ezzor/Dura Euphoros, to reach the middle Euphrates) and appear in Mesopotamia

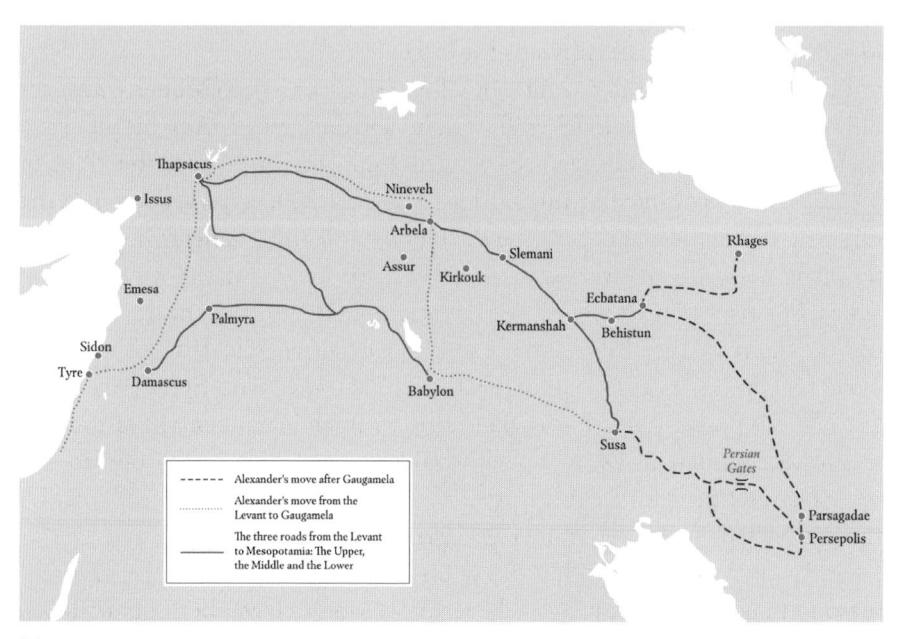

Map 9.

following the opposite direction from the one Darius had (most probably) taken in 333 BC starting from Babylon. As a result, Darius could not afford to move northwards and have Alexander emerge at his tail, reversing the events of Cilicia, and threaten Babylon. He had to stay put and try to oppose Alexander's crossing (had he had such a wish, which is doubtful) by some dispatch; the contingent of Mazeus.

The army of Alexander was not the same force that crossed the Hellespont and roamed the width and length of Asia Minor. At some time after the Battle of Issus, but definitely in Egypt, the lean and mean army created by Philip II (Diod XVI.3,1–2) was no more. Luxury and extravagance were the order of the day (Plut Vit Alex 40,1), as the loot captured in Damascus was taken along (Diod XVII.35) and a full system for administering the conquered lands while on campaign was developed, similar to but lighter than the Achaemenids. It is true that during the siege of Tyre and the campaign to Egypt the family of Darius, and thus the heavy baggage train, is never mentioned; they might have been left in Damascus and brought to Egypt by sea, in Memphis, when Alexander arrived there. Or Alexander had them reside in Damascus under the protection of Parmenio and took them along when returning from Egypt to invade Mesopotamia. But in any case he could not follow the short Lower Road to Mesopotamia, through Palmyra and the desert; it was too unsafe, too difficult and too risky. He had to move northward, to Syria (from Damascus to Homs/Emesa, Hama, Aleppo) and cross the Euphrates at Thapsacus (Monerie 2019), probably located at or near Jarablus (**Maps 5 and 9**).

Knowing in advance he could not take the Lower Road (Monerie 2019) of Palmyra (see solid lines in **Map 9**) – a solid and easy guess given his planning and his army status – he had dispatched engineers to prepare the crossing of Euphrates by constructing bridges (Arr III.7,2); a very good fake, it might have been. Fake or not, the deployment of such elements implies that powerful detachments were stationing there for the security of such valuable assets, but also to forestall any Persian attempts to cross westwards and take him at the rear once more, after the bitter experience at Issus. Such units were definitely the allied cavalry, left precisely to defend Syria (Arr Anab II.13,7) but possibly the Thessalians also, as there is no mention of them in Egypt (Strootman 2012) and they would be invaluable in the operational manoeuvres that could develop should Darius achieve a comeback earlier than expected, while Alexander was preoccupied in Phoenicia and Egypt. In all honesty, Darius did not know his intentions, nor would he have any reason to take any risks; he would keep a position to cover both possibilities.

Possibly Alexander was quite happy to find Persian loyalists from the whole empire concentrated and assembled within reach, to crush them in one battle (Diod XVII.56,4), but this was only one plan of action. As mentioned previously, although he meticulously created and projected the image of a bold, even reckless, impatient and dashing general, he was not entirely such (Fuller 1958). The storming of the Cilician Gates (Arr. Anab. II.4,3) and the prompt engagement at the Granicus (Arr. Anab. I.13,6) were testaments of his dashing and daring. The final action in Pelion (Arr. Anab. I.6,9–10) and the attempt at Mindus (Arr. Anab. I.20,5) were bold, night actions to catch enemies off guard; but the action in Halicarnassus proper (Arr. Anab. I.20,2 and I.22,7) and the one in Thebes (Arr. Anab. I.7,10) were patient, leisurely siege actions, not very rapidly nor astutely pursued. When unnecessary risks, in the form of naval engagements, emerged, he had been really cautious and did not respond to repeated challenges (Arr. Anab. I.18,6). The surprise winter campaign of 334 BC (Arr. Anab. I.24,3) was followed by weeks of inaction in Cilicia (Arr. Anab. II.6,4), prolonged sieges in Tyre and Gaza and a really comfortable schedule in Egypt, which resulted in almost two years between the second and the third major battles.

This behavioural inconsistency was showing a leader having all the needed qualities and using them with discretion, thus increasing the uncertainty of the enemy. Consequently, when Alexander crossed the Euphrates at Thapsacus (Arr Anab III.7,2), neither he nor Darius were looking for a head-to-head clash in equal terms, a set-piece battle. They intended to capitalize on any possible advantage they had or they could create, and deny their opponent any such opportunities. Darius now believed what the late Amyntas, son of Antiochus, the renegade-become-mercenary who perished in Egypt (Arr Anab II.13,3) had told him before the Battle of Issus (Arr. Anab. II.6,3&6), that Alexander would come himself to meet him in arms, and intended to build up all possible advantages: from a new model army (Diod XVII.55,1) through better selection of the battlefield (Diod XVII.53,3), improved tactics, full use of technology and technical resources (Diod XVII.55,2 & 53,1) to a smartly executed opening campaign of exhaustion laid in the path of his opponent (Diod XVII.55,1). An advance force of 3,000 cavalry and 2,000 Greek mercenaries under Mazeus, the satrap of Syria (Arr Anab III.8,6) and thus perfectly familiar with the terrain, was guarding the crossing of Euphrates (Arr Anab III.7,1) and actively contested the bridging, but was repelled a bit too easily once Alexander arrived there, and retreated towards Babylon, from the road roughly following the Euphrates, the Middle Road (Monerie 2019). He was evidently trying initially to buy time so as to devastate the eastern bank of the river and then to lure Alexander towards their main force, most probably through barren and devastated land, along the eastern bank of the Euphrates (Marsden 1964) to bring his forces hungry, exhausted and out of breath to the battlefield (Engels 1980a).

Darius, previously engaged in the Royal Postal Service (Badian 2000), was the one man with the most intimate knowledge of his vast empire, in terms of geography and transportation. The events reported and the intentions discussed in the following parts of this work focus on the understanding that Darius wanted Alexander to take the Middle Road, from Thapsacus to Babylon, and not the Upper, to the east bank of the Tigris (**Map 9**), as maintained by other scholars (Boardman 1999). Which means that the devastation mission carried out by Mazeus was not meant to discourage Alexander and send him to the Upper Road, but, combined with a measured retreat, to entice him into pursuit along the devastated terrain.

If Darrius was to intercept Alexander at the eastern bank of the Tigris, on the Royal Road, this would mean the latter's approach from Jarablus/Thapsacus through Sanliourpha – Qamishli-Mosul – Erbil/Arbela – Kirkuk to Kermanshah, a crossroads leading to two vital areas, Northeast to Ecbatana in Media through Behistun (the road of Khorasan); and Southeast to Susa and then Persepolis. Darius' massive host could cover these directions by deploying Northwest anywhere from Kermanshah to Mosul (he actually settled for Arbela), but then Babylon would be exposed to a dashing rerouting of the invaders' much nimbler army. There was no question of risking a siege of Babylon by the conqueror of Tyre, especially since Achaemenid caution had reduced the defences of the city to discourage revolts by the natives; nor any option to starve out the invaders in Mesopotamia, the main part of the 'Fertile Crescent'.

Alexander had no intention of playing by Darius' rules, and instead of dashing towards Darius in the general direction of Babylon by the Middle Road (Monerie 2019), Southeast from Thapsacus, as Cyrus the Younger had done after crossing the Euphrates (Xen Anab I.4,11), he moved away from the Euphrates river (dotted line in **Map 9**) until he crossed the Royal Road and taking it he continued east (Stein 1942), following the Upper Road (Monerie 2019) which ended at Susa (Her V.52). This move took him to an area with relatively cool weather and adequate resources of water and fodder (Arr Anab III.7,3). Having arrested the Persian scouting party who revealed that Darius was east of the Tigris and intended to intercept Alexander's crossing (Arr Anab III.7,4), he pressed East-Southeast (Stein 1942) and forded the Tigris with difficulty and danger but without opposition (Arr Anab III.7,5; Diod XVII.55,3–6). Neither Darius was there, nor the crossing was contested; most probably the prisoners had been planted to misinform Alexander on the whereabouts of Darius (Russell 1999; Engels 1980a), conceivably to deter him from crossing the Tigris and thus to subtly guide his advance Southeast west of the Tigris, through the devastated Mesopotamia and away from the crossroads at today's Kermanshah, which lead to Ecbatana through Behistun or to Susa. There can be no other reason for supplying such misinformation, as Darius was not in a position to prevent a crossing of the Tigris.

After the crossing, Alexander afforded his troops some days of rest before advancing for four days (Arr Anab III.7,8) and approaching the ruins of Nineveh, the major crossroads in the area (Stein 1942) where he was tipped off by his own scouts about a Persian mounted force. Alexander deployed for battle; further intelligence elaborated on the strength of the enemy detachment, now estimated at about a thousand horse (Arr Anab III.7,7), obviously dispatched either for reconnaissance-in-force or to check possible crossing points and perhaps intercept Alexander's crossing, or both. Alexander gave chase personally with a flying detachment including the Royal Squadron, another squadron of the Companions and the Paeonian scouts (Arr Anab III.8,1); a competent and sufficient counter-reconnaissance task force. They intercepted the enemy. Most probably the Paeonian prince Ariston killed their commander in a duel reminiscent of jousting (Curt IV.9,24–25; Plut Alex 39,1) and this put the rest to flight. The Macedonians gave chase, killed and apprehended some whose horses were too tired (Arr Anab III.8,2), an indication that the Imperials were intercepted after a forced approach. This time the intelligence reported that Darius was rather close by, and under the circumstances Alexander established a properly entrenched camp and from there he moved to Gaugamela, where Darius had deployed. Alexander in this case took only the combatants, in the dead of night, intending to fall upon the enemy at dawn (Arr Anab III.9,1).

This northward and then eastward dash was a strategic master-stroke. It nullified all the preparations Darius had made along the expected convergence path, in the SE direction from Thapsacus. Additionally the Macedonian army had a cooler walk south of the Armenian mountains (today's Kurdistan) instead of the scorched Mesopotamia, which most probably would have been stripped of fodder and other supplies (Arr. Anab. III.7,3). Thus, Darius' exhaustion strategy failed. But it also created a crisis: the dashing and unpredictable character of Alexander and the superior mobility of his army allowed, at least in theory, a chance to repeat the storming of the Cilician Gates on a gigantic scale. He could, after following the eastern bank of the Tigris, reach a position to burst through the Behistun pass at the Zagros mountain range to Media, following roughly the escape road selected by

Darius after the battle (Arr Anab III.16,1) and from there to the heartland of Persia, with only over-aged militia in position to intercept him. Even these would be in anything but high alert, as the gigantic Imperial army was supposedly between the Zagros range and the invader.

Darius had been trying for years to transfer the war into Greece (Arr. Anab. II.1,1; Diod XVII.30,1), a strategy which worked superbly against the Spartans in 395 BC (Xen Hell IV.2,1–3). Instead of this, Ecbatana in Media and then Persepolis, the secret royal city, the hearth of the Achaemenid rule, could be stormed, outraged and violated by the agile and flying Macedonian army while the host of the King of Kings was lurking between Babylon and Susa, gleaning the supplies of the Fertile Crescent.

This threat made Darius move his gigantic host in anger Northeast to Gaugamela (Arr Anab III.8,7), in order to counter this move (Marsden 1964). His army being largely made up from eastern contingents, it would have been much better in terms of time and logistics to have them assembled in the vicinity of Arbela, had he intended to tackle Alexander there, squarely on the Royal Road, near a large city with workshops and enjoying access from four bearings of the compass for supplies and units to flood in. But he had no such intention originally, it was a forced move. Still, a successful one.

Alexander would make no attempt at forcing a narrow mountain pass, such as Behistun, in the relatively densely populated Zagros range with the royal army close by. The said army also barred the Royal Road to Susa, a possible target of Alexander. The latter in theory could bypass Babylon and go for Susa, by simply following the Royal Road. However, the morale of the Achaemenid host would have suffered a blow already. They were found to rush to intercept after a surprise development, instead of waiting for an exhausted enemy at their comfortably established base at Babylon (Diod XVII.53,1). This was emotionally unsettling and wrecked morale. Similarly, all the preparations of the battlefield and the logistics set in place were abandoned and eliminated from the equation overnight. The scales were coming towards levelling, but there was still a long way to go.

Preparations and intentions
The Persian side

Darius was proving a smart and intelligent man with good reflexes. His gigantic host (Arr. Anab. III.8,6) moved relatively fast to avert the threat to the Motherland and impose an all-out battle instead of a contest by manoeuvrability and generalship, i.e. the territorial warfare practised for 100–120 years by the Greeks. Alexander would have to fight it out with a huge disadvantage in numbers over a battlefield selected and prepared by the enemy (Arr. Anab. III.8,7), although not as advantageous and well-groomed as the previous position near Babylon.

Although the battle order of Darius fell at the hands of the Macedonians after the end of the battle (Arr. Anab. III.11,3), it is usually maintained that the Persian army was mainly cavalry, due to the eastern contributions and the slaughter of dependable infantry vassal units at Issus (Arr. Anab. II.11,8). Still, the massive Mesopotamian levies were infantry, as were big parts of Median and Persian national armies and the gigantic host of the Achaemenid kingdom was reportedly infantry-heavy by almost 20:1 at Gaugamela (Arr. Anab. III.8,3–6). Though contrary to the total number at Issus as corroborated by the numbers of Xenophon and Herodotus, by estimating two major recruiting areas for Darius III (**Map 3**) instead of four for Artaxerxes II (Xen Anab I.7,12) and six for Xerxes (Her VII.82), at Gaugamela the numbers of the full host seem out of any context. One should expect two recruitment areas, for 600,000 at most, possibly with all the auxiliaries and attendants, non-combatants included (Kambouris 2022a,b).

The cavalry, though 40,000 (Arr Anab III.8,6), is half that of Xerxes in 480 BC (Her VII.87) which could be attributed to the loss of half the realm and the heavy casualties at Issus (Arr Anab II.11,8). The survivors operated in Asia Minor, behind enemy lines, and it is doubtful whether they were able to take the long way home from the road of Pteria, through Armenia in the general direction Ankara – Erzurum – Tarbriz – Hamadan or even Ankara – Kayzeri – Malatya – Nineveh (dotted and dashed/dotted line respectively in **Map 5**), to rally under the Imperial standards for the Battle Royal.

The new, longer arms, spears and swords developed by Darius (Diod XVII.53,1) were most probably issued to the native infantry (Patchen 2014), which had performed very poorly at Issus, in stark contrast to the cavalry and the Greek mercenaries. The ranks of the latter were depleted after the battle and their recruitment became impossible (Arr. Anab. II.8,5 & II.13,1). But in any case the *xyston* lance of the Companion Cavalry outranged the hoplite *dory* spear, not to mention the reach of the *sarissa* pike. A longer spear would allow the Imperial line infantry to ward off at least the Macedonian heavy horse that had cut through its phalanx with annoying ease at Issus, at least according to the established interpretation of events, i.e. assigning the thunderous charge of Alexander (Arr Anab II.10,3) to the Companion Cavalry.

Here some attention is required. Diodorus mentions longer swords and spears (Diod XVII.53,1) but does not mention for which arm and which troopers. All the host? Impossible. Cavalry? Double that. There is not one line in any report of the battle suggesting that a new, longer spear had been issued; the feeling one gets is that in such a case Alexander would have been defeated, as the facial thrusts by the Macedonian lances along with the horses used to shove the enemy (Arr Anab III.14,3) is the most powerful image of Arrian's description of the battle. Nor would the Scythians, being allies and not Imperial troops, or the conservative Bactrians, take up a new weapon, alien to their skill sets and traditions. The Persian cavalry, taken out at Issus by the tactics of the Thessalians (Arr Anab II.11,3), not by any superior armament, would have also been reluctant. After all a new weapon cannot be introduced in cavalry, a most diversified arm, in less than a year, the time Darius had to outfit and train his army. Such intensive training courses are, on the other hand, compatible with infantry; Philip trained and raised a new model army in one year as mentioned above. Thus the new weapons were for infantry and a limited number, probably Persian, at that and definitely been around for some time to have time to train.

The issue with the spear is clear: the Macedonian cavalry *xyston* produced a range and lethality advantage over infantry, even against hoplite infantry. It was this detail, not the massive *sarissa*-phalanx that destroyed the Imperial host at Issus. There is nowhere any notion on any advantage enjoyed, much less exploited, by the Macedonians concerning the sword. The fight did not come to the sword except as a backup, and actually Alexander suffered a thigh wound due to one (Arr Anab II.12,1). Thus there is no such Macedonian advantage. Then why did Darius issue longer swords, along with the spears?

The answer must have been that Darius (re)introduced to his army the Iphicratean. It is the troop type characterized by longer sword and spear compared to the Greek hoplite, and Darius must have somehow revived the idea, be that from any captain of his mercenaries, or by any other source. He must have been reminded that Iphicrates had developed this troop type in Persian Imperial service, most probably, to produce men able to stand against the hoplites. Thus, with the hoplite being obsolete, especially *his* hoplites, he must have outfitted his 'hoplitised' Kardaka, who survived at Issus, with the Iphicratean kit, making in some months the evolutionary steps of some decades. These troops must have been the Persian infantry intermingled with cavalry (Arr Anab III.11,3), now able to tackle the Companions so as to stop them and support the *asabara*. These troops were not meant to face the phalanx. The surviving Greek mercenaries, who gave a hell of a fight at Issus (Arr Anab II.10,6–7) would undertake this task (Arr Anab III.11,7), this time assisted by the scythed chariots that were expected to disorganize and breach the phalanx to a vastly greater degree than the river had done at Issus (Arr Anab II.10,5).

And to top the tactical adaptations, Darius mixed infantry and cavalry units as already mentioned (Arr Anab III.10,3), with the clear intention to fight together, supporting each other, a concept simply preposterous for the *asabara* mentality some months before. The arming of Persian peasantry was not something unheard-of; they were a martial master race and soldiering was their prerogative and honour; thus Darius was not upheaving the social order as occasionally maintained (Badian 2000; Patchen 2014). But *mixing* them, this was something different.

At Gaugamela the Persian intention is double and doubly obvious: their deployment, contrary to Issus, indicates an intention for envelopment by the wings, instead of the caterpillar formed at Issus, which may be considered mistaken, at least by the results (Boardman 1999). The disposition, and in this the new weapons must be included, namely the swords and spears, (Diod XVII.53,1) and also the new weapon systems, the elephants and, especially, the scythed chariots (Arr Anab III.11,6), clearly indicates the intention to counter frontal charges delivered by qualitatively superior forces. Such charges were expected either at the left flank, as had happened at Issus, if Alexander was to match the Persian front, or at the centre. The latter was a correct intuition of Darius, perhaps suggested to him by the proceedings of the Battle of Granicus, but also by guessing that an army at the order of magnitude of the one he faced at Issus, anchoring its left wing, as it did with the sea at Issus, would have its right wing directly opposite the centre of his mega-host. Something similar had happened with the army of

Cyrus the Younger against the host of Artaxerxes II at Cunaxa. Thus, the centre, always of concern as the King was stationed there, was reinforced, and so was the left wing, with elite armoured cavalry and the majority of the scythed chariots. This was the defensive aspect of the Persian army. Having judged the Macedonian army invincible frontally, even if the best infantry of the time, the Greek mercenary hoplites, was to rush in at a disturbed phalanx front, as at Issus (Arr Anab II.10,5–7), the offensive now was to develop from the flanks, not the front. The deployment in an extended front intended to do this, contrary to the deployment at Issus, which was meant to trample and steamroll over the Macedonians (Arr Anab II.6,5).

Darius discontinued the Greek tactics, at least the ones he had tried at Issus. The defensive positioning of a hoplite or pseudohoplite phalanx behind a river (Arr. Anab. II.8,5–6), the palisades to protect accessible positions (Arr. Anab. II.10,1) and the cavalry posted at the flanks (Arr. Anab. II.8,10) in *parataxis* were all Greek, not Persian traits. The same may be said for the deep battle formation (Arr. Anab. II.8,8). Palisades in the battlefield were the specialty of the Thebans against the Spartans for 20 years (389–371 BC), as were very deep infantry formations (Thuc IV.93; Xen Hell VI.4,12 & IV.2,18). But he did try the tactical combination of infantry and cavalry, as already mentioned.

The deployment (Arr Anab III.11,3–7) was in three lines: The first line was divided into separate groups: only cavalry, scythed chariots and elephants. Behind it, one continuous battle line was deployed, made by the Army of Media to the right under Mazeus; of Persia to the left under Bessus and an almost separate small army in the middle, the division of the King. Finally, the third line, the Babylonian Army, politically rather suspicious, were the reserves (Sarantis 1977). It consisted of Babylonians (who hated the Persians), Uxians (who were never totally subjugated), Sitaceneans and the inhabitants of the Red Sea (our Persian Gulf). Alexander's army numbered 40,000 infantry and 7,000 cavalry (the largest he had ever led).

The mini army of the Imperial command centre

The position of Darius was at the middle of his host but not in the first line. Contrary to Xerxes he was deploying for battle, and could perhaps see some action but it was a matter of responsibility for the sovereign to be well-protected. He was not a trooper, and this mentality had passed to the imperial Greeks. The Spartans always had the war-king deployed in battle surrounded by his bodyguard, the *Hippeis* (Knights). In the fourth century they used elaborate drill not to have him exposed at the extreme right or at the van (Xen Const Lac XIII.6). But the Athenian Iphicrates was saying he was the brain of the army and not an accomplished fighter but a commander. Thus there were Greek examples of war-leaders commanding from behind. Not in the Macedonian army; no matter how attractive in theory that could seem (Wrightson 2010), the evidence shows otherwise. And not only in the mentality of the troops accepting and celebrating such a leader, which might have been heroic or traditional value. It is evident that it was happening as a rule. At Gaugamela many Macedonian commanders were wounded (Arr Anab III.15,2). The demise of a phalanx general at Issus in the thick of fight (Arr Anab II.10,7), plus one chiliarch of the Hypaspists in Tyre scaling the wall first, plus the duel of a light horse commander, Ariston, *phylarch* of Balkan Allies and dependants, before Gaugamela (Plut Alex 39,1) all indicate leaders actually fighting as a rule. Ptolemy in India personally engaged with an Indian *raja*, in a territorial battle over some hill. All the above show this was the norm in every setting and operation, siege, pitched battle, or territorial warfare. It was not just Alexander, they were all like this, and Philip had been incapacitated by being in the danger zone at least twice.

To counter this, Darius was covered by his Guards unit. Arrian's report, indirectly from the Persian plan, mentions one guard unit of infantry, the Applebearers (Arr Anab III.11,5) and one of cavalry, the Kinsmen – *Anusiya* (Arr Anab III.11,6); in Xerxes' times there were two of each, one of noblemen, one of the entire nation (Her VII.40,2–41,3) and this could have been the model for the original formation of the Macedonian Hypaspists under Philip.

Darius had two units of Greek mercenaries to his left and right (Arr Anab III.11,7) guarding his flanks, as he expected Alexander to try to approach him personally from that direction. They were a shadow of their former mass, but perhaps still numbering more than the Hypaspist Corps of Alexander. Additional units were present, but their distribution is not mentioned; they are only catalogued. The vanguard was heavy cavalry of Persian and Indian aristocrats, plus chariots, and the elephants were earmarked for positioning there as well, although they were not deployed for the actual battle. Two more units deserve attention. The Mardian archers are mentioned, implying a deficiency in archery in the Persian regulars; else there is no reason to mention them specifically and position them at the entourage of the king. The other unit of special interest is the transplanted Carians (Arr Anab III.11,5) who must have been outfitted in their original attire, as hoplites, thus reinforcing the dwindling numbers of mercenary hoplites and perhaps being issued with the new, longer lances (Diod XVII.53,1). It is not known how, when, why or which Persian King had brought a Carian population from the coast to the heart of Asia. They could have been rioting radicals, as were the Eretrians of 490 BC brought back as slaves by Datis (Her VI.119,1), while their city was still active in 480 BC (Her VIII.8,1), or the descendants of some such radical elements of the Carian participation in the Ionian Revolt, an insurgency resolved mysteriously and almost amicably in 494 BC, at least in some cases (Her VI.20), and proven almost benign for the empire, after a resounding success against Imperial forces at Mylasa, off Pedasus (Her V.121). Or they could have been loyalists, pro-Persians, moved to security once the climate in Ionia was deemed unhealthy, although it is difficult to find a date for this condition.

One may well ponder upon any association with the later incident of the wholesale slaughter of the transplanted population of Didyma that the army of Alexander found happily residing (Curt VII.5,28–35). Their fate implied they were considered both traitors and sacrilegious by pedigree and not poor uprooted chattel slaves, victims of cleansing and retribution. This fact sheds another light, very different what is widely known about the extinguishing of the Ionian revolt and the loot and razing of the major spiritual centre (Her VI.19,2–3), the oracle and temple of Apollo at Didyma. The version as we understand it is that the holy precinct was ruthlessly violated and the treasure plundered by the troops of Darius I, after suppressing the Ionian Revolt, but Curtius reports that Xerxes had transplanted said priesthood to the depth of Asia (Curt VII.5,28); Xerxes at the time was regent at Babylon. In his days as king there was nothing to explain the transplantation of mainland royalists; the Greeks liberated the islands, not the mainland cities. Even if they did, in 479 BC, the sanctuary was razed in 493 BC. Thus, neither the transplantation of the clan of the ministers and keepers to the depths of Asia in this latter date may be explained, nor the savage treatment they suffered, after more than 150 years later, meaning some five generations. Something amounting to foul play, perhaps instrumental in the removal of the treasure (which the insurgents pondered upon confiscating and using to fuel their cause and man their fleets and armies) and/or the ultimate defeat may be implied (Heliopoulos 2019).

A new troop once more

The Persian infantry is prominent in its absence from the three great battles of Alexander. At the Granicus there was none, or none was used. At Issus, it is possible that it had a central role if the hoplite Kardaka were indeed another name for retrained Persian conscripts. And at Gaugamela, once more it is mentioned as a matter of fact, at an obscure line in the narrative. True, if at Issus it had been instrumental and suffered massive casualties, its role at Gaugamela would have been limited by definition and necessity. Wouldn't it?

Darius identified correctly that Alexander was striking the centre of his army from the right wing of his own battle line, thus hitting the left flank of the imperial centre. At Gaugamela Darius had obviously an epiphany that Alexander would try the same trick *somehow*. Alexander would do anything to surprise him but in the end this would be his signature and decisive move. This is why he posted his wildcard, the once more retrained Persian infantry, with long spears (in Iphicratean mode) and intermingled with cavalry, to his left. He expected to intercept the Companions and the infantry that would directly support and follow them with a similar mix of his own. There is no other way to explain why in his huge battle order it was only there that he deployed cavalry intermingled with infantry; and the few dependable infantry he extracted from the slaughterhouse of Issus at that.

Although the new spear would outrange the *xyston* of the Companions, it did no such thing with the infantry *sarissa*. There was no way Darius could create a pike phalanx in so little time and without any preliminary work on the subject. The pike needed different skills and dexterities for which he had no such experts, nor could he bestow on his conscripts another major change of weapons and attitude. Thus, the phalanx was to be faced by other means, the one that had given it some bruising at Issus, i.e. the mercenary hoplites, but this time with more breaches and gaps, opened not by chance but by another weapon system, the scythed chariot.

Darius was correct: Alexander found a way to seed uncertainty but in the end he advanced obliquely and did exactly what Darius expected him to do. It was the genius of the young Grecian King that he did it with a twist: his preliminary manoeuvring and assaults exposed the flank and he did not strike the Persian cavalry-infantry complex; he infiltrated to flank it and rolled it up from the side with his oblique phalanx; he never directed his frontal attack onto these troops. Whether some portion of his phalanx did take these troops head on cannot be surmised; the phalanx had a definite range, penetration and density advantage and would have swept cavalry and infantry before its hedge.

The army of Alexander

The spacious plain of Gaugamela allowed the deployment of the Persian host to an astonishing width. This fact denied any thought that the Macedonian army might match the enemy front by elaborate deployment of units, as done at Issus (Arr Anab II.9,3) and, to be accurate, at Marathon 490 BC (Her VI.111) for the first time. At Issus the resulting reduction in depth or density was a constant source of consternation for Alexander (Arr. Anab. II.9,3 & 4) and possibly the reason for the spontaneous gap which led to the bitter fighting between Greek mercenaries of the Persians and the phalanx (Arr. Anab. II.9,4–6). Thus, at Gaugamela Alexander deliberated differently – to form his army deep and more compact, impervious to frontal assaults and penetration. The difference in width would be irrelevant; since Darius' line would be much longer, Alexander intended to cover it by manoeuvring across the enemy front. By making his formation compact, Alexander succeeded in making a Persian breakthrough harder, inviting flanking attempts by the Persians on both flanks and ensuring precision and perfect coordination in the execution of manoeuvres and drill by the whole army.

The army of Alexander at Gaugamela is a third larger than that of the invasion force, obviously due to massive reinforcement instalments, totalling at the very least 8,750 troops of which 7,200 were infantry. From the 35,000-plus invasion force (Arr. Anab I. 11,3) Alexander fielded some 47,000 at Gaugamela (Arr Anab III.12,5), which means that massive casualties in the previous years and operations, as suggested (Bosworth 1988) are unlikely. The latter figure must refer to a grand total, with support units, such as the engineer corps (artillery and siege parks, bridging, fording, roadcutting and building units and sappers) plus baggage train or logistics and general support. These included the attendants of the High Command headquarters, the scientific cadre, the civil administrators, religious, treasury, courier, medical and financial personnel. They cannot be estimated, but all these were most probably left behind when the clash at Gaugamela was imminent, at the carefully established main camp, which was guarded closely (Arr. Anab III.12,5), as they could not participate in a pitched battle where the opponent could retake the initiative even if originally he had forfeited it to precipitate a battle at the field of his own choosing.

The core of Alexander's host was the Macedonian national army, in modern parlance both the King's army and the territorial army. Massive Macedonian reinforcements had not yet arrived except for the class of 333 BC, a mere 3,000 infantry and 300 cavalry, which had joined the army in Asia Minor, at Gordium (Arr. Anab. I.29,4) in spring 333 BC. These troops allowed the introduction of tertiary units in both arms to be deployed at Issus later that year. Since then, only allied and mercenary contingents had arrived, although there is some argument against this conclusion as drawn by reading Arrian (Brunt 1963); this line of thought provides for replacing the casualties and absentees *and* increasing the total force. Thus, the phalanx regiments were six according to Arrian (Arr. Anab. III.11,8–10), plus the three Hypaspist chiliarchies (Arr Anab III.11,9), and the Companion Cavalry. The latter (Diod XVII.57,1; Arr. Anab. III.11,8) was made up of seven squadrons and the Royal Squadron. The Macedonian light cavalry and archers should have followed a consistent binary force structure. Thus, the arm of the archers was probably divided in two units and the Macedonian archers are explicitly mentioned as a different unit than the Cretan archers at Issus (Arr. Anab. II.9,2–3), a fact compatible with what happened at Gaugamela.

The deployment of Alexander was unlike the deployment of Miltiades at Marathon, who lined up at the same length as his enemy – actually a standard in hoplite battles, in order to avoid flanking (Kambouris and Bakas 2021). Alexander opted for a solid and compact formation, opposite the right half of the Persian army (**Figure 12.1**). This made irrelevant the preparations on the Persian left wing, intended solely against him and the elite units he was leading to decide the action, and would frustrate his enemy who would try to make amends in the nick of time to its probably unresponsive huge force. Alexander's main battle line was divided into left and right operational commands (**Figure 12.2A**), himself commanding the right and Parmenio the left as usual, and included three main parts. In the centre, the Macedonian phalanx was made up, from left to right, of the *taxeis* of Craterus, Amyntas (under his brother Simmias), Polysperchon, Meleager, Perdikkas, Coenus, (which is the exact line-up at Issus) and, importantly, *two* chiliarchies of the Hypaspists under Nicanor (Arr Anab III.11,9–10). Heavy cavalry was posted on both sides (Arr Anab III.11,8 & 10), a standard Greek *parataxis* arrangement. And this is the central part.

In the left wing (of the central part, this must be underlined) there were the Thessalian horse under Philip and next to their right, all the way to the phalanx, the allied Greeks cavalry under Erigius (Arr. Anab. III.11,10); the latter were probably six squadrons from different city-states or leagues of the alliance. Most probably these were Peloponnese, Achaia, Phthia, Malis, Locris, Phocis (Diod XVII.57,3), with 'Peloponnese' being a bit unclear. To the right wing, after the Hypaspist Corps, the Companion Cavalry under Philotas was positioned in seven regular squadrons (under Glaucias, Ariston, Sopolis, Heraclides, Demetrius, Meleager and Hegelochus) plus the Royal Squadron under Cleitus the Black at the extreme right (Arr Anab III.11,8). According to Diodorus, there was still another squadron between the Royal one and the seven regular ones: the 'Friends' (*philoi*) of the King (Diod XVII.57,1), possibly a transfer of Persian custom and obviously non-territorial recruitment, but probably the bodyguard or a misunderstanding, as Friends and Companions in Greek are equivalent to the term *Hetairoi*. The fact that Philotas, the Commander of the Companion Cavalry, is attested as in charge of such 'friends' corroborates the possibility of misinformation, evident also in the terminology as Diodorus retroprojects the term *hipparchiai* instead of the correct *ilae*. A screen of 500 selected archers and 2,000 javelineers (the latter being a mixed force of Greeks under Balacrus and half the Agrianians) was thrown in front of the Companion Cavalry (Arr Anab III.12,3).

The right part of Alexander's deployment was a massive flank guard of one heavy cavalry unit and two light cavalry regiments, plus light and heavy infantry. All these were arranged in three successive lines and posted at the right and rear of the Companions' heavy cavalry. The flank guard was canted back after the end of the battle line as a precaution against outflanking, although this was the obvious. Arrian brilliantly underlines that this arrangement allowed contraction or extension of the battle order as necessary (Arr Anab III.12,2). The former, in a completely open battlefield needs some explaining. It is obvious that the intended meaning is the proper mission of a flank guard, to prevent flanking, but in this case, given that the phalanx was deployed so as to be able to fight on both fronts (front and rear) the flankguard was most probably expected, should the need be, to form the outer side of a rough square and thus allow fighting under total encirclement.

This arrangement was almost symmetrical in the two flanks and a repeat of the arrangement of the special purpose task group at the Granicus, as updated at Issus, to include the minimum of Macedonian units so as not to divert or weaken the main effort. And this is the less obvious mission, at least of the right flank guard, namely to open the way for the strike group under Alexander. The right flank guard consisted of six units in three lines. Behind the heavy cavalry at the extreme right were the squadrons of the light cavalry and a bit to its rear were the infantry units: the second half of the Agrianian javelineers (under Attalus, the unit commander), who always supported the onslaughts of the Companions. Next to them and aligned, were the Macedonian archers (under Bryson) and next to them the 'Old Mercenaries' under Cleander (Arr. Anab. III.12,2), which can be identified with 4,000 mercenary Greek infantry which Cleander had raised himself and brought to Alexander during the siege of Tyre (Arr. Anab. II.20,5).

Supposedly these were the mercenaries who had participated since the beginning of the campaign, (Arr Anab III.12,2) but this is not true; as mentioned they came after the Battle of Issus. Even if one overlooks – for no good reason – the report of Diodorus assigning 5,000 Greek mercenaries to the invasion force of 334 BC (Diod XVII.17,3), mercenary units of Alexander are mentioned after Ephesus (Arr Anab I.18,1), while some 300 mercenaries in Persian pay are pardoned and enlisted in Alexander's army off Miletus (Arr Anab I.19,6), while a massive force of 3,000 mercenaries stayed in Caria to contain the Persian garrison (Arr Anab I.23,6) after Alexander left the region. Cleander with his mercenaries did not join the army in the first instalment of reinforcements in 333 BC in Gordium, where draftees from Macedon were assembled plus some allies (Arr Anab I.28,4) but, as mentioned earlier, during the siege of Tyre (Arr Anab II.20,5). Thus, these mercenaries were not from the beginning with Alexander, nor the first ones in the campaign under Alexander; but the ones *not* left behind in garrison duties may well have been incorporated into Cleander's command.

Two units of light cavalry were posted in front of the mercenary infantry, at the right the Paeonian lights under Ariston and at the left the Scouts of Aretes. The unit of heavy cavalry posted before them were Greek mercenaries under Menidas (Arr Anab III.12,3). These must be the force of 400 mercenaries under the same Menidas son of Hegisander who joined Alexander at Memphis, sent by his regent Antipater (Arr. Anab. III.5,1). This means they were a relatively new unit, virtually unbled.

At the left wing, next to the Pharsalian squadron, the best and largest of the Thessalian cavalry, were the Thracians of Sitalces, probably normal peltasts, experts with the javelin, and next to them an allied force under Coiranus and even further to the left the light Odryssian horsemen under Agathon (Arr Anab III.12,4). These are a Thracian tribe (Webber 2001). In front of them were the mercenary cavalry under Andromachus (Arr Anab III.12,5). These are probably the 'Achaean mercenaries' (Diod XVII.57,3). Next to the Thessalian cavalry Diodorus assigns the Cretan archers (Diod XVII.57,4) and not the Thracian javelineers, but both of them is the best bet, in symmetry to the arrangement of the right flank guard. This contradicts Arrian who does not mention Cretan archers at all in this battle.

There seems to be no heavy infantry on the left flankguard. Coiranus, however, who commands an allied cavalry unit, according to Arrian's explicit reference (Arr Anab III.12,4), begs for some attention. First, allied Greek cavalry led by Erigius had been positioned next to the Thessalian cavalry (Arr. Anab. III.11,10); Erigius is elsewhere mentioned as the Commanding Officer (CO) of allied cavalry (Arr. Anab. III.6,6). Two regiments of allied cavalry are not likely. Then, in Egypt, a 'Calanus' takes over the command of the allied infantry, because their commander Balacrus is to stay behind (Arr Anab III.5,6). 'Calanus' is not a Macedonian name and may be a mistake for 'Caranus'. Possibly a series of misspellings produced Calanus and Coiranus out of the correct name, that is Caranus, as the capital letters R and L look alike in the ancient Greek script (and a miswritten 'a', in poor handwriting could be 'oi' in Greek lowercase scripts). Caranus is a well-known Macedonian name. Many names differ in spelling depending on the ancient author. Such cases include, without being limited to, Polyperchon-Polysperchon and Menidas-Menoitas, perhaps due to copying errors in Alexandria. If this is the case, then the allied hoplite infantry of southern Greece is right here, in the flank guard assigned to Parmenio, making it very similar to the corresponding formation of the right.

Thus the Macedonian heavy infantry accounts for 12,000, the archers for perhaps 1,000 more, the heavy cavalry for a bit less than 1,400 (1,200 Companions and 200 of the bodyguards if they were also fighting mounted) and the light scout cavalry for an unknown number, but perhaps at 400 to 600 (Strootman 2012); the number of Macedonians is hardly 15,000, less than a third of the 47,000 grand total (Arr. Anab. III.12,5). If attendants are added, who had an active role in combat, at least at this battle (Arr. Anab. III.13,6), there were at the very most one for each cavalryman and one for every 10 infantrymen (Front Strat IV.1,6), that is some 3,000 men (the bodyguards included), pushing the total to 18,000, of whom 2,000 were cavalry.

The Macedonian troops are the main battle line at Gaugamela. Two massive flank guards are expressly described and are comprised mostly of non-Macedonian units, with few light cavalry and light infantry exceptions. These formations were at a field strength of approximately 6,000 for the right flank guard and probably an equal number for the left, pushing the total to 30,000, without counting the respective servants that may have participated. The allied infantry under Caranus at the left flank guard could be 7–8,000 shields as its initial strength was 7,000 (Diod XVII.17,3) and some reinforcements from the League must have come, as the Eleans joined at Gordium (Arr Anab I.29,4). This takes the figure to 35,000 or 42,000 if one servant per hoplite had been allowed, as per standard Greek practice in hoplite armies (Her IX.29,2). And this is all of the army of Alexander which took part in the battle. Arrian speaks of a double phalanx, behind the first echelon, but he only mentions one of its units by name, the Royal Hypaspists (Arr. Anab. III.13,6).

The usual explanation is that the second echelon (Arr. Anab. III.12,1) is made up of southern Greek hoplites, especially allied ones (Devine 1975; Griffith 1947) who are omitted from the narration due to biases of the primary sources of Arrian, especially Ptolemy. That may be; though Cleitarchus, the chief source of Diodorus (Steele 1922; Prandi 2012) was a resident in Alexandria under Ptolemy I. Still, eliminating the whole body of such troops is a bit too much, especially for Arrian who is a soldier and understands the nature of things.

In Alexander's three battles against the Persian state, a force was always left to guard a base, a camp or a bridgehead, or to secure the rear if things do not develop as wished. Thus, at the Granicus the bridgehead and the beached ships of the invasion fleet must have been heavily guarded for any surprises and only a fraction of the available heavy infantry participates in the battle, the Macedonians (Arr Anab I.14,2–3). At Issus, where every last trooper was needed, an infantry rearguard was available on the left to plug any breach by the Persian cavalry (Arr Anab II.9,3). At Gaugamela a well-fortified camp, less than a day's march from the battlefield (Arr. Anab. III. IX.1 & III.XII.5) had been established and maintained. Arrian specifies that Alexander took his troops with only their weapons to the field at Gaugamela (ibid.), aiming for – or feinting – a dawn attack (Arr. Anab. III.9,2).

It is more than certain that the elaborate train of siege equipment, pack animals, artillery, the prisoners of war, possible hostages, the captured family of Darius and the acting court of Alexander which practically administered the conquered lands and Macedon were not dragged along on this forced march towards Darius, implemented by the combatants. All these elements were left behind to the base camp (Arr Anab III.9,1), along with a considerable force of Thracian infantry for their protection, for the defence and security of the camp, and for guarding the prisoners (Arr Anab III.12,5). The fate of base camps was occasionally decisive both before and after Alexander, as at Marathon 490 BC (Her VI.114–5), Cunaxa 401 BC (Xen Anab I.10,18–19), Aegospotami 404 BC (Xen Hell II.1,28), Himera 479 BC (Her VII.167; Diod XI.22,1–2), Plataea 479 BC (Her IX.70), Thermopylae 191 BC (App Syr. IV.18–19), Magnesia 190 BC (App Syr VI.36).

Advancing and Manoeuvring

Alexander may have tried, with a short night march, to surprise the enemy and attack Darius at dawn (Arr Anab III.9,2), before the latter had completed his deployment; he had done it in Pelion and was to repeat it at the Persian Gates (Arr Anab III.18,6), but Darius was tipped off in time of his approach and hastily formed his battle order. Darius had no properly entrenched, secured, fortified camp (Arr Anab III.11,1). This could have been due to the size of his army, or since he had arrived, in haste, not long before Alexander and had had no time to properly make his arrangements (Marsden 1964). Moreover, perhaps the nature of the terrain where he had encamped provided a degree of safety (Stein 1942), and it was selected for this reason in mind, but it was not enemy-proof. Darius was concerned of some nocturnal surprise. Xerxes almost lost his life in one such (Diod XI.10), Mardonius his army and career and Daurices his life and his army (Kambouris 2022a-c) and so on. But it seems that the Kings of Kings had decided that fortified camps were beneath their dignity. Not all the Persians; but the Emperors did so.

Alexander came into visual contact when about 5 kilometres away and emerging over a hill range. He stayed his force and did not attack upon deployment. Up there he was secure from enemy cavalry and chariots; he had the higher ground with better troops, thus enemy infantry was no threat, either. And, of course, massive hosts such as Darius' are not very manoeuvrable and even less mobile; they roll along a smooth battlefield or launch attacks; they do not charge headlong upon sight of an enemy, especially in rugged terrain. Thus, it is not that Darius showed no initiative and was defensively minded (Sarantis 1977). He *had* no initiative as the enemy was more manoeuvrable and swifter, and thus dictated the range and kinetics of the engagement.

And then Alexander inspected and reconnoitred the battlefield in detail the previous day (Arr Anab III.9,5); and he spotted the uneven ground at the edge of the prospective battlefield. This mission was carried out by the entire Companion Cavalry and skirmishers (Arr Anab III.9,5), which was actually the arrangement used for field cavalry engagement as at the Granicus and Issus. Major cavalry actions were supported by light infantry skirmishers, and thus Alexander's cavalry was either looking for a fight, or was ready for one so as to conclude the detailed reconnaissance without hindrance by enemy cavalry groups. The move and the attitude produced every indication of the intent and preparation of night action, be that a raid or a major offensive. Arrian says Darius' camp was not well protected and safely entrenched (Arr Anab III.11,1) – a sign it was occupied for a short time before the arrival of Alexander with priority assigned to battlefield shaping, although other explanations have been suggested above.

And this was the reason for keeping his troops in battle order, to avert the night raid advised by Alexander's staff (Arr. Anab III.11,1 & 9,3 respectively). Lacking an entrenched camp and generally being uncomfortable with nocturnal operations (Xen Anab III.4,34–5), the Persians spent the night on high alert, in position (Arr Anab III.11,1). They only trusted arrangements such as spiking the field, or at least certain areas, with traps and caltrops (Curt IV.13,36). It is understood that traps might have been a legitimate concern for the Macedonian staff (Arr. Anab. III.9,4), but they actually were not planted throughout the field, as they would have marred the perfectly laid and managed Persian battlefield – although correct emplacement could conceivably shape and not mar it. These devices could also – or mostly – have been employed to protect the royal camp, as it was not fortified (Arr Anab III.11,1).

The reconnaissance would have made the specifics of such spiking clear to Alexander (Arr Anab III.9,5), which means that he quite simply was not in favour of a night action in this particular case, an action expected by Darius. But there was no reason to oblige the Sovereign by letting him know.

After this, Alexander had his army rest and sleep in the safety of the rugged ground of the hill range. He bluntly refused to engage in a night fight in an unknown field with an opponent vastly larger and more familiar with the terrain, despite the clear advantage of the Greeks in night operations. In addition, he secured a tremendous advantage. He exhausted the Persians who were kept deployed in battle order and awake through the night (Arr Anab III.11,2), as had happened at Salamis in 480 BC (Her VIII.76). He would fight with a rested army against the exhausted, if vigilant, enemy. Since surprise had failed, he would fight it out in set-piece battle, strictly conventionally, but with as many advantages as possible. From rested troops versus unrested to the familiarization with the battlefield and the perception of the order of battle and thus intentions of the opponent already deployed in full sight, and from an elevated position at that (Boardman 1999); a favour Alexander, despite his gallantry, was not to return. It is difficult to find more of Sun Tzu.

Next morning, Alexander slept heavily into the day (Plut Alex 32,1; Diod XVII.56,1–2). His intentional 'oversleeping' was to stall and so unnerve and wear down the Persian host further. At the time the all-night-long exhaustion was beginning to have an effect, Alexander formed up and descended to the level ground. His enemy had no time to react by changing disposition, even if he could understand what Alexander was doing since the latter's troops and command structure were responsive, resilient and enduring enough, physically and mentally.

At this point another issue arises. Alexander spent the night at a summit (Arr. Anab. III.9,4) steep enough to provide security from the Persian mobile units, that is chariots, elephants and heavy cavalry (Arr. Anab III.8,6). According to Arrian, he had taken only the assault units with nothing but their weapons (Arr Anab III.9,1–2). But somehow he spent quite some time there and a tent is reported, along with meals for the troops (Arr Anab III.10,1); thus he *could* have established an advanced camp, but due to the terrain, this camp could not be stormed by cavalry units, a conclusion important for discussing later the despoiling of (one) Greek camp by Darius' cavalry.

The stay on the summit means that Persians would be able to see his order of battle as he descended to the plain. Perhaps he judged that they simply had no time to reform, nor the mental and command reflexes. Or he may have deployed to his final order of battle after descending to the level ground. This is consistent with the canted back flanks or flank guards, which require some level space behind the main line. It is reported that all preparations regarding the battle order were completed on the eve of battle (Arr Anab III.9,3–4). The units took their assigned positions, as a result, in the day of the battle, by default. When the signal was given the advance started in earnest.

It is a bit difficult to understand how the elaborate positions of the units were assumed on such ground. On the other hand, the detailed reconnaissance-in-force (Arr Anab III.9,5), giving birth to some interesting lore (PseudoCal Rom Alex 177–82), plus the realization that the Persians were not to make changes but stayed their position overnight, meant that the planning, the missions, the arrangements were finalised and the orders were issued in advance.

In any case, at the latest when off the summit the army of Alexander was in position. Darius' precaution to reinforce the centre was vindicated; the enemy line was compact, not extended, to avoid breaching by his strike arms. Its murderous right flank, where Alexander was with his elite cavalry, was opposite to the Persian centre (Arr Anab III.13,1). As the Greek advance started, the massive host, half-asleep from unending hours at the same spot, both men and animals, came alive. This exhaustion and agitation is a possible reason for the elephants not being present, being temperamental animals and very frustrated by inaction while not at ease. Darius was thus going for a flank decision, by his left under Bessus. And there, there were problems.

Alexander this time had readied the greatest surprise, a masterpiece of drill and tactics. His army did not advance forward. It advanced diagonally (**Figure 12.1**). This was achieved by a half-turn of men and beasts as they stood, and the whole battle order would move obliquely, changing the projection of its front onto the enemy army always to the latter's left. It is not reported when the Achaemenid High Command understood what was going on, and, although the battle order of Alexander could well move in one block, it is conceivable that by timing the initiation of the advance (each trooper starting to march one step later than his comrade to his immediate right, see **Figure 12.3**) or by any other trick of a drillmaster, he might have *developed* the line obliquely (not only *moved* obliquely), which would greatly perplex the enemy and pose some spatiotemporal difficulties in engaging his weaker, denied left. The special mention of maintaining total silence so as to precisely follow orders (Arr Anab III.9,7) was a given for Greek armies since Homer's times (Hom Il III-8/9) but in this particular case the use of drill differentially, so as to deny the left without opening gaps during an oblique movement, should be seriously considered (Parpas 2014). This was unprecedented, and startled the enemy, troops and high command alike, seeing something unbelievable. When exactly the two dimensions of the Greek advance, the diagonal approach and the denial of the left were apperceived by the enemy, cannot be surmised. But the Imperials had not anticipated it, and their window of opportunity to do anything was quickly shrinking. It is not understood what exactly Darius' fear had been. Being flanked was less of a danger; his host was too enormous for flanking to have a consequence, but a reverse at a point could well spread panic as a wildfire. To allow the Macedonians to skip the prepared ground, and thus shirk his chariot charge (Arr Anab III.13,2) was also a possibility, but how fatal could that be? He had a gigantic host, he did not *need* the chariots. It seems Darius

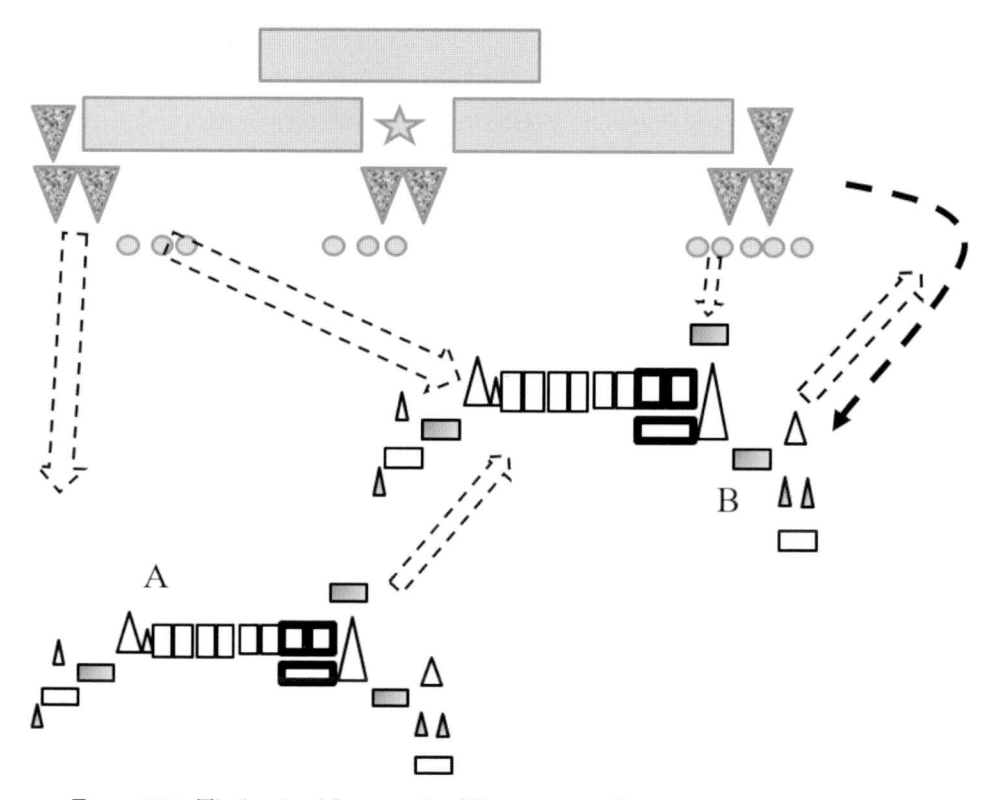

Figure 12.1: The battle of Gaugamela – The sequence of events.
Alexander's compact formation barely exceeds one half of the Persian front (A), but by advancing in an oblique direction (perhaps also in oblique order, not depicted here) it covers the full enemy front in time and threatens with flanking the enemy left (B). Frustrated, Darius attacks with his first-line units. Bessus has to extend to the left to avoid flanking, and thus is exposed to sudden charges by Alexander's flank guard units, (spearheaded by Menidas' heavy mercenary cavalry) while still in redeployment and suboptimal position and formation. His scythed chariots attack the Companion Cavalry and the rightmost of the phalanx, to no avail, and thus the Persian left is exposed for Alexander's attack with a complex cavalry and infantry wedge.

At the meantime, the oblique advance exposes Parmenio's left flank and Mazaeus, at the Imperial right wing charges to engage it from front, flank and rear, while the Persian centre does so frontally. While Mazaeus pins the Greek left, while the right storms to the attack, there are gaps exploited by the said Imperial cavalry at the centre. The second echelon of the Macedonian phalanx about-faces to receive the rear attacks as instructed. Mazaeus sends a cavalry detachment to turn the exposed Greek left wing and gallop far to their rear, back to the main camp, so as to free the prisoners, and especially the Royal Family.

was simply kicked off his mental balance and frustrated, a killer move by Alexander who had learnt his lesson from Leonidas and Themistocles: the mind of the *karana* was the Achilles' heel of gigantic Persian hosts, on land and at sea.

The river crossings and reconnaissance-in-force

Alexander used the main road north when starting from Egypt; this northward trek, even if there was an alternative track, would bring him to meeting the expected reinforcements Amyntas was conveying from Macedon. It was also suitable for the baggage train; the monstrous baggage train of his victorious troops, which was now their household, prize and loot. The crossing of Euphrates was achieved through elaborate preparations resulting in bridges thrown by the Macedonian engineers at the correct spot at Thapsacus, the regular crossing point. It was a rather official and leisurely affair. It was contested rather reluctantly by 3,000 cavalry and 2,000 Greek mercenaries (an interesting combination by itself) under Mazeus, a most capable commander (Arr Anab III.7,1), as would later become clear. For long his presence had denied the completion of the bridges to the eastern bank, but, mysteriously, he retired when Alexander arrived. The bridges were finished promptly and the Greek army crossed. Alexander gave limited pursuit with a contingent, a fact Arrian does not mention but the interrogation of Persian scouts (Arr Anab III.7, 4) means that they must have been apprehended somehow, somewhere.

Probably understanding a bait when seeing one, Alexander broke contact and until his enemy got wind of the fact, his army had moved North and then East and could not be located by the patrols of the Imperials. It was an arduous job to try to re-establish contact; Alexander's cavalry was exceptionally well-versed in counter-reconnaissance/counter intelligence and the attitude of Alexander, to assign the utmost importance in attacking enemy scouts, screens and vanguards and use his own in force and diligence shows focus (Engels 1980a). With the Tigris, things were different. Darius had a gigantic host, but could not use it to manoeuvre and conduct territorial war. His host was for pitched battle. For other missions he used detachments. The force he sent this time constituted legitimate opposition: 1,000 cavalry (Arr Anab III.7,7), not much less than the strength of the Companions and Alexander headed against them with the Royal Squadron, one more squadron of Companions and the Paeonian scouts (Arr Anab III.8,1), a close match. This Imperial detachment was to intercept the crossing or at least stall him until Darius could properly occupy his new position and make his preparations; this is the only reason he would have sent a large cavalry force alone, to hastily occupy the passages and contest the crossing. Similar forces must have been dispatched to other places suitable for crossing. On the Euphrates, Darius wanted to lure Alexander through barren ground to his position (Marsden 1964). On the Tigris he wanted to stall him so as not to be bypassed and see Alexander penetrating to the Iranian plateau, especially Media. Darius had been satrap in Armenia (Badian 2000); he knew the landscape in the north and the assets and liabilities for the empire. When Mazeus lost contact he must have guessed, correctly, that Alexander was going east to cross the Tigris and outmanoeuvre him. The expediency and difficulty in fording and crossing the Tigris (Arr Anab III.7,5) from an army renowned for its engineering corps and feats suggests he was on a schedule and in a hurry; all show his intention to conduct manoeuvre warfare and perhaps to cross the Zagros to steal the access through Behistun, or to race to Susa.

Alexander's counter-reconnaissance force, as mentioned above, was massive but if one judges numbers objectively, it was a force intended for high mobility, to counter the main mode of action of the Persian cavalry when operating independently. To achieve that, and for a large force of 1,000 cavalry, possibly as much as the cavalry brought to Marathon under Datis, he needed enough troops, especially since he had to plan for an engagement without the support of light infantry; they would be a mobility liability for the long-range pursuit and engagements inherent in massive counter-reconnaissance missions. Despite the advantage in engagements provided by attached infantry, for long-range, high-speed action it was simply unable to follow, and Alexander expected no major action, just some engagements and pursuit. Darius valued his cavalry and wanted every single man for the Battle Royal he planned, thus when overtaken by the developments his cavalry retired and showed no intention to engage, especially under disadvantageous conditions, most probably including, but not restricted to, exhaustion from galloping to intercept the Macedonians.

The elaborate reconnaissance mission on the eve of the Battle of Gaugamela included the whole of the Companion Cavalry plus the light infantry (Arr Anab III.9,5) to familiarize the troops *and* mounts with the terrain, to reconnoitre it exhaustively and with an eye to engage in limited combat in mostly limited space, if need be. Thus, infantry could intervene properly and augment the cavalry; it is important that Arrian's wording seems to imply the sum of the light infantry, along with the sum of the Companion Cavalry.

> It is obvious that in all three battles, and contrary to some views that identify differences in the strategic attitude of the Imperials (Patchen 2014), they did nothing but mobilize, select a defensive position and wait. They never moved to intercept. There is no difference among the satraps allowing Alexander to move unhindered from the Hellespont South to Aeolis and the coast or Southeast to Sardis (**Map 2**); Darius remaining still in wait in Sochi while Alexander roamed Cilicia, and Darius and his host waiting at Babylon while Alexander was conquering and organizing Egypt and all his territorial gains. At both Issus and Gaugamela Darius finally moved once his patience and time – or supplies – had become critical (in the former case) or his position irrelevant (in the latter case).

The clash

The commanders of different parts of the Persian front were just as stupefied, especially the commanders of the wings. Deliberating was taking time, the window was shrinking fast, their frustration increased. The chariot groups moved into action immediately, so as not to lose their target. On the Persian right, the target was much to the side and the chariots might have become irrelevant, as there is no report of their use, although this is far from proof that they did not engage. In the middle, the chariots of the Persian centre charged directly to the Macedonian phalanx. On the Persian left, suddenly the chariot crews found themselves in position to attack, but for a limited time, and were unleashed against the flank guard and the Companion Cavalry, as they were coming into their horizon (Arr Anab III.13,2).

At the same time, whether on their initiative or under central command by Darius, who would have reacted on reflexes, the vanguards of the wings moved to pin the enemy. But on the left, the cavalry might have had to redeploy, not to lose the advantage of extending beyond the Macedonian right. By extending to the left, the Imperial left vanguard left a gap at its previous position – nothing important as the main line was in position. What was of importance was that the lateral movement had turned them to a column moving perpendicularly to the axis of attack of the enemy; they presented their flank to the strike unit of the flank guard on Alexander's right. Alexander was in no race mood; he was advancing briskly but nothing more than that; and seeing the opportunity he launched an attack, just to agitate the enemy and shake their confidence through the psychological advantage of the charge (**Figure 12.1B**). The Greek mercenary cavalry under Menidas actually delivered the first blow, by charging onto the transforming enemy vanguard cavalry as it exposed its flank in an effort to extend the front (Arr Anab III.13,3).

It was a suicidal charge in terms of numbers; just the Bactrians of the vanguard were 1,000 horse, most probably the cavalry guard of Bessus himself, while Menidas commanded something like 400 (Arr Anab III.5,1). When one considers that he also faced the Scythians, it was a very risky proposition had it not been for the surprise, the geometry and the momentum. Still, numbers did tell. But having pinned their target, Menidas' men allowed the mercenary infantry of Cleander to approach unchallenged, along with the Paeonian light cavalry. The combination was vindicated time and again. The mercenaries were a numerous force but it was the synergy, not the numbers,

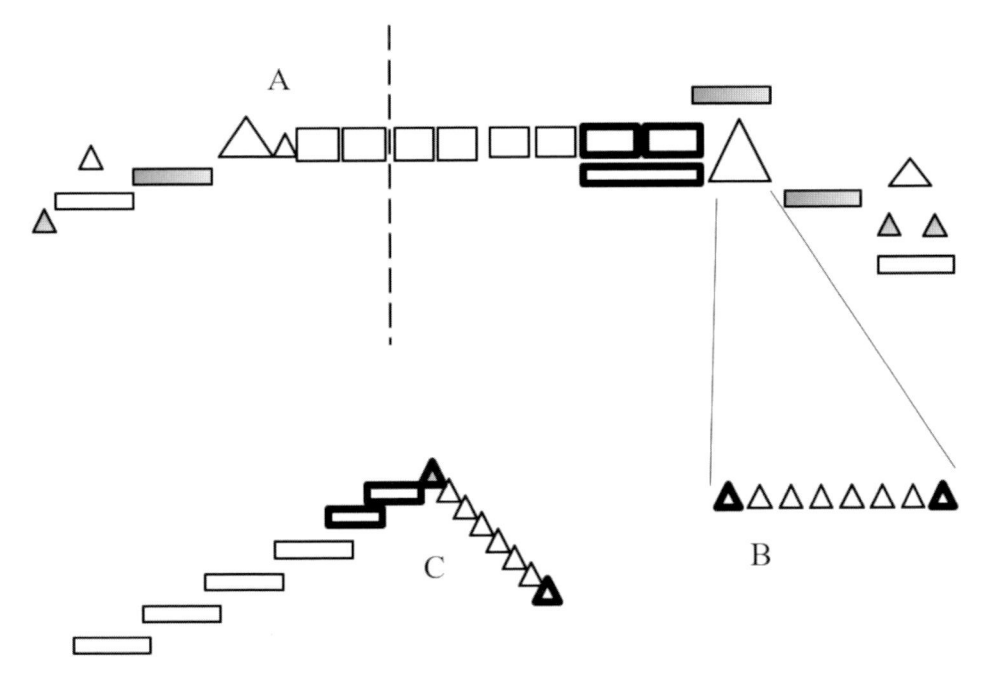

Figure 12.2: The battle of Gaugamela – Alexander's deployment.
A. Alexander's battle order as per Arrian, with flank guards denied and made up by heavy cavalry, light cavalry and heavy infantry. The quintessence of Greek combined arms warfare.
B. The unique deployment of the Companion Cavalry, with two divisions of the Royal Squadron (of equal or unequal size) as per Rezpka 2008, to the two flanks of the corps.
C. A possible arrangement of the assault wedge mentioned by Arrian, made up by Companion Cavalry squadrons and phalanx regiments *en echelon*.

Triangle: cavalry (dashed: light, hollow: heavy, thick line: elite/Royal Squadrons). Rectangle: infantry (dashed: light, hollow: heavy, thick line: elite/Hypaspists). The Companion heavy cavalry under Philotas is directly supported by light infantry fighting as *hamippoi*.

that broke the enemy. Sensing defeat the commander, Bessus, launched all he had and stopped the rout. The fight was rekindled.

By sending masses of cavalry to overcome the combined force pitted against him and disrupting his mission, Bessus thinned his line against Alexander. At that point Alexander ordered the last reserve of the flank guard in: the lancers under Aretes (Arr Anab III.14,1), the same name as the young officer who assisted the king in the Battle of the Granicus (Arr Anab I.15,6). The charge at the flank of yet another oriental cavalry column moving laterally, this time by long, cavalry *sarissa* lances couched underarm must have made quite some impression as it used dash and collision. Frederick the Great insisted that a cavalry charge should be executed by small-sized horses and small-statured horsemen, instead of bulky ones (Burn 1965), so as to develop maximum speed and thus momentum against enemy cavalry and infantry, which was the key to successful physical shock cavalry tactics (Sears & Willekes 2016). Indeed, the impact was decisive. The Persian line cracked there, and the engaged cavalry that steamrolled over the flank guard was checked. And Alexander, at his position, promptly turned his units and formed them in depth, now aiming 90 degrees left from his original advance vector; obliquely, as at the Granicus, and right into the gap. He charged in a wedge with cavalry and infantry, smashed the Persians after some extremely violent fighting and, approaching Darius, the sovereign again had to flee.

As mentioned, the basic drill that enabled the surprising battlefield manoeuvre of Alexander had been most probably the original turn at 45 degrees right; practically, a half-turn 'spearwards' (Arr Ars Tact XXI.1) and then advancing. A similar, oblique advance, but by cavalry only, and for a short distance in full gallop had been executed at the Granicus (Arr Anab I.14,7). The idea for the advance at Gaugamela is simple; the formation, though, is more obscure. As already mentioned, the whole battle line might have been moving simultaneously (**Figure 12.1A**), which would present as little challenge in timing between divisions as possible. On the other hand, moving *en echelon*, with different divisions starting the march successively, with a set delay, and not simultaneously, would produce the added and highly desirable effect of denying the left, where envelopment was to be expected, for as long as possible.

Once the manoeuvre at a slant had repositioned the Macedonian army laterally opposite the Imperial left wing – and possibly beyond – Alexander's own left would have become *highly* exposed. This fact dictated taking some risk in moving the line in iterations, which was more difficult than moving it en bloc (**Figure 12.1A**). It was more demanding in terms of timing and coordination and a much more sinister proposition: it afforded ready-made breaches if an Imperial looked from the side, at some angle, and could charge from such a direction, obliquely. But the ascertained and immediate danger was the flank attacks, easy to launch, and readily so from a force deployed with just this in mind. Launching cavalry, the massive, cumbersome armoured cavalry of Persian and subject feudal lords sideways to penetrate to the gaps between successive phalanx *taxeis* was not so great a danger; seen from straight ahead, the phalanx was presenting a continuous front; small lateral empty spaces, the standard between successive divisions, would have been presented. If the unexpected was to happen, the infantry divisions could always align, to actually form a continuous front.

The command reflexes of the Persians and the haste in reacting to the move of Alexander, all beg the question of the character of the uneven ground at the left of the Persian battle line (Arr. Anab. III.13,1–2). If it was rough enough to cause mobility problems for cavalry, how did Bessus shadow Alexander (Arr. Anab. III.13,1–2) in the lateral move? How did he do this and why, if the terrain was unsuitable for cavalry? Most probably it presented problems to the deployment of the chariots only, as clearly suggested by Arrian's wording (Arr Anab III.13,2). Thus, Alexander's lateral move would simply take him out of the threat of the scythed chariots, on terrain where infantry and cavalry would face no particular problems and would be able to manoeuvre at will.

The move of Alexander would threaten to mar the Persian plan in two ways: (i) by getting out of the killing field of the chariots, and (ii) by assuming position suitable for him to launch a flanking attack. True, with a decent opposing commander it would not *enable* Alexander to actually do either. Most probably his aim was to stimulate these reflexes and cause a commotion in the Persian line so as to create a weak point to charge *at*, not *around*, and craft internal flanks in the enemy battle order, to strike at. At Issus, a straight charge did the trick, with the stout *xyston* lances of the Companions offering the edge against the *hoplon* shield and simple *dory* spears of hoplites, both Kardaka and Greek mercenaries (Arr Anab II.8,6). But at Gaugamela the new, longer Persian offensive arms might have been a reason for creating a weak point *before* launching a charge. It was a case not dissimilar to the Battle of the Granicus, where an initial charge disrupted the Persian line, caused redeployment and provided a foothold and a weak point for further exploitation by the main offensive thrust (Arr Anab I.15,1 & 3–4 & 7). At Gaugamela it was the same on a massive scale, with the move itself leading to countermoves that would expose some point or other, whereas the successive charges and countercharges between the Persian left flank and the right flank guard of Alexander (Arr Anab III.13,3–4 &14,1)

would keep any threat away from the main offensive task force, till the opportunity presented itself for the decisive charge (Arr. Anab III.14,2). All the interceptors were to be engaged against the escorts, as modern airmen would say. The bombers were free to wreak havoc.

On the contrary, Mazeus, the Persian commander of the right, flanked the Macedonian left easily as the rightward move of Alexander gave him even more leeway, and at the same time he dispatched a cavalry detachment to raid the main Macedonian base – obviously from the corridor the Macedonians were leaving between their extreme left and the hill range as they were veering rightwards. Diodorus' account (Diod XVII.59,5–8) states as objective for this operation the retrieval of the Persian royal family. The successful assault implies the fortified main camp; no way would such a cavalry operation succeed against a position uphill.

As Mazeus' main force thundered on the Macedonian left, with no mention of chariots, the geometry of his attacks did not allow the flank guard any 'cheek to slap'. The Imperials hit the Greeks almost at a right angle, if not to the flank, and engaged in close quarters combat. Parmenio was not able to avert the attacks and received them. The greater experience of his troops with long shafted weapons permitted them to fight against the odds and keep his command intact; though, not to complete his mission. He could not keep up with the advance of Alexander and his force, intended to attack Darius from the front, and he was not available for the decisive action.

Arrian, after an interesting account of how things developed at the wing of Alexander, which caused the collapse of the Imperial centre, describes an independent action at the centre. The Imperial mounted vanguard there, of whose commander we hear nothing, did not launch headlong on the *sarissai*, but through the gaps in the phalanx, that were formed due to the pinning down of the left. The rather inexperienced Simmias, leading the *taxis* of his brother Amyntas, checked his advance. Amyntas had been dispatched to Greece to conscript soldiers (Arr Anab III.8,9) and was hopelessly late for the battle; this was a good reason for Alexander to have kept stalling for months, expecting a massive body of reinforcements and the return of a most proficient general. Either due to camaraderie so as to assist the badly pressed left (Arr Anab III.14,2) or, possibly, because he was attacked and pinned as well, commanding the second-leftmost phalanx *taxis*, Simmias stopped in his tracks. Thus, instead of a gap to its left, another breach was created at his left (Arr. Anab. III.14,4). This is the usual interpretation of the facts (Sarantis 1977) but it is perhaps mistaken or unjust. Simmias was under the direct command of Craterus, Commanding Officer of the *taxis* at his left and chief of the whole infantry of the left (Arr Anab III.11,10).

This implies not only the infantry of the allies set in the flank guard and – possibly – the light infantry, but most probably at least one more phalanx infantry *taxis* than his own; and Simmias' was the closest by (Arr Anab III.12,9–10). Simmias might have been ordered by Craterus to act in such a way; to check his advance so as to assist him, possibly to tilt 90 degrees to the right and form a rectangle with the rest of the operational command of the left, so as to endure the massive Persian onslaught. The flawless career of Craterus shows that Alexander did not consider this action of Simmias, his direct subordinate, as an error in judgment of Craterus. He may have pinned it to Parmenio, or not, but under the conditions Alexander did not chastise his two infantry generals for acting as they did.

No matter how and why it opened, the breach in the phalanx was a fact; it may have evolved to only one, very wide, if Simmias rearranged his command to seal the right flank of Parmenio's command. Or, if he simply slowed his advance, there may have been two lanes, on his left and right flanks. Through this breach or breaches, Persian units, definitely *not* the elite units of the Great King's entourage, poured through the Macedonian phalanx (Arr. Anab. III.14,5) to attack it in the rear. The penetrating Persian mounted units, turning right, must have enveloped the Macedonian left which would have to deploy defensively to fight fully encircled and was pinned down for good.

A breakthrough by enemy cavalry is reported by Arrian (Arr. Anab. III.14,5). It was engaged by infantry on the field that about-faced to meet the threat and proceeded against it, while the cavalry was not expecting to receive an attack (Arr. Anab. III.14,6). This implies directly that these Imperials attempted to storm the advanced camp at the hills (Arr. Anab. III.14,5), or no camp at all.

Indeed, these Imperial cavalry units may have made the surprise of the day and turned around to hit the phalanx from the rear. Alexander's second echelon infantry units that about-faced and engaged these mounted Imperial troops (Arr Anab III.14,6), could not have caught cavalry galloping all the way to the advanced camp on the hills, where there were no camp followers, nor prisoners (Arr Anab III.15,5). Much less could they have followed a mounted enemy to the main, properly fortified and guarded camp, deep at the rear, at sixty stadia (Arr Anab III.9,1–2) – something less than 12 km – where any prisoners would have been kept. Perhaps Arrian was confused and considered the true and successful camp raid of the Imperial cavalry (of the right wing, sent by Mazeus) as the result of an infiltration of cavalry at the middle of the phalanx. The latter actually allowed the Persian cavalry to assault the rear of the phalanx. Thus, the second phalanx echelon reversed promptly to receive this attack at their rear, not to give chase to galloping cavalry across an open plain (Arr. Anab. III.14,6).

These Persian units, attacking the Macedonians from the rear, would have been reversed, regarding the front of the main Imperial battle order. So, they witnessed first-hand the collapse of the left Persian flank, and the centre, after the flight of the King of Kings, which was leaving them behind enemy lines. This condition should have made them bound to retire fast and in poor order, through the gap(s) they emerged from. These units must have been the ones accidentally intercepted by Alexander and his Companions when they aborted the pursuit of Darius and turned left to assist their pressed left wing (Arr. Anab. III.15,1–2). Although the assistance of Alexander to Parmenio never materialized due to the chance encounter with the retreating Imperial cavalry of the centre, said retreat, the rout of Darius and the dissolution of their army checked the cavalry of the Persian right. Many of them were Armenians and Cappadocians, nominally pledged to Alexander, especially the latter, but remained true and loyal to Darius III, their former Satrap before he became emperor. With Darius, a war-hero, in flight, they had no allegiance, no heart, and felt betrayed and disappointed. They just vanished once the Thessalians of Parmenio took a breath and counter-attacked with their murderous rhomboids (Arr Anab III.15,3; Diod XVII.60,8). This settled the issue, which would have remained unresolved for as long as Alexander fought with the massive elite cavalry of the centre. The mass and consternation of the Orientals of the centre, with the courage of desperation, helped them escape, despite horrific losses in the melee with the better equipped Companions, who were not better armoured, though. The demise of some sixty Companions (Arr Anab III.15,2) shows a fierce fight. They amount to the majority of the fatalities of the troops under Alexander (Arr Anab III.15,6), being more than half an original squadron and 40 per cent of the tertiary ones.

Arrian dwells briefly on the turning point of the battle, the action developed by the combined arms attack of Alexander. He never mentions which enemy unit he fell upon, neither himself and the cavalry nor any of the phalanx brigades. His report of a combined phalanx and Companion cavalry wedge (Arr Anab III.14,2) is most unsettling: the solutions suggested to date (Devine 1983) befit rather a show than a tactical reality under pressure.

Arrian's description of an infantry wedge (Arr Ars Tact XXIX.5) is inapplicable here as the phalanx was deployed laterally: any other deployment, although possible by the tertiary organization of the *taxeis* (**Figure 2.1**), would nullify the tactical surprise prepared meticulously by Alexander's staff for the scythed chariots and is not warranted by the sources. A slanted,

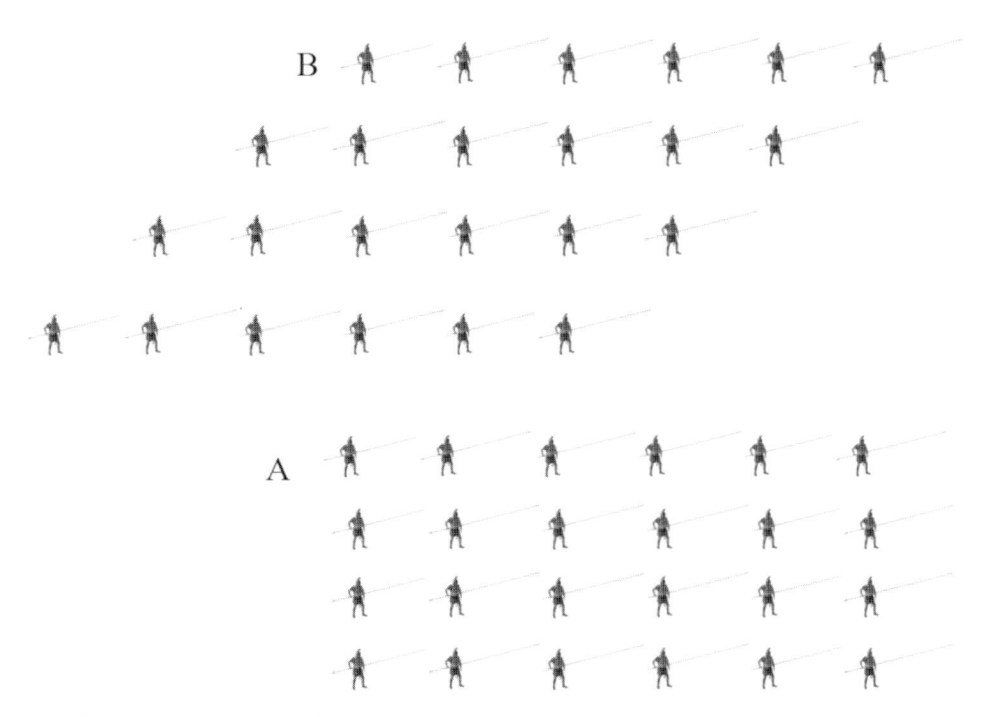

Figure 12.3: Oblique order.
A possible model for a slanted front in an infantry formation. Each file starts its advance lagging one step from the one at its left.

oblique formation with every man lagging a step behind his rightward respective number (*parastates*) might have been possible (**Figure 12.3**) but remains improbable.

On the other hand, cavalry wedges for the charge of the Companion Cavalry are easy to depict. Arrian clearly mentions them as a Macedonian practice since Philip; he does *not* imply a Scythian origin in the Macedonian use, despite the usual liberal interpretation (Arr Ars Tact XVI.6–7). Each fifty-strong subunit of a squadron forms a wedge (**Figure 1.2**). Though, how these wedges were deployed in squadron and higher echelons is debatable: the tertiary organization of squadrons allowed a wedge of three wedges, a line, or a column. The latter is possibly the *ilae orthae* – literally 'squadrons in column' (Arr Anab IV.14,7). Even a slanted line, one side denied, is plausible (**Figure 1.3**). The arrangement of seven squadrons is even harder to contemplate.

The only sure thing is the incorporation of light infantry to support the charging cavalry – the units which initially screened the Companion Cavalry from the chariot attack with extreme effectiveness, shooting the teams, the crews and probably the vehicles themselves to pieces (Arr Anab III.12,3).

Neutralising the chariots

The first recorded Greek encounter with the novel weapon of the Persian Empire, the scythed chariot, is at the Battle of Cunaxa, 401 BC (Xen Anab I.8,10). It was a resounding success for the Greeks, who had their infantry part lines and thus evade the physical contact of the charge. Whether similar chariots had been used by the Assyrians and are implied in the prophesy by the Oracle of Delphi to the Athenians, a monumentally defeatist proclamation (Her VII.140,2) cannot be surmised (Nefedkin 2014). But the weapon was used with some success, in a somewhat different context, most probably against hoplites as well, in Dascylium in 396 BC (Xen Hell IV.1,17–19). The success is confusing, as the drill was known and the survivors of Xenophon's army were serving in this Spartan army and thus must have passed the knowledge.

Even weirder is the ease of defeating this new arm at Cunaxa in 401 BC. The Greek mercenaries show no surprise, no doubt, and no hesitation; as if they had long drilled such manoeuvres for this very reason. It is possible that their employer, Cyrus the Younger, had tipped them off on the subject as he himself had twenty scythed chariots in his army (Xen Anab I.7,10). To suggest that the Greek commanders, especially the Spartans, borrowed some scythed chariots and tested them in simulations and military exercises to accustom their men and officers and develop tactics against them, is a bit far-fetched, but remains a valid possibility. In any case when encountering them in battle they are not surprised, nor stupefied; it is a known contraption by then, while there is no mention of it during Xerxes' invasion, where contingents with chariots (Her VII.86,1–2 & 184,4) obviously use conventional, non-scythed models (Nefedkin 2014).

It is a somewhat expected question why Darius III had not deployed such an arm before; after all in 396 BC they were deployed by a satrap, within his satrapal levies and forces. The Achaemenid conscription system had provisions for estates from which chariots were drawn (although not necessarily scythed ones), similar to estates supporting cavalry and infantry (actually, 'bowmen') conscription (Manning 2021). The above suggests that scythed chariots could have been deployed at the Granicus and even more so at Issus. But they were not. In both cases the Persian deployment behind a riverbank made their use impossible; but at the latter campaign the battlefield of choice was wide, the plain of Sochi, without hindrances and perhaps suitable for such use. But they are not reported. Not reported because they were not deployed at Issus is a possibility; but if so where were they? They might have been unable to cross the Gates of Amanus – a rather dubious reading of the events – but even so, where were they left – or sent? Back at Damascus with the non-combatants?

It is possible that the arm had been considered obsolete by Darius' staff, especially his Greek mercenaries who knew the drill to neutralize them. But after Issus, where it became obvious that the cavalry of the Macedonians was a threat to undisturbed, solid hoplite phalanxes, the idea returned with a vengeance (Griffith 1947). It might have been of dubious value against infantry, although the pike phalanx was no hoplite phalanx and was more cumbersome with the *sarissa* lowered into assault position: manoeuvring must have been carried out with the *sarissa* upright (Connolly 2000) and levelled just prior to attack, making timing vital (Parpas 2014). But the heavy cavalry, especially when dense and in-depth, as in assault formations, was a suitable target. Thus the arm was reconstituted between the Battles of Issus and Gaugamela and deployed in the latter, with special precautions not to be more threat for their own troops than for the enemy. Contrary to views considering it good mostly against infantry (Nefedkin 2014), it was intended and deployed against cavalry also, as in there the disarray it would cause would be far greater and the target, the legs of the mounts, softer and more massive.

At Gaugamela Alexander understood exactly the conditions of the scythed chariot use and its threat potential; it was his gift to look at the enemy and understand the intentions, liabilities and assets with one look (Fuller 1958). No surprise he did not attack upon sight when he arrived at dawn at the hill range; he had noticed the contraption from the higher, superimposed position – along with other Persian novelties – and wanted to ponder upon them, especially after reconnoitering the field in detail (Arr Anab III.9,5). At least the chariots would operate better in shaped battlefields, and he had to understand the extent and the location of said shaping operations by the Persian engineer corps.

Alexander must have reached the aforementioned conclusions himself and understood that the problem was mainly a chariot attack against his cavalry (Arr Anab III.13,5). The infantry was well-drilled and ordered to open ranks (Arr Anab III.13,6), as at Cunaxa (Xen Anab I.8,20). To do so, they had to keep the *sarissai* upright, so as not to impede the ranks in front of each other. Thus, there was some window of vulnerability, with the phalanx units presenting lanes that could be exploited as gaps and with their weapons in such disposition, in order to allow the mobility drills, that they were of no use. No wonder he took, in this very battle, the utmost care to have his orders followed promptly (Arr Anab III.9,7). His troops had to open ranks, let the thundering chariots through, return to position and perhaps deliver a charge or close ranks to more dense formation and present their weapons to assault position, so as to counter an enemy charge by cavalry and perhaps light infantry discharging missiles. It was a simple but most difficult trick and needed split-second decisions (Parpas 2014) but also brisk, immediate, clear orders and prompt, responsive execution. This is why the charging chariots suffered no reported casualties when going through the phalanx (Arr Anab III.13,6). The *sarissai* were held upright not to impede the movements of the phalangites (Connolly 2000) and thus were unavailable to skewer horse and crew, as would have been expected (Kagiavas Torp 2014). Once through, and their momentum expanded – perhaps in order to about-turn for another charge from the rear – the chariots were vulnerable to light infantry and servants following the phalanx (Arr Anab III.13,6), who could shoot them with javelins or actually board them, by taking the bridles and attacking the crews while at a stop or low speed. Not one chariot survived this treatment; the ones captured at the camp of Darius after the battle (Arr Anab III.15,6) must have been the ones not committed, possibly from the right wing, or the ones repulsed by the missile barrage.

As already mentioned, with the cavalry it was much more complex; horses could not respond with the accuracy infantry does, and have more limbs exposed. Alexander used a not very Greek approach; a screen of missile fire. He had few archers, but more than enough javelineers (Arr Anab III.13,5), and the javelin packed more impetus. A good shot may throw a crewman off the chariot, cause pain and thus rearing to an – armoured – horse or mess with the driver's handling, even if achieving no penetration and puncture wound. This hail of missiles would also disorientate crew and team and slow them down, and perhaps disrupt the formation – obviously a line charging dead ahead. Disrupting the formation would mean vehicles running into each other, manoeuvring in order to avoid doing so and thus lose momentum and speed, exposing their sides to the light infantry who, after the volleys, were to press home a running attack in open order and skirmish, with the objective to approach a vehicle at low speed, take the bridle and stop or change course to the horses, or cut down the team or the crew or, at the very least, cut

> and destroy the reins, making the horse panic uncontrollably and thus either run apart and have the vehicle thrown out of balance, or change course to the direction of least opposition and noise; i.e. backwards, to their own troops (Diod XVII.58,4). Even if not impacting the latter, their mission would have been aborted and the teams would refuse to resume the offensive, even if the advance of the enemy line had allowed them the time and space to do so.

The use of light infantry to support cavalry may be assumed at the Battle of Issus, though it is not directly attested either as an event or as a consequence and outcome. But it is explicitly mentioned at the Granicus, and with great effect (Arr Anab I.16,1) while such light infantry units were directly under Philotas, the Companion Cavalry commander (Arr Anab I.14.1).

The effect of Alexander's attack (Arr Anab III.14,2) was devastating. It is impossible to recreate the geometry of the final engagement, but one could contemplate that Alexander positioned his strike group at right angle with the Persian order of battle and thus flanked it practically to extinction. This would account for the short and desperate fighting, with all measures taken by Darius failing singularly to keep away the phalanx and the Macedonian cavalry. Whether Alexander at some point fell onto conscript Persians of the left or the royal units of the centre, or the term *Persians* is used *sensu lato* for the Imperials, remains unresolved. What is important is that Alexander and his cavalry used the weight and mass of their horses to shove their adversaries (Arr Anab III.14,3). At first sight, or rather reading, this would have been more effective against infantry as the Imperials had larger mounts than the Greeks; but as already mentioned, the very experienced and well-versed in cavalry operations Frederick the Great prioritized dashness over mass in shock cavalry action, and considered the latter as perfectly applicable against both cavalry and infantry, a view vindicated in the Napoleonic Wars (Sears & Willekes 2016). The Macedonians also struck at the faces of the enemy with their *xyston* lances (Arr Anab III.14,3); this may apply to both cavalry and infantry, especially heavily shielded infantry, as are the hoplites. There is no mention of Alexander and his entourage coming to grips with the Greek mercenaries; perhaps Darius fled before they were engaged or committed. And the last clue is that in this case the phalanx came within sight of Darius and proved frightening and lethal; this implies either a frontal approach squeezing Darius from two directions and thus greatly increasing his frustration and causing panic; or a sideways approach from an angle that

The novel tactics I: Double-edged phalanx

Arrian mentions a double phalanx at the Granicus (Arr. Anab. I.13,1), without any other comment, as he only provides the disposition of the Macedonian phalanx before the action (Arr. Anab. I.14,1–3), regarding the heavy infantry. But since this excerpt refers to the approach of the army, not to the final battle order, it could be explained away as the Macedonian phalanx set in double depth; or the *taxeis* of the phalanx deploying their *lochoi* in tandem (**Figure 2.1A**). Thus, the double phalanx may be explained as a marching disposition, to be deployed in single-line battle order with one or other *Paragogi* drills (**Figures 6.4 & 6.6**) once at the river bank. Still, no whereabouts are mentioned for allied infantry units, nor for mercenary infantry, which implies either placement as a rear phalanx (Arr Anab I.13,1), a true second line, or having left these divisions back at the bridgehead to provide base security. The former option is bolstered by Arrian, when referring to Parmenio (Arr Anab I.13,3) stating that Alexander's army outnumbers the opposite force in infantry – the Persian infantry being estimated at less than 20,000 southern Greek mercenaries (Arr Anab I.14,4).

But at Gaugamela the double phalanx is explicitly elaborated to a double-*edged* one (Arr Anab III.12,1), a term adequately explained by the same author (Arr Tac XXIX.1) as a formation presenting two fronts facing at diametrically opposite sides (**Figure 12.4**). Additionally, the tactical purpose and the relevant orders are clearly mentioned (Arr Anab III.12,1), at least part of its operational employment is attested (Arr Anab III.14,6) and one of its units is mentioned by name: the Royal Hypaspists, which eliminate Persian scythed chariots after the latter pass through the phalanx openings (Arr Anab III.13,6). Moreover, allied infantry under Caranus is securing the left flank guard (Arr Anab III.12,4), and the mercenary infantry under Cleander does the same for the right flank guard (Arr Anab III.12,2).

Thus, the hazy second phalanx line cannot have been made up by any other units as usually suggested (Devine 1975; Griffith 1947), which would have shadowed the first line units, the Macedonian phalanx *taxeis*. Cohesion, coordination of front and rear units and, most importantly, troop availability issues make such propositions highly improbable. Rather, a true second *phalanx* line might be a better guess, a concept up to a point felt but not fully explored previously – actually long before (Delbruck 1920). The Macedonian infantry *taxeis* might have been deployed, each in two echelons, the front one made up of two 500-man *lochoi*, the second one by the third *lochos* (**Figure 2.1D**). The rear *lochoi*, deployed to half depth, so as to cover a front equal to the two front ones (**Figures 12.4 & 12.5**), would form a real second phalanx, of decreased depth but equal front, shadowing the move of the first echelon and ready either to plug any breach or to reorientate rearwards to meet a threat from the rear (**Figure 12.5**). Thus, any breach and encirclement might be tackled, contrary to some views which insist on considering such eventuality outright destructive and fatal (Wrightson 2012). This disposition weighs heavily on *lochos* commanders (*lochagoi*) for ordering such evolutions, which means that the taxis cannot advance further and is pinned down to hold off the attackers. This explains Alexander having them in the briefing before the battle, to give orders and explain the plan (Arr Anab III.9,6).

The most obvious drill to achieve about-facing must have been, at the time, the Macedonian Countermarch (Arr Tact XXIII.2 & XXIV.1), but the Laconian Countermarch might have been better suited if the front echelon had already been in contact (Arr Tact XXIII.3 & XXIV.2). The Macedonian army emphasized drill due to its origins dating back to the legacy of Iphicrates in Macedon (Aesch II.26–29) and to the days of Philip II as a hostage in Thebes (Diod XVI.2,2–4). It must be noted that the double-phalanx, needing drill to countermarch half its troops to orientate them to the rear (**Figure 12.5**), is a different thing than the double-edged phalanx mentioned above, which has the troops in-position and simply needs those of the rear echelon to about-face as they stand, in order to present the front inverted (**Figure 12.4**). This disposition is much faster in reaction, but as the rear echelon is inverted regarding the disposition of troops, it makes its use to address any needs of the front line, i.e. to plug a breach, inapplicable.

The same applies to the Hypaspist Corps. Arrian refers to the two units of the corps, the Agema and the Hypaspists as the rightmost units of the first echelon of the phalanx (Arr Anab III.11,9). The third unit, the Royal Hypaspists, is mentioned later, when they were tackling scythed chariots having passed through the phalanx (Arr Anab III.13,6). Thus once more the most plausible model is a two-echelon deployment, with two chiliarchies of the corps in the front and the third at the rear, covering equal front with the two front ones by sacrificing half its normal depth.

The novel tactics II: the Embolon (wedge) at Gaugamela

At Gaugamela Alexander presented another surprise for his enemy. It was to be the ultimate one, it was an assault formation Arrian describes as a 'wedge' (the Greek term is *embolon*) which was made of Companion heavy cavalry and phalanx infantry. This was part of an elaborate tactical scheme that gave him the victory, along with some heavy fighting and the known equipment imbalance.

The Greek word is generally translated in English as 'wedge' although the meaning, literally, is 'ram'. And the latter meaning is, generally speaking, the more correct, especially in functional terms. The rams of the Greek warships were not always pointed, occasionally they were blunt to maximize rupture of the enemy planking.

The term itself had evolved between the time of Arrian and the fourth century BC. Arrian has a logical problem: to use the term in the context of the fourth century BC, or as he himself understands and uses it, in a contemporary context. This causes great consternation between historians and makes the recreation of the battle sequence a nightmare.

To attempt to address the issue, one has to start with the 'double-phalanx', which is presented above; it was not a 'double-phalanx', once more the English does injustice to the Greek, and once more Arrian's current knowledge and terminology, half a millennium after the battle, pose challenges. The other thing is to understand the deployment of the Companion Cavalry. It has been argued convincingly (Rzepka 2008) that eight Companion Cavalry squadrons is an anomaly: one is the Royal Squadron, but seven regular squadrons (Arr Anab II.11,8) is an issue: without pondering on the maths of troop numbers, one has to accept that the military system was straightforward, based in numeric streamlining, and standardized. Thus, if Alexander had six infantry commands, it would have been a bit inconsistent to have seven cavalry ones, and this number refers to regular, not special units. This anomaly is coupled to another (ibid.), that in this case Arrian refers to Royal Squadrons (Arr Anab III.11,8), emphasis on the plural; a once-off mention in the work of Arrian. To have divided the Royal Squadron so as to put one part (not necessarily one half) at the usual, extreme right under Cleitus the Black, its Commander, and another part to the left of the cavalry array (**Figure 12.2B**), under Hegelochus (Arr Anab III.11,8), is a most insightful suggestion (Rzepka 2008). Alexander could then lead his attack by any of the two parts.

Coming to the heart of the issue, which is the key for the planning, execution and resounding result of this battle, one has to ponder upon *Embolon*. The term in a tactical context appears with Xenophon, who uses it to describe a cavalry formation at the second Battle of Mantinea in 362 BC; a formation that charges home on to an intact phalanx and tries to breach it. It does not attack in the flank or rear – as was common – but head-on. It has been convincingly shown that charging a phalanx is perfectly doable for well-trained cavalry (Sidnell 2007; Sears & Willekes 2016; Charles 2015). The result is not a foregone conclusion and depends on a number of factors.

Xenophon, on the other hand, knows of separate occasions of deep formations, actually columns, of both cavalry and infantry. In Dascylium he reports a cavalry formation of excessive depth (Xen Hell III.4,14) and in Asia a hoplite such formation is called '*lochoi orthioi*' – 'companies deployed in column' (Xen Anab IV.8,11–14). As these formations are rectangular, they were rather assault columns; *Embolon* is wedge-shaped. Thus in Xenophon a cavalry *Embolon* (Xen Hell VII.5,24) implies *wedge*, not column. In the context of infantry, it most probably suggests an oblique order, as the infantry of Epaminondas in the second Battle of Mantinea, in 362 BC. These troops after being formed in an *Embolon* (Xen Hell VII.5,22), are explicitly mentioned to perform a deep hoplite column attacking 'as a trireme' (Xen Hell VII.5,23) but, at the same time, present an oblique front, part projected part denied (ibid). Although at the time the assault column was some prodigy since the phalanx, the line was the order of the day – literally – for centuries, assault columns described by Homer as 'towers' (Hom Il IV-334) were well-known to tacticians and had been used by the 10,000 in 401–400 BC (Xen Anab IV.8,11–14). Epaminondas was a philosopher (Diod XVI.2,3), meaning a scholar; and he could well have been inspired by the Homeric descriptions coupled to the Persian practices recounted by the veterans of the Asian campaigns since the Battle of Cunaxa. As Philip was residing as a hostage in Thebes, among the friends of Epaminondas, he might have decided to study Homer more deeply and been inspired, and this could have resulted in creating the Macedonian pike phalanx (Diod XVI.3,2) from existing raw materials: the Thracian very long spears: *sarissai* (the word *sarissa* is possibly Thracian and if so it refers to these exceptionally long spears) and the Iphicratean *peltast*, with some differentiations.

Fast forward to the ancient tacticians: some decades to and even centuries later, *Embolon* means 'wedge' and thus its use in historical context may be misleading. For example, there are accounts of Epaminondas using *infantry* wedges (Devine 1983; Xen Hell VII.5,22; Arr Ars Tact XI.2). Moreover, the term was used thrice by Arrian: in the first case at Pelion (Arr Anab I.6,3) it is an infantry formation of the Phalanx, much better understood in the context of 'column'. The second case is a Persian cavalry unit at the Granicus (Arr Anab I.15,7), where the column formation as described by Xenophon (Xen Hell III.4,14) is a plausible interpretation. And the third case is a mixed, multi-unit formation at Gaugamela (Arr Anab III.14,2), which could well have been the first instance for such a contraption.

As underlined most succinctly (Devine 1983), to tacticians the cavalry wedge may be formed by one unit or more, a solid formation or a hollow formation of some different dispositions. In infantry, it is always a hollow, multi-unit formation, although the multi-unit clause could be doubted. Thus, at Gaugamela, Alexander most probably created a multi-unit wedge, one side being cavalry, the successive squadrons of the Companions (in unknown deployment, perhaps side-by-side) denying their right, so as to secure themselves against the enemy engaged by the right flank guard and in position to engage such enemy. The left side was the infantry divisions, having their two subdivisions side-by-side (the third was in a second line, see the discussion on the double phalanx above) and advancing with the right projecting and the left denied, so the latter could ward off the units of the Persian centre (**Figure 12.2C**). The tip was the second part of the Royal Squadron, under Hegelochus, where Alexander himself was posted to lead the attack. Bursting through the Persian main line, as it was weakened by preliminary action, the wedge must have turned left to flank the entourage of Darius, taking the enemy formations in the side and causing mayhem to the mixed cavalry and infantry units of the ethnic Persians, but to other units as well, including half the Greek mercenaries. Possibly a portion of the cavalry units turned right and dissolved the Bactrian units, engaged already, which must have been the first to flee. Already half-beaten by the successive charges, the rupture of their line had them cut off before Darius had to flee. No wonder they were among the survivors (Arr Anab III.16,1) and thus formed the nucleus of the troops Darius was able to rally, with ominous consequences therefore. Whether or not part of the *embolon* turned right, the leftward sweep of the main part not only put Darius and his entourage to flight, which became immediately apparent to his units that had encircled the Greek left, destabilizing them, but also threatened to cut off any retreat. Especially the Imperial cavalry, with the slaughter it had suffered at Issus (Arr Anab II.11,8), was quick to take the hint and to flee.

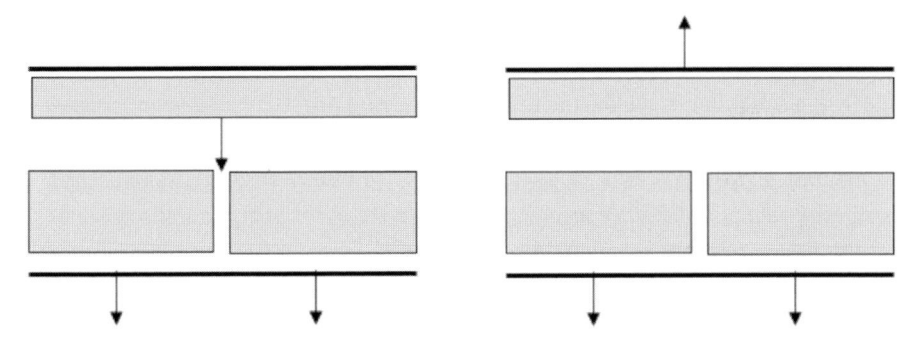

Figure 12.4: The wording of Arrian for the Macedonian phalanx at Gaugamela (Arr. Anab. III.12,1) suggests a textbook double-edged phalanx, as introduced in Ars Tactica XXIX.1 by the same author. This means the second echelon is deployed with the best troops (file leaders, bold black line) at the very rear and file closers directly behind the file closers of the first echelon. The advantage is the prompt reaction to the rear threat; men have simply to about-face individually. The challenge is that this format offers little – if any – support to the main effort.

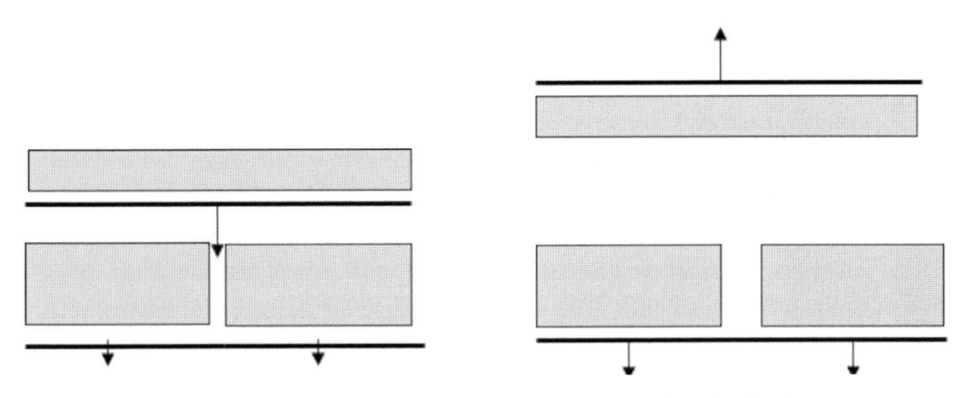

Figure 12.5: The tertiary basis of phalanx organization as proposed in this book suggests a conventional double phalanx at Gaugamela which could become double-edged by executing a countermarch (the file-leaders are shown by the bold black line). The third *lochos*, in half depth, double width, followed the other two *lochoi* of the *taxis* as a second echelon, which were in normal depth side-by-side (thus forming the first echelon), covering their rear in full. In this way it is ready to assist in the main effort and if the need be, transform to meet rapidly any threat appearing to the rear.

allowed a nice, terrifying aspect and brings to mind the last phase of the Spartan victory at the first Battle of Mantinea, 418 BC (Thuc V.73).

It is not clear whether the flight of Darius and the collapse of his entourage brought about the collapse of the units engaged with Alexander's right flankguard. The last attack by Aretes' lancers had broken some units at the tail of the formation and Alexander's penetration, whatever form that might have taken, would have made an impression; the Macedonians were at their tail, cutting them off from the rest of the army. Being already engaged they might have not had the nerve to wait it out while fighting themselves; the penetration was a most ominous evolution. Thus, they might have broken and fled before the collapse of the centre. Arrian lists Menidas among the wounded of the action of the Macedonian right wing against the returning Achaemenid squadrons from the central penetration, which means that the cavalry that engaged the right flank guard was left unpursued alone to flee, or was pursued by some of the light Imperial cavalry launched against it, possibly to assist in helping. It would have been a standard mission of light cavalry to pursue in depth, especially in order to secure the flank of other units engaged in a different direction.

The storming of Alexander's base camp

The issue at hand arises from the very different narratives of Arrian and Diodorus on the subject, which seem mutually exclusive, as are other parts of their respective works. Still things are not as they seem.

The latter describes a deep, planned raid to free the Persian prisoners and especially the royal family, sanctioned by Mazeus, the cavalry commander of the whole army and executed by two units (2,000 Cadusians and 1,000 Scythians) by flanking the Macedonian left (Diod XVII.59,5–8; Plut Alex 32,3). The former considers Mazeus the commander of the right Persian flank, not the cavalry commander, and assigns the raid to Persian and Indian cavalry units (Arr Anab III.14,4–5) penetrating through a breach in the phalanx line. Moreover, Arrian maintains that the rear echelon of the Macedonian army about-turns, pursues these two units and defeats them after the camp has been stormed (Arr Anab III.14,6). As they flee, these riders accidentally crash onto the Companion Cavalry which has turned left to assist the hard-pressed Macedonian left wing (Arr Anab III.15,1) and a major engagement ensued at point-blank range, with many casualties on both sides.

This clearly does not seem plausible, on open ground, to pursue cavalry with infantry and somehow be able to overtake it. Arrian probably reports two different actions, not necessarily connected. First, a penetration and raid by Indian and Persian horse, but while the Indians are indeed counted within the elite units of the Persian centre (Arr Anab III.11,5–6) and are not mentioned or counted anywhere else, the Persians may be also elite units from the centre, that is the Persian cavalry guard (ibid.), but they might be equally well regular units from the left wing (Arr Anab III.11,3) or any cavalry unit of the empire, in a *sensu lato* use of the adjective 'Persian'. After all, the elite guard cavalry of the centre would have been reluctant to leave the King to execute a raid or even a charge against conventional, rank-and-file targets. It is important that when such cavalry returns and is engaged decisively by Alexander's wheeling right wing, the Parthians are mentioned amongst them, who are part of the right wing of the main Persian battle line (Arr Anab III.11,4).

Then, Arrian narrates a bitter encounter between the Macedonian cavalry and Indian, Persian and Parthian horse (Arr Anab III.15,1), without any more explanations. The Parthians are not counted among the cavalry which broke through and stormed the Macedonian camp (Arr Anab III.14,4–5). Thus it is most probable that the Companions engaged Persian, Indian and Parthian squadrons fleeing the field, without any connection or participation to the camp raid. Moreover, the Persian squadrons may well have been from the left flank (Arr Anab III.11,3), the regular cavalry intermingled with infantry, and not the elite units from the centre.

Could Diodorus' account be reconciled with the above? Up to a point, it could. The detailed account of Arrian should be preferred to the much more educational, epic, biased and anachronistic, sensational narrative tale of Diodorus as a rule. Still, in this case the comparison is more balanced. Diodorus mentions the positioning of Cretan archers which do not feature in the account of Arrian. Diodorus has them positioned at the left wing (Diod XVII.57,4), which was their position in Arrian's account of the Battle of Issus (Arr Anab II.9,3), making it a very dependable and reliable reference. He also details fully the composition of the Greek allied cavalry at Gaugamela (Diod XVII.57,3) while he keeps it positioned exactly where Arrian puts it as well (Arr Anab III.11,10).

On the contrary, Diodorus and Arrian disagree over the command of a phalanx *taxis*. The detailed account of Arrian, over the feudal-hereditary leadership of the unit (Arr Anab III.11,9) and the central point it had in the battle (Arr Anab III.14,4–5) make Arrian's reference more dependable than Diodorus' plain narration (Diod XVII.57,2). By the same token, Diodorus' account for the raid (Diod XVII.59,5–8) is more attractive as it gives more definite details and a perfectly plausible reasoning in intention and execution, while Arrian's account is shady and does not even clarify the target – the fortified, main camp sixty or more stades (12 km) away (Arr Anab III.9,1–2) or the provisional camp on the hills, less than 30 stades (6 km) from the scene of the main battle (Arr Anab III.9,3–4). Thus, Arrian's account should be generally preferred, but not always; in many cases it is wanting, plain and simple (Griffith 1947).

A very important issue, at the heart of the present discussion, is the identification and positioning of both Scythians and Kadusians, who executed the deep raid or search and rescue mission (Diod XVII.57,5–8). The Sacae, the only contingent which might be identified with the Scythians mentioned by Diodorus as above, are positioned at the right wing by Arrian (Arr Anab III.11,4). This is weird, they are explicitly mentioned (Arr Anab III.8,3) as following Bessus' command as allies and should thus have been deployed at the left wing – the extreme left to be more specific, where more of their nation had been positioned (Arr Anab III.11,3). Actually, another Scythian unit – possibly Dahae – was deployed with the Bactrians at the left wing, but was engaged against the left flank guard of Alexander and would thus have been unavailable for the raid.

Similarly, the Cadusians are positioned in the left wing (Arr Anab III.11,3), although Arrian clearly states that they came along with the Medes, who were positioned at the right wing (Arr Anab III.11,4). It is understood that the written deployment plan, recovered by the Macedonians and referred to by Arrian (Arr Anab III.10,3), in some cases was not followed – at least on the day of the battle. The most obvious such case is the elephants which were intended as an extra asset against the Companion Cavalry at the centre (Arr. Anab. III.11,6). In that era they must have been simply ridden by two- to four-man teams (the mahout included) shooting bows and/or throwing javelins (Nossov 2008). However, they did not participate in the actual battle, as they are missing from any account; possibly due to incompatibility with horse cavalry not trained to cooperate with them, but being weary is a valid possibility as well (ibid.). The latter could be due to their expedient move from Babylon to Arbela into desert climate, or to being deployed and staying immobile overnight, a very frustrating condition even for a very patient animal.

Still, the positioning of the Scythians and Cadusians remains problematic, especially regarding their intended use by either Mazaeus or the Persian High Command. It cannot be determined whether this had been an ad hoc task force organized by Mazaeus, a dispatch of available units at an opportune moment of the battle, or a standing order to the army for any unit finding itself in position suitable to execute this rescue mission – with a hefty reward.

It is a most reasonable assumption that the raid was launched against the main Macedonian camp, sixty or so stades away (Arr Anab III.9,2). It is there that the Persian royal family and the prisoners would have been kept, along with unfit or unreliable troops (Arr Anab III.9,1). Out of sight of the battle, the guard might have been less alert. If the Thracians (Arr Anab III.12,5) were assigned to this main camp, and not to the provisional one on the hill range, the low alertness would be understood. Thracian national units were not renowned for their vigilance and discipline.

Chapter 13

After Gaugamela

Measured and weighted

The Battle of Gaugamela was a masterpiece of planning and execution. The plan correctly anticipated reverses and provided accordingly. It was meticulous, played well the psychological card and the tactical and technical superiority of the troops of Alexander's army. Keeping large numbers of the opponent occupied by small detachments and making Darius expend his options and reserves early is a token of high competence, not the opposite (Diod XVII.60,1; Griffith 1947). The same must be said regarding Alexander's personal involvement in combat. Criticism for abandoning his position of a general for the one of petty officer or trooper is inaccurate. It is rather intended to exonerate military elites who gave up the glory of participation for the security of managing and commanding (Delbruck 1920). Taking on the Persian Empire was an unbelievable feat needing the belief, devotion and exceptional participation of his men. His leading by example made it happen (Fuller 1958), struck terror within the Persians and legitimized the victory, as it would have done for Cyrus the Younger 70 years earlier (Xen Anab I.8,26).

Arrian is very specific in making a distinction between Darius' portable treasury and the major baggage train, retinue and even his personal kit –the moving palace – that was left at Arbela, (Arr Anab III.15,5), quite some distance from the prospective battlefield, and his established camp at Gaugamela (Arr Anab III.15,4). The latter was not properly defended and fortified, unlike Alexander's main camp (Arr Anab III.9,1). The arrangement of Darius is similar to his comfortable disposition at Sochi, with the treasury and heavy baggage at Damascus, in-theatre but rather far to his rear. The point is whether fortified camps were not an SOP in his army, possibly due to its size, or it was not implemented in this case due to lack of time. This is definitely not absolute; he had time enough to shape the terrain so as to prepare killing fields for his chariotry. But he may have prioritized one need over the other; this means he may indeed have moved his army to Gaugamela and his logistics to Arbela from Babylon under duress, when Alexander broke off to the east after crossing the Euphrates. The camp was captured by Parmenio, to free Alexander for the resumption of the pursuit of Darius (Arr Anab III15,4), while the major base at Arbela was taken by Alexander the next day (Arr Anab III.15,5).

Herein lies an interesting issue, whether Darius tried to make something less of his defeat after his flight from the field. He may have tried to rally his troops under his banner after the battle. He most probably had made no arrangements for defeat; he *had* to win and defeatism is a terrible initial investment, although it may prove invaluable. At Issus it must have been out of arrogance that he had made no such arrangement. In any case, in both battles Alexander was able to penetrate to the heart of his battle order, which meant that his armies were not destroyed but dispersed in different directions, depending on the closest egress route (Parpas 2014). Darius fleeing towards Media was perhaps not scheduled, but of necessity: this egress route was accessible and politically sound; going to Babylon would expose him to hostile locals and hot pursuit, with few prospects of survival. His dissolved host ran in whichever direction each thought accessible; in the chaos he could not have contemplated how he could assist the flight of his troops, but for the preservation of the bridges leading to Media (Patchen 2014).

Thus, at Gaugamela when given a respite by Alexander, he might have gained some distance and tried to rally his troops at Arbela (Curt V.1,3–4); whether to issue orders and directives for the future or to continue the battle is uncertain. At the moment he fled, his wings were engaging in earnest and at least on the right rather successfully. He might have not noticed that the collapse was prompt and total, or he hoped to find an opening.

This obvious opportunity arose because Alexander broke off the pursuit to assist Parmenio and his left wing (Arr Anab III.15,1) but eventually had the opportunity to smash major, relatively intact forces that were fleeing, especially elite-rated cavalry (Arr Anab III.15,1–2). Thanks to the proceedings, this distraction did not lead to the loss of the entire Macedonian left wing which eventually survived and counterattacked (Arr Anab III.15,3). This line of events was catastrophic; the disaster became a slaughter as the whole of the Macedonian army engaged in the pursuit and took a bloody revenge for the hardship and terror of the battle (Arr Anab III.15,6). Thus the units leaving in the same direction as Darius were wholly disheartened and perhaps nothing but hordes of dispirited fugitives. Additionally, Alexander resumed the pursuit in earnest (Arr Anab III.15,3); he could not capture Darius, he knew (although if the latter tried to rally the distance could be covered) but he did want to wholly eliminate present and future dangers from this army. The hotter the pursuit, the worse the nightmares of the survivors – and the fewer their number. And, of course, taking intact the enemy base and baggage was of immense importance, not only for reasons of money and income; intelligence was for the Macedonians of Alexander a most important form of spoils (Engels 1980a) as indicated by finding the written deployment plan at the Imperial headquarters (Arr Anab III.11,3).

Darius' flight to Media was perhaps not scheduled, but of necessity: it was accessible from the position he had found himself at, and it was a politically sound choice, near his previous satrapy, Armenia, amongst good subjects, the Medes. It was also through a road ill-suited for the heavy baggage of the conqueror, a true escape path.

To the victor the spoils

Darius supposes that Alexander will collect the prizes he has won (Arr Anab III.16,2), as he did after Issus, and will not engage in hasty strategic pursuit. Alexander had proven to be a very considerate and prudent commander as evidenced by twice not rushing into the offensive; neither the summer of 333 BC, when Darius expected him at Sochi (Arr Anab II.6,3–4), nor the previous day, when it was taken for granted that he would launch a night attack to even the odds (Arr Anab III.10,1–2). So Darius' choice is to flee to Ecbatana by the road of Khorasan, through Behistun (solid line in **Map 9**), where he might raise the semblance of another army, especially from Bactria, the cradle of the Achaemenid rule, and Armenia, his own seat of feudal power (Badian 2000) and through associations with landlords and feudalists. He could also hope to save Persepolis by mobilizing the Persian militia (Xen Cyr I.2,14). Babylon, with its deep anti-Persian feelings was lost, especially with its native troops fleeing the field of Gaugamela after being beaten on it. Their impression would have made them rather face the defeated and broken Persian overlords than the victorious Macedonians. Susa was of questionable loyalty; although not so resentful as Babylon, being a royal city, after some massacres at the hands of Darius I (DB 72, 75), it was impossible to defend against Alexander.

Babylon was lost to the Persians, but not won by Alexander by default. If he bypassed it to chase Darius, upon his return it might not be Gates Open and disturbing views of autonomy could have surfaced and entice the populace. Its amazing fortifications could repulse Alexander for some time and in the heat of summer this was to be an existential problem. Unfortunately for the Persians, most of their forces had been slaughtered at Gaugamela and there were not enough soldiers for such operations, especially in Babylon with the unfriendly population and the vast expanse of its walls; but the *natives* inspired and mobilized to defend their city, many as they were to properly man the fortification and using the abundance of supplies would suggest an unsavoury situation for the victors.

In any case, Alexander did not allow power gaps and such temptations, nor the looting – or extraction – of the Achaemenid treasures. Then he needed to reward and rest his army in abundance, not to take them on a campaign in the Zagros Mountains immediately after such an ordeal, while the riches and comforts of Babylon were at hand. Even during the battle Alexander must have realized that taking Darius' head did not guarantee his success in gaining the empire if he was to suffer severe casualties; this is why he paused the pursuit to assist his crumbling left wing. And he was right. Although the Persian army disintegrated on the field and their system of power would have collapsed with the death of the Emperor in the hands of an invader, making ridicule of the Mandate of Heaven which was the motto of the dynasty, there would be many contenders and surrogates to claim a fresh start. The populace of the empire would accept the verdict of the battle, but not the different, affected systems of power; they would muster any vigour to resist. And in order to vanquish such opponents, and to preserve his conquests, especially from the temptation of centrifugal forces, Alexander needed his army in excellent condition, with top morale, glorified, fed and satisfied, with few casualties and regrets. Alexander would go to Babylon to collect his spoils.

The local resentment coupled with the awe from the battle meant that there was no way the Achaemenid authorities, possibly Mazeus who retreated there after the battle, would be able to defend it under siege. The – warranted – Persian distrust must have deprived the city of key elements for defending its walls so as to discourage insurgencies (Bosworth 1988). Still, the charms of the city would delay and unnerve the victorious Macedonians, saving Darius some valuable time to try to salvage what he could (Patchen 2014). Indeed Alexander this time capitalized on the impression created by his victory and was received as a liberator in Babylon and confirmed as King of the World, a proclamation made probably at Arbela, mere days after the battle (Parpas 2014; Hammond 1989). The populace, the clergy, the authorities came out of the city to welcome him and deliver the city, the citadel and the treasure (Arr Anab III.16,3); there were no questions regarding self-governance, independence and so on. The Babylonians were only offered beneficial measures and a respect for all their traditions (Arr Anab III.16,4), which delighted the populace more than the clergy; once in the city, for Alexander the populace was the most important element, as the fighters were raised amongst it.

The Battle of Gaugamela ended Alexander's war against the Persian Empire – at least in the purely military aspect. There was no Empire, although there was Persia and its nuclear states (Media and Elam) and its eastern provinces (Patchen 2014). Alexander had no idea how important one of these provinces was; it was Bactria, the hidden heart of the empire. But from the moment he occupied the capital of the empire, Susa, with its treasure, etiquette, prestige and significance, the empire was over. From then on, his operations were aimed at securing this state of affairs, by preventing Darius and other Persian aristocrats from challenging his conquests by raising another large army, and subduing satraps who showed tendencies of autonomy, independence, insurrection and resistance to his prerogative as won in battle; the sceptre of the empire. The army that Darius contemplated raising later while in Media and Bessus would be mostly conscripted from the Upper Satrapies (Diod XVII.73,2), areas which were backward and vehemently Mazdaic. Their holy mission would be the *liberation* of the conquered Persia and not its *defence*.

As long as Darius remained alive and free, Alexander could not appropriate the throne of Persia. The power yes, but not the title. Darius' clever move meant that Alexander was between two embryonic and evolving threats: the national army of Persia that would be assembled by the leadership of the aristocrats and the authorities of the nation (Xen Cyr I.2,5 & 9); and the Imperial host from other, loyal nations, that would be raised by Darius himself. Troops loyal to his person or his mantle or his religious stature. Alexander could move immediately and dismantle or prevent the creation of one, but not of both. He did not have enough forces to divide into two major strategic objectives in opposite directions (**Map 9**); his dividing the army had always been at the operational level at the most.

In the unlikely event Alexander was to give chase, Darius could defend Behistun or even ambush Alexander there – a good reason for Alexander to have opted for a Battle Royal in the first place, instead of sneaking into the pass. After all, he had given up four days to Darius to settle in position, so he would not have to enter Behistun; Alexander had feinted a move there, he did not mean it. If Alexander was truly going for Behistun, then and only then could Babylon be retained by Mazaeus. If the city was left undisturbed and bypassed by Alexander or if assigned to secondary forces, as had happened with Damascus after Issus (Arr Anab II.11,10), it might resist.

This might, just might, have allowed the evacuation of the treasure of the war chest, which was a most potent weapon (Fuller 1958; Ashley 1998): at the time Alexander was fighting at Gaugamela, a massive anti-Macedonian coalition under Spartan leadership had taken the field and caused a major reaction by Antipater, the regent of Alexander in Macedon (Arr Anab I.11,3). He used his entire army and all the alliances so as to crush the neo-Medizers, which meant a major threat (Diod XVII.63,1). There were many fighters in Europe that would take the field against Macedon for some gold.

The Persian army was dissolved, but was not utterly destroyed. It suffered heavy losses, especially regarding morale, which plummeted and never allowed any open confrontation again. The elite, aristocratic-feudal cavalry corps was decimated at Issus: their flight due to the precipitous exits, the panic and their weight and bulk ended in disaster. A third of their number were slain, obviously not battle casualties, but victims of hot pursuit; stabbed by pursuers, trampled underhoof by their comrades or fallen in ravines (Arr Anab II.11,8). At Gaugamela they tried to disengage early but fell on Alexander's cavalry (Arr Anab III.15,1–2) and suffered a most vigorous pursuit (Arr Anab III.15,5).

Without their *asabara*, Persia, as well as Media, were not defenceless. Their terrain, rugged and mountainous, was immensely suitable for prolonged guerrilla warfare, as well as regular territorial campaigning with multiple lines of defence in choke points, such as mountainous passages and fortified cities. An asymmetric, hybrid campaign by Darius had to begin on Persian soil. The Persians did not share the advanced perception of the territorial war of the fourth century Greeks. This was obvious by the inability of any Imperial unit other than the mercenary Greeks under Memnon to face the corresponding kind of warfare conducted by Philip's vanguard. But they could certainly present a strong and determined defence against the relatively few Greeks that were expected to invade, and subject them to attrition.

Darius could hope that in Ecbatana in Media he could find refuge for a long time and gather loyal forces (Arr Anab III.19,1). It was an advantageous position, between two loyal districts, Armenia and Bactria with facilities for transportation and logistics. Even if Alexander pushed in that direction before Darius was fully prepared, the latter could easily retreat eastward, through the Caspian Gates and the Elbruz Mountains, to the Upper, i.e. northeastern, Satrapies (**Map 9**).

Alexander, always cautious and a master of aggressive psychological operations (PsyOps) led his army to Babylon in battle order (Arr Anab III.16,3), to press home the message of the battle. Mazeus was discouraged from any thoughts of a sudden sortie he might have entertained, and the locals from any thought not involving full cooperation with the new master of Asia and his army (Arr Anab III.16,3). The sojourn in Babylon lasted a month (Diod XVII.64,4), to rest the men, offer them recreation, and organize the conquered territories; Alexander even sent a satrap to Armenia (Arr Anab

III.16,5), although the region had not been officially conquered, while it had sent strong cavalry detachments to Darius for the Battle of Gaugamela (Arr Anab III.11,7). It was the satrapy of Darius (Pathcen 2014) and the shock of the battle enticed it to submit, at least in appearances, which were evidently shed at some pretext and opportunity. The fact that Alexander's successors invaded and properly conquered it after his death is very informative; it was the one and only operation they undertook in common before launching themselves at each other's throats.

Alexander would not stay in Babylon for too long though; the city was corrupting a warrior's spirit, a fact that could lead to uneasy conditions where conspiracies thrive. Darius perhaps hoped for such a development, a Secret Warfare solution (Arr Anab III.19,1), very dear to the Achaemenids (Arr Anab II.14,5) and there was much to do in not so much time. It was the turn of Susa. Susa was the seat of the Persian government. There the Royal Road ended. There, the Medizing Greeks of some importance flocked to betray their homeland for gold or spite to the King of Kings. And at this point, Alexander enters the nucleus of the Achaemenid Empire, the western part of the Elam, the Sushan. From now on he cannot pose as liberator, but he can image himself as social reformer or vindicator of local dynasties and oppressed religious factions.

Alexander had secured an almost friendly reception and the peaceful surrender of Susa, city, population and treasure (Arr Anab III.16,6), for immediately after the Battle of Gaugamela he had the good sense to send a special detachment with a confidante of his to negotiate the surrender of the city and secure the treasury and the public order. He was there in 20 days after he started from Babylon, more than two months after he had won the battle; it was too soon for Darius and any loyalist to have undertaken any action. After all, Darius *wanted* Alexander to stay south of Zagros, to spend much time there, and for this he might have used his treasure and ordered compliance to his local regents so as to sap the fighting spirit of the Macedonians with luxury and riches. What he needed was time and Alexander took the bargain; he gave him but little, for too steep a price in gold.

The Persian treasure allowed generous rewards and thus spared the city from a most deserving loot and pillage session. Susa was to be spared and forgiven as an Imperial capital, possibly to remind the population of the atrocities of Darius I and to kindle the Elamite memories of the city that would be flattered by Alexander paying respects to the memory and policies of Cyrus, a figure not wholeheartedly revered by the Achaemenids and their priesthood (Farahmand 2015). This example, and the proceedings in

Babylon, suggested to other cities to do the same and open their gates (Fuller 1958). In Susa, Alexander settled the royal Persian family. More importantly, the massive reinforcements expected and sorely needed for the Battle Royal at Gaugamela caught up with him at Susa, three months late. But now he would need them more.

This possibly catastrophic delay made Alexander expect no further such reinforcements and make do with local human resources from then on (Olbrycht 2011), until a bit before his death, eight full years later, when he ordered a whole new army under Antipater to come to replace the discharged veterans sent home under Craterus (Arr Anab VII.12,4).

Chapter 14

In the Heart of Persia

The cradle of the Persian nation was Persia, with Persepolis and Parsagadae, east of Zagros. It is important that before Alexander no reference is made by Greek writers to Persepolis, the Secret City of Darius I, made to spite the heritage of Cyrus the Great (Mousavi 2005). In Herodotus there is no mention of the city, although many Greeks had visited the depth of Persia. Possibly its name in Persian, *Parsa* was confusing as it would be similar or identical to Greek ears for the Greek name of the region, *Perses* (meaning *Persia*) and the people, *Persai* (Persians): this is the word for the city in Arrian (Arr Anab III.22,1). The city is referred to as *Persepolis* by Diodorus (Diod XVII.69,1).

Alexander thought that he knew all he needed, with Persians like Artabazus residing at his father's court (Diod XVI.52,3). He had to invade Persia to conclude the conquest and had some debts long overdue to settle – with interest. He was not to outrage the city of Cyrus, Parsagadae, although Cyrus had been the first Persian to rule Greeks. But Cyrus was a very amicable figure in the Persian folklore, well-respected by the Greeks since Herodotus and revered by Xenophon and Alexander knew that by honouring him and imitating him (Burliga 2014) the Persians would be flattered and less reactionary. To pin the enmity to the Achaemenids, the line of Darius I, was a very ingenious policy of Alexander – and Persepolis, the Secret City of the former was focal in this context.

In Persepolis there were favourable conditions for the defence of the inner heart of the empire and thus a determined effort was planned. It was the last hearth of Achaemenid Persia and its treasures. After conquering Persepolis, Alexander could turn his attention to Darius once again. Having conquered Darius' wealth, country, family and palaces, he needed his crown and mantle; the King Must Die. Darius would actually be a fugitive, not a monarch, from the moment Alexander arrived in Persepolis. Until then, he still retained the title of Great King, and was simply challenged by Alexander whose achievements deprived the crown of Darius of power and significance and made it a useless piece of fabric, but it was still a piece of fabric with enormous prestige, especially in the East.

As a consequence, the Medizers' revolt under Sparta, deprived of its rich Persian sponsorship, was destined to dwindle. The affairs back in Greece were now not a priority for Alexander. They were inconsequential, with the exception of the availability of more mercenaries. But they were important to his men, who had families there, especially the Southern Greeks of the Alliance of Corinth, much more exposed to anti-Macedonians, both factions and states.

Alexander set out from Susa for Persepolis relatively quickly, to allow as little time as possible for the organization of any kind or resistance. Such measures by the defenders could include, without being limited to, raising troops, restoring morale, consolidating some force structure and fortifying locations of interest. He correctly believed that survivors from Gaugamela would be instrumental in such efforts with their knowledge and experience, once properly motivated and stiffened by the existential threat. Whether he understood the possible role and potential of the Persian militia is not clear. After all, they would have been still under the cumulative shock of a number of disasters, from the resounding defeat in battle to the fall of the first capital and the bigger city of the empire.

The Zagros range defined the frontier of the realm of Persia and its plateau (**Map 9**). The mountainous area of Uxiana was the first contact with the folk of the Persian nations: the mountaineers were truly unruly and not under any regent or Satrap. Additionally, the Highlander Uxians were receiving tolls from the Great King for his travels between Susa and Persepolis, with his enormous retinue (Arr Anab III.17,1), while their lowland kin were squarely under the jurisdiction of the satrap of Persia and healthily submissive (Diod. XVII.67.3). There were many such mountainous foci of autonomy in the Achaemenid Empire, and their importance is overlooked. Not necessarily a sign of Persian incompetence, but rather a healthy policy for breeding and raising mercenaries and, even more to the point, a safeguard of the Great King so that the safekeeping of some important passages would not be left to possibly unreliable Satraps and officials, prone to corruption and insurgency (Sekunda 1992). The mountainous peoples, under certain conditions, were much more reliable though uncontrollable, as the Byzantines believed and practised.

A typical lightning campaign against the highlander Uxians was carried out, turning the heavily guarded main passes with elite infantry (Arr Anab III.17,2–3) and leading to total submission after some slaughter (Arr Anab III.17,4–5). The lowlanders had been less of a sport (Bosworth 1988), if they needed any campaigning at all (Fuller 1958); Curtius (Curt V.3,2–12) refers to it, Arrian does not.

The Persian gates

Alexander's move from Susa to Persepolis was definitely intended to unsettle the enemy; Darius had every reason to suppose that Alexander would spend much time west of the Zagros, between Babylon and Susa (Arr Anab III.19,1) but eventually he *would* venture there to finish the job. It was by no means a surprise, thus Alexander had somehow to compensate for its predictability. He decided for a move to Persepolis as soon as possible, making Time the wildcard; he had few other options, really.

In effect it was a forced move; Persia had to be invaded, the treasure confiscated and the scores settled. Perhaps leaving early from Susa rather than staying the winter was one way of keeping the enemy unsettled and catching them off guard. He followed his usual practice, and after the submission of the Uxians he took the more mobile units for a forced march whereas heavier formations and the baggage train under Parmenio were lumbering forward from the main route connecting Susa to Persepolis (Montagu 2000); the eastern extension of the Royal Road, the Road of Shiraz (Fuller 1958) which allowed carriages of quite some size and weight, such as the ones used by the retinue of the King of Kings.

The short itinerary, through the steepest road (Stein 1940), was followed by Alexander's detachment which was practically the entire Macedonian field army (Arr Anab III.18,1). It was a gamble, to take the shortcut and emerge to Persepolis before defences were prepared and manned, while the obvious invasion was coming from the main road. Thus Parmenio was a bait, a distraction, and the enemy was surely kept informed of his approach, possibly for his estimated time of arrival also. But in this case Alexander overplayed his hand. He possibly knew that Darius was in Media, most probably trying to raise a new army. Whether he knew there was an opponent, defending Persia, and who he had been, is a guess, but he must have had some information. It turned out not to be accurate information.

First, the narrows of the shortcut, the Persian Gates, were held in strength and properly fortified; the opponent had been busy, something typical of Achaemenid administration but even more of Darius. The commander was Ariobarzanes (Arr Anab III.18,2); his relationship to a son of Darius III by the same name from his first marriage, while satrap of Armenia (Patchen 2014; Badian 2000), is uncertain, but the name should be underlined, and the same goes with the activity, method and attitude. Of course, Ariobarzanes was the name of one of the three sons of the elder and very capable and loyal Artabazus (Arr Anab III.23,7).

He had built a wall to cut the narrows completely (Arr Anab III.18,2). He was obviously well-informed of the practices of Alexander, especially his storming of the Cilician Gates and believed Alexander would be rather dashing than cautious at this time, betting on the effects of the shock and awe of his victory. Ariobarzanes must have deployed the militia of Persia; the numbers in Arrian, 700 cavalry and 40,000 infantry (Arr Anab III.18,2) are the highest. Both options indicate a wholesale slaughter of the national Persian elements of the army. The *asabara* were practically exterminated, although it might have been the nature of the terrain, or their lack of faith in the commander; they were nobles, after all. But the infantry, 40,000 out of an estimated 120,000, the registered male Persians available for military service at home, (Xen Cyr I.2,15) indicates that the national infantry, obviously the Kardaka, had been obliterated. Alterative figures from other sources reporting 25,000 foot and 300 horse (Diod XVII.68,1; Curt V.3,17) do not change the basic facts and impressions; quite the opposite. Ariobarzanes, whether bearing the title of Satrap (Arr Anab III.18,2) or not, as Persis was no conquered land to need a Satrap, was also amply provided for; his supplies must have been more than adequate.

Alexander did no reconnaissance – very untypical of him. Had he become cocky and careless or had he been really in a hurry? Perhaps both; he would have never allowed himself sloppiness and carelessness if not in the greatest hurry. In this case speed was not enough, nor delivering.

Alexander may have ordered a most unwarranted, too risky attack (Arr Anab III.18,3); or Ariobarzanes executed an ideal ambush, (Curt V.3,17–19). The result is the same; Alexander was repulsed, probably hit also by siege engines and catapults deployed in a field context (Arr Anab III.18,3), a gimmick he was himself a master of as proven already in his Balkan campaigns (Arr Anab I.6,8). He was repulsed with some loss and according to one tradition, not mentioned by Arrian, he was frustrated with the attitude of his men, who fled the field ignominiously due to their arrogance being shattered by the spirited Persian defence in advantageous terrain. So infuriated had he been that he withdrew full body armour and issued half-cuirasses, so as to have their backs exposed and dare not turn them to the enemy (Pol Strat IV.3,13). True, the Persians had no access and possibly no nerve to approach for a close kill. Was it the terrain or the awe and terror that the Macedonian army inspired, especially when CQB was concerned, that kept the Persians at a distance? It could be a combination. Though, in any case, pelted by all kinds of missiles the Macedonians retreated some 3.5 km through the narrows, a true trap, with minimal damage; the tales of disaster advanced by some scholars (Bosworth 1988) are just that: tales. There is not one clue to indicate anything but a reverse; true, this is how the Achaemenids presented the events at Marathon to outsiders. But this parallel is unwarranted without further substantiation. It is not impossible, not even improbable. Simply, not suggested by the reports and fact descriptions in terms of figures, not sensational wording by Curtius. Once out of the trap, the Macedonians camped nearby to recuperate and study the situation.

The massive reinforcement of the Macedonian army due to the new recruits that Amyntas finally brought to Susa (Arr Anab III.16,10) had seriously degraded cohesion and performance; Alexander was lucky not to have them for the Battle at Gaugamela. They had no time to be integrated. Alexander knew he had no reason to press the issue in the Persian Gates frontally (Bosworth 1988); morale was low and prospects allowed no optimism. He needed another approach, he knew his Battle of Thermopylae, he blamed himself for stupid arrogance, he understood that Xerxes was not an incompetent and found himself in the same position: his problem now was not Persepolis, it was his baggage train that moved slowly along a road where it could be ambushed and destroyed in detail (Fuller 1958). The difference in the figures for the troops of Ariobarzanes in the sources implies either that they were deployed and guarded other passages as well (Bosworth 1988), or that a sizeable part of his forces was detailed against any attempt from the main road, where Parmenio was moving slowly. In any case, the Persians could move along internal lines as they occupied the central position. The position at the Persian Gates could be kept with a fraction of their force and the rest could move fast to engage Parmenio and then back to stiffen the defence at the Gates (Ashley 1998). Ariobarzanes was the first Persian who seems to have scored a success against Alexander.

Alexander, after crossing the Tigris had moved South-Southeast, to Babylon and Susa (Arr Anab III.16,3). The road that Darius followed to Ecbatana, the Road of Khorasan was not accessible; too far to the Northwest and he had no time, Parmenio was moving into a potential trap. He must had been the bait, the distraction, the obvious danger so as Alexander would storm the narrows unopposed, but Ariobarzanes saw through it and destroyed the hook. Ariobarzanes could now go for the bait. To destroy Parmenio would be marvellous, to stop him in his tracks just as good, but to delay him would be still beneficial. It bought time for Darius to gather a large army, while evacuating the vast treasure of Persepolis to Ecbatana or to the east, to finance further resistance. Darius was resilient, he had not given up hope or bellicosity. Whether the Uxian resistance was spontaneous or further instigated by Darius and/or Ariobarzanes one cannot tell. The former sounds more probable as they asked for tolls (Arr Anab III.17,1). After their failure (Arr Anab III.17,4), Ariobarzanes did have a fighting chance. The quality of troops and the morale are important, but his rather small force of a maximum of 40,700 men (Arr Anab III.18,2) one should notice that was a bit less than Alexander's total army at Gaugamela, 47,000 men (Arr Anab III.12,5), and definitely more than the troops facing him outside of the straits.

Thus, as mentioned above, Parmenio, instead of unlocking the situation by going the long way around, might be encountered by a significant portion of the army of Ariobarzanes that would relocate along the road, while a cover force would be more than enough to dissuade or repulse Alexander. The latter had to storm the Persian Gates or bypass them but Ariobarzanes was still there, with most if not all his forces. Alexander had to destroy this force then and there. Obviously the Persian expected a new assault with his full force and wanted to defeat it decisively before moving against Parmenio. This provided a window of opportunity for Alexander.

He does not attack so as not to offer the moral boost of a second victory and thus keeps Ariobarzanes still there, nailed. The objectives are to breach the Gates, to eliminate any danger for Parmenio, to occupy Persepolis before the treasure is evacuated (Ashley 1998) or looted, but also to exterminate Ariobarzanes' army so as not to worry in the future for the whereabouts of said army, nor the boasting of its men for scoring a bruising reverse to the unconquerable invader.

Alexander was the Avenger of the Warriors of the Persian Wars. He enlisted local help to take precipitous tracks around the fortified position (Arr Anab III.18,5), a reversal of the Battle of Thermopylae (Howe 2015). But Alexander changed the sequence: he took a considerable part of the outflanking force with him, to secure the route, and especially all subsequent crossings, bridges and straits to Persepolis, to keep the road under control and allow swift access there, while the pinning elements under Craterus create a false image of inaction (Arr Anab III.18,4). This shows that Alexander is excellently informed on the topography, distances and perhaps possible resistance by enemy activity. These detachments, under Coenus and Amyntas (Arr Anab III.18,6), are not only to keep the passages free for him to access Persepolis, but will entrap fugitives from the army of Ariobarzanes that may retreat, flee or move tactically.

This division of force totally changes the nature of Alexander's deployment. Actually he does not send a force to bypass and turn the position so as to unlock it as did the Persians in Thermopylae. He leaves a pinning force under Craterus out of the Gates and manoeuvres with his *main* force behind the enemy, to deploy on two fronts in four groups, of which one under himself will strike the enemy from behind, a second under Ptolemy will entrap the fugitives and the other two under Amyntas and Coenus will pave the way for the doubly vital objective, the city of Persepolis.

Surprising in the dawn all the outposts and sentinels (Arr Anab III.18,6–7), Alexander attacks the enemy camp with a vastly inferior force and signals to Craterus with the pinning force to advance (Arr Anab III.18,8). This is a much more decisive action than Thermopylae had ever been. No word, no warning, no chance to fight back and very few survivors. Total surprise, total victory, total annihilation (Arr Anab III.18,9). Persia will not cause him any more problems and the ghosts of Leonidas and the 300 in crimson, along with the Thespians of Dithyrambus and Demophilus in black (Her VII.222 & 227), may now rest.

Vengeance delivered

Alexander captures Persepolis and Parsagadae, confiscates the treasure of the Persian kings and empties the vaults of the Achaemenids before delivering vengeance. For the hundreds of burned, pillaged and levelled sites throughout Europe and Asia, Greek or not, the murder of his father, the conspiracies against himself, Alexander finishes the Persian wars the way Ahura-Mazda likes: with a magnificent fire that purges the blood of millions and turns Persepolis to cinders. Miletus, Eretria, Athens and their slaughtered inhabitants who simply wanted nothing to do with the Mazdaic benevolence may now rest as the debt is paid in kind (Arr Anab III.18,11). No matter the criticism, Alexander beacons the message that there is no temporary occupation of Persia, but that the Persian state – not just the Monarch – is no more. It has fallen and pays for its crimes against Greeks, Babylonians, Egyptians, Thracians, Scythians Phoenicians and so many others who considered him a liberator and avenger (Arr Anab III.18,12). Now Persia has a new, alien, master and is a conquered land.

Alexander always maintained that he was conducting a war of retribution and revenge. He should, thus, have levelled all the cities of Persia proper and amongst them Parsagadae, the city of Cyrus. *He* was the first Persian to enslave Greeks (Her I.141) and to initiate a lasting war against them, not only in Asia but also in Europe. It was against the Spartans who intervened for the Greeks of Asia. Cyrus declared that he would do with the latter as he pleased and then deal with the Spartans (Her I.153,1). Since the war was kindled between the Spartans and Cyrus, Alexander finishing it while the Spartans were fighting *for* the Persians would have been weird.

Not so weird. Cyrus was not an Achaemenid. The vehement Zoroastrians that commandeered his throne hated his policies, perhaps himself too, but could not do much to erase him from history; he was the father of the Persians (Her III.89,3). But they did mar his memory. They made another royal Persian city, Persepolis (Mousavi 2005), to throw Parsagadae into oblivion or at least insignificance. And they launched propaganda as to how glorious a conqueror Darius I had been. Looking at the map this is outright ridiculous and the campaigns in Scythia and Greece are ample proof. Thus, if the Spartans were assisting the bloodline of Darius, not of Cyrus, they may have felt OK, especially since the disowned and disenfranchised stallion king of theirs, Cleomenes I, was responsible for the clash with the Empire under Darius I (Kambouris 2022a,b).

Not profaning the city and sepulchre of Cyrus (the latter was not to happen even for the worst enemy; Greek religion forbade making war against the dead) Alexander became tolerable by many Persians. He confiscated the treasure of Parsagadae, possibly the spoils of the war of Cyrus with Lydia, Babylon and of course, Media. Parmenio had advised sparing Persepolis too, to be likable to the natives and since they now owned the place; by torching it Alexander was a raider, not a conqueror (Arr Anab III.18,11). This is all weird; Parmenio belonged to the old guard and they were in favour of looting every enemy city, and so they accused Alexander of being too soft and cooperative to the Persians, who were the defeated party. This all makes no sense: there is no way a people being the master race of the world for some 250 years felt OK towards a conqueror who made them subjects to some of their previous subjects. If their royal city was spared, they would have somewhere to look, hope, pray and rally. By turning it to ashes, it was a powerful message that their reign had ended and was not to come back.

With Darius III, with his royal and religious insignia, being at large, the best man in Persia to conduct territorial and guerilla warfare as he had been in the Royal Postal Service (Patchen 2014; Badian 2000), Alexander was absolutely right. Darius was at Ecbatana, in theory likely to cut Alexander off, and with plenty of treasure. Months later, he had with him, in his eastwards retreat from Ecbatana – or flight, it is perhaps a matter of perspective – some 10,000 men and 7,000 talents from the treasure of Ecbatana (Arr Anab III.19,5). More than enough to stir trouble in the East-Northeast. Bactria and the even more remote Sogdiana were ideal for mounted guerrilla warfare, and Darius knew that well. They had a large and warlike population dispersed in the wilderness and not urbanized but concentrated around mountain fortresses, extremely inaccessible to enemy encroachments and more so to heavy formations with huge baggage trains. The population was prosperous in their pastoralism and, having suffered some casualties at Gaugamela, they had a taste for revenge and a decent morale, bolstered by their ardent beliefs and their faith in feudal and family ties. More troops might come from the subject Indians or from further away, from independent India. And of course, there was also Scythia, with the many and warlike warriors to hire, tempt, invite, etc. to confront Alexander (Arr Anab III.25,3); warriors that distinguished themselves at Gaugamela and ever ready for hire, by the promise of cash or plunder. This meant a hard and arduous campaign to assure that the crown and the empire would go to Alexander and his conquests were secure and ever expanding.

But the Greek allies were not there to fight for his possessions, they were fighting for vengeance and the deletion of the oriental threat. They had no motive and many of them would have no nerve; the ones wishing so, would re-enlist, the others were decommissioned with honour (Arr Anab III.19,5).

Alexander and Zarathustra

Alexander was the son of a priestess – or a very zealous worshipper of the Divine (Plut Alex 2,6) – and a very well-groomed prince, with excellent tutors (Plut Alex 5,4–5 & 7,2). The episode with the philosopher Diogenes in Corinth (Plut Alex 14,2–5) may be real or not, but it shows undeniably his fascination with the Cynic ideals and attitudes. Other sources show him an accomplished Cynic, along with his close entourage (Heliopoulos 2019), a fact hushed in almost all official histories for any number of reasons. This does not mean he was not a very devoted believer of Zeus; many people of high intelligence are very critical, disapproving or even ready to ridicule religious beliefs once they are not *their* beliefs; this tendency is obvious in all the Christian literature with polemic to other religions, especially polytheistic.

Alexander, thus, was devoted to his paternal pantheon (Hammond 1989 & 1997) or at least pretended very convincingly to be so. He performed all rituals expected from him (Arr Anab III.25,1; Plut Alex 29,1 & 33,1) as the head of state and high priest of his people (Bradford 2000). Genuinely pious or not, he knew perfectly well how to use the religious issues to his advantage politically. Given the fact that he and his entourage were all Panhellenists (Tarn 1948) he had perceived at least the conquest of Asia Minor, the limit of this school of thought (Isocr Philipp 120), as his objective and developed the blueprints of a policy. But as he was also a Cynic, it is possible if not probable that his ambition was set, from the very beginning, much wider than the Panhellenic ideal, which was unsustainable. Without dissolving the empire, Asia Minor could not be held; once a generation of competent Greek commanders and troops was in Hades, wave after wave of Imperial troops and gold would flood the area. When crossing the Hellespont, Alexander most probably meant to take Susa and Persepolis, nothing less (Fuller 1958), contrary to the beliefs of esteemed scholars (Tarn 1948). This is clearly his opening move when landing to Troy, to cast his spear so as to consider *Asia* (not *Asia Minor*) taken by the spear (Diod XVII.17,2). He had studied his Xenophon (Burliga 2014) and thus knew that Babylon was a rather conservative target, conceivably attainable within a yearly campaign, but most probably a bit longer, considering all the variables. This was not taking into consideration the unreliability of his own fleet, which led to a 12-month diversion to the south, although he must have considered an Egyptian campaign from the first moment.

Being a Greek he also knew everything there was to know about factions and social unrest; being the student of Aristotle (Hammond 1997) he was empowered in using logic, but also perfectly versed in political science; his tutor wrote political theory, the voluminous *Politics*. An immensely useful handbook on how to manipulate communities by the assets and liabilities of their governance, if studied with a generous dose of cynicism.

Thus, when the authorities of an area, after an initial attack of flattery, respect and goodwill were not cooperative enough, some social strata were found to side with Alexander to undo them. This could be a class struggle, as in Bactria (Heliopoulos 2019), or a new religion. Alexander and his staff, when facing the stiff resistance of the Brahman clergy (Engels 1980a) and their social network in India, discovered a heresy, or rather a socio-philosophical outcrop, Buddhism, and supported it with all their might so as to undermine the Brahmanic establishment, with great success. Alexander was a sage and saint of Buddhism, and the same went with some of his successors, especially the renowned Milinda Maha, Menander the Great (Heliopoulos 2019).

Being of such disposition he took on the mantle of the liberator and avenger not only of the Greeks, but of all nations and faiths outraged by the Persians which secured to him, along with a firm control of the governors, acceptance, cooperation and unprecedented loyalty (Hammond 1997). This international *persona* and the resulting attitude – a most needed propaganda adaptation once outside the belt of dense Greek populations in Asia Minor – was extremely helpful: he was quick to identify the religious liabilities and vulnerabilities of the Achaemenid establishment. He knew for example the laws of succession and coronation. Under Darius I the monarch was sanctified and regicide was a sacrilegious crime, not simply a crime against the State as in all monarchies. Thus, if Darius III had fallen in battle, Alexander was in line for acquiring his title, by right of conquest; not only his kingdom and secular authority. But for this to happen he had to be recognized and confirmed by the clergy of Ahura-Mazda, or Darius had to forfeit his throne to him in an official way. As in his campaign Alexander was adopted by – or adopted himself – many fallen and disrespected deities, from the Gods of Egypt to Bel-Marduk of Babylon, he became the embodiment of evil for the Mazdaic clergy long before he invaded Iran. The depictions of Alexander with two small ram's horns, set onto his diadem, are usually considered an influence from his visit to the oracle of Amun in Siwa; the truth is that such attire was also compatible with the Carneian persona of the god Apollo, greatly revered throughout classical Greece and particularly in Macedon. With Apollo and Amun, the latter revered in Macedon, Sparta, and Thebes, the image of Alexander with the two horns, 'Iskander dul-carnein' (notice the similarity of the last word in sound, if nothing else, with the Greek 'Carneios', the personality of Apollo celebrated by horns and forbidding the Spartans to take the field at a set date) passed to the Mazdaic subconscious as the embodiment of Evil. When such beliefs were transmitted to others, in the syncretism of the Roman Empire, the horn-bearing version of Satan must have presented itself and been adopted by the Christians. Other deities, such as Pan, might well have been the raw model for the Christian version of the Fallen Angel and Lord of Hell, but the Mazdaic caricature of Alexander is a valid candidate.

Thus, Alexander had to bypass any intervention of the Mazdaic clergy to appropriate the mantle of Darius and be acknowledged by the Persians and other nations of similar beliefs; but if the Persians accepted him, it was almost a done deal, as they were the guardians of the faith. Or so he thought. He wanted to arrest Darius and to make him prostrate and forfeit his divine and regal prerogative so as to legitimize his claim (Ashley 1998). Thus, when Bessus murdered him and assumed the mantle, prompting the whole eastern part of the empire not to yield to the Conqueror, despite the demise of the previous ruler (Olbrycht 2011), Alexander was outraged. Claiming the mantle for himself by right of conquest he was right to consider Bessus an impostor. Alexander must have been proclaimed King of the World at Arbela, after the battle of Gaugamela (Plut Alex 34,1). Having captured the nation, the country, the capitals, the regalia, and the symbols of power and faith, while keeping in custody the family of Darius (Parpas 2014) he was right to consider that he had substantiated his claim.

But Bessus was more than a satrap and an impostor. He was a *Macista*, the designated successor (Heliopoulos 2019) and Alexander perhaps ignored it. Bessus was the satrap of Bactria (Arr Anab III.8,3). As a token of respect to the cradle of Mazdaic Zoroastrianism, which supported the ascension of Darius I to the throne, the satrap of Bactria, at least since the reign of Xerxes (Her IX.113), was the Heir Apparent to the throne, the Macista (Garcia-Sánchez 2014). His status was something like the vice-president of the USA. If the reigning monarch perished he was in line for the succession, if the Crown Prince was underage or unsuitable. He had to be confirmed by the nobles and the army and sanctified by the clergy, but he was in a prime position for the throne, except if there was an adult Crown Prince. It is true that this arrangement may have predated Xerxes, even Darius; Cyrus the Great had installed his younger son, Smerdis, in Bactra, and the senior, the Crown Prince Cambyses, in Babylon, exactly as was done by Darius I. When Cambyses was proclaimed dead, Smerdis – or his imposter – stepped up the throne with a minimum of fuss; this could have never happened had he not been designated heir (Kambouris 2022a).

In the case of Darius III, the Crown Prince, Ochus, was underage and in the hands of Alexander (Patchen 2014), thus Bessus, the Macista, was in line for the crown. If Darius forfeited the crown or was slain, Bessus was his successor (Bosworth 1980b). It was not a coup that he and his associates demanded the crown for him; the coup was the demand for Darius to forfeit.

In there was the catch: the Macista had not a free hand for regicide. If the King died, or if he forfeited, it was OK. But he could not kill him. Once Darius was slain, things were a bit complicated: if he had resigned for Bessus, he would obviously not have been slain. Thus, being slain as he was, consisted a proof that it happened before forfeiting his mantle or resigning from office and due to his refusal to do so. It was a regicide. If committed by Bessus, he was automatically a regicide and excluded from the official and automatic passing of the crown and mantle. If by one of his friends, he was also responsible; it was exactly the kind of development Darius I wanted to avoid when sanctifying the mantle of the King and the office. The sacrilegious nature of the regicide was expansive and thus Bessus was not blameless for the crime – not to mention that the perpetrator was sacrilegious and then he could no way lead a religious campaign of devoted Mazdaic Zoroastrianists. But the chief Priest of the Mazdaic clergy, Kidinu, pretended he had seen no evil and confirmed the automatic transition of power to Bessus the Macista (Heliopoulos 2019). Bessus in this way became King and was legitimized under Ahura-Mazda to wear the cap upright, as only the King was allowed to (Arr Anab III.25,3). Alexander considered this resolution of the High Priest high treason, dereliction of duty and participation in the crime of regicide and sacrilege and perhaps many other things and reacted swiftly: he executed Kidinu and perhaps a large number of his ministers, and that by torture, obviously by abiding to the Imperial protocol (Heliopoulos 2019). It is important to note that the Bactrians, nobles and populace reacted to these events by mass rebellion under some pretext (Arr Anab IV.1,4–5), since the cradle of Zoroastrianism was Bactria (Heliopoulos 2019). But the Persians did not: they sided with Alexander and there was no rebellion or insurgency in Persia. Whether the horrific casualties in battle or something else, for example the legitimacy of Alexander's claim under the conditions was causal to this docile attitude is not obvious. But the fact is that somehow, standing among legitimacy, terror, impotence and a hidden reverence for Cyrus, the long-neglected non-Zoroastrian King and father-figure (Farahmand 2015), the Persians had no taste for following Bessus and his savages, and, when the time came, they were quick to torture him for his crime against a decent King (Diod XVII.83,9; Arr Anab IV.7,5), *their* Last King.

Chapter 15

Game Over

The goodwill of the Persians, on the other hand, once their arrogance was humiliated and their psychology rebooted, was something advantageous if not necessary for the stability of Alexander's newly acquired realm. Thus, Alexander paid respects to the sepulchres of Cyrus, spared his city and only confiscated the treasure (Arr Anab III.18,10). And then he started for Ecbatana, the Last Capital. Darius had not managed to gather the size of the forces he hoped for in Ecbatana when Alexander decided to finish the job and take care of this loose end. Darius expected the prudent Alexander he had met to consolidate his gains beyond the Zagros. If so, Darius would be residing (**Map 9**) at a central position on the northern axis of the Persian Empire, from Cappadocia in Asia Minor to the most distant satrapies in Central Asia, Sogdiana and India. There were vast resources he could call upon and he could strike anywhere along a greatly extended front, roughly running West to East, even in central Asia Minor to cut the access to Macedon or even invade Europe. Darius also had a contingency plan: if Alexander was to push to Ecbatana, probably by moving Northwest from Susa to enter Behistun and follow the road of Khorasan, Darius could defend it and if pushed back, he could retreat, in iterations, to the east (Arr Anab III.19,1). Darius was a resilient monarch with a plan. And he had a hidden asset: Alexander had no idea that the hearth of the Achaemenid religion and ideology was not seated in their holy city, Persepolis. It lurked deep in Bactria, the birthplace of Zarathustra; not dissimilar to Greece, where Delphi were much more important than the great cities, Athens, Sparta, Corinth and Thebes. The headquarters of Alexander and the Panhellenists of his staff simply had no clue on this subject.

By summarily subjugating Persia and razing Persepolis Alexander approached Darius from a least expected direction at a rather unexpected time, with more means at his disposal, a considerably reinforced army due to the new recruits that arrived, and a vast moral advantage. What was much worse was that having Persia under his spear, he made sure that no ethnic Persian reinforcements would rally in Ecbatana under the standard of Darius; neither uncommitted reserves nor survivors of Gaugamela. With their homes and families under the Macedonian yoke they would not venture to fight under a monarch soundly beaten twice, as if accursed. This fact defeated Darius' cause. Ethnic Persians were virtually absent from Darius' host. They were one of the two ethnic groups most loyal to him; the other was the Armenians, raised from his own satrapy. Thus, Darius' position amongst the still fighting Achaemenid nobility and their resolute followers was weakened (Arr Anab III.21,1 & 4). The religious parameter, an asset in political terms, was his greatest liability. The Bactrians, the Mazdaic nucleus of the empire were a backward, strictly feudal people (Curt IV.6,3) much more devoted to their satrap Bessus (Diod XVII.73,2) than to the King, especially once the King was abandoned by his own people and was evidently not favoured by the Lord of the Truth, Ahura-Mazda, previously the protector of the realm. The innovations, the foreigners, the way he gained the crown, all and any might have sat the wrong way with the deity. What is worse, with the Persians not rallying in any numbers under his standard, nobody else did. His retinue were some enemy mercenary infidels if not godless hoplites (Arr Anab III.21,4), possibly traitors and certainly not liked by the Lord of the Truth, and themselves, the true believers.

Darius knew his position was difficult but not desperate; he had to initiate his plan for retreat to the east (Arr Anab III.19,4). He would collect an army there, by sacrificing his last capital and treasure. The feudal lords did not like moving far from their estates when things went sour, and thus if he approached them at Bactria he would entice them to join en masse more easily. As Alexander expected to find him with an army – in this respect both players had committed the same mistake in their calculations – he was approaching slowly, in battle order (Arr Anab III.19,3). The ever cautious Alexander was there. It could be that deserters were planted by Darius to inform Alexander of a great army, so as to make his approach slower and cautious and buy Darius time and distance; or it might have been an army that disintegrated before it ever fought. The bottom line is that Alexander was late but took Ecbatana as if in a school excursion, plus the treasure except for some taken by Darius to fuel his guerrilla campaign (Arr Anab III.19,5). Alexander being in Media, the central area of the northern belt, meant that Armenia had been cut off from Darius, even though not properly subjugated. He could venture there no more, nor receive any kind of assistance – a dubious proposition once he was not able to entice his own blood, the Persians.

Alexander further understood that the Medes were not particularly fond of the Achaemenids, something known for centuries (Diod XI.6,3). They had no reason to nurture affection for the people that made them subjects from masters, especially after some slaughters when they rose in rebellion

(DB 24–25 & 31–32), nor had they excelled in any of the three encounters with the Macedonians. Alexander, always quick to grasp the feeling of a people, especially through his secret service, the geographers and the financial department that decided and implemented purchases and other transactions, took a most important decision.

Ecbatana would be his base for his endeavours in the east, a vast depot and transportation hub. He was to follow Darius in the west-east direction and bring the rest of the empire under his sceptre. And Ecbatana, at a suitable position, securely fortified (Arr Anab III.19,7) and obviously with a rather friendly population was selected for this role. With treasure being transported there from all the occupied vaults, the treasury of the empire was established there under Harpalus (Arr Anab III.19.7), a morally vile but also brilliant financial official. Military barracks, training grounds and other support facilities for receiving and billeting reinforcements, recruits and expeditionary forces were established. Parmenio was posted as the warden of this base of utmost strategic significance endowed with a massive force of 6,000 Macedonian infantry plus mercenaries (Arr Anab III.19,7).

The allied troops, including the Thessalian cavalry which had a special personal relation with Alexander as their *Tagos*, were demobilized and their units disbanded, as the punitive campaign was declared over by Alexander. They were paid in full (Arr Anab III.19,5) and then some, to act as living advertisements for the conquest of the Far East, Alexander's own project. They were also encouraged to re-enlist to his own, personal army (Arr Anab III.19,6). The army of Alexander, not of Macedon, nor of the League of Corinth. It was the end of Alexander the Great Avenger who bowed out of the scene in triumph, while Alexander the Great Conqueror was introduced to the world and to the Ages. A brief moment in history, with tremendous consequences.

Bibliography

Ancient Sources
Aelian, *Varia Historia*
Aeschines, *On the Embassy*
Aeschylus, *Persai*
Anaximenes FGrH llVA.
Appian, *Syrian Wars*
Arrian, *Anabasis*
Arrian, *Ars Tactica*
Q. Curtius Rufus, *Historiae Alexandri Magni*
Diodorus Siculus, *Library*
Encyclopedia Britannica 1911, 1911_Encyclopædia_Britannica/Philip_II.,_king_of_Macedonia https://en.wikisource.org/wiki/1911_Encyclopaedia_Britannica/Philip_II.,_king_of_Macedonia
Frontinus, *Stratagems*
Herodotus, *Histories*
Homer, *Iliad*
Homer, *Odyssey*
Isocrates, *Philippus*
Justin, *Epitome*
Nepos C, *Lives of Eminent Commanders*
Pausanias, *Description of Greece*
Plato, *Laches*
Pliny, *Naturalis Historia*
Plutarch, *Vitae Parallelae*
Plutarch, *Moralia*
Polyainus, *Stratagems*
Polybius, *Histories*
Pseudo-Callisthenes, *The Romance Of Alexander the Great*. Wolohojian A.M. (transl.) Columbia University Press 1969
Strabo, *Geographica*
Theophrastus, *Historia Plantarum*
Theopompus, FGrH115 F348.
Thucydides, *History of the Peloponnesian War*
Xenophon, *Agesilaus*
Xenophon, *Anabasis*
Xenophon, *Constitution of the Lacedaimonians*
Xenophon, *Cyropedia*
Xenophon, *Hellenica*
Xenophon, *Hipparchicos*
Xenophon, *On Horsemanship*

Contemporary Scholarship

Anderson JK 1991. Hoplite Weapons and Offensive Arms. In: Hanson VD (ed.): Hoplites: The Classical Greek Battle Experience. Routledge 2003, 15–37.
Andronicos M 1970. Sarissa. *Bulletin de Correspondance Hellénique* 94(1), 91–107.
Anson EM 2015. Counterinsurgency by Alexander. In: Howe T, Garvin EE, Wrightson G (Eds): Greece Macedonia and Persia. Oxbow Books, 94–106.
Anson EM 2013. Alexander the Great: Themes and Issues. Bloomsbury Publishing.
Anson EM 2010. The introduction of the sarisa in Macedonian warfare. *Ancient Society* 40, 51–68.
Anson EM 1981. Alexander's Hypaspists and the Argyraspids. *Historia: Zeitschrift für Alte Geschichte*, 30(1), 117–120.
Anson EM 1985. The Hypaspists: Macedonia's Professional Citizen-Soldiers. *Historia: Zeitschrift für Alte Geschichte*, 34(2), 246–248.
Arslan M 2019. The Asia Minor Campaign of Alexander and the Battle of Issus. In: İren K, Karaöz C, Kasar Ö (Eds): The Persians: Power and Glory in Anatolia. Anatolian Civilizations, Vol 6, Yapi Kredi Yayinlari, 136–157.
Ashley JR 1998. The Macedonian Empire: The Era of Warfare under Philip II and Alexander the Great, 359 – 323 BC. McFarland.
Badian E 2000. Darius III. *Harvard Studies in Classical Philology*, 100, 241–267.
Best JGP 1969. Thracian peltasts and their influence on Greek Warfare. Wolters-Noordhoff.
Boardman AP 1999. An Analysis of the Generalship of Alexander III of Macedon: Undermining or Underlining Greatness? MA Thesis Department of Classics, University of Durham.
Bonner RJ 1910. The Boeotian Federal Constitution. *Classical Philology* 5(4), 405–417.
Bosworth AB 1973. Astheteroi. *The Classical Quarterly* 23(2), 245–253.
Bosworth AB 1997. A Cut too many? Occam's Razor and Alexander's Footguard. *Ancient History Bulletin* 11(2–3), 47–56.
Bosworth AB 1980a. A Historical Commentary on Arrian's History of Alexander 1. Clarendon Press.
Bosworth AB 1980b. Alexander and the Iranians. *Journal of Hellenic Studies* 100, 1–21.
Bosworth AB 1988. Conquest and Empire. Cambridge University Press.
Bradford AS 2000. With arrow, sword and spear. Praeger Publishers.
Burliga B 2014. Xenophon's Cyrus, Alexander φιλόκυρος. How carefully did Alexander the Great study the Cyropaedia? *Miscellanea Anthropologica et Sociologica* 15(3), 134–146.
Brunt P 1963. Alexander's Macedonian Cavalry. *Journal of Hellenic Studies* 83, 27–46.
Buck RJ 1972. The Formation of the Boeotian League. *Classical Philology*, 67(2), 94–101.
Burn A 1952. Notes on Alexander's Campaign. *Journal of Hellenic Studies* 72, 81–91.
Burn AR 1965. The Generalship of Alexander. *Greece & Rome* 12(2), 140–154.
Campbell DB 2011. Ancient Catapults: Some Hypotheses Reexamined. *Hesperia* 80(4), 677–700.
Campbell DB 2003. Greek and Roman Artillery 399 BC–AD 363. *New Vanguard* 89. Osprey.
Charles MB 2011. Immortals And Apple-Bearers: Towards A Better Understanding Of Achaemenid Infantry Units. *The Classical Quarterly* 61(1), 114–33.
Charles MB 2012. The Persian Kardakes. *Journal of Hellenic Studies* 132, 7–21.
Charles MB 2015. Achaemenid elite cavalry: from Xerxes to Darius III. *The Classical Quarterly* 65(1), 14–34.
Connolly P 1981. Greece and Rome at War, Prentice-Hall.
Connolly P 2000. Experiments with the *sarissa* – the Macedonian pike and cavalry lance – a functional view. *Journal of Roman Military Equipment Studies* 11, 103–112.
Dahm M 2019. Macedonian Phalangite vs Persian Warrior. Alexander confronts the Achaemenids, 334–331 BC. Combat 40. Osprey.

D'Amato R & Salimbeti A 2018. The Etruscans. Elite 223. Osprey.
D'Amato R & Salimbeti A 2011 Bronze Age Greek Warrior. Warrior 153. Osprey.
D'Amato R & Salimbeti A 2017 Early Iron Age Greek Warrior 1100–700 BC. Warrior 180. Osprey.
Delbrueck H 1920. Warfare in antiquity Volume 1. Reprinted University of Nebraska Press, 1990.
Devine AM 1975. Grand Tactics at Gaugamela. *Phoenix* 29(4), 374–385
Devine AM 1983. Embolon: A Study in Tactical Terminology. *Phoenix* 37(3), 201–217
Devine AM 1986. Demythologizing the Battle of the Granicus. *Phoenix* 40(3), 265–278
Du Plessis J 2019. 'Synaspismos' and Its Possibility in the Macedonian Styled Phalanx. *Akropolis* 3, 167–183.
Ellis JR 1975. Alexander's Hypaspists Again. *Historia: Zeitschrift für Alte Geschichte*, 24(4), 617–618.
Engels D 1980a. Alexander's Intelligence System. *The Classical Quarterly*, 30(2), 327–340.
Engels DW 1980b. Alexander the Great and the Logistics of the Macedonian Army. University of California Press.
English S 2002. The army of Alexander the great, Durham theses, Durham University.
Esposito G 2020. Armies of Ancient Greece Circa 500 to 338 BC: History, Organization & Equipment. Pen & Sword Books.
Farahmand A 2015. Darius the Great Zoroastrian versus Cyrus the Emperor. https://authenticgathazoroastrianism.org/2015/04/06/darius-the-great-zoroastrian-and-cyrus-the-emperor/
Fields N 2007. Thermopylae 480 BC. Campaign 188. Osprey.
Freewalt J 2014. Battle report: Alexander the Great's Siege of Tyre – 332 BC. The Wars of Ancient Greece and Macedonia – HIST612 A001 American Military University. https://www.academia.edu/6606428/Battle_Report_Alexander_the_Greats_Siege_of_Tyre_332_BC
Fuller JFC 1958. The Generalship of Alexander the Great. Eyre & Spottiswoode.
Gaebel RE 2002. Cavalry Operations in the Ancient Greek World. University of Oklahoma Press.
Garcia-Sánchez M 2014. The Second after the King and Achaemenid Bactria in Classical Sources. In: Antela-Bernárdez B & Vidal J (Eds): Central Asia in Antiquity: Interdisciplinary Approaches. Oxford University Press, 37–43.
Garlan Y 1994. Warfare. In: Lewis DM, Boardman J, Hornblower S, Ostwald M (Eds):The Cambridge Ancient History, vol. 6, The Fourth Century B.C. Cambridge University Press, 678–693.
Green P 1991. Alexander of Macedon, 356–323 B.C.: A Historical Biography. University of California Press.
Green P 1998. The Greco-Persian Wars. University of California Press.
Green P 2007. Alexander the Great and the Hellenistic age. Weidenfeld and Nicolson.
Griffith GT 1947. Alexander's Generalship at Gaugamela. *Journal of Hellenic Studies*, 67, 77–89.
Griffith GT 1963. A Note on the Hipparchies of Alexander. *Journal of Hellenic Studies*, 83, 68–74.
Griffith GT 1979. In: Hammond NGL and Griffith GT (Eds): A History of Macedonia II: 550–336 BC. Clarendon Press, 711–712.
Hadjidaki E 2012. The battle against Alexander from Crete during the c. 4th BC. Acta of Conference: Alexander, the Greek cosmos – system and contemporary global society. The Greek thought series, Thessaloniki. Academy Of Institutions And Cultures, 102–112.
Hammond N GL 1991. The Various Guards of Philip II and Alexander III. *Historia: Zeitschrift für Alte Geschichte*, 40(4), 396–418.

Hammond NGL 1994. Philip of Macedon. Johns Hopkins University Press.
Hammond NGL 1997. Arrian's Mentions of Infantry Guards. *Ancient History Bulletin* 11(1), 20–24.
Hammond NGL 1989. Alexander the Great: King, commander and statesman. Bristol Press.
Hammond NGL 1966. The kingdoms in Illyria circa 400–167 BC. *The Annual of the British School at Athens* 61, 239–253.
Hammond NGL 1992. Alexander's Charge at the Battle of Issus in 333 B.C. *Historia: Zeitschrift für Alte Geschichte* 41(4), 395–406.
Hammond NGL 1997. The genius of Alexander the Great. University of North Carolina Press.
Hammond NGL 1990. The Macedonian state. Oxford University Press.
Hammond NGL 1994. Macedonia before Philip and Philip's first year in power. *Meditarch* 7, 13–15.
Hammond NGL 1998. Cavalry Recruited in Macedonia down to 322 B.C. *Historia: Zeitschrift für Alte Geschichte* 47(4), 404–425.
Hanson VD 1983. Warfare and Agriculture in Classical Greece. University of California Press.
Hanson VD 1999. The wars of the ancient Greeks. Orion.
Head D 1992. The Achaemenid Persian Army. Montvert Publications
Heckel W 1986. Somatophylakia: A Macedonian 'Cursus Honourum'. *Phoenix* 40(3), 279–294.
Heckel W 1992. The Marshals of Alexander's Empire. Routledge
Heckel W 2012. The Royal Hypaspists in Battle: Macedonian hamippoi. *Ancient History Bulletin* 26, 15–20.
Heckel W & Jones R, 2006. Macedonian Warrior. Alexander's elite infantryman. Warrior 103. Osprey.
Heliopoulos GZ 2019. The Chimerae of War. Bartzoulianos [In Greek].
Heliopoulos GZ 2002. Catapults. Communications SA [In Greek].
Hencken H 1950. Herzsprung Shields and Greek Trade. *American Journal of Archaeology* 54(4),294–309.
Howard D 2011. Bronze Age Military Equipment. Pen & Sword Books.
Howe T 2015. Introducing Ptolemy: Alexander and the Persian Gates. In: Heckel W, Müller S and Wrightson G (Eds): The Many Faces of War in the Ancient World. Cambridge Scholars Publishing.
Humble R 1980. Warfare in the ancient world. Book Club Associates
Juhel P 2009. The Regulation Helmet of the Phalanx and the Introduction of the Concept of Uniform in the Macedonian Army at the End of the Reign of Alexander the Great. *Klio* 91, 342–355.
Kagiavas-Torp A. 2014. The Changing Role of the Phalanx Infantry between 490 and 323 B.C. Department of Classics and Ancient History, Durham University.
Kambouris ME 2023. The Trojan War as Military History. Pen & Sword Books.
Kambouris ME 2022a. The Rise of Persia. Pen & Sword Books.
Kambouris ME 2022b. The High Tide: Persia Triumphant in Greece. Pen & Sword Books.
Kambouris ME 2022c. The Persian Ebb. Pen & Sword Books.
Kambouris ME et al 2014. Drill and Tactics of Epameinondas's Theban Phalanx in the Second Battle of Mantineia 362 BC. *Archaeology and Science* 10, 121–132.
Kambouris ME et al 2015. Greco-Macedonian Influences in the Manipular Legion System. *Archaeology and Science* 11, 145–154.
Kambouris ME et al 2019. The Hypaspist Corps: Evolution and Status of the Elite Macedonian Infantry Unit. *Archaeology and Science* 15, 19–30.

Kambouris ME & Bakas S 2021. The battle mechanics of the hoplite phalanx. *Nuova Antologia Militare* 2(6), 3–43.

Kambouris ME & Bakas S 2017. Gaugamela 331 BC: the triumph of tactics. *Archaeology and Science* 13, 17–32

Kambouris ME 2014. Warfare in Mycenaean Times: the Iliad as a Paradigm and the Applications Emerging for Experimental Archaeology. *Archaeology and Science* 10, 221–230.

Kambouris ME 2000. Ancient Greek Warriors, Communications SA [In Greek].

Keyser PT 1994. The Use of Artillery by Philip II and Alexander the Great. *The Ancient World*, 25(1), 27–59.

Kholod MM 2018. The Macedonian Expeditionary Corps in Asia Minor (336–335 BC). *Klio* 100(2), 407–446.

Kleymeonov AA 2015. Asthetairoi: Alexander The Great's attacking guards. *European Journal of Science and Theology*, 11(5), 67–75.

Konijnendijk R 2014. Iphicrates the Innovator and the Historiography of Lechaeum. In: Sekunda NV & Burliga B (Eds): Iphicrates, Peltasts and Lechaion. Foundation for the Development of Gdańsk University, 84–94.

Krentz P 1985. The Nature of Hoplite Battle. *Classical Antiquity* 4(1): 50–61.

Lane Fox R 1980. The Search for Alexander. Little Brown & Co.

Llewellyn-Jones L 2012. King and court in ancient Persia 559–331 BCE. Edinburgh University Press.

Lock RA 1977. The Origins of the Argyraspids. *Historia: Zeitschrift für Alte Geschichte*, 26(3), 373–378.

Manning S 2021. Armed Force in the Teispid-Achaemenid Empire. *Oriens et Occidens* 32, Franz Steiner Verlag.

Markle MM 1977. The Macedonian Sarissa, Spear, and Related Armor. *American Journal of Archaeology* 81(3), 323–339.

Markle MM 1978. Use of the Sarissa by Philip and Alexander of Macedon. *American Journal of Archaeology* 82(4), 483–497.

Marsden EW 1964. The Campaign of Gaugamela. Liverpool University Press.

Matthew CA 2015. An Invincible Beast. Pen & Sword Books.

Matthew CA 2012. A Storm of spears. Pen & Sword Books.

Matthew CA 2013. Towards the Hot Gates. In: Matthew CA & Trundle M (Eds): Beyond the Gates of Fire. Pen & Sword Books, 1–26.

Meiklejohn KW 1938. Roman Strategy and Tactics from 509 to 202 B. C. *Greece & Rome* 7(21), 170–178.

Miller MC 2006/7. Persians in the Greek Imagination. *Mediterranean Archaeology*, 19/20, 109–123.

Miller MC 2004. Athens and Persia in the Fifth Century BC: A Study in Cultural Receptivity. Cambridge University Press.

Milns RD 1982. A Note on Diodorus and Macedonian Military Terminology in Book XVII. *Historia: Zeitschrift für Alte Geschichte* 31(1), 123–126.

Milns RD 1976. The army of *Alexander* the Great. In: Badian E (Ed): Alexander le Grande: image et réalité. Entretiens Hardt 22, Vandoeuvres, 87–136.

Milns RD 1971. The Hypaspists of Alexander III: Some Problems. *Historia: Zeitschrift für Alte Geschichte*, 20(2/3), 186–195.

Milns RD 1967. Philip II and the Hypaspists. *Historia: Zeitschrift für Alte Geschichte*, 16(4), 509–512.

Milns RD 1966a. Alexander's Seventh Phalanx Battalion. *Greek, Roman and Byzantine Studies* 7(2), 159–166.

Milns RD 1966b. Alexander's Macedonian Cavalry and Diodorus xvii.17.4. *Journal of Hellenic Studies* 86, 167–168.
Monerie J 2019. Invading Mesopotamia, from Alexander the Great to Antiochus VII. In: Da Riva R, Lang M, Fink S (Eds): Routes and Travellers between East and West. Zaphon, 155–186.
Montagu JD 2000. Battles of the Greek and Roman Worlds. Greenhill Books.
Mousavi A 2005. Why Darius built Persepolis. *Archaeology Odyssey* 31, 22–51.
Nefedkin AK 2011. A Note on the Late Phalanx of Alexander the Great. In: Sekunda NV, Noguera Borel A (Eds): Hellenistic Warfare 1. Fundatión Libertas 7; Instituto Valenciano de Estudios Clásicos y Orientales, 65–71.
Nefedkin AK 2014. Once More on the Origin of Scythed Chariot. *Ancient History Bulletin* 28(3–4), 112–118.
Nefedkin AK 2006. The Tactical Development of Achaemenid Cavalry. *Gladius* 26, 5–18.
Noguera-Borel A 1999. L' evolution de la phalange macedonienne: le cas de la *sarissa*. Ancient Macedonia Sixth International Symposium, Thessaloniki Vol. 2, 839–850.
Nossov K 2008. War Elephants. New Vanguard 150. Osprey.
Olbrycht MJ 2011. First Iranian military units in the army of Alexander the Great. *Anabasis* 2, 67–84.
Panovski S & Sarakinski V 2011. Memnon, the Strategist. *Macedonian Historical Review* 2, 7–27.
Parpas AP 2013. Alexander the Great. The Dissolution of the Persian naval supremacy 334–331 BC. CreateSpace Independent Publishing Platform.
Parpas AP 2014. Alexander the Great in Erbil. CreateSpace Independent Publishing Platform.
Parpas AP 2015. The Siege of Tyros. The decision to resist Alexander in 332 B.C. – A religious or a geopolitical decision? CreateSpace Independent Publishing Platform.
Patchen J 2014. Redefining Darius. Baker University.
Petitjean M 2017. Mathematics of War: Some thoughts on the cavalry embolon and the lost Technê taktikê of Posidonius. 4th International Congress of Hellenistic Armies, 25–9–2017, l'Universidad Nacional Autónoma de México. https://www.academia.edu/34719985/The_mathematics_of_war_some_thoughts_on_the_cavalry_embolon_and_the_lost_Techn%C3%AA_taktik%C3%AA_of_Posidonius
Prandi L 2012. New Evidence for the Dating of Cleitarchus (POxy LXXI.4808). *Histos* 6, 15–26.
Raaflaub KA 2013. Early Greek Infantry Fighting in a Mediterranean Context. In: Kagan D, Viggiano GF (Eds): Men of Bronze: Hoplite Warfare in Ancient Greece. Princeton University Press, 95–111.
Rahe PA 1981. The Annihilation of the Sacred Band at Chaeronea. *American Journal of Archaeology* 85(1), 84–87.
Randall K 2012. Pezetairoi: Infantry Reform in the Time of Phillip II. Korean Society of Greco-Roman Studies, 1–18.
Ray FE 2009. Land battles in 5th century B.C. Greece. McFarland & Company Inc.
Recaldin J 2011. What Was The Main Purpose Of The Ephebeia? MA Dissertation, School of Archaeology and Ancient History, University of Leicester.
Russell FS 1999. Information Gathering in Classical Greece. The University of Michigan Press.
Ruzicka S 1988. War in the Aegean, 333–331 B.C.: A Reconsideration. *Phoenix* 42(2), 131–151.
Rzepka J 2008. The Units of Alexander's Army and the District Divisions of Late Argead Macedonia. *Greek, Roman and Byzantine Studies* 48, 39–56.

Rzepka J 2012. How Many Companions Did Philip II Have? *Electrum* 20, 131–135.
Salimbeti A & D'Amato R 2014. The Carthaginians. Elite 201. Osprey.
Samuels M 1997. Alexander the Great and Manoeuvre War. https://www.academia.edu/15306853/Alexander_the_Great_and_Manoeuvre_War
Sarantis Th 1977. Alexander the Great. Alkyon [In Greek].
Sears MA & Willekes C 2016. Alexander's Cavalry Charge at Chaeronea, 338 BCE. *The Journal of Military History* 80, 1017–1035.
Sekunda N 1984. The Army of Alexander the Great. Men-at-Arms 148. Osprey.
Sekunda N 1986. The Ancient Greeks. Elite 7. Osprey.
Sekunda N 1989. The Persians. In: Hackett J (Ed): Warfare in the Ancient World. Guild Publishing, 82–103.
Sekunda N 1992. The Persian Army 560–330 BC. Elite 42. Osprey.
Sekunda N 1994. Seleucid and Ptolemaic Reformed Armies 168–145 BC, Volume 1: The Seleucid Army. Montvert Publications.
Sekunda N 1995. Early Roman armies. Men-at-Arms 283. Osprey.
Sekunda N 1998. The Spartan Army. Elite 66. Osprey.
Sekunda N 2000. The Greek Hoplite. Warrior 27. Osprey.
Sekunda N 2001. The Sarissa. *Folia Archaeologica* 23, 13–46.
Sidnell P 2007. Warhorse: Cavalry in Ancient Warfare. Bloomsbury Academic.
Snodgrass AM 1967. Arms and Armour of the Greeks. Cornell University Press.
Stein A 1942. Notes on Alexander's Crossing of the Tigris and the Battle of Arbela. *The Geographical Journal* 100(4), 155–164.
Strootman R 2012. Alexander's Thessalian cavalry. *Talanta* 42–43, 51–67.
Steele RB 1922. Cleitarchus. *American Journal of Philology*, 42(1), 40–57.
Tarn WW 1948. Alexander the Great Volume 1, Cambridge University Press.
Tarn WW 1921. Heracles Son of Barsine. *Journal of Hellenic Studies* 41, 18–28.
Taylor R 2021. The Greek Hoplite Phalanx. Pen & Sword Books.
Thompson M 2007. Granicus 334 BC Alexander's First Persian Victory. Campaign 182. Osprey.
Van Wees H 1997. Review of N. Sekunda 'Seleucid and Ptolemaic Reformed Armies 168–145 BC. Vol. 1: The Seleucid Army under Antiochus IV Epiphanes' *The Classical Review*, 47, 356–357.
Warry J 1991. Alexander 334–323 BC. Conquest of the Persian Empire. Campaign 7. Osprey.
Warry J 1980. Warfare in the Classical world. Salamander Books.
Waterfield R 2006. Xenophon's Retreat: Greece, Persia, and the End of the Golden Age. Belknap Press of Harvard University Press.
Webber C 2001. The Thracians 700 BC–AD 46. Men-At-Arms 360. Osprey.
Webber C 2003. Odrysian Cavalry Arms, Equipment, and Tactics. In: Nikolova L (Ed): Early Symbolic Systems for Communication in Southeast Europe. BAR S 1139 Vol. 2, 529–554.
Westlake HD 1936. The Medism of Thessaly. *Journal of Hellenic Studies* 56(1), 12–24.
Wrightson G 2010. The nature of command in the Macedonian *sarissa* phalanx. *Ancient History Bulletin* 24, 71–92.
Wrightson GCL 2012. Greek and Near Eastern warfare 3000 to 301 BC: the development and perfection of combined arms. PhD Thesis, University of Calgary.

Index

Achaemenid, 5, 7–8, 12, 18, 22, 39, 43–4, 45, 49, 51, 54, 56–7, 59, 62, 66, 68, 76, 94–6, 101–102, 104, 111, 115, 117–20, 122, 126–8, 132, 141–9, 152–6, 158, 162, 167, 169, 177, 180, 186, 189–91, 193, 205, 207–208, 224, 236, 246, 252–3, 256, 258–60, 264, 268, 271–2
Achaia, 217
Aegae, 20
Aeolis, 138, 140
Agathon, 123, 219
Agesilaus, 35, 69, 96, 99–106, 108–15, 118, 128, 139–41, 145, 155, 194, 197
Agrianian, 112, 124, 171–2, 218
Akinaka, 36–7
Amanic Gates, 138
  see also Gates of Amanus
Amun, 192–3, 268
Amyntas, 20, 30, 49, 58–9, 62, 64, 122–6, 171, 180, 190–1, 193, 199, 201, 204, 217, 226, 232, 262–4
Antigonus, 29, 171, 200
Applebearers, 12, 50, 54, 95, 212
Arcadia/n, 24, 52, 104, 112
Archelaus, 60, 62, 103, 198
Aretes, 128, 135, 218, 230, 246
Argead(s), 15, 56, 64
Ariobarzanes, 45, 260–3
Armenia, 111, 137, 153, 196, 200, 208, 227, 252, 255, 260, 272
Armenian(s), 154, 206, 234, 272
Arsames, 140, 156, 166
Arshtibara, 45, 51
Arsites, 108, 142
Asabara, 3–4, 8–9, 46, 66, 101, 125, 127–8, 133–5, 140, 167, 169, 171, 178–9, 210, 255, 261

Assassination, 103, 107
Assassins' Creed, 103
Attalus, 62, 106–107, 115, 140, 142, 218

Bactria, 118, 252, 254–5, 265, 267, 269–72
Bagoas, 189
Behistun, 205–207, 227, 252, 254, 271
Bessus, 211, 224–5, 229–31, 248, 254, 268–70, 272
Boeotian helmet, 7
Brasidas, 6, 19
Bridgehead, 23, 105–10, 112, 115, 117, 120, 140, 142, 145, 220, 240
Buckler, 25, 29, 89, 93

Callas, 109, 112, 123, 140, 200
Caltrops, 222
Caria, 137–8, 144, 148, 151–3, 155, 160, 185, 196–8, 218
Catapult, 68
Chaeronea, 9–10, 60, 93, 104, 136, 174
Chalcidian, 34
Chalybes, 21
Charidemus, 45, 155
Chariot(s), 45, 55, 71, 133, 179–80, 210–11, 213, 221, 223–5, 228, 231–2, 234–8, 240–1
chariotry, 70–1, 250
Cilician Gates, 138, 155–6, 158, 179, 181, 200, 204, 206, 261
Cleitarchus, 120, 127, 220
Cleitus the Black, 9, 30, 128, 132, 217, 242
Coenus, 62, 65, 124, 154, 171, 217, 263, 264
Companion cavalry, 9, 12, 26, 133, 234
  see Companions

Companions, 5–7, 9–10, 14–16, 18–19, 28, 51–5, 58, 60–1, 65, 93, 96, 112, 122, 125–7, 130, 132–3, 135, 162, 170–6, 188, 206, 210, 214, 217–19, 226, 231, 234, 244, 247
Corinth, 104, 154, 259, 266, 271, 273
Corruption, 259
CQB, 35, 40–1, 43, 125, 127, 158, 261
Craterus, 62, 124, 172, 188, 217, 232–3, 257, 263–4
Cretan archers, 36, 171, 216, 219, 247
Croesus, 97, 137, 159
Cuirass, 7, 10, 14, 25, 29, 31–2, 37, 42–4, 130
Cunaxa, 56, 118, 167, 169, 211, 221, 236–7, 243
Cynic, 266
  cynicism, 267
Cyprus, 102, 140, 163, 180, 190
  Cypriot, 139, 147–8
Cyrus the Great, 97, 137, 141, 163, 258, 269
Cyrus the Younger, 24, 51, 99, 118, 122, 205, 211, 236, 250

Damascus, 111, 158–60, 162, 164, 181–2, 184–5, 202–203, 237, 250, 254
Dascylium, 105, 115, 118, 122, 137–8, 140, 151–2, 195, 200, 236, 243
Dirk, 32, 36–7, 76
Dorylaeum, 137, 151

Elam, 196, 254, 256
Elamite(s), 50, 256
Embolon, 9, 242–5
Epaminondas, 6, 21–2, 67, 69, 79–80, 99, 121, 167, 243, 244
Ephebeia, 35
Ephesus, 102, 106, 137, 139, 142, 218
Epilektoi, 35, 52–4
Erigon, 6, 54

Frederick the Great, 178, 230, 239

Gates of Amanus, 155, 158–61, 163, 179–81, 200, 237

Gaza, 183, 185, 189, 202, 204
Gordium, 58, 137–8, 151, 153–4, 170, 196–7, 216, 218, 220

Halicarnassus, 138–9, 142–5, 148–51, 160, 185–7, 189, 194–5, 197–200, 204
Hellespontine Phrygia, 140
Herodotus, 3, 5, 36, 37–9, 41–4, 46, 49–50, 54, 57, 95, 108, 118, 143, 157, 208, 258
Hipparchiai, 217
  see also Hipparchies
Hipparchies, 12, 14–15
  hipparchy, 12–14
Hoplitodromos, 26, 34, 76, 83
Hoplomachoi, 34
Hydaspes, 13, 53, 59
Hypaspist Corps, 12, 18, 50–1, 54, 56, 58, 95, 123, 125, 174, 188, 212, 217, 241

Iphicrates, 6, 20–1, 30, 64, 95, 210, 212, 241

Jason, 15, 67, 103, 155

Kamax, 10, 135
Karana, 107–108, 114, 117–18, 120, 141–2, 144, 164, 225
Kardaka, 38, 41, 44–6, 210, 214, 231, 261
Khorasan, 205, 252, 262, 271
Kidinu, 270
Konos, 26
Kopis, 22, 30, 33

Leonidas, 35, 96, 101, 159, 197, 225, 264
Linothorax, 25, 32, 34, 38, 43
Lochagoi, 22, 241
Locris, 121, 217
Looter, 45
Lower Road, 157–8, 181, 187, 198, 201–203

Macista, 269–70
Malis, 121, 217

Mardian archers, 213
Mardonius, 42–3, 125, 139, 155, 201, 221
Mazeus, 203–205, 211, 226–7, 232–3, 246, 253, 255
Meleager, 62, 123, 154, 171, 217
Memphis, 185, 187, 191–3, 202–203, 218
Middle Road, 138, 157, 198, 204–205
Miletus, 110, 132, 139, 142–5, 147–8, 157, 186, 195, 218, 264

Nicanor, 52, 55, 123, 127, 217
Nineveh, 138, 163–4, 200, 206, 208

Ochus, 168, 182, 269
Odryssian, 123, 219
Orontobates, 143–4, 148, 151, 160, 196–7
Oulamos, 7

Palmyra, 157–8, 181, 187, 202–203
Parataxis, 122, 169, 211, 217
Parsagadae, 258, 264, 265
Pavisarii, 36
Peltast(s), 20–1, 60, 243
Perdikkas, 6, 19, 28, 30, 62, 124, 171, 217
Persepolis, 37, 205, 207, 252, 258–60, 262–5, 267, 271
Persian Gates, 12, 45, 68, 221, 260, 262–3
Pharsalus, 15, 113
Philotas, 55, 112, 123–4, 127, 170, 217, 229, 239
Phocis, 217
Pilos, 26, 34
Pixodarus, 143–4, 148, 151
Pteria, 137, 139, 153, 208
Ptolemy, 62, 120, 125, 127, 154, 171, 184, 198, 212, 220, 263

Queen Ada, 143

Rhomboid, 8, 15–17, 30, 32, 171, 177

Sagaris, 36
Sardis, 49, 100, 105, 118, 137–42, 151, 153, 191, 195, 201
Scouts, 13, 15, 122–3, 132, 135, 163, 170, 218
Simmias, 62, 217, 232–3
Siwa, 190–3, 268
Sochi, 157–8, 161, 236, 250, 252
Spara, 5, 27, 36–40, 43, 92
  sparabara, 3, 19, 28, 31, 36–40, 43–5, 50, 66, 69, 94
Spithridates, 9
Sun Tzu, 223
Syenessis, 140

Takabara, 43–5
Tetrarchia(i), 7, 80
Thapsacus, 179, 202–206, 226
Tigris, 138, 153, 205–206, 226–7, 262
Tripolis, 157, 180, 190, 197
Troad, 129, 138, 140, 151
Tyre, 65, 68, 140, 157, 180, 183, 185–7, 189, 191, 202–205, 212, 218

Upper Road, 138, 205
Uxiana, 259
Uxians, 57, 211, 259–60

War chest, 111, 146, 181, 254

Xyston, 10, 14, 16, 27, 128, 133, 135, 171, 174, 209, 214, 231, 239

Zagros, 206–207, 227, 253, 256, 258–60, 271